John Haslet:
A Useful One

by
Fred B. Walters

to my wife Lil and our family

Cover: Painting shows Colonel John Haslet leading the First Delaware Continentals off Dover Green, painted in 1915 by Stanley Arthurs, courtesy of the Delaware State Archives.

Contents

Introduction

My American history professor at the University of Pennsylvania, Dr. Thomas Cochran, believed that history was best learned through the lives of the principal figures of the period under study.

But does it always have to be the principals? What about the next rank of players, those people Historian Whitfield Bell of the American Philosophical Society referred to as the "useful ones?" Shouldn't their story be told?

Mightn't the reader better understand the period under study through the life of a person more like a neighbor than an icon?

In his book, "The Colonial Physician and Other Essays," Dr. Bell wrote: "*The Franklins and the Jeffersons on the one hand, the scoundrels and the killers on the other, are all well known; they crowd history's galleries. But (*the people) *who keep alive the ideas other men conceived and hold together the institutions other men create . . . They are the ideal trustees, the perfect friends. They are the useful ones . . .*"

I've chosen to write about a hero of the American Revolution under the working title, *John Haslet: A Useful One.* It is a story of a husband and father, preacher and physician, politician and patriot. It was on the battlefield, however, that he established his place in history.

Unfortunately, people like Haslet also are the forgotten ones.

Consider that Paul Revere might have been among them, too, if it weren't for Henry Wadsworth Longfellow.

Caesar Rodney, Delaware's political leader, made a midnight ride that was more significant, over a much longer distance and in a severe storm—from Dover, Delaware, to Philadelphia—to cast a decisive vote for Independence on July 2, 1776. It is part of Delaware folklore, but who knows about it outside that state?

Suppose Longfellow had written: *"Listen, my children, learn, at my knee, of the midnight ride of Caesar Rodney,"* instead of that line about the other fellow? (A tortured rhyme, I admit, but the point is that a good publicist makes a great deal of difference.)

I've included that ride in my story because Rodney was an important part of Haslet's American life.

In an 1875 speech to the Delaware Assembly, the Hon. William Gustavus Whitely said: *"John Haslet, who has been truly called the father of his regiment, lived at the outbreak of the war in Dover. He studied medicine and practiced it with much success in Kent County. He was tall and athletic and of generous and ardent feelings . . . He was a leading Whig and evidently Caesar Rodney's right-hand man; the one he depended on to get the people right on the question of independence, as well as raising and enlisting soldiers to fight for it."* (Emphasis mine.)

Granted this was a hometown fan. But consider the judgment of Washington Irving in his biography of George Washington:

> *"Colonel Haslet . . . distinguished himself through the campaign by being foremost in services of danger. He was a gallant officer, and gallantly seconded by the Delaware troops."*

Or Page Smith, in Volume I of his Bicentennial History:

> *"The American losses* (at Princeton) *were far less than the British, but Washington lost officers he could ill afford to lose, among them General Mercer, killed trying to rally his men, and Colonel Haslet, who had emerged as one of his steadiest, most reliable officers."*

And Mark Tully, in his essay on the performance of His Majesty's 55th Royal Regiment of Foot at the Battle of Princeton:

> *"Washington . . . lost several of his key officers . . . Colonel John Haslet was dead—his Delaware Regiment had been one of the finest fighting units of the entire war . . ."*

This from Lt. Col. Henry Lee of Virginia:

> *"The State of Delaware furnished one regiment only; and certainly no regiment in the Army surpassed it in soldiership."*

I first ran across Haslet many years ago in Christopher Ward's excellent two-volume study of *"The War of the Revolution."*

Names of many little-known heroes flit through the pages, but the name that captured my attention was Haslet's as commander of the Delaware Continentals.

I'm not sure now exactly why. Perhaps it was Ward's description of his battlefield feats, or the fact that he died on the battlefield at Princeton with a note in his pocket from George Washington ordering him home to recruit a new battalion. Haslet had stuffed the note in his pocket and followed Washington to one more battle. Or perhaps the legend that Washington wept over his corpse piqued my curiosity.

My research has taken me to the state archives in Dover, Delaware, and Harrisburg, Pennsylvania, (colonial Delaware was part of the province of Pennsylvania); to the offices of the Kent County Recorder of Deeds and Register of Wills (Dover); to the Morris Library of the University of Delaware (Newark); to the Historical Society of Delaware (Wilmington); to the Milford Historical Society (Haslet lived in that area before it was a town); and the Presbyterian Historical Society of America (Philadelphia).

The Pennsylvania State Library yielded a great deal of information, including the journals of the Delaware Assembly when Haslet was a member and an account of a court martial board on which Haslet sat shortly after his arrival in New York in August, 1766.

The University of Glasgow verified his graduation and supplied me with the names of his professors. The Presbyterian Historical Society of Ireland (Belfast) sent me the dates of his ministry, a little bit of family background and notes on his problems with his Ulster congregation.

The National Archives found a few records of his military service. The Internet provided quick answers to spot questions.

I was helped very much by a distant Haslet kin, Michael Higgins of Belfast, descended from John Haslet's uncle William Haslet. Higgins helped with the genealogy, fed me tidbits he picked up in his own research, advised me on the geography of John Haslet's home area (largely unchanged) and made sure dialogue conformed to "Irish-speak." The thick file of e-mails between us attest to the great contribution he has made to my research and his encouragement to pursue the Haslet story.

I read every issue of the *Pennsylvania Gazette* from 1757 to 1777, the period Haslet lived in America, and issues of other Philadelphia newspapers that might contain information the *Gazette* missed.

John Haslet: A Useful One

Letters to and from Caesar Rodney provided a lot of insight to the political events of the period and included his last letter, written only a day or two before his death. I also obtained copies of Haslet's few existing letters from the Delaware Archives. Sadly, the research failed to produce any letters to or from his wife or any family members.

I read a lot of books about the events, the life style of the time, and pieces of other books. That included books about colonial medicine (he practiced medicine) and colonial attitudes towards death, since his corpse was left on display in Philadelphia for a time after his death at Princeton until, in the words of *The Delaware Journal* in July, 1841, "corruption, and the worm, claimed their own, when it was quietly laid away among strangers, with scarcely a mark to designate its resting place." (The *Journal* was reporting on the ceremony removing Haslet's remains from Philadelphia to Dover, the opening chapter in my manuscript.)

A book about George Read, a contemporary of John Haslet, contains the anecdote that Haslet's oldest son inadvertently learned of his father's death from a passing messenger who stopped to talk to the minister at the church where the son was playing with other boys; and so on.

Despite all my research, this is not meant to be a scholarly study.

As the pieces accumulated, I began to imagine what Haslet's life might have been like and I decided I would write about that life as I imagined it to be.

I've taken the fragments, pieced them together and expanded on them to create what I think is a credible account of Haslet's life in America. Like an anthropologist, I've added flesh to the bones, providing dialogue, of course, but dialogue often borrowed from letters, minutes of meetings, depositions, etc. My chapter notes explain my reasoning for each of the assumptions I've made in this story.

It was reported that Jemima Haslet "died of a broken heart" after she heard of his death, a comment that attests to his role as husband. Young Joseph fled in tears from the playground where he heard of his father's death, a vignette that says something about his role as a father. Little else is known about these roles in his life, but they would seem to support the family life I imagined for him.

None of my assumptions represent leaps of fancy. For example, the musters show he was seriously ill in September and October of 1776, following the Battle of Long Island. It's logical that the battalion surgeon and second-in-command visited him and I've written a scene based on that assumption, but including information of historical record.

In fact, throughout the manuscript, I've used these assumptions to advance the story and to bring contemporary events to the reader's attention.

A lot of people have contributed to this work. Michael Higgins I've already mentioned. The folks in Milford, Delaware—particularly Dave Kenton—have given me support and encouragement beyond anything I ever expected. Kenton was the point man of that support and his research, as a realtor, helped establish where Haslet lived and when he moved into his final home. Dave—and through him the Milford Commission on Landmarks and Museum—have become my partners in bringing this story to print.

In the year I spent reading the Philadelphia newspapers of the period Haslet lived in America (Delaware did not have a newspaper of record during those years), Bob Mason, Richard Hill and Kenny Chase in the newspaper room at the State Library of Pennsylvania in Harrisburg were of immense help.

My other research at the Pennsylvania library was made fruitful by the efforts of John E. Geschwindt, Depository Libraries Advisor; Alice L. Lubrecht, Director, Bureau of State Library, Office of Commonwealth Libraries, and Tim Kreider, Emily Geschwindt and Dave Hueison.

During my frequent visits to the Delaware archives in Dover, Clifford Parker, Bruce Haas or Heather Jones were available when I asked for help.

The Morris Library at the University of Delaware was also a great source of information, thanks to Iris Snyder, Associate Librarian; L.Rebecca Johnson Melvin, Associate Librarian; Rhonda Hennrich, receptionist, Special Collections; and Melissa Clarke in Microforms.

At the Historical Society of Delaware in Wilmington I had help from Connie Cooper, Ed Chichivichi, and Ellen Rendle.

At the Military History Institute at the Army War College in Carlisle, Pennsylvania, I received the valuable assistance of John Sponaker and Michelle Davis.

I found important fragments of Haslet's life at the Presbyterian Historical Society of America in Philadelphia, thanks to the help of Susan Flacks and Norotha Robinson, staff, and Bob Blades, volunteer.

These other people also helped me find pieces of information during the years of research: Brian Costa, Kent County, Maps Section; various staff at the office of the Register of Wills in the Kent County Court House; and Jack and Jane Jones, and Georgiadee Sandstrom at the Family History Center (associated with the Mormon Church) in Dover.

I made one trip to Annapolis and Kim Alder at the Maryland Hall of Records was frequently at my side helping me find information.

Chuck Fithian, historian for the State of Delaware gave up some of his time to discuss the project and help me interpret some of the arcane language of 18th century wills.

And, of course, there were people in Ulster and Scotland who provided important facts about my subject: Higgins, of course, and Robert Bonar, assistant secretary of the Presbyterian Historical Society of Ireland who provided information about Haslet's ministry and first marriage, and Simon Bennett, assistant archivist, University of Glasgow who supplied notes about the faculty during Haslet's matriculation.

I must give thanks to the folks at BookMasters, Inc., in Mansfield, Ohio, for advancing my manuscript from draft to bookshelf. Shelly Sapyta opened the door and Kristen Butler escorted the manuscript through to completion. There were, of course, editors and designers on staff who contributed to its final form.

Since I felt it was important to the story to give Haslet a family life, I also want to mention my own family. My sons Bruce and Kevin and my daughter Kathy and their spouses monitored the progress of their father's book as did those among my 10 grandchildren and two great grandchildren old enough to have an interest.

Finally, there is my invaluable editor, my wife Lil, a person with a voracious and eclectic reading taste who went over the whole manuscript to provide her special insight and love of books to the Haslet story.

Chapter One

Going Home

It was a remarkable Fourth of July commemoration; remarkable for the fact that thousands of Philadelphians turned out to honor a stranger.

He was not from Philadelphia, nor even from Pennsylvania, but from neighboring Delaware—and from southern Delaware, besides, about 100 miles away. At the time this took place, that was a considerable remove.

Furthermore, he had been dead for more than sixty-four years.

On the other hand, he was a war hero, killed at the battle of Princeton on January 3, 1777.

The year was 1841 and the stranger the Philadelphians were honoring was John Haslet.

Poets and biographers can lift the shroud of obscurity from the names of forgotten heroes. But few of these heroes have that good fortune and certainly not John Haslet of Delaware.

Consider Paul Revere and his famous midnight ride in 1775. It's doubtful many of the people gathered to honor Haslet in 1841 had heard of Revere, since Henry Wadsworth Longfellow didn't write his ode until 1863. Haslet's mentor, Caesar Rodney, made a historic midnight ride too. It was much longer and much more arduous. And it was much more significant because of its effect on the vote for independence on July 2, 1776. There was no bard to celebrate it, however, so it's another almost forgotten deed of the Revolution.

Sure, the people knew about Washington, Jefferson, Adams, Franklin, and the other founding fathers who were the soul of the American Revolution. They knew almost nothing about people like Haslet who were its spirit.

1

Historian Whitefield J. Bell Jr. of the American Philosophical Society commented, "The Franklins and the Jeffersons on the one hand, the scoundrels and the killers on the other, are all well known; they crowd history's galleries. But [the people] who keep alive the ideas other men conceived and hold together the institutions other men create. They are the ideal trustees, the perfect friends. They are the useful ones . . ."

Such a useful one was John Haslet.

He shared the Delaware stage with Rodney and people like John Dickinson, Thomas McKean, and George Read during those tumultuous years when Britain's North American colonies went through the paroxysms that led to the ultimate political act of revolution.

These were Delaware's men of vision. Perhaps it's appropriate that their words proved enduring. Haslet shared their visions; he worked to implement them in the years leading up to the war. It was his actions in battle, though, that brought this Irish immigrant his greatest acclaim.

Unfortunately, recognition erodes with time; the calendar replaces memory as the recorder of deeds. It leaves no room for the record of Haslet's life as a husband, father, preacher, physician, political leader—a life useful for the patriot cause in the twenty years from the time he emigrated from Ireland until his death at Princeton on the third day of January in 1777.

At the Fourth of July celebration in 1841 he would have one last flare of public adulation before fading back to the footnotes of history.

Delaware had decided it would commemorate the deeds of this almost forgotten hero as the centerpiece of the state's Fourth of July celebration in this year 1841, in hopes this might revive the spirit of '76.

The best remembered Haslet in 1841 was Joseph Haslet, as it had been only some eighteen years since he died, during his second term as governor. Joseph, by the way, was John Haslet's oldest son.

The decision to honor his memory was forced upon the legislature, prompted by the practical consideration of a permanent resting place for Delaware's war hero.

His remains had been in a grave in the old First Presbyterian churchyard in Philadelphia nearly all of these years. Now, the commercial interests in a growing city of 95,000 people had overwhelmed the spiritual interests of the dead. The church had yielded to commercial need long ago. Now, only the cemetery located on Bank Street, just off High (Market) Street between Second and Third, was standing in the path of progress.

Haslet's body had been brought to Philadelphia shortly after a British soldier had shot him dead as he was rushing to the rescue of a fallen general and friend, Hugh Mercer.

In an acceptable practice of the day, their bodies were brought to the city and laid out on the town common, displayed as inspiration to the living.

The living in Philadelphia certainly needed that inspiration and, even more so, courage. A few weeks earlier, when the advancing British army had reached the east shore of the Delaware River, concern among Philadelphians gave way to confusion and panic. Many threw their possessions into wagons and fled the city. Even the *Gazette* and *Journal* newspapers left town.

Having served the purpose, the bodies perforce were buried in the First Presbyterian churchyard in simple caskets provided by the Continental army quartermaster.

In 1783, the Delaware Assembly belatedly voted to place a monument over the site of Haslet's grave.

That would have been the end of the story until commercial development intruded on the supposed eternal resting place of the dead.

Delaware's legislators decided in January of 1841 to bring Haslet's remains back to Dover for reinterment in the Presbyterian churchyard. Obviously it would be necessary to add some ceremonial flair to the event. And why not, they decided, use the occasion to capture the feeling, the sound, the euphoria of those exciting days when the men of vision and the men of action risked their lives and fortunes in the nation's fight for independence from Great Britain. It was a melancholy fact that people had lost interest in that founding generation's ideals, in the cost of independence.

The legislature appointed a three-man committee to work out details with church and city officials in Philadelphia. Notices were sent to appropriate organizations in Delaware and Pennsylvania.

The Haslet notice came before the Hibernian Society in Philadelphia at its April 16 meeting. The meeting's priority was consideration of the society's participation in the city's April 20 tribute to the recently deceased President William Henry Harrison. It turned out there was little interest in Harrison but a lot of interest in John Haslet. Participation in the April 20 ceremonies was left to the individual member's discretion. But John Haslet was a son of Ireland. Obviously, members felt, something special was needed to honor "a son of the old sod."

From that point the Hibernian Society took charge. By its June 17 meeting, the society had developed plans for a grand commemoration. Philadelphia's tribute would exceed even that planned by his home state.

And so it was that on Friday, July 2, 1841, two brigades of the Pennsylvania militia and assorted leading citizens gathered on the warm, sunlit morning to escort the remains of Colonel John Haslet, commanding officer of the First Delaware Continentals, to the Arch Street wharf on the Delaware River where the steamship *Kent* would then take them to Dover.

His remains had been exhumed from the old churchyard the day before, transferred to a new casket—the decay of years made this a very delicate task—and moved to the church's new site on Washington Square.

The Hibernian Society had provided a beautiful, new, mahogany casket. It was lined with salmon-colored silk held in place by silver-headed nails. Silver ornaments added a splendid finish. Over the coffin was placed a black drape and the national flag with its twenty-six stars.

Philadelphians were given one last opportunity to pay their respects as the casket waited in the new Presbyterian church for the commemoration to begin. Then, at eight o'clock, the pallbearers from the Hibernian Society gently lifted it from its pedestal. Somberly the entourage walked from the church to the waiting hearse and lifted the casket into place.

The pallbearers took their places beside the carriage, flanked by members of the elite First City Troop. This unit's presence was a singular honor. It had become tradition for the First City Troop to take a conspicuous place in parades, major funerals, and any major ceremony where a display of military splendor would add cachet. It dated back to that time in 1775 when an earlier detachment of the First City Troop escorted George Washington from Philadelphia when he left to take command of the new Continental army at Boston.

The First City Troop also had fought at Princeton. Their unit flag was placed beside the Stars and Stripes on Haslet's casket.

4

The casket in place, the escorts ready, Major General Robert Patterson, commander of the Pennsylvania militia, himself Irish born and a member of the Hibernian Society, called his troops to attention.

Two cannons on the square fired a salute, the signal for the march to begin.

The cortege began its slow, steady march. Grooms led each of the four horses pulling the hearse. Clattering hoofbeats and muffled drums set the cadence for the procession. Bells pealed softly, their clappers also muffled. The military bands began playing solemn airs.

The general provost and his staff took the lead, followed by the first military band. Next came two companies of the Washington Guards, then the German Washington Artillery, followed by a second band, the Washington Greys, the Philadelphia Greys, another band, the 102nd Regiment and seven more militia companies. The remainder of the First City Troop fell in behind. Then came General Patterson and his staff, preceding the hearse.

As the hearse moved from the square, a line of carriages fell in behind, with the clergy and local judges in the first followed by the carriage with Hibernian Society President Joseph Tagert and the three members of the Delaware committee: Representatives William Huffington and Gardner Wright and Senator Charles DuPont.

After that came the federal judges, the officers of the army, navy and marines.

The members of the Hibernian Society followed on foot, green sashes over their mourning clothes.

Next in line were the citizens of Delaware living in Philadelphia, led by Colonel Thomas Robinson.

Robinson's role added a particular irony to the honors.

At the time of the Revolution, a prediction that someday a member of the Robinson family would serve as chief marshal in a tribute to John Haslet would have been dismissed as nonsense. Robinson's grandfather, also Thomas, had been Haslet's most daunting adversary in the turbulent times of the '70s. Like most American political leaders of the time, the elder Robinson had opposed the acts of Parliament that led to the disaffection of the colonists. However, he remained steadfastly loyal to King George III. As disaffection grew into rebellion, the conflict of loyalties was irreconcilable. Robinson chose the side of loyalty to the king and organized opposition to the patriots and independence.

There were many, often violent, confrontations in those tumultuous times. Ultimately the elder Robinson had been forced to flee to a British warship, then to Nova Scotia. He returned to Delaware after the war and died quietly. His son Peter and grandson Thomas, however, became prominent lawyers in Delaware.

Citizens from Maryland, New Jersey, and Pennsylvania filled the final ranks of the long column.

It was a truly splendid sight, the colors of the uniformed soldiers and of the sashes, banners, flags, and other paraphernalia of the participants flashing along the procession as it moved along the two-mile route, up Walnut, over Thirteenth, down Arch to the wharf.

Thousands upon thousands of Philadelphians leaned from the windows of their homes and gathered on the sidewalks to witness the spectacle.

They had learned from the newspapers that Haslet was born and reared in Ireland, emigrating to Delaware about 1757. There he became a practicing physician. The stories said he also was a leader of the patriot movement, that he had organized, trained, and led one of the elite regiments in the Continental army, and that he had been killed in battle.

That was enough to justify the citizens' participation. And, after all, this was a Fourth of July celebration and this was a magnificent pageant. It renewed a sense of pride in all those patriots who created this wonderful new nation, bursting with the hubris of its youth.

At last the column arrived at the Arch Street wharf, where the SS *Kent* awaited its honored passenger and his escorts. Whiffs of steam from its engines floated over the crowd in the still July air, the noise of the engines a reminder that the journey was only half completed.

A stage had been set up at the wharf and when the last of the marchers arrived and settled into place, Philadelphia Alderman John Binns walked to the front to deliver the eulogy.

The crowd grew silent and attentive as the alderman began.

"We are assembled to pay the homage of our high consideration to the memory of one, who, in the darkest days of our perilous struggles, took up arms in defense of Independence; one who bravely fought and gloriously died."

Binns dwelt briefly on another fallen hero recently honored, President Harrison. Then Binns went on, his voice expertly measuring his phrases and playing the crowd.

Service in the Continental army, he said, "has been a passport to honors and emoluments in every state of our proud Republic."

Then he invoked the name of George Washington, "the one pure, one peerless, priceless patriot, that glorious patriot who commanded when Haslet fell and who, even in the hour of victory, watered with his tears the corpse of the gallant soldier."

Mention of the revered Washington stirred the first show of emotion in the crowd. In the years since Washington's death, his life had been so sterilized by writers and politicians that his personality had become barren, lifeless, even trite. The image of a tearful George Washington was startlingly human. At the same time, his feelings for John Haslet certified for the crowd that Haslet was worth all this adulation being bestowed by their city on an out-of-town hero.

Binns went on to invoke the martial spirit indigenous to the holiday, his voice rising:

"To do honor to these remains we are here surrounded with all 'the pride, pomp and circumstance of war;' the officers of the army and of the navy, and volunteers, prompt to do homage to their departed fellow soldier, and equally prompt to emulate his example."

His voice rose higher:

"Soldiers, elevate on high your eagles; give to the breeze your Stars and Stripes and if your country calls, bear your 'star-spangled banner' to the battlefield, where it was borne and upheld by Haslet, and if you cannot bear it victorious as he did, die nobly in its defense."

Almost as if it had been rehearsed, the militia flag bearers raised their banners.

This was stirring Fourth of July oratory, conjuring images of brave soldiers carrying tattered battle flags into the ranks of a suddenly fearful enemy amidst the roar of cannons and muskets, routing the foe in the name of the United States of America.

It was time now for Binns to pay respect to his sponsors.

"The deceased, Colonel John Haslet, was a native of Ireland, a gentleman of talents, who had received a liberal education, and was by profession a physician. An association of his countrymen, the Hibernian Society, are among those now gathered 'round his remains—clods of the valley—which once were animated by as daring and patriotic a spirit as ever gave life to the image of his Creator. That society have appointed me to discharge the duty I am now performing—and which would indeed be but indifferently performed if I did not take occasion to say that the members of this society, their countrymen, and all Irishmen are proud on proper occasions, to make known that their Montgomerys, their Haslets, and their Irvines, best blood of Ireland, has been freely shed to serve the good cause of 'The Land of the Free and the Home of the Brave.'"

And, finally, Binns turned to the object of today's honors, speaking now in reverential tones:

"The state of Delaware, the near and much respected sister of Pennsylvania, adopted John Haslet. Before the Declaration of Independence, he raised and mustered a regiment at Dover, at the head of which a few days after the declaration, as its commanding officer, he marched to headquarters and placed it under the orders of Washington. The people of Delaware had marked the ardent patriotism, the fearless courage, the devotion to the public weal which characterized every act of Colonel Haslet, and they selected him to take command of as brave a regiment as ever fought for Independence. He proved altogether worthy of their confidence; he led her sons where honor and fame were to be achieved; he set them a glorious example and at the battle of Princeton, poured forth his life's blood. The state of Delaware, having enrolled the name of Haslet with her Reads and her Rodneys, will no longer permit his remains to be entombed in another state, even though that state be Pennsylvania. The constituted authorities of Delaware on the twenty-second day of February last, made arrangements to take all that remains of her heroic son to her own bosom, to deposit his relics in their own soil, and to raise over them a monument to her own glory, to cherish the remembrance of his virtues and to stimulate others to great and glorious deeds."

Now his voice rose again to bring the crowd's attention to his closing remarks:

"To you, gentlemen, who, on this interesting occasion represent the state of Delaware, are about to be surrendered the precious relics of one of your many distinguished sons; your legislature have wisely determined to take them home and to bury them deep in the soil which he had cultivated and in defense of which he nobly died."

Then he spoke softly, solemnly:

"To you gentlemen, they are now committed; deposit and reverence them, and teach your children to reverence them as the remains of him who was patriotic, great and good; thus shall you, and they, be an honor to your country."

The assemblage applauded warmly. The strings of patriotism had been expertly plucked by a master orator. He had made Haslet one with the crowd.

Now it was Assemblyman William Huffington's duty to acknowledge the favors Philadelphia had bestowed on Delaware's hero. Huffington was co-chair of the committee appointed by the Delaware Assembly to arrange Haslet's return.

He complimented Binns on his remarks, thanked the Hibernian Society, General Patterson and his militia brigades, the other distinguished citizens and the ordinary citizens of Philadelphia for the splendid tribute.

Some embellishments of the achievements of Haslet and his men were in order.

"The Delaware Continentals fought bravely and proudly from Long Island to Camden, South Carolina," Huffington said. "Their immortal journey into the annals of military history, to fame and glory began in July 1776 when John Haslet led 800 stalwart patriots of Delaware off to join the Continental army.

"More patriotic Delawareans would follow that original regiment of heroes. And five years later, barely fifty straggled home."

Huffington paused to allow time for that awesome statistic to have impact.

"Its soldiers defended their new country, the cause of independence, of freedom, in some twenty to thirty battles. They shed their blood in all of them. Few commands gave as much to this country as did the Delaware Continentals."

He credited John Haslet with creating this remarkable regiment, training it and leading it into battle. He mentioned the day in July, 1776, when Haslet addressed his assembled soldiers and instilled in this group of uncertain volunteers a sense of mission.

"John Haslet stood before them," explained Huffington, "and spoke to them in words electric and persuasive. He told them he had neither gold nor power to offer them. But he promised them eternal fame and the eternal gratitude of the nation. He reminded them of the circumstances that had led to the separation of the young colonies from the mother country, of the many grievances that had persuaded the Continental Congress independence was the only recourse.

"He spoke of the coming conflict as a crusade for man's right to worship God according to his own conscience, to enjoy the fruits of his labor in the fields and businesses without worrying about a confiscatory government thousands of miles away, to be free from an arbitrary power that would cut off his commerce as punishment, station foreign soldiers in his villages and even his homes to enforce its will. He drew a vision of a free, bountiful, happy America should this crusade succeed.

"By the time he finished, determination replaced doubt on the faces of his soldiers.

"They then marched smartly off to Philadelphia, on the road to glory, this heroic Irishman leading the way.

"Delaware has not seen John Haslet since he left. For, after fighting bravely in several campaigns from Long Island to Trenton, he fell in his last battle, one of only a handful of soldiers still left among the hundreds of the First Delaware Continentals who marched off that July day sixty-five years ago.

"The new Delaware Continentals raised after Princeton carried the spirit of the First Continentals and the soul of John Haslet to the very last battle of that glorious fight for independence.

"It is a sad footnote to the life of this heroic soldier that his widow barely survived him, dying of a broken heart shortly after she learned of his sacrifice. We understand Jemima Haslet's grief because Delaware felt it, too."

That romantic, emotional footnote to this noble life they were honoring once again stirred the crowd. Huffington continued:

"In taking him back home, we know you who have honored his memory will miss him, too. But you could not have done more honor to this hero, to Delaware, to the Commonwealth of Pennsylvania, indeed, to the United States, than the tributes poured from the hearts of your citizens today. Thank you."

The dignitaries on the stage stood up. The militia came to attention.

The hearse was moved carefully onto the deck of the *Kent*. A delegation from the Hibernian Society boarded, followed by the militia units that would accompany the casket to Dover. General Patterson joined them, as did the Delaware delegation and representatives of the other states.

The lines were freed and the SS *Kent* moved away from the wharf and headed down the Delaware River. In 1757 John Haslet had sailed up that same river to his new homeland in North America.

Chapter Two

The Capture of Fort Duquesne

More than a year after he arrived in America, John Haslet marched into Fort Duquesne on Pennsylvania's western frontier on November 25, 1758, part of a 2,500-man force of American militia and British regulars led by Brigadier General John Forbes.

The expedition's arrival was hardly a triumphal one. You could tell that from the soldiers' faces: some solemn, some angry, some shocked. Over the final three miles they had witnessed the horror of the massacre that befell comrades several weeks earlier. Plainly visible in the darkening twilight were the bodies of nearly 300 of their comrades who had been slain in a September 11, 1758, assault.

The forests, their tree limbs bare and gray, gave grim embellishment to the macabre scene.

After five months of hacking and scraping a road through 200 miles of dense forests and rugged mountains, felling trees, moving boulders, occasionally skirmishing with Indians lurking in the woods, the expedition now marched grimly towards the fort.

Most of the corpses had been scalped. The heads of some soldiers of the Royal Highlanders had been impaled on poles and their kilts wrapped around them as skirts, the Indians' particular insult, suggesting the soldiers were women, not warriors.

A twelve-year-old boy who had been a prisoner at the fort for two years described how the Indians had gathered some of the prisoners onto the parade ground of the fort, tortured them, scalped them, then burned them alive. The boy said the French seemed to enjoy the savage ritual, describing the chanting as "Indian music."

Premature death was a familiar experience in colonial times: it sometimes came as a plague, it frequently dashed out of the woods to the chilling war whoops of attacking Indians, it often attended the bedside at the moment of childbirth.

Nevertheless, the sights presented to the marching column stirred deep emotions in the marching column. Members of the Royal Highlanders roared with outrage at the treatment of their dead comrades.

Members of Haslet's own battalion were among the dead and he muttered half aloud as he walked through the scene of carnage:

"A monument to French humanity. They didn't even have the decency to bury our dead."

The dead were among 800 soldiers from the Pennsylvania and Virginia militias and the Royal Highlanders, led by Major James Grant of the Royal American Regiment in the September battle.

Grant's detachment was only supposed to reconnoiter the site to help plan for the final assault. But Grant was brash and dreamed of glory.

Duquesne was an important objective in a three-pronged offensive against French positions in North America in 1758. Major General Sir Jeffrey Amherst, newly appointed by Secretary of State William Pitt as commander of British forces in North America, planned to capture the forts that stood as gateways to Canada, to the Great Lakes, and to the Ohio Territory. Located at the point where the Allegheny and Monongahela Rivers joined to form the Ohio, Fort Duquesne stood as a formidable sentinel on the water route between French posts in Canada and the Ohio Territory. And water was the preferred means of travel.

Amherst was rewarded during the summer with the conquest of the French forts at Louisburg in Nova Scotia, and at Frontenac, where the St. Lawrence River flows from Lake Ontario. The only setback was an attack on Fort Ticonderoga. The assault against this key post between Canada and New York failed with heavy losses.

There remained Fort Duquesne.

Grant—as he would prove in subsequent years—understood how laurels in battle brought fame and fortune. Capturing Fort Duquesne would surely bring acclaim to this thirty-eight-year-old soldier.

He deployed most of his force in the woods and out of sight of the fort then sent a party to the perimeter of the fort, taunting the occupants to come out for a fight. When they did, it was Grant's plan to feign a retreat until the pursuing enemy stumbled into an ambush.

He had been led to believe there were only about 200 French soldiers and Indians in the fort. But substantial reinforcements had arrived just the day before. It was Grant's detachment, not the enemy, that was ambushed and Grant himself was captured. However, he was more fortunate than his soldiers. The French protected him and other officers from the Indians, then sent them immediately off to Montreal where Grant eventually would be released.

In the next two decades, Grant would rise through the ranks of the British army and serve as a member of Parliament (as did many English officers). As the colonists grew restive over rule from London, as their objections escalated to the point of threatening rebellion, Grant boasted in Parliament that with 5,000 men he would march from one end of the North American colonies to the other and squelch the opposition. The disdain for colonial militia which he developed during the French and Indian War never changed. Indeed, it could be argued that failure of the militia to follow his instructions had led to the debacle at Fort Duquesne in September of 1758.

And on an August day in 1776, on Long Island, Major General James Grant and Colonel John Haslet of the Delaware Continentals would meet again, this time as enemies, not comrades.

But in 1758 there were no thoughts of rebellion, let alone independence, among the provinces. The colonists supported the British government in the war against the French and served willingly under British officers.

Forbes, forty-eight, Scottish born, would not repeat the mistakes of Brigadier General Edward Braddock in 1755, particularly Braddock's casual dismissal of the fighting abilities of the French and their Indian allies. Braddock had lost nearly two-thirds of his 1,500-man army and himself was mortally wounded in an ambush near Duquesne on July 7.

Forbes was more deliberate, more open to advice from those familiar with frontier warfare. The formal battle array in an open field was not the style in this theater. His careful plan was to advance through the frontier in stages, stopping at several points along the way to construct forts and supply depots. Forbes also was a seriously ill man, even before he left Philadelphia, and trusted his second-in-command, Colonel Henry Bouquet, to carry out his orders. Bouquet, a Swiss mercenary, was a very skilled Indian fighter and an able commander. He and the general communicated by letter, Bouquet sending back reports of progress and problems, and Forbes responding with his observations and orders.

Before the expedition could march, however, there was the question to be decided of which route to take: over the old Braddock Road from Fort Cumberland, Maryland, or over a road started but not completed from Carlisle on the Pennsylvania frontier.

At the heart of the dispute was the advantage to be gained by speculators in the Virginia and Pennsylvania colonies interested in developing the Ohio Territory.

The outspoken twenty-six-year-old leader of the Virginia militia, Colonel George Washington, advocated the route taken three years earlier by Braddock. All the road needed was repair, Washington argued. He had been an aide to Braddock and barely escaped with his life in the 1755 battle.

Opponents, of course, disagreed, claiming the Braddock road was in hopeless disrepair. Furthermore, Forbes' expedition was using Carlisle as its base and, therefore, the route through Pennsylvania would be shorter.

Bouquet sent out engineers to survey the Pennsylvania route and they sent back word that there was easy passage over the Allegheny and Laurel Hill Mountains.

Forbes and Bouquet were convinced that the dispute was nothing more than provincial politics which the officers of His Majesty's forces should ignore. Forbes wrote to Bouquet at one point that he considered it "a shame for any officer to be concerned in" what he described as Washington's "scheme" to affect the decision over the road. Bouquet responded that the Virginia officers publicly advocated the Braddock road "without knowing anything of the other, having never heard from any Pennsylvania person one word about the road."

So, in late July, Forbes gave the order to proceed with the route through Pennsylvania.

When the Pennsylvania route turned out to be more troublesome than expected and it became obvious the expedition wouldn't reach Duquesne until the fall, Washington couldn't resist writing to Bouquet on August 28: "We might have been in full possession of the Ohio by now if, rather than running ourselves into the difficulties and expense of cutting an entire new road . . . Braddock's road had been adopted."

Washington learned to be more diplomatic when he became commander-in-chief of the Continental army of the United States of America.

Forbes, meanwhile, had to stop frequently to rest and regain his strength. When he did feel well enough to move, he had to be transported in a litter slung between two horses. And thus he arrived at Duquesne to find reward for the pain he suffered and satisfaction for his careful planning.

In reality, the Forbes army didn't really conquer Duquesne; the French abandoned it. By the time the expedition arrived, the French were miles away, headed either for settlements down the Ohio River or to forts near the Great Lakes.

Forbes' victory was tempered by the devastation he witnessed, the fort in ruins and the mutilated bodies of so many of his soldiers left to nature's disposition.

Writing to a friend, Francis Allison, on November 26, Haslet reported:

"We arrived at six o'clock last night, and found it in a great measure destroyed. . . . There are, I think, thirty stacks of chimneys standing, the houses all burnt down. They sprung one mine, which ruined one of their magazines. . . . They went off in such haste, that they could not make quite the havoc of their works they intended."

Forbes studied the scene. There was sorrow in his face and sadness in his voice when he finally commented to Bouquet, "There's been so much British blood shed needlessly on these grounds. Our brave soldiers and officers were not well served by their commanders here."

Bouquet nodded in agreement, uncomfortable at remembering the general's disapproval over Grant's expedition. (When he learned of the disaster, Forbes had written to Bouquet that he "could not well believe that such an attempt would have been carried out without my previous knowledge and concurrence." Bouquet had tried to explain that the mission had been prompted by an urge to stop Indian attacks on parties working outside the army's advanced base at Fort Ligonier. Grant had suggested he take a large party and go straight to the source of the trouble, presumably Duquesne, and Bouquet agreed, insisting, however, that it was only to be a reconnoitering mission.)

Forbes was still bothered by Grant's folly.

"His thirst for fame brought on his own perdition and jeopardized our expedition," he said. "He had approached me at Carlisle, asking for a command, but I suspected his motives. Even though he promised to be prudent and to avoid risks, my suspicions led me to deny his request.

"I don't doubt his indiscretion here led to last month's attack on Loyalhanna."

Emboldened by the defeat of Grant's detachment, a 600-member force of French and Indians attacked Fort Ligonier on the Loyalhanna Creek on October 12, 1758. The assault lasted three hours. The attackers drove the defenders into the fort but failed to penetrate the stockade. So, they broke off the battle. The French made another pass at the fort during the night but then gave up the effort and returned to Duquesne.

Twenty-three defenders were killed and thirty-six were wounded. Another sixty-two soldiers were listed as missing, mostly those who had been away from the fort on guard duty. The attackers' casualties were not determined.

Bouquet described the result as "humiliating." He reported to Forbes on October 15: "A thousand men keep more than 1,500 blockaded, carry off all their horses, and retire undisturbed with all their wounded and, perhaps, ours, after burying their dead. This enterprise, which should have cost the enemy dearly, shows a great deal of contempt for us."

Forbes, who had received an account from someone else, was more sanguine: "I am very glad the enemy's visit has turned out near as fruitless to them as ours was to us under Major Grant," he wrote to Bouquet, "and hope at least by this they will see we can fight."

Nevertheless, after Loyalhanna, Forbes was having second thoughts about attacking Duquesne. He had about decided to postpone the assault until spring when Indian scouts reported the astounding news that Duquesne had been abandoned.

The expedition pushed on. And now the arduous journey had been at last marked with success.

It was time to get on with securing the gain.

First, however, the soldiers went about the task of burying the dead.

In the course of scouring the woods, they also found bones they surmised were those of Braddock's soldiers. These, too, were gathered for burial.

The most poignant finding was what appeared to be the inter-twined bones of two people in the woods. They were thought to be the remains of Colonel Peter Halkett and his son, James, a lieutenant, who had been killed almost simultaneously in the massacre of Braddock's army.

Another son, Brigade Major Francis Halkett, chief aide to Forbes, arrived as the soldiers studied the scene.

"This most certainly was your father and brother," an officer said. "I understand they fell together, that your father was killed first and your brother right after, falling on your father's body."

"Yes," Halkett replied. "I recognize my father's peculiarly shaped tooth. It's something he used to make a great show about."

Halkett's face grew pale and he started to fall, one of the soldiers grabbing him to steady him. Halkett uttered a barely audible moan, but nothing more. He regained his composure, turned, and left.

While the soldiers went on about the grim task, Forbes and Bouquet met with their commanders to plan the next moves.

"First," Forbes began, "I will declare a day of prayer and thanks-giving for our success."

Turning to Bouquet, "Please note it for your orderly book."

He paused while Bouquet made notes, then continued:

"We'll rename this fort in honor of William Pitt."

There were nods of approval from the assembled officers.

Pitt, as secretary of state, had taken over direction of the war against the French in 1757. Until then, the war had been going badly for the Eng-lish, and King George II decided to form a new government under Thomas Pelham-Holles, Duke of Newcastle, with Pitt as the secretary of state. Pitt was the real power in the administration and his energy, enthusiasm, and leadership skills infused the war effort with a new dynamism.

"We'll build an even grander fort here than the French," Forbes continued.

He turned to Colonel Washington and Colonel James Burd of the 2nd Pennsylvania Regiment:

"You will provide soldiers to garrison the fort, 200 from each regiment.

"Colonel Mercer of Pennsylvania will be in command."

Forbes and Bouquet had already decided on that choice, hoping it would be acceptable to Washington because he and the Pennsylvanian were known to be friends. Hugh Mercer, in command of Pennsylvania's Third Battalion, had been left behind to protect Fort Ligonier, but was regarded as a very able soldier and leader. Washington's first choice probably would have been his own Colonel George Mercer but it was true that he and Hugh Mercer were friends, dating back to earlier battles. Washington believed he could at least persuade Hugh Mercer to be neutral in any disagreements between the two provinces over access to the Ohio Territory.

"Colonel Mercer is a fine choice," Washington agreed.

Despite his youth, Washington's opinions carried great weight because of his experience on the frontier and his previous engagements with the French. In fact, some blamed the start of this whole war on Washington, recalling how he had led forty Virginia militiamen in an attack against a French outpost in western Pennsylvania in late May, 1754.

At the time the two nations were technically at peace, but Virginia, after all, was subject to English rule and direction.

With Washington's acquiescence, Forbes turned to Bouquet:

"Colonel, see that arrangements are made to keep Fort Pitt supplied through the winter. I'll send a courier to Sir Jeffrey to tell him of our plans. As soon as conditions permit, instruct Colonel Mercer to see to the building of a fort here that will do honor to Mr. Pitt, a fort that will stand as a symbol of British power in North America. I want a grand fort."

"I'll not leave here until I'm satisfied your wishes will be fulfilled," Bouquet responded. "I'll see to provisions for the garrison. And I'll assign Captain Gordon as chief engineer."

"A fine choice," Forbes agreed. Harry Gordon was a member of the 60th Regiment with an excellent reputation as an engineer.

"I expect to leave in a day or so for Philadelphia," Forbes said. "I'll make it my personal responsibility to see that the assembly there is prompt in meeting its commitments to sustain our presence in the frontier."

Earlier in the year, Forbes had threatened to abandon the expedition and leave the Pennsylvania frontier to the French and the Indians if that colony's legislature was not more dependable in providing the wagons for transport and the forage and supplies for the teams and soldiers. But he felt Virginia, the most populous of all the colonies, also was delinquent in its efforts.

"Colonel Washington, I'll count on you to do the same with Governor Fauquier at Williamsburg."

He paused for effect: "Your colony's assembly hasn't always been timely in providing its share of the support."

Washington showed no emotion, replying calmly:

"Virginia has always supplied the men and means demanded of it and will continue to do so."

The two men left it at that and the meeting disbanded.

For Haslet, the arrival at Duquesne was a different milestone.

He had been mostly rootless in the months since his 1757 arrival at Philadelphia from the port of Londonderry in Ireland's province of Ulster.

At first he found temporary lodging among cousins that had immigrated earlier and were now living along the Pennsylvania–Maryland border.

As a graduate of the University of Glasgow and an ordained Presbyterian minister, he soon made himself available to various congregations in the rural area. It was common practice for settlers to establish a congregation as soon as there were enough neighbors to warrant it. Consequently there were far fewer ministers than there were congregations.

A man with Haslet's background supplied their needs very nicely. He had served a church in Ballykelly, County Derry, for the five years preceding his emigration, also marrying the daughter of the previous minister. But the death of his wife in childbirth in 1752 shook his faith and for most of his ministry the effects marred his spiritual service to his people. They, in turn, responded with indifferent support to his material needs. The combination of spiritual ennui and material deprivation finally influenced his decision to emigrate. He left it to his father to pursue the debt owed by the congregation.

(It took several years before the Presbytery of Derry was able to enforce payment of the debt.)

Although the challenge of settling into a new world was invigorating, Haslet found the return to the pulpit unsatisfying. He found respite in the Pennsylvania militia, recruiting a company of mostly fellow Irish immigrants among the congregations. On April 28, 1758, he was commissioned a captain in the Second Battalion.

Haslet was over six feet tall, lean, muscular, and very handsome, a fact often noted by the young women in his home townland of Straw and in neighboring townlands like Drumneecy and Camnish. The women who followed the Forbes expedition—wives, girlfriends, cooks, seamstresses and so forth—would readily agree with the women back in Ulster. The young man had a charm that made people feel comfortable, that made friends of the men and admirers of the women.

Now, however, shelter was the immediate problem. The Duquesne contingent had marched off from Fort Ligonier with light supplies, leaving their equipage behind. Improvising shelter from the debris from the fort, they made camp as comfortable as the weather and circumstances allowed.

The men relaxed now by a fire, conversation among them casual, mostly about home, the future. Among them was Captain John McClughan of the lower counties militia. Haslet, anticipating that his enlistment in the Pennsylvania militia would soon come to an end, felt it was time to consider a permanent home in America and McClughan would influence that choice.

The "lower counties of the Delaware" referred to the counties of New Castle, Kent, and Sussex along the Delaware River. They had functioned as a semiautonomous colony for half a century, subject only to the authority of the Pennsylvania governor and executive council. The three counties had created their own legislature because of their dissatisfaction with the Pennsylvania Assembly and what they perceived as its indifference to the needs of the lower counties.

Their militia had marched with the Second Pennsylvania Battalion and Haslet had found McClughan engaging company. The man constantly talked of the benefits of life along the Delaware. He himself had settled in New Castle County after emigrating from Ireland.

"John, if you have no other plans, you should consider finding a plantation in the lower counties," McClughan said. "There is much land available and it is fertile; there is much game; the waters are filled with fish and shellfish. There are many fine rivers and streams in the lower counties for commerce with places like Philadelphia; even, perhaps to the West Indies or Europe. There are endless opportunities for a clever man like yourself."

"Sounds very attractive," Haslet answered. "I just haven't made up my mind. Maybe I'll return to preaching. There are many Presbyterian meeting houses without a minister. I am, after all, ordained. And preaching the Lord's word sustained me very well after I first arrived in this continent. I just haven't a clear idea at this point."

"There are meeting houses in the lower counties, too, that need a minister," McClughan said.

"Well, if the Pennsylvania regiment is disbanded, I'll consider it."

They sat silently for a while, engrossed in study of the flames in the camp fire.

"What do you think of that young Virginia colonel?" McClughan broke the silence.

"Washington?" Haslet stopped to collect his impressions." He seems a stalwart leader. His age seems to be of no consequence to the men under him. There's something in his bearing, in his mien that commands respect. And he's as fine a horseman as I've ever seen."

"I find him a difficult man to approach," McClughan said.

"I've not had any reason to deal with him," Haslet responded.

"They say he's quite different with the ladies," McClughan said, smiling. "They say he's as graceful in the ballroom as he is on a horse."

"I suspect we'll hear more of him in the years ahead," Haslet commented.

Conversation gave way to contemplation, the flames somehow seeming to illuminate the visions in their minds until, one by one, the tired men moved to their shelters to seek the release of deep sleep.

In December, 1758, the Pennsylvania legislature did, in fact, disband its militia, except for a few hundred men needed to garrison Fort Pitt and other frontier outposts. Haslet returned to Lancaster County and resumed supplying the scattered Presbyterian congregations there and in neighboring areas.

Forbes, meanwhile, returned to Philadelphia where he was honored with a grand celebration. But his illness finally ended his life in March of 1759. Brigadier General John Stanwix was appointed to succeed him and a new call went out for militia levies. Haslet once again recruited a company and returned to the frontier.

This time, however, the service was mostly uneventful, his time spent in road building and escorting supplies to the various outposts. There were only minor skirmishes with the Indians, most of whose tribal leaders had decided to cast their lot with the British, perceiving that the time of French hegemony in the west was ended.

At year's end, Haslet once again was faced with decisions about his future. He had learned that a man with a university education could easily set up practice as a doctor in America and so he decided that's what he would do. Living nearby in Pennsylvania he had visited the lower counties often enough to agree with McClughan that they would be a good place to settle.

He chose a place along the Mispillion River that marked the line between Kent and Sussex counties.

There was indeed need for ministers in those counties, so he continued to supply the meeting houses there as needed while he built up his practice of medicine.

Two years had now gone by since his arrival from Ireland. He was ready to establish himself in this new world and he set about doing that with a determination that would make him a leading figure in the colony.

Chapter Three

Jemima

John Brinckle shifted restlessly in his bed, his fever and pain making it difficult for him to focus on instructions he was giving to the man seated beside the bed.

At the age of sixty-six, he had lived a long life by colonial standards; it was time now, he had decided, to draw his will, as friends and family had urged. He remembered that his friend Henry Molleston, whose only daughter Brinckle had married, had made it a point to have a will drawn just before his death eighteen months earlier.

That was how John Haslet came to Brinckle's bedside on September 25, 1764. Although he was a newcomer to the neighborhood along the Mispillion River in lower Delaware—setting up practice as a physician only four years prior—the thirty-six-year-old Haslet's imposing physical appearance had brought him notice and his charm and intellect had quickly won him friends in the community, many of whom were, like himself, immigrants from Ireland.

Also, Haslet was college educated and had impressed his neighbors with his knowledge of many things, including the law. He had come to Brinckle's bedside as physician, but the man's condition was beyond an eighteenth century physician's powers; drawing a will was not.

Brinckle's ancestors had come to the area in the late 1600s and were early on players in the political life of the colony. A Brinckle ancestor was involved in the 1704 split with Pennsylvania when the three Delaware counties formed their own legislature. Both John Brinckle and his uncle served in the colonial assembly; in fact John Brinckle had served fifteen years.

Now, Haslet sat at the bedside of John Brinckle, making notes as the ailing man haltingly gave instructions for the disposition of his estate.

Brinckle was perspiring heavily. Dampened sections of his night-gown clung to his body and the dampness spread to the folds of linen bedclothes.

"I want to leave most of my land to my sister Sarah's children, Spenser Cole and his sister, Emilia," Brinckle said.

"I've raised them as my own children since their father died," he explained. "Neither my first wife, Susanna, nor Jemima have blessed me with children." His disappointment was plain. Jemima, Henry Molleston's daughter, and Brinckle had been married long enough to accept they were going to be childless.

The plantation where he built his home would go to Spenser, along with an adjacent tract, some 375 acres in all. Another 1,000 acres would be split between Spenser and Emilia.

Brinckle has done well, Haslet thought.

"You must make provision should either of the Cole children die before you do," Haslet advised him, at the same time thinking that was unlikely.

Brinckle thought about that for a while.

"Well, if Spenser dies then his share will go to the oldest male heir of my eldest sister."

"And if Emilia dies?" Haslet prodded him.

Another pause while Brinckle considered that possibility.

"In that case, her share will go to Spenser."

His slaves would be distributed among the two Cole children and his wife Jemima. She also would get the furniture along with a horse, livestock, and the furniture she brought with her when they married.

Money from the plantation and twenty cows, calves, ewes, and lambs would be used for Spenser's education. Jemima and Reyneer Williams, brother of his first wife, would be administrators.

One of his slaves, a horse, and a portion of his crops would go to friends and in-laws.

He decided to allow a tenant, Joseph Nichols, to keep the profits from his acre of land in exchange for forty shillings a year.

Williams would get his clothing, buttons, and ring.

He would forgive fees due him as a justice from persons possessing assets less than £12.

"Whatever is left," Brinckle continued, "can go to my niece Penelope Williams, and to Spenser and Emilia and their older sisters, Sarah and Mary.

"That's everything, John. I trust you to put all this in proper form."

"You may rest in peace with the Lord that your estate will be distributed as you wish," Haslet assured him. "But please don't be discouraged about your health, John. Don't anticipate passage to the kingdom of God, however welcome it may seem. You've made the proper preparations for that passage, so let's attend to this life. I think prayers for your recovery would be in order."

Haslet's education for the ministry asserted itself at times when situations seemed beyond control of the temporal world. Brinckle's life certainly seemed beyond any mortal assistance.

Haslet took the man's hand in his, bowed his head, and began to pray. Brinckle was silent, merely staring at the ceiling. His hand felt lifeless to Haslet, who feared the patient was slipping more quickly than expected.

However, Brinckle was breathing quietly, and after a few minutes, Haslet turned to a table by the window and began translating his notes into a formal document. When he had finished, he began reading aloud:

"Here's what I've written for you, John."

Brinckle raised himself feebly in his bed as Haslet read aloud:

"In the name of God, Amen, I, John Brinckle, sensible of the uncertainty of human life in general and of the weak and sick condition in which the Divine Providence hath at present placed me, and being sound in my judgment and understanding, do recommend my soul to the God of all mercy, order my body to be decently interred, when it shall please his wisdom to call me hence . . ."

Brinckle motioned for him to stop. He did not feel like talking about his will.

"Is Curtis here?" he asked after a long silence. Curtis was a cousin and had been summoned because of John Brinckle's condition.

"He and Sarah are downstairs with your wife," Haslet replied. "I'll go get them and send them up. Why don't you read this while I'm gone."

"All right, but please keep the terms of my will secret until we've done with it."

Haslet put the draft of the will by Brinckle's side and left.

Shortly thereafter, Sarah and Curtis Brinckle entered the sick room.

"How are you doing, John?" Curtis asked his cousin. Curtis, fifty-seven, was nine years younger than Brinckle.

"I'm going as fast as I can," came the feeble response.

His cousin's obvious distress shocked Curtis.

They talked for a while, until Haslet returned to the room.

"Have you had a chance to look this over, John?" Haslet asked, picking up the paper lying apparently untouched on the bed.

"It's not right, doctor. It's just not right."

Brinckle appeared agitated. He snatched the paper from Haslet and threw it behind him. Fever and pain had deprived him of his senses, Haslet concluded.

"All right, John," Haslet said. "I'll make some changes."

He left the room.

The younger Brinckles remained to talk to John Brinckle about family and friends, news of the neighborhood.

"How is he, doctor?" Jemima asked as Haslet came into the kitchen.

"Not well, Mrs. Brinckle," Haslet responded. "I am afraid his time is very short, that the good Lord may call him before not too much more time.

"He seems to be confused about the will, although it is exactly as he proposed. I'll write a new copy and present that to him. I'll tell him I've made some changes, according to his wishes. In all honesty, I am concerned that we will lose him before he can put a proper close to this."

"I'm sure you are doing your best, doctor.'

She busied herself for several minutes about the fireplace and for the first time Haslet studied her closely. In all his previous visits, she had remained in the background, dominated by her much older husband.

She was an attractive young woman, trim, fair of face, brown hair coursing from under her cap and tied in a bun. Catching his glance, she broke the silence:

"Would you like some breakfast?"

"Thank you. That would be welcomed. I'd almost forgotten about food."

He smiled: "It's been a long night and my stomach is beginning to make urgent demands for my attention."

She placed a bowl of oatmeal in front of him, along with a spoon.

"I have a choice of venison or sausages, doctor," she added. "What would you like next?"

26

In the custom of the day, she had several courses cooking in the large fireplace.

"Sausages would be fine."

Haslet noted with approval that Jemima Brinckle kept a fine kitchen. Pots and kettles not involved in her cooking were hung neatly on hooks by the fireplace. There were racks for the eating utensils and an array of plates, bowls, and cups—some of pewter—were organized neatly on a sideboard adjacent to the fireplace. The door to the Dutch oven revealed a warm loaf of bread just about ready for the table.

Jemima placed a helping of buckwheat cakes alongside the sausages and was pleased to find Mr. Haslet seemed to enjoy her cooking.

He did indeed. Mrs. Brinckle, he thought, was an excellent cook.

As she served the various courses, Jemima glanced at the young man at the table, curious about this person in whom her husband had placed such trust. She had seen him before; he had visited the house on a number of occasions and he was active in the little community of plantations along the Kent-Sussex County line. But she had never exchanged more than brief greetings with him.

Haslet's homeland in Ulster
Photo by Michael Higgins

"You're from Ireland, I've heard." It was part question, part assurance that he wasn't a complete stranger to her.

"Yes, from the northern part of the country, in the province known as Ulster."

"What is it like in Ireland?"

"It is different. More like Pennsylvania with rolling hills, mountains, farmland. My family lives in the Roe Valley, in a townland called Straw. It's between Dungiven and Limavady in County Derry."

Except for the alluring thought of faraway places, the names meant nothing to Jemima. She only knew that Ireland was an island, and that it was close to England.

"It is beautiful, perhaps the most beautiful part of Ireland," Haslet continued. "Its people tend to get lyrical when they talk about it, as you may have noted. In fact, there's been many a song inspired by its beauty and history."

Jemima refilled his coffee cup in silence, letting his memories run their course. After a time she asked:

"Are you married?"

"I was. She died in childbirth a dozen years ago."

"I'm truly sorry. Did the child survive?"

Talk of children was difficult for Jemima. She felt it as a personal failure that she and John Brinckle had not conceived any children. Haslet caught her quick glance at a small, child-size chair in the corner.

"The child is a girl," he said, recapturing the young woman's attention. "We named her Mary but everyone knows her as Polly."

"And where is she?"

"She's with one of my uncles in Ulster. I intend to bring her over as soon as I can provide a proper home for her. Soon, I pray."

"Do you have any family here, doctor?"

"Two brothers. My brother William and I sailed together in 1757. Our brother Joseph came over about a year ago."

"And where are they living?" she asked.

"William is in Maryland, in Caroline County. Joseph is living now with cousins in Pennsylvania—the same family I stayed with when I first arrived—but is talking about moving into Queen Anne County."

"Do you see them much?"

"I've seen William several times since the war. Joseph I saw soon after he arrived but not since."

"Did you come from a large family?"

"In fact, there are many Haslet families in Ulster," he said.

"In my own family I have another brother and two sisters back home. I have many uncles and cousins living nearby, in a place called Drumneecy. You'd find lots of Haslets if you visited Ulster."

"Does your family go back a long way in Ireland?"

"Yes, but I was told my ancestors actually came from Holland a couple hundred years ago to escape religious oppression. They probably settled for a time in Scotland before crossing to Ulster."

This was too much history, too much geography for Jemima. She returned to her favorite theme: family.

"Are your parents alive?"

"Yes, my father is a merchant and farmer in the townland of Straw."

"My father died a couple years ago," Jemima said. There was silence for a while, then she added: "Our family was very close with the Brinckles."

She sensed the unspoken question of how a young woman like herself came to marry a man so much older.

That thought had, in fact, entered Haslet's mind, but he decided it would be indiscreet to voice it.

There was another period of silence as Jemima busied herself around the kitchen. Finally, she returned to the table where Haslet was busily writing out the will.

"You were in the war, I understand."

"Yes, I served with the Pennsylvania regiment in '58 and '59."

"Are you planning to settle here permanently?"

"Yes. In fact, I went up to Philadelphia in July two years ago—1762—to bid on some land over between the Mispillion and Swan Creek. Two hundred fifty acres. I'm still waiting for my bid to be approved in London by the partners. There are several of them, but I assume they would take the recommendation of their agent in Philadelphia. Also, there were several parcels—11,000 acres in all—and I suppose dealing with all that land adds to the delay. As you can suppose, I'm anxious to be settled."

Jemima was curious that this handsome, charming young man had remained single these past twelve years. She wondered about the woman who had been the other half of "we." What was she like to attract this handsome young man? What was there about this other woman that Haslet passed all these years without finding a new mate?

Widowhood was common to both men and women but the young ones usually remarried quickly after the loss of their spouse.

The thought struck her that she faced the prospect of widowhood herself. Her mind drifted to thoughts of her own future. There was no further conversation between them. Haslet finished rewriting the will and stood up.

"Perhaps this version will satisfy your husband."

She did not demonstrate any curiosity about the will and Haslet returned to the upstairs bedroom.

"I must review this privately with John," Haslet told the younger Brinckles, "then I will ask you to return to witness his assent."

Curtis interrupted to remind Haslet about his cousin's intent to take care of his tenant, Joseph Nichols.

"That is done and in the will," Haslet answered.

"And he's often mentioned he wants to leave his clothing to Reyneer."

"That's also been included."

Satisfied, Curtis went back downstairs.

It was only another short time before Haslet called down: "Would everyone please come up here?"

There was an ominous tenor in his voice. They were not surprised when they entered the room to find John Brinckle had died.

Haslet suggested they all pray together and led them in supplication to God to care for their departed spouse and kin.

Then he turned to Jemima: "Mrs. Brinckle, do you need any further help from me?" he asked. She merely stared at the body on the bed, her feelings concealed. Memories of their short life together occupied her mind. She could think of nothing to say and merely shook her head.

For now, however, according to the custom of the day, she would have to prepare her husband's body and make the arrangements for its burial

When the will was offered for probate two weeks later, Jemima Brinckle, accompanied by counsel, contested it. Kent County Deputy Register of Wills Caesar Rodney heard testimony from Haslet, from Curtis and Sarah Brinckle, and from a friend of Brinckle.

Haslet testified that he felt Brinckle was sound of mind at the time he dictated notes for his will. The younger Brinckles related details of the day Brinckle died and what they knew of his intentions about his property. The friend, Thomas Parke, added that Brinckle had told him he intended to take care of the Cole children. But Parke had not seen Brinckle for the six months before his death. At the end, Rodney concluded there was insufficient witness to the will and ruled in favor of the widow.

Thus Jemima came to manage the vast plantation. She managed it well, assisted by her brothers and by Reyneer Williams. Williams, who had married the Cole children's older sister Penelope earlier in the year, took the Cole children under his care.

John Haslet frequently stopped by the plantation to see if Jemima needed any help. Gradually, interest became more than that of a concerned neighbor. He was impressed by Jemima's ability to manage affairs, but the pleasure of her company became more of an attraction.

Chapter Four

Wedding Plans

The morning sun was still low in the sky as John Haslet arrived at the Brinckle plantation, his first stop of a busy day. Visits to some of his patients and an important meeting at the Three Runs Church, also were to be part of his day. But the first stop concerned a very personal matter.

In the months he had been visiting the plantation since Brinckle's death in late 1764, his interest had changed. His visits started out as an effort to help the attractive young widow with managing the property, but this soon became the kind of self-deception one practices to divert the mind from emotions that demand more serious commitments.

He dismounted, rehearsing silently one more time what he would say to Jemima Brinckle, and turned his horse over to the Negro boy Tobe.

By now the slaves on the Brinckle plantation all knew Haslet. The older and wiser ones perceived he could be more than just a visitor someday. On this day in the early fall of 1765 the young man was going to confirm their perceptions.

Jemima was, as usual, busy in the kitchen with sundry chores, assisted by Sarah, Phyllis, and Jean, three of the eleven slaves on the plantation.

Her face revealed that this visitor was someone special, and her voice as she greeted him was quite a bit more than just cheerful. He returned her welcome, greeted the servants, then asked them to leave. This they promptly did, smiling because they suspected why he had asked to be alone with the mistress of the plantation.

"Mrs. Brinckle," he began, as usual using the more formal address as a check on his feelings for her. He took a deep breath.

"Jemima," he said, a shy smile crossing his face. She was not used to that because she had never seen him as a shy man. She was startled by this familiar address and looked him square in the face, trying to guess his thoughts.

"I've been coming to this place for about a year now, to give you what help I could in keeping things in order." He paused at an after-thought. "As if you really needed any help."

"Oh, but I did, doctor, I did. And you've been most helpful. Believe me, I appreciate all that you've done for me in helping to look after things. Did you have doubts?"

She looked at him curiously, but he was looking into space, obviously searching for words, again something that surprised her. Her pulse beat a little faster as she realized this was not going to be an ordinary visit.

"Thank you," he responded and proceeded to the point of this visit.

"For some time now, I've found your company more appealing than helping with the plantation. Helping you has become an excuse, not a purpose."

Once again, he took a deep breath.

"I would like to make it a permanent arrangement, Jemima. I've been a single man now for several years. After my wife died, I wasn't interested in any of the women I knew in Ireland. And since I arrived in America I suppose I've been more concerned about getting established than about a family. But I've been in this country more than seven—in fact, for eight—years. And even if I had just arrived, my heart would have led me to this decision."

Jemima continued to look directly at him, but her heart was beating faster. She recalled all she had learned about him, thinking about her response to the question she suspected would be forthcoming. The response would be easy. She had decided some time ago she would like this man to take her as his wife.

"I've grown quite fond of you, Jemima. In fact, I'm in love with you. Would you consent to become my wife?"

She blushed, looking away now to await an appropriate period before responding.

"Yes, John, I'll marry you," she answered finally. "I fell in love with you a long time ago and hoped this time would come. You would make me a very happy woman—a very fortunate woman."

They looked at each other for a while. Their hands locked, then Haslet pulled her toward him and their lips met. The passion so long subdued overwhelmed them and prolonged their kiss.

After a few minutes, they sat silently on the bench by the big oak dining table, facing the fireplace, her head resting on his shoulder, substituting feelings for conversation.

"Well," he said, finally. "We've much to do, much to plan."

Jemima straightened up.

"Will we live here?" she asked, a moment of practicality intruding into her thoughts. She had found comfort, independence, in this place and for the first time had to confront the possibility she would leave it. Besides, she knew he owned no land himself.

"For a while," he responded and noticed her relief at his answer. "I really would like to have a place of my own. I've been looking at some property over by the Fairfield and Longfield tracts. And I still have my bid in for another piece of land in that same area."

"That's a very nice area," she agreed.

After a bit, he spoke again.

"I'd like to bring my daughter Polly from Ireland."

Jemima had considered that possibility when she thought about her prospects of marrying him. She was a bit apprehensive, but stepparenting was common to colonial men and women and she was not aware of any problems any of the stepmothers she knew had.

"Of course," she said. "She should be with her father."

Jemima looked directly at him: "I'll treat her as my own child."

The prospect of motherhood, even stepmotherhood, elevated her spirits. She also hoped she and John would have many children of their own. That made her frown slightly, because she wasn't sure whether her failure to have children to that point indicated she was barren.

"Letters from family and the dispatches in the newspaper speak of much violence in Ireland," he elaborated. "I would be much more comfortable having her with me where she can grow to womanhood in peace and security."

She didn't feel he needed to justify his decision about Polly. She asked instead: "Is Ireland a particularly violent country?"

He smiled ruefully.

"We Irish have a way of expressing our opinions forcefully," he explained. "When we get upset, our blood tends to rule our minds. There are many things upsetting my countrymen now—absentee landlords for one. They're forced to farm land owned by people they never see and who, therefore, never care about them. There are also religious problems. The Church of England rules all. A person can gain no advancement without swearing allegiance to that church. That puts us Presbyterians—and, of course, the Catholics—at great disadvantage."

She noticed a hard edge in his voice, accented by the firm set of his jaw.

"But violence?" she said. "What kind of violence?"

Violence—robberies, burglaries—was not unknown to the colonies, particularly in the cities like Philadelphia, on the roads and along the frontier.

He spoke of something different.

"About a year ago, a dozen or so English soldiers were escorting prisoners to the jail in County Kilkenny when they were attacked by several hundred members of a gang that are called the White Boys."

"White Boys?" she interrupted. "Why that name?"

"They wear white shirts," he explained. "I understand their officers have white bands in their hats. There was much slaughter on both sides. It was quiet for a while but now, I understand, the White Boys are still active."

He told the story straightforwardly, without any indication of judgment on his part.

"Is Kilkenny near your home?"

"No, it's in the southern part of Ireland. I tell the story merely to illustrate the kinds of violence that make me concerned about my daughter. It is a violence bred by resentment over absentee landlords, denial of rights to those who don't belong to the privileged class or the privileged church.

"Feelings are no less strong in my part of Ireland. There we have a group called the Oak Boys whose behavior is not unlike that of the White Boys. We haven't heard of any activity from them lately, but I fear we may at any time."

Sensing discomfort in Jemima, he smiled and changed the mood: "In love, passion is not a bad thing at all." She blushed at the meaning.

They talked about the wedding. It would be a simple affair, at Three Runs Presbyterian Church, with the Reverend Alexander Huston, the new pastor, presiding. Houston, a native of Dublin who had studied for the ministry at the College of New Jersey, had been at Three Runs since August of 1764.

"I've been thinking about the Cole children, too," Haslet said. "Your late husband was very concerned about his niece and nephew. After all, he did raise them and treated them as if they were his own children. It would be an injustice to his memory if we left the sole burden of raising them to Reyneer Williams."

Williams had been married to John Brinckle's sister and after she died married Penelope Cole, the older sister of Spenser and Emilia Cole. He had taken Spenser and Emilia to live with him after John Brinckle died.

"I've been concerned about them, too," she said. "I fear they misunderstood my intentions about them when I challenged my late husband's will, but I've been so busy with the plantation I confess I've almost forgotten them. I'm ashamed."

Haslet had never asked for an explanation of her challenge to the will he had helped draft. She did not offer an explanation then, nor now. He already had decided it wasn't important to him.

"There's time enough to make amends," she said. "There's money in this land that can be turned over to them. I believe that would satisfy the spirit of John Brinckle's intentions for the two children."

Haslet readily agreed and over the next three years they would provide over £700 for Spenser and Emilia Cole's support.

Their arms around each other's waists, they walked outside to talk to the slaves.

"Dr. Haslet will be coming to live here permanently and will be the new master of the plantation," she announced as the men, women, and children gathered in the yard.

"That's wonderful news, ma'am," Sarah responded for the group.

"Yes, wonderful," echoed Gosman, the senior male.

"We'll live here for a while," Haslet added, "then Mrs. Brinckle and I will find our own place. It will be in this area."

There was no response. There was nothing the slaves could do about that anyhow, but each wondered what that might mean for him or her. Would they move to the new plantation? Would they become property of new owners of the Brinckle plantation? Or would they be sold off to other owners? These concerns they reserved for later, when they were alone among themselves.

"Tobe, would you please bring my horse?" Haslet asked the boy.

Turning to Jemima: "I'm going to visit some of my patients. Then there's a meeting at the church this evening about a tax the British government has imposed on the colonies. It has created much displeasure everywhere, in all the colonies."

In a prescient moment, Jemima suspected politics would play a much larger role in her future than it had in the past, that she would remember her life with John Brinckle as a tranquil period of her adult life, even though Brinckle had been politically active. However, during the years of her marriage she always had found things to do, absenting herself except to keep the men's thirst and appetites satisfied. And now, John Haslet hinted at a more contentious political environment.

While Tobe held his horse, Haslet reentered the house with Jemima. They looked fondly at each other. He kissed her warmly.

"I am a very happy man," he said.

"And I a happy woman," she responded.

Haslet left the kitchen, mounted and rode away.

The tax he referred to in his conversation with Jemima was the Stamp Act and it had, indeed, stirred colonial emotions as nothing else had since the colonies were settled.

Chapter Five

The Seed of Rebellion Is Planted

The relationship between the English government and its American colonies had been close and supportive through the French and Indian War. But it had been an expensive war and by November of 1763, the year in which the Treaty of Paris formally ended that war, King George III impressed upon Parliament the need to raise money to pay for it.

So, in 1764 the government began a long term policy of seeking to bolster revenues from these colonies, a policy that would destroy their historic ties.

First off, the government decided to strengthen the enforcement of the old laws regulating colonial trade, laws that were often ignored because smuggling was a lucrative part of colonial commerce.

Laws long unenforced seem more obnoxious when they are suddenly given life.

Parliament also voted to impose new duties on certain imports to the colonies. Among other things, the Revenue Act of 1764 (also known as the Sugar Act) imposed a heavy duty on the import of Madeira wine, a colonial favorite, while favoring wine imported from England. It also extended restrictions on trade, notably with the French and Spanish possessions in the Caribbean which had been active trading partners with the colonies

The colonials had always conceded Parliament's right to regulate trade within its empire. However, this act blatantly declared it was intended to "raise revenue" and the colonists assumed that was something their assemblies had the exclusive right to do.

Parliament also considered a tax on legal documents and printed material such as newspapers, to be collected through stamps, but decided to wait to see how the new trade impositions would work.

Over the holiday period at the end of 1764, government leaders, meeting with the king, decided to proceed with what became known as the Stamp Act.

Prime Minister George Grenville summoned a delegation of colonial agents, headed by Pennsylvania's Benjamin Franklin, to his office on February 2, 1765, to ask about their respective colonies' positions.

Franklin, only recently arrived in England, had first heard about the possibility of the tax while still in Philadelphia and at first looked favorably upon the idea, a posture that cost him some political support later. Now, however, he was very aware of the growing opposition back home.

After the men were seated and greetings stiffly exchanged—the agents already had an inkling of the reason for the meeting—Grenville asked for their opinions about colonial reaction.

"I believe they will strenuously resist," Franklin responded, "and I fear the consequences on our relationship will be like the sun setting on the horizon."

Grenville frowned with displeasure at what seemed like an impertinence.

"I don't doubt," Franklin continued, "that Parliament is the supreme legislature of the empire. Many of my friends in America, question, however, whether it alone can decide how American colonies will pay to support their part of the empire. I think it also is worth noting that while Parliament claims the right, constitutionally, to tax Ireland, it does not exercise that right. I should think Irish liberties would be endangered if Parliament did tax them. I have the same objections and some even stronger against your taxing America."

Franklin was determined to be as candid in his presentation as his very agile mind would allow.

"I don't believe it is necessary," he continued, warming to his argument. "There are other ways of raising all the money there requisite for public service. These other ways have succeeded in the past. In fact, the colonies have in general showed the utmost alacrity to contribute to the common cause. While we accept that Parliament is supreme we also believe there should be bounds on the extent of its power over the British subjects in America.

"And if the majority of Parliament think they ought not to set these bounds, then they should give representation in Parliament to the American colonies. They have done so formerly to much less considerable parts of the British dominions. If they don't, I shall think the liberties of America in danger and the liberties of Great Britain, too. Colonial liberties cannot be injured without danger to Great Britain's liberties as well. I do not say the liberty of America will be lost merely because it has no share in the election of members. But if the government renders the colonial assemblies useless or unnecessary, America will lack the means it now has and that every other part of the British dominions has, to defend its rights against those who would burgle those rights. I thank God, that hasn't happened yet."

Grenville sat at his desk, staring with the blank expression of a closed mind, but his eyes flickered at what seemed an odious comparison of the members of Parliament to common burglars. Just as quickly his impassive look returned.

In nearly a quarter century as a member and most recently as its leader, he had heard complaints about Parliament's exercise of its powers over and over again and just as easily dismissed them. After all, when the rebel John Wilkes dared to criticize the king in an issue of his newspaper, he had been jailed, expelled from Parliament, and now was living in virtual exile in Europe. Wilkes was a popular figure and large segments of the population had demonstrated against the government but Grenville's reaction was good riddance!

He also was well aware of the respect Franklin, just turned fifty-nine, enjoyed in England as well as in America. The American moved easily among intellectuals and common folks, aristocrats and working classes. His company was enjoyed by all. He was even a member of the Royal Society and had been honored by them. In truth, the government ministers were envious. It would delight Grenville to put this colonial in his place.

"Gentlemen," he finally said. "The government wants only to adopt those measures we think are fair and satisfactory to all parties. We considered alternatives last year and concluded a stamp tax would be that measure. It was put aside in deference to the feelings at the time that it might not be well received in America. However, we have concluded we have no better way to satisfy the needs of this government to meet its obligations to all the citizens of its empire, those living in America and elsewhere as well as those living in this land.

"We feel the stamp tax is the proper way to raise the revenue to defray the costs of protecting the colonies from invaders and from the savages along its frontiers. There has been some opinion that Parliament should not be imposing taxes on faraway citizens who are not fully represented in that body. However, Parliament has passed many, many measures dealing with the affairs of the colonies, without any real objection from any of you. We don't see how imposition of the stamp tax is any different."

There was a hint of a smile on his face, the smug look of someone who has just made a telling point. Then he played his final card.

"Of course, if some other method is proposed that would produce the satisfactory assistance, I would not object. However, I would point out that I suggested last year, when this tax was first considered, that you agents survey your colonies for alternatives."

"I beg your pardon, sir," Franklin interrupted, "but I doubt if your suggestion gained much circulation in the colonies." The other agents nodded agreement. Franklin chose not to mention his own earlier approval.

Grenville's face grew stern at the suggestion he might not have been truthful about this supposed earlier approach. He was anything but what former Prime Minister William Pitt had called the "Gentle Shepherd" as he paused to control his rising anger, then asked:

"Suppose we leave it to the colonies to determine revenue measures on their own. Can you agree on the proportions each colony should raise?"

The agents looked at each other and confessed they could not. After all, united action was uncommon among the colonies.

"Well," Grenville concluded, "absent an alternative, I shall propose to the committee on ways and means next Wednesday, the sixth, that the House of Commons adopt the stamp tax."

There was a moment of silence. The agents awaited Franklin's lead but the elder statesman had no further arguments. In many respects, the issue of the stamp tax was a distraction to his real mission for the Pennsylvania Assembly. He had come to ask the government to take control of Pennsylvania from the Penn family, reflecting years of unhappiness among some political leaders in that colony over the family's rule. However, the Stamp Act had become an issue consuming his time and thoughts since his arrival. Now, one more appeal—possibly the last appeal—had, obviously, failed.

"Thank you for your time, sir," he said.

"Thank you for coming, Dr. Franklin, and you other gentlemen. Good day."

The act was passed overwhelmingly by the House of Commons and endorsed shortly thereafter by the House of Lords. King George gave his approval on March 22. The tax—to be paid on licenses, legal documents and newspapers—would be effective November 1.

It was late April and early May when ships arriving from England brought the news to America.

Now, to the smoldering resentment over the 1764 measures, the Stamp Act added spark. Further, the government had given to the admiralty courts the right to try violators, which meant trial without jury.

Although the colonists were not totally surprised—there had been rumors for a long time of Parliament's intention to impose revenue measures on its North American colonies—the emotion of the colonial reaction surprised everyone.

The weekly newspapers were filled with stories about actions from Boston to Charleston to resist this tax on newspapers and legal documents

Feelings grew stronger that while the government in England had the right to determine the support it needed from the colonies, it was the right of the colonies to determine the means of that support. Their reasoning simply stated was: if the government could decide arbitrarily what property of the colonists could be taxed, then no property was safe from seizure, and their liberty, happiness, and security existed only at the pleasure of people thousands of miles from America.

Colonial displeasure was displayed almost immediately.

The government had decided it would appoint colonials to the important post of tax collector, hoping that would placate the colonies. It was a forlorn hope. In Philadelphia, a mob surrounded the house of John Hughes, a member of the Pennsylvania Assembly who had been named tax collector for that province and the three lower counties, and threatened him with harm unless he disavowed the appointment. To stress the point, they burned him in effigy. Similar scenes played out across the colonies from the Carolinas to Massachusetts.

It was against this background of growing unrest that the people from the Mispillion area gathered at Three Runs in the fall of 1765.

Early arrivals had gathered in small groups making idle conversation when Haslet walked in. There was a large crowd from both sides of the Mispillion, from Sussex as well as Kent, mostly male with a sprinkling of wives and widows who found politics a welcome diversion from the never-ending household chores. It was a time for exchanging gossip, discussing items in the newspapers.

Some stopped Haslet as he walked in, knowing the young doctor to be bright and well-educated, one who traveled extensively, often a source of information, one whose stories were spiced with wit.

"Doctor, I've read in the Philadelphia papers about a device they say can capture lightning, to prevent it from entering a house," one man commented. "Have you learned anything of it on your visits there?"

"It's an act of God," a second man interrupted. "Men shouldn't interfere with heaven-sent messages."

"I have heard about 'lightning rods' in Philadelphia," Haslet said. "They've had people killed by this lightning, but so have we for that matter. The rod is a very simple device: an iron rod is fixed to the roof to attract the lightning and then a metal wire carries it harmlessly to the ground. They have been using them in that city for several years. Dr. Franklin has conducted many experiments on the phenomenon of thunderstorms and the dangerous flashes; he calls them electrical fluids."

His listeners nodded. Franklin was well-known as a man of great scientific curiosity and knowledge.

"Whether or not you put one on your own house," Haslet continued, "I suppose depends on whether you believe the lightning was sent to open the gate to the next life. But it seems to me that if that is the case, a great many summons are wasted."

He left the group to its own deliberations and moved on to sit down on a bench beside the Rev. Alexander Huston.

"Alex," he said, "I want you to know that I've asked Jemima Brinckle to be my wife. We want to have the wedding here, a simple wedding, and have you preside."

"That's wonderful news, John," he responded. "I'd be delighted to officiate. Let me add my congratulations, too. She's a fine lady. And quite attractive as well. You two will make a handsome couple. And you should have beautiful children."

For a moment and not for the first time, Haslet's mind considered the question whether Jemima Brinckle could bear children. That concern had delayed his decision to ask her to marry him.

His thoughts were interrupted by the arrival of William Killen, accompanied by Caesar Rodney and another man. Killen, an elder of the church and a lawyer, would preside over the meeting.

Haslet liked Killen and they were in the early stages of what would become a strong friendship.

"John, I read that a couple of doctors have opened a medical school at the College of Philadelphia," Killen said after greetings were exchanged.

"Yes, I read about them. Shippen and Morgan. They have excellent reputations."

"You know them, then?"

"I know Morgan, John Morgan. He was a regimental surgeon in the French and Indian War. I met him then. He's the son of a Philadelphia shopkeeper. I understand he is a protégé of Benjamin Franklin, which certainly is very helpful to getting along in Philadelphia. Franklin, I'm told, paid the fees to have Morgan admitted to the Royal Society of London. He's even been licensed by the Royal College of Physicians."

"I know Shippen," Rodney added. "His father, William senior, is a very prominent physician in Philadelphia. The young Shippen studied extensively abroad. He became very interested in childbirth and studied it while he was in England. Since his return to America he has been able to convince many women to favor him over a midwife to deliver their children."

Shippen's acceptance into these very private moments marked a distinct deviation from conventional colonial practice favoring midwives to assist at childbirth.

The other arrival with Rodney and Killen interrupted at that point.

"My brother should point out that he was delivered by a man— our father—according to the favorite family tale. It was midnight and our parents had no other choice."

"Forgive me," Caesar Rodney said to Haslet. "This is my brother Thomas." Caesar Rodney, thirty-seven, was the oldest of eight children and Thomas, twenty-one, the youngest.

Haslet acknowledged the younger Rodney.

"He's right," Caesar Rodney agreed. "My father was the midwife at my birth and I guess I'm none the worse for it."

"Back to Shippen," Caesar Rodney continued, "I recall being told he studied medicine at Edinburgh."

"As did Morgan," Haslet added.

"I've heard they license physicians in England," Killen said.

"Some," Haslet answered, "but the Royal College of Surgeons recognizes very few doctors and only graduates of Oxford and Cambridge. It takes forever to complete the course—fourteen years, I understand. Outside London, incidentally, you'll find the opinion that the two English schools are not nearly comparable to the medical schools on the continent.

"My university—Glasgow—and Edinburgh offer an excellent medical education. I was exposed to some of their teachings when I attended at Edinburgh and that has helped me set up my own practice. But you can earn a medical degree from Glasgow and Edinburgh without actually attending the school. All you need to do is write to them with the endorsement of two physicians, present an acceptable thesis, and pay the necessary fees. I suppose for that reason they are denied the prestige of other schools."

"Perhaps, in the future, all doctors will have to be educated," Killen said, chuckling.

Haslet laughed.

"I don't really know, William. Certainly education is a good thing, but then if everyone became educated, who could practice law?"

Killen smiled and Rodney, also a lawyer, laughed heartily.

"Well, it is time to get the meeting started," Killen said. He and Rodney took seats in the front of the church.

Also Irish born, Killen was five years older than Haslet. He had immigrated as a teenager, in 1737, and settled in Delaware, where he took up the practice of law when he reached adulthood. He was admired as a man with a sharp and retentive mind, of strong moral principles and professional scruples.

Rodney, the third generation of his family to live in Kent County, had been a political force in the county for a decade. He held several offices at this time, including justice of the peace, recorder of deeds, register of wills and member of the Delaware Assembly. He was tall, slender, and slightly younger than Haslet.

Lanterns along the walls seemed to grow brighter as the dusk grew deeper. The benches in the Three Runs church were now filled.

Killen opened the discussion, explaining the details of the tax.

"In less than a month—November 1—your business with the courts will cost a great deal more. And the increases won't be going to lawyers, but to London. You will pay anywhere from three pence to ten shillings—per page—when you file with the courts, for whatever purpose. That includes wills, petitions, remonstrances, declarations, certificates, writs, affidavits, and so forth."

He paused for the crowd to absorb the information, then continued: "But it's not just court filings.

"A diploma or degree will cost you £2. You will pay 20 shillings for a license to sell liquor, £4—£4!!—to sell wine." Killen emphasized that point since wine was a favorite drink.

"Surveys will cost you anywhere from six pence to a shilling, six pence—per page—depending upon the size of the land. Your newspapers will cost one shilling per page, which means anywhere from four to eight shillings each edition. There will be a charge on advertising, which I don't recall right now. And, take note, the tax must be paid in sterling. The act goes on and on like that. I think you begin to see the vileness of this unconscionable action by the members of Parliament."

Payment in sterling would add to the cost of the tax paid in colonial currency, which held less value.

To this point, the people had been silently attentive to Killen's explanation. There was a stirring in the audience now, signs of indignation.

"What can be done about it?" asked one of the audience. "Doesn't Parliament have the right?"

"Some will argue that it does," Killen answered. "Many of us don't think so, however. We believe Parliament has the right to regulate commerce among its colonies all over the empire. We believe it has the right to determine what is needed from each colony to defend against its enemies. But we equally believe each colony has the right to examine the demands the government places upon it and to determine how its citizens can best meet those demands."

Killen was more animated now, pounding his fist on the lectern to emphasize his points.

"There is an additional issue here and that is the right of a citizen to have charges against him heard by a jury of his neighbors. Under this act, the lords of the admiralty are given the right to hear the charges under the Stamp Act. There is even the possibility the accused might be sent to their main venue in Halifax for trial, separated from home and family for no one knows how long."

Anger flashed through the audience.

"Is there anything we can do?" one asked.

"We hope to appeal to the conscience of Parliament," Killen said. "Mr. Rodney can elaborate on that."

Rodney rose to his feet.

"There will be a meeting in New York to pursue a plan of action," Rodney said. "Each colony is sending representatives. I've been appointed to represent Kent County. New Castle is sending Thomas McKean and Sussex County is sending Jacob Kollock.

"The most likely course will be to draw up a petition to submit to Parliament in which we will argue our position, appeal to the reason of the members of the Commons and the Lords, and ask that the act be repealed, that the colonies themselves decide on the proper revenue measures to meet their obligations to the Crown."

There were skeptical looks here and there and a man in the front row asked: "What happens until then?"

"Such are the feelings in the colonies that the immediate action seems to be to resist implementation of the tax. Citizens in Boston, Providence, Newport, New Haven, and the Carolinas all have confronted the appointed tax collectors demanding they refuse their assignments. I suppose you are aware of the action a crowd took in Philadelphia against John Hughes?"

There were murmurs of approval. That old adage that actions speak louder than words was heartily endorsed by this crowd (and throughout the colonies).

"Stamps have been delivered to Boston but authorities there had to spirit them away to the fortress for safekeeping. They have not been distributed. There is talk the courts will cease to function rather than submit to the government plan.

"Some merchants and traders have suggested a boycott of trade with England as a forceful way of making our objections strike home. Those in the lower counties will be meeting soon in New Castle to consider joining this movement. Many others throughout the colonies were already unhappy about last year's trade restrictions, particularly in prohibiting trade with the French and Spanish islands in the Caribbean. They feel the additional burden of the tax will further ruin them."

"And we expect Parliament to take a reasoned approach to this kind of response?" offered another man, obviously skeptical.

"They'll pay attention if we knock them hard enough," commented another man.

Laughter broke out in the room and heads nodded in appreciation.

"Perhaps we should bypass the legislature and go directly to the king," suggested another. "He is our sovereign. He has expressed concern for the welfare of all his people over and over. If we find the members of Parliament without a conscience, perhaps we would find the king would give us a more sympathetic reception."

"That is a possibility we will be considering in New York," Rodney said. "In the meantime, we've organized committees to coordinate whatever action we determine is best. They'll see that there is proper deliberation before anything is done and then see that the word is spread around so we can be united in whatever we do."

The audience applauded. The meeting broke up.

In October, the merchants and traders from the three lower counties did vote to join the boycott movement spreading through the colonies, agreeing to refuse any imports until the act was repealed.

The Sons of Liberty in Sussex County went further. At a meeting in Lewes they called the Stamp Act unconstitutional, saying it was destructive of the natural rights and liberties of Americans. County officials, lawyers, and the collector of customs were summoned and persuaded to pledge to ignore the tax. The group then took possession of the county magazine and fired the cannon to celebrate their action. They also, however, drank toasts to the king for it was unthinkable to the loyal citizens of Sussex County that the king could have been a party to the obnoxious Stamp Act. That was an omen of a dichotomy that would sunder the leadership in Sussex and other parts of North America when opposition to the English government's edicts turned to rebellion.

Court business throughout the three counties—indeed in many parts of the thirteen colonies—was suspended in the uncertainty over whether to honor the tax or pretend it didn't exist. Finally, the following February, at the suggestion of Thomas McKean, Delaware courts decided to resume business and ignore the tax.

By then the British government had become alarmed at the overwhelming and fervent opposition from both the colonies and from English merchants concerned about loss of business. The colonies were gradually catching up with the Caribbean islands as sources of income from trade and the more astute among the English merchants realized North America would soon surpass the islands in importance.

The government repealed the tax, but not without resentment over the challenge to its authority and what it considered the ingratitude and impertinence of the British subjects across the sea.

Chapter Six

Joyful News

The colonial reaction to the Stamp Act surprised the government in London.

In truth, the government had been patronizing towards British Americans, indifferent to their feelings and to the changes taking place in its North American colonies.

That was strikingly illustrated during the debate in Parliament on the Stamp Act, when Charles Townshend, an influential member of Prime Minister George Grenville's administration, dismissed the colonists as people the British had "planted" in America, people "nourished by our indulgence." To which Colonel Isaac Barre, who had fought in North America during the French and Indian War and was mindful of the reasons that many people left home and endured the dangers of an ocean voyage for a try at a new life, retorted: "Planted by your *care?!* No, your *oppressions* planted them in America!"

The flood of petitions against the act were at first ignored by Parliament, which also took sour note of the Virginia House of Burgesses' claim to have the sole authority to tax Virginians (a claim which the colony later tried to back away from).

The fourteen resolutions adopted at the Stamp Act Congress in New York in October 1765 reaffirmed the colonies' loyalty to the Crown, but asserted their rights to all the liberties of Englishmen, inveighed against the stamp tax and the trade restrictions. The congress' resolutions, of course, were ignored in London as were all other entreaties from the colonies.

John Haslet: A Useful One

When complaints from English merchants and manufacturers about a loss of business due to the American boycott were combined with the news from America, however, Parliament had to face political reality.

Moreover, there was a new ministry in power, one more receptive to the complaints. The previous August, King George III had replaced Grenville with Charles Watson-Wentworth, the second marquess of Rockingham, as prime minister, the fifth prime minister in as many years. It was family not politics that turned the king against the Grenville ministry; the king felt Grenville had slighted the Queen Mother in legislation providing support of the royal family.

When Parliament assembled in January 14, 1766 for a new term, the King indicated it was time to reconsider the stamp tax. He informed the members that he had ordered his governors and military commanders to deal with the colonial unrest, then he added:

"If any alterations should be wanting in the commercial autonomy of the plantations, which may tend to enlarge and secure the mutual and beneficial intercourse of my kingdoms and colonies, they will deserve your most serious consideration."

Since the party in power generally prepared the royal address, it was taken as a signal to act on repeal of the stamp tax. Accordingly, when the members of the House of Commons returned to their chambers to consider their response to the king's message, as tradition demanded, repeal immediately intruded on the proceedings.

There was a great deal of anger within the chamber against the unruly subjects in North America, but the colonies had their defenders, among them the celebrated Great Commoner, William Pitt. As secretary of state during the French and Indian War, Pitt's oratorical skills and energetic leadership had inspired the British to the triumphs that wrested Canada and all of the land between the Appalachians and the Mississippi River from the French. It was expected he would be named Earl of Chatham and move on to the House of Lords, but to the surprise and delight of many, he appeared in Commons to participate in the debate over repeal.

He was fifty-seven now, still handsome and lean. Chronic ill health had left him frail, but he quickly showed he had not lost his ability to phrase his positions eloquently. His health had prevented him from attending a year ago when Parliament passed the Stamp Act and he referred to that in his opening remarks. Now, when he rose to speak, the chamber grew respectfully silent. Members suspected this might be his last appearance as one of them.

He went quickly to the point:

"It is a long time, Mr. Speaker, since I attended in Parliament. When the resolution was taken in this house to tax America, I was ill in my bed. When the act passed, I was ill in my bed. If I could have endured to have been carried in my bed, so great was the agitation of my mind for the consequences, I would have solicited some kind hand to have laid me down on this floor, to have borne my testimony against it. It is my opinion that this kingdom has *no* right to lay a tax upon the colonies."

George Grenville and his supporters sat glumly on their benches, but other members were enraptured.

Pitt inserted a dash of conciliation:

"At the same time I assert this kingdom has authority over the colonies to be sovereign and supreme in every circumstance of government and legislation whatsoever. They are the subjects of this kingdom, equally entitled with ourselves to all the natural rights of mankind and peculiar privileges of Englishmen, equally bound by the laws and equally participating of its constitution."

Then, his voice rising, he returned to his acerbic attack:

"The Americans are the sons, not the bastards, of England!"

A mix of applause and disapproval reverberated through the chamber. Pitt waited until the reaction ended, then continued:

"According to the constitution of this free country, taxation is no part of the governing or legislative power."

The Grenville side hissed disapproval but there were murmurs of approval on the ministry's side.

"There is an idea in some that the colonies are virtually represented in this house. I would fain know by whom an American is represented here? Is he represented by a knight of a shire of any county in this kingdom? Would to God that respectable representation were augmented to a greater number! Or, will you tell him he is represented by a representative of a borough? The idea of the virtual representation of America in this house is the most contemptible notion that ever entered into the head of man. It does not deserve serious refutation.

"The commons of America, represented in their several assemblies, have ever been in possession of the exercise of this their constitutional right of giving and granting their own money. They would have been slaves if they had not enjoyed it. At the same time, this kingdom, as the supreme governing and legislative power, has always bound the colonies by her laws, by her regulations, restrictions in trade, in navigation, their contents. Here, then, I would draw a line."

Grenville waited for the shouts of approval to die down, then rose to respond.

He decided he would pass over the arguments about taxation and virtual representation and dwell on what he considered the unacceptable reaction in America to the stamp tax.

"Mr. Speaker, I am seriously disturbed by the failure of the current ministry to let this body know of the heinous behavior of the colonials to our very justifiable desire to have them provide the revenue for their own support and security. There has been rioting, violence upon the king's officers.

"They began in July and now we are in the middle of January. When our king spoke to us in December, these acts in America were described only as 'occurrences.' They are now grown to disturbances, to tumults and riots. I don't doubt they border on open rebellion and if the doctrine we hear today be confirmed, I fear they will become a revolution. If the government over them is dissolved, a revolution will take place in America."

Rockingham gave a sound of disbelief, but Grenville moved on:

"It cannot be denied that this kingdom is the sovereign, the supreme legislative power over America, and taxation is part of that power. It is a power that has been exercised over others who are not represented here. It is exercised over the East India Company, the merchants of London, the proprietors of the stocks and over great manufacturing towns. It was exercised over the palatinate of Chester and the bishopric of Durham before they sent any representatives to Parliament.

"When I proposed to tax America, I asked the House whether any gentleman would object to the right. I repeatedly asked it and no man would attempt to deny it. Protection and obedience are reciprocal. Great Britain protects America; America is bound to yield obedience. If not, tell me when the Americans were emancipated?"

There was sarcasm in his voice as he added: "When they want the protection of this kingdom they do not hesitate to ask it."

The indignation in Grenville's voice was warmly approved on his side.

"That protection has always been afforded them, in the most full and ample manner. The nation has run itself into an immediate debt to give them that protection and now they are called upon to contribute a small share towards the public expense! An expense arising from themselves! They renounce your authority, insult your officers and break out, I might almost say, into acts of open rebellion.

"The seditious spirit of the colonies owes its birth to the factions in this house."

Grenville looked accusingly across the floor at his opposition and his eyes fastened on Pitt.

"Gentlemen are careless of the consequences of what they say, provided it answers the immediate purposes of opposition. We were told that we trod on tender ground. We were bid to expect disobedience. What was this but telling the Americans to stand out against the law? Also to encourage their obstinacy with expectations of support from home."

Grenville altered his voice to mimic colonial leaders:

"'Let us only hold a little,' they would say, 'our friends will soon be in power.'"

He paused, took a deep breath and concluded:

"Ungrateful people of America!"

Grenville was flushed with anger as he finished, his supporters cheering. Pitt sat impassively in his seat, contemplating his response. He rose again, but another member objected that the speeches of Pitt and Grenville were not appropriate, that the only subject before the House should be its response to the king's speech.

Member George Onflow interjected:

"Mr. Speaker, I submit that both honorable gentlemen have appropriately placed before the House a subject that was very much implied in our sovereign's remarks. Therefore, their remarks are very much to the point."

The speaker agreed. From the benches came shouts of "Go on! Go on!"

A trace of a smile crossed Pitt's face.

"Gentlemen. Sir," he began, "I have been charged with giving birth to sedition in America. They have spoken their sentiments with freedom against this unhappy act. That freedom is described as a crime. Sorry I am to hear the liberty of speech in this House imputed as a crime, but the imputation shall not discourage me. It is a liberty I mean to exercise. No gentlemen ought to be afraid of exercising it. It is liberty by which the gentleman who calumniates it might himself have profited. He ought to have desisted from his project. The gentleman tells us America is obstinate, America is almost in open rebellion. I rejoice that America has resisted!"

The House erupted with loud boos and cheers, the members competing to drown out the opposition voices.

"I am no courtier to America," Pitt continued as the clamor faded. "I stand up for this kingdom. I maintain that Parliament has a right to bind, to restrain America. Our legislative power over the colonies is sovereign and supreme. When two countries are connected together like England and her colonies, the one must necessarily govern. The greater must rule the lesser, to rule it but not to contract the fundamental principles common to both."

Pointing to Grenville:

"The gentleman understands not the difference between internal taxes and external. I cannot help it. But there is a plain distinction between taxes levied for the purposes of raising a revenue and duties imposed for the regulation of trade for the accommodation of the subject, even though some revenue might arise from the latter."

Pitt measured these words carefully, his arms slashing for emphasis, his voice at full volume.

"The gentleman asks: 'When were the colonies emancipated?' I desire to know when were they made slaves?"

Cheers and whistles mingled with hisses and boos as he sat down.

The debate continued for hours, ending in a vote expressing the sentiment of the Commons—the Stamp Act should be repealed. More than a month would pass, however, before the decisive vote was taken—at 2 A.M. on February 22, 1766, after an eighteen-hour debate. The vote was 275–167.

Bells rang throughout London all day. Shops, coffee houses and taverns lit candles, as was the custom to observe joyful news.

But the government would not ignore the reports of rioting in Boston against the tax, of colonial mobs preventing the tax collectors from distributing their stamps—indeed from even accepting their office—of decisions to boycott trade with England. And it certainly would not concede the colonists' position that Parliament did not have the right to tax them. In all the celebration, little note was made of the fact that while Parliament had repealed the despised tax, within a week it also passed the Declaratory Act, asserting its right to pass laws over the colonies.

Final approval of the repeal came in March and was quickly endorsed by the House of Lords. King George signed it on March 18. More than 100 American merchants visiting in London traveled by carriage to St. James to witness the signing.

The first, unofficial, news reached Philadelphia in late March by a circuitous route. A news item in a Dublin newspaper contained a letter from a member of Parliament to his Irish friend saying that "everything relating to the affairs of America was settled, that the Stamp Act was repealed." This wasn't yet a fact, but the message was printed in a newspaper in Cork, Ireland. Copies of the newspaper were carried aboard ship to Oxford on Maryland's Chesapeake Bay. From there the dispatch found its way to Philadelphia in the stagecoach service by way of New Castle, Delaware.

It was printed in the Philadelphia *Gazette* of March 27, a black border surrounding the item to catch its readers' eyes. Even before the newspaper appeared, the word had spread throughout the city. Bells began to ring. That night bonfires were lit and the citizens celebrated appropriately, including toasts to the royal family and America's friends in Parliament.

However, joy was tempered by the concern that the information was only hearsay.

Now came a long period of uncertainty, waiting for the official word. It reached Philadelphia on May 19, aboard the *Minerva,* out of Poole, Dorset, a port in southern England on the English Channel.

It had taken the *Minerva* eight weeks to make the voyage. When she dropped anchor in the Delaware River off the city of Philadelphia, anticipation prompted the shipping agent to row out to board her. A ship's officer handed him an official copy of the repeal, with the imprimatur of the Crown printer, and he hastened ashore with it.

It happened that John Haslet was in Philadelphia, checking on progress on his 1762 bid for land in Kent County. He and Dr. Francis Alison were dining at the London Coffee House at Front and High streets when the agent burst in.

Alison was the Presbyterian minister-educator who had been Haslet's first contact when he arrived in America six and a half years earlier. He was a native of Donegal and, like Haslet, had been educated for the ministry at Glasgow. Alison, now sixty-one, had immigrated when he was thirty. Since his arrival he had established the renowned New London Academy in that rural Pennsylvania village. (The academy eventually moved to Delaware and became the University of Delaware.) He then was invited to run the Philadelphia Academy and was named its vice provost when it became the College of Philadelphia. He also was a leading minister in the Presbyterian church.

They looked up at the loud intrusion from the doorway.

"It's official!" the agent shouted, so excited he had to pause to catch his breath. "It's official! I have a copy of the law repealing that damned tax. And it has the imprint of the king's own printer. Let me read it to you."

The babble of conversation at the many tables in the crowded tavern ceased. Merchants and traders from the second floor exchange filed down the stairs to the main room. The overflow spilled out into the street where passersby attracted to the excitement joined them. The silence was a striking contrast to the normal babble of voices in the tavern as people listened attentively while the agent read the words on the paper in his hand.

"And it has the king's seal," he concluded.

There were loud cheers. Drinks were poured.

"Who brought this news?" a patron shouted over the din.

"The ship *Minerva,* from Poole," someone responded.

"Where's the captain?"

"He's still on his ship. His name is Wise."

"Fetch him," someone shouted. "He should share in our joy. And let's take up a collection for the crew."

A hat was quickly passed around the room, filling with paper currency. Its owner and some companions hurried out of the tavern and down to the wharf where they met Captain Wise coming ashore.

"Captain," one of the delegation announced, "your presence is requested down the street at the London Coffee House. The people wish to thank you for the wonderful news you've brought us."

While the collection from the tavern was shared with the crew, Captain Wise headed up Front Street. The clamor was attracting patrons from other taverns and the street filled with a happy crowd. The captain, now surrounded by people, moved down the cobblestone street almost like a cork in a stream. The news had spread like a brush fire and bystanders cheered as the mob surged by.

In the meantime, the owner of the London Coffee House had ordered a large bowl of rum punch. The captain was promptly handed a cup when he entered.

"I drink to America," he said, raising the cup, "and may she prosper as a righteous and proud member of the glorious British empire."

"Hear! Hear!"

"Let's give the captain a present," declared one of the crowd. Again there was an enthusiastic response. Someone produced a felt hat with a gold lace band, quickly procured from an adjacent shop.

"Captain, we would like to present you with this hat," someone said, "as a reminder of our appreciation of the great news you've brought us this day."

Captain Wise took it, placed it on his head, and smiled.

"This is a fine headpiece," he said. "I'll wear it proudly and when people admire it, I'll explain that it's a token of gratitude from his majesty's loyal subjects in America." More cheers reverberated through the tavern and the streets outside.

Haslet and Alison sat quietly enjoying the moment.

"This is wonderful news, John," Alison commented. "There's been so much turmoil, so much unhappiness, I feared for our province and what the authorities might do to force us to comply with that pernicious tax. I'm relieved the government has decided it was all a mistake and has moved to heal the wounds."

"I am, too, Francis," Haslet responded. "But I wonder if this is the end of it. I've read the dispatches from England. It's been obvious the government was going to back away from this particular tax; there was too much pressure from the merchants there. It's equally clear the government hasn't yielded on the point of taxing the colonies.

"I'm afraid the issue really isn't resolved. There remains the question of revenue to pay for the troops stationed here, for the maintenance of the Crown officers, for paying the debt the government says it incurred to fight the last war. Will the government now leave it to us to raise the money it says it needs? Or will they make another attempt at imposing a revenue measure on us? If they do, I believe the colonies will be just as violently opposed as they have been to the stamp tax."

Alison sat silently, reflecting on the issue. He was an ardent supporter of colonial rights. He sighed. "Perhaps you're right, John. Let's enjoy this moment, however."

They watched the crowd continue in its revels with Captain Wise. Other officers from the *Minerva* had arrived and were offered a generous cup from the punch bowl. After long moments of celebration, the din subsided to the point conversation could resume at the various tables.

"I understand Charles Inglis is leaving the Anglican mission in Dover for Trinity Church in New York," Alison said to Haslet. The church's official status in the British Empire made news of its churches a prime topic among the Presbyterians, principal rival to the established church in the middle colonies.

"Yes, so I've been told. It's not unexpected. He had accepted the New York church two years ago but his wife died as he was preparing to leave and for one reason or another, he was persuaded to stay on."

The Irish-born Inglis had been teaching in Lancaster, Pennsylvania, when he was called to England to be ordained by the Church of England's Bishop of London and sent by the Society for the Propagation of the Gospel in 1759 to mend the Anglican church's sagging fortunes in Kent County.

"Sad about his wife," Alison said. "She was so young."

Haslet nodded agreement, then Alison observed: "Dr. Inglis has done wonderful work for his mission during his time, hasn't he? How many years?"

"Seven years. Yes, you're right, he has worked hard.

"When he arrived he said the church was in deplorable condition, its congregation noted more for drunkenness than spiritual fervor."

The two men thought with some quiet satisfaction about Inglis' discomfort when he began his mission.

"Well, the church is in fine condition now," Haslet resumed. "What's more, there are three Anglican churches in my county now and all seem to be thriving. I should note, however, that our Presbyterian churches outnumber them and continue to grow."

Haslet lowered his voice to a conspiratorial whisper: "But if the truth be known, I think some of Dr. Inglis' colleagues are a bit envious and resentful at the Presbyterian success."

Alison smiled at the thought. "I like to think we have a more powerful message of salvation."

"I think it's a wonderful thing for religion to be in so many homes and so many hearts," Haslet said.

Alison nodded agreement and they sat quietly again, observing the fading celebration around them until Alison broke the silence.

"Will you be staying over another night?"

"No," Haslet responded. "I must stop off at New Castle on my way home. I'm expecting my daughter Polly to arrive from Ireland any day now. According to the last letter from my family in Ulster, she was to leave from Londonderry in early April. You know those sailing dates are always uncertain, but if she did leave around the scheduled time, she should be arriving at New Castle soon. I've left instructions there for her travel to my plantation in Mispillion."

"How does Mrs. Haslet feel about that?" Alison asked.

"I think she's looking forward to it," he answered. "She's wanted children and has regretted she and her first husband weren't able to conceive. Of course, we still hope to have children of our own. In any event, I've been hoping for the day when I'd be settled enough to bring Polly over and that day, thank the good Lord, is near at hand."

"I think it's a fine woman who is eager to raise another woman's child," Alison commented. "You must feel blessed."

"I do," Haslet said and a contented look spread across his face.

"How did you make out with the land company today?" Alison asked.

"All they could tell me is that there were a great many lots involved and it's taking time for the partners in London to process the bids," Haslet answered. "There are, after all, something like 11,000 acres to be settled. Several bids have been approved since the auction more than four years ago, but none since the end of 1763. I haven't been able to find out why, but I can only hope they'll resume action on the pending bids soon—mine among them."

"I'll pray for that, too," Alison offered. "By the way, have you heard that John Morgan has formed a medical society and is proposing that it license physicians?"

"Yes, but I don't know how successful he'll be. Too many people will view it as an effort to turn the practice of medicine into an exclusive club reserved for a chosen few. The very name of 'medical society' suggests that."

Haslet stood up, finally.

"I've enjoyed our visit together, Francis, but I really must be getting along. A boat is about to leave for New Castle and I want to start my journey home. I plan to stay overnight in New Castle to check on the arrangements for my daughter."

He extended his hand to Alison.

"You've been a wonderful host for my visit to Philadelphia. I hope you'll allow Jemima and me to reciprocate your generosity at our plantation."

"Perhaps, I will, John. God speed you on your journey and bless you with a joyful reunion with your wife and daughter."

Alison walked with him to the river.

"Do you know Robert Cross, the minister at First Presbyterian Church?" he asked as they walked along.

"Yes. In fact, you introduced me to him when I first arrived in '57. I don't believe I've seen him since. He was born near Ballykelly, my church when I was ordained in Ulster. Why?"

"I'd forgotten about that meeting in '57. Well, he's very ill, not expected to live much longer."

"He's lived a long life," Haslet said.

"I think he's seventy-seven," Alison said.

"If I had the time I'd look in on him," Haslet said, "but I must be going."

They shook hands and Haslet joined a group boarding a shallop at the pier.

It was late afternoon as he entered his house two days later. Jemima was busy in the kitchen. She was delighted to see him, making that clear when she embraced him, and he returned the feeling.

"I had little success in Philadelphia," he informed her. "There's still no word on the tract over by Swan Creek. But I did have a nice visit with Dr. Alison and caught up with the news. He's very busy at the college, which seems to be expanding. And the Stamp Act has been repealed, to everyone's joy. Dr. Alison and I were having dinner at a tavern when the word arrived and you would have been excited at the happiness of the crowd."

He described the scene to her and was rewarded with her pleased reaction. His enthusiasm was her measure of the importance of any political news he brought her.

"I stopped over at New Castle yesterday and checked on the arrangements for Polly," he continued. "The shipping agent there will see to overnight accommodations at an inn and a carriage to bring her and my cousin William to our plantation. I left details how to find us, just in case they have mislaid the instructions I sent to them before they left."

Jemima listened as she resumed her kitchen chores, waiting for the opportunity to reveal an important piece of news of her own. She barely restrained her excitement when she finally spoke.

"Polly will not be the only child around here," she said and paused.

It only took a moment for Haslet to understand the import of her remark.

"You are with child?" he said, almost shouting.

She nodded and happiness very nearly exploded in her. "My time has passed for a couple of months now and there can be no doubt there is life inside me."

He grabbed her in his arms. "Oh, Jemima! That's just wonderful. The Lord is blessing our marriage. If you are as happy as I am you must be ecstatic."

She could only nod again as emotions overwhelmed her. Tears filled her eyes and she was happier than at any moment in her life, partly because she now knew she could conceive and partly because of her husband's joy at the news.

The two hugged each other. They said nothing but let their love and happiness nurture in the closeness of their embrace.

Chapter Seven

Polly

John Haslet was in the fields with his slave Dollar, discussing things he had read in a book about husbandry, when Dollar's glance shifted over Haslet's shoulder, focusing on the road into the plantation.

Haslet turned to follow Dollar's glance. A carriage was moving through a cloud of dust and he could make out two figures, one appearing to be an adult male, the other a teenage girl.

With the realization of their identities, he began sprinting across the fields.

The carriage had reached the house and its passengers debarked by the time he arrived. Jemima was starting to greet the visitors when he scooped the girl into his arms and embraced her.

"Polly! Polly!" He repeated her name over and over, hugging her tighter at each mention of her name. She hugged him back, tentatively at first, then more eagerly, tears wetting the smile on her face. She could not muster enough breath to speak. She had anticipated the reunion with her father and imagined it in many different ways. The reality exceeded anything in her dreams.

Finally, he released her and stood back to take a good look at the thirteen-year-old adolescent he last saw as a five-year-old.

The changes in her were striking to him. She was already showing signs of her womanhood. She also was tall for her age and her fair hair framed a face with high cheek bones and hazel eyes, adding to her physical attractiveness.

The girl was both pleased and startled at his effusive greeting. It was a marked contrast from the moroseness that she remembered after her mother died.

POLLY

Polly had gone to live with Samuel Haslet, her father's uncle, but her father had made it a point to visit her as often as his duties as minister in the church in Ballykelly permitted. Despite his effort to be cheerful, however, she remembered the sadness that often came over him as they strolled hand-in-hand along the roadside or sat and talked in Uncle Samuel's parlor. And even though she was barely five years old at the time, the shock when he took her on his lap and explained to her why he was going to go away to another land and the tears they both shed had remained as vivid memories.

"I promise you, my dear little one," he had said, "that we will be together again. It may take some long time, but it will happen." It was almost more than a little five-year-old could tolerate.

Then he was gone. A long time did pass before Uncle Samuel Haslet sat down with her one day to talk about a letter from her father in America. There had been others, but this one was special.

"Your father wants you to go to America to live with him and his new wife," Samuel said. "He lives in a place called Three Runs in County Kent. It's in the province of Pennsylvania." He added, a note of sadness in his voice:

"My son William is planning to go to live in America, too, and he'll go with you and see you safely to your father's home."

It was much for a young girl to absorb. A new land. A new family. And there was the voyage across the ocean. She had heard the adults talk about the hardships of the long voyage, living in cramped quarters. Sometimes there were violent storms that tossed the passengers about their quarters below deck. And sometimes the storms were so severe a ship would sink. It was a frightening prospect.

All the fears, the homesickness were forgotten at the joyful reunion. Haslet abruptly realized he had been ignoring his cousin William.

"William," he said, "what a fine young man you've become. You were barely in your teens when I saw you last and now look at you."

William was in his early twenties, about the same age as John's own brother William when the brothers sailed for America in 1757. Cousin William was a few inches under six feet tall, brown-haired, slender but fit looking. He'll be able to endure the hard life on the frontier, Haslet thought. His Uncle Samuel had written of William's plans to go west after he finished his visit with his Delaware cousins.

"Thanks so much for bringing Polly to America," Haslet said to him. "God has blessed me by bringing her—both of you—safely to my side. There's so much joyfulness in me I can't find the proper words to express it." Haslet's voice choked and he stopped talking.

Jemima gently interrupted.

"John, you're overwhelming these young people. Please, folks, come into the house. Let me offer you something to wash away the dust from your trip. I know you've been a long time on the road. Perhaps you'd like a little cheese or meats? It will be a little while until dinner."

Polly turned to Jemima, seeing her fully for the first time. She had wondered for months what her stepmother would be like, what life in her new home would be like.

"May I do something to help?" Polly asked, because she could think of nothing else to say and becoming helpful seemed the logical way to start this new relationship.

The Ulster accent forced Jemima to listen intently.

"My goodness, you sound just like your father when I first met him," she said, cheerfully. "I could barely understand what he was saying."

They all laughed.

"You've had a long, tiring trip, dear," Jemima continued. "Just rest for now. After I get a few things started cooking I'll show you your new home."

They settled around the kitchen table and Haslet immediately started questioning about family and friends in Ireland.

"My parents," he said, "did you see them before you left and how are they?"

"We did see them a few days before we left for Derry to board our ship," William said. "Both seemed healthy. Your father is as vigorous as ever, John, and your mother just the same. We also saw your sister Mary at Derry before we sailed. Her husband John Kyle is doing very well and their little Ann is almost seven now and a very active child. Your brother James is going into the seed business in Coleraine.

"We also saw your father's old friend, Cumoighe O'Cathan. You'd never know he's in his seventies. He still goes to your father's store to buy his seeds and hardware, exchanges yarns with your father and they discuss the prices of cattle, pigs and sheep in the market at Limavady. What a fine person he is. It's easy to see why your family has such great respect for him."

"O'Cathan is a descendent of a famous clan that ruled over my part of Ireland long ago," Haslet explained to Jemima. "He bought his seeds at my father's store and was a great story-teller. He knew more Irish history than any person I knew. Of course, my father always chided him that he made up most of his stories about the exploits of his O'Cathan ancestors."

"And your father?" He returned to William.

"He has slowed some. He still goes shooting on Benbradagh and Loughermore and fishes in the Roe, but he complains about his bones not being up for the strain."

"No problem with the landlords about the hunting and fishing?"

"No," William said, "Ogilby has been very generous in these matters. He's been a very tolerant landlord. He's also helped many of our young people to emigrate."

Mention of the Ogilby family reminded Haslet of the control the landed families had over Irish life, something he had all but forgotten since he arrived in America.

Memories of his own childhood flitted through his mind.

"And the Roe? How about the flooding?

"It seemed to me that the Roe flooded every year," Haslet told Jemima. She was hovering around the fireplace, attaching pots of food to hooks on the lug pole that spanned the width of the fireplace, placing meats on three-legged skillets that sat above the coals in one corner of the fireplace, occasionally moving the meat with a long fork or lifting a pot off its hook to test its contents, moving pots to different length hooks to vary the cooking time. Polly was fascinated, watching her.

"There's not been bad flooding for a while," William responded. "The rains have not been so heavy for a few years."

William continued describing events at home and Haslet listened. Some were familiar from the letters, but hearing them in the rhythm of his native dialect made them far more real, fresher, than words on a piece of paper. Haslet could close his eyes and see everything clearly, imagine he was back in the Roe Valley. And, of course, no one had aged one day in his mind, a small consolation for the separation.

Jemima finally reached a point in the meal preparation that she could take time for Polly.

"Come, Polly. I'll show you around," she said.

"Did they tell you, John, that my father has seen to it the roof on the church at Bovevagh has finally been rethatched," William said, picking up the conversation as Jemima and Polly left the room.

"That old roof has been in need of replacement for years," Haslet said. It was the Haslet family church.

"By the way, were you aware that your old congregation at Ballykelly has been feuding with your successor, John Neilson?"

"My brother James has written to me about that." Haslet responded. "It was not an easy congregation. You may know I had difficulty with them. That was one of the reasons I decided to leave for America. They were negligent in providing support for their minister. In fact, it took my father and the intervention of the synod to get them to make up their arrears. And that took years. I know the synod refused to allow a new minister until they settled that account."

"Well, in a very short time after they called Neilson they began complaining he was unorthodox," William said. "The synod disagreed, so the members simply locked him out of the church. He's moved on to Dublin."

"I hadn't heard that," Haslet responded.

"Yes, there was talk before I left that they were looking at an American-born clergyman to take over. A Benjamin McDowell, I think. He was visiting relatives in County Antrim and was invited to preach at Ballykelly. The members liked him and it was said before I left that they're going to offer him the calling."

"Where did he study?"

"I think they mentioned the College of New Jersey and also Glasgow. He was born in a place in Jersey called Elizabethtown."

"The College of New Jersey is in Princeton," Haslet commented. "Started by Presbyterians."

William went on to talk about relations in Upper and Lower Drumneecy, near Haslet's home area. There were many Haslets spread over that part of County Derry.

"Did you know, John, that our cousin Charles has a brother-in-law living not far from here, as I understand it."

"A brother-in-law?"

"Yes, you remember he married Marge Harris?"

"I think that happened after I left."

"Well, Marge's brother John Harris left for America and Marge is looking after his house. It's said he's operating a ferry between Lancaster and Cumberland Counties. Do those names sound familiar?"

"Yes. They're not too far away; in fact, Lancaster County is where your cousins live. My militia company served in that county for a while in 1758. Cumberland is just across the river, the Susquehanna River."

While John listened to William's talk about home and their voyage, he observed Jemima and Polly moving around the house and listened for some words, sounds that would hint at how they were getting along. At times they were out of sight, but he could hear their movements in the downstairs and upstairs rooms. Occasionally he could hear them laughing and that was reassuring. Finally, they returned to the kitchen. Jemima was explaining the functions of the various fireplace tools, the location of their kitchen utensils and other furnishings.

Their conversation was relaxed, cordial, but it would take a while, Haslet realized, for a truly close relationship to develop between these two women in his life.

"Dinner will be ready shortly," Jemima announced. "I hope your first family meal in America will be special and I've tried to make it such."

"I have no doubt it will be special," Polly said, unsure what to call her stepmother.

Jemima sensed the uncertainty and thought there would be time enough for that, deciding to let the matter resolve itself naturally.

"Polly, would you bring the plates and cups and bowls to the table, please? And the knives and spoons." Polly fetched them from the cupboard Jemima had shown her a little while earlier and placed them on the table, now covered by a neat linen tablecloth.

"You're growing into a beautiful woman, daughter," Haslet said. She stood alongside Jemima. Haslet thought they would make a splendid mother-daughter portrait. Someday. Someday. Polly's smile was especially charming, reminiscent of her mother's smile. The memory brought a smile to his own face and Jemima, guessing at his thoughts, commented:

"If she looks like her mother, then her mother must have been a very beautiful woman."

Haslet nodded, then pulled Jemima to his side and bussed her on the cheek.

"Obviously, I have been blessed with beautiful women in my life."

He enjoyed the moment, then turned back to William.

"Your plans, I understand, are to settle in Pennsylvania."

"Yes, I plan to stay with our cousins in Faggs Manor until I can establish myself. That's in Lancaster County, as you've mentioned. I'll do whatever is necessary to make a home in America for myself and, if so blessed, for my family."

"I stayed with them when I first came here," Haslet said. "They're fine people. You'll enjoy their company and feel quite at ease with them."

"You stayed in Faggs Manor?" William asked.

"Yes. Not for long, however. The British and Americans were fighting the French on the frontier and I raised a company of men to join the Pennsylvania Regiment. A fine group, too. And you can imagine Ireland was well represented when you are enlisting men to fight."

Haslet said it with pride, which the others shared, even Jemima, who had gotten used to Haslet's pride in his ancestry.

"You have quite a plantation here, cousin," William said. He had a little trouble with the word "plantation." In Ireland that referred to a group of trees. Still, "farm" hardly described the size of his cousin's land, not in the ordinary Irishman's concept of farm.

"Yes. It was Jemima's first husband's plantation." Haslet said. "He was a very successful man, as you can tell. Jemima took over the management when he died and now, of course, I'm helping her."

"Helping," Jemima scoffed, "as if John Haslet would ever allow himself to be a mere helper."

Haslet went on:

"Some years ago I bid on some land a few miles from here and I'm waiting for the bid to be processed. Incidentally, Jemima, I'm told Brady's bid for the adjacent property has been approved. The Bradys have let it out that they've decided they don't want to develop it and are going to offer it for sale. You and I must discuss it, but I think I'd like to make an offer to the Bradys."

Finally, Jemima announced dinner was ready for the table.

Haslet offered a blessing.

"Merciful God, we thank Thee for delivering my daughter and cousin William safely to our table. I pray their lives in America will be productive, that they grow in love and service to You and to their families and communities. Thank You also for the blessing of this food."

The group set to eating.

"Tell us about the voyage," Haslet said. William filled the dinner table conversation with an account of their mostly uneventful, forty-five-day trip across the Atlantic from Londonderry to New Castle.

Polly was pleased to note that her stepmother was a fine cook. William noticed, too, and it would be mentioned in the letter he would write home. His report on John's American wife would be eagerly shared by Haslet kin wanting a more detached view of Jemima Haslet than John had given them.

William stayed over for a week. John briefed him on American crops, American customs, American opportunities.

Meanwhile, Polly picked up on the domestic chores that would help assimilate her into her new life but the first really broadening experience was a trip to Dover with her father and stepmother to settle the Brady purchase.

Jonathan and Mary Ann Brady had signed the Pennsylvania Land Company deed for 128 acres along the Mispillion River on August 4, 1766. On August 27, it was signed over to the Haslets for £170, 2 s.

Now she had time for a more leisurely exploration of the Kent County area. On her trip from New Castle weeks earlier she was so concentrated on the forthcoming reunion and the experiences of the just-completed voyage that she barely noticed this new country.

Haslet expounded on his plans for the property as he and Jemima, whose pregnancy now was obvious to all, rode home in their carriage, Polly between them, taking in the sights along the King's Highway.

There were scattered plantations in the first few miles out of Dover. One particularly caught her eye.

"Who lives there, father?" she said, pointing off to the left.

"That's the Dickinson family plantation." he said. "John Dickinson owns it, but he doesn't live there now. He's a lawyer who spends his time in Philadelphia."

"Philadelphia?"

"That's a city about ninety miles north of here, the capital of Pennsylvania and the biggest city in America. Our governor lives there and just comes down to the lower counties when our legislature meets in New Castle. I guess Mr. Dickinson has no plans to come back here because he's a member of their assembly, not ours. Anyhow, he's rented his property. His family has owned this land for probably a hundred years, but the home you see was only built about twenty-five years ago. Before that the family lived in Maryland. His father built the home, but he's dead now and there are no other family members living here."

Polly was impressed. There was a large, two-story brick house and another, smaller brick building. She counted four barns, a building with a stream running through it ("a dairy house," her father explained when she asked), and assorted other buildings scattered around the grounds. Hundreds of acres had been cleared for planting and she noted several trees in orderly rows that her father identified as apple and peach orchards.

"Did Mr. Dickinson rent the slaves, too?" Polly asked.

"He did offer them," Haslet answered, "and he described them as remarkably honest and well-behaved. And he said he would want them cared for by a 'good-natured, humane man.'"

"Are your slaves honest and well-behaved, father?"

"Certainly."

"Is it unusual for slaves to be honest and well-behaved?"

Haslet laughed. Jemima added: "No less so than anybody else."

As they bounced along the road and left the Dickinson plantation behind, the landscape filled with woods. Signs of human life ceased to exist.

A thought crossed Polly's mind. "Father, are there any Indians in those woods?"

He laughed. "No, dear one. The Indians moved away from the lower counties many years ago. The closest tribes now are a few days' ride from here. They once owned the land we live on and, in fact, the whole of the lower counties. But the people bought the land from them and all the Indians have moved on."

That wasn't quite true. A tribe known as the Nanticokes remained in southern Sussex County. (In fact, they would survive to modern times.) But the main nation of Indians, the Leni Lenape, or Delawares, had moved north and west.

"Why did they leave?" she asked, "and what about the land they lived on? Did they own it? Did the settlers buy it from them?"

"They realized the white settlers lived much different lives than they did and it became obvious they either had to adapt to our lifestyles or move on. So they chose to move on and they sold their land to the settlers.

"The Dickinson plantation that you saw awhile back was part of a tract that two brothers, the Walkers, bought from an Indian known as Christian some years ago. It became known as the 'Brothers Portion.' They paid three match coats, twelve bottles of drinks and four handfuls of powder for it. Dickinson bought his land from the two brothers. Our friend William Killen that you met in Dover owns another 400 acres of that same tract."

70

A strange way to do business, Polly thought. Maybe I'll understand it better when I've lived here longer, she said to herself, but for now I'll just let it go.

"Have the settlers always come from England and Ireland?" she asked.

"Well, at first there were the Dutch and the Swedes," he said. "Then the English came and the king—Charles II was king then—granted huge tracts of land in America to a man named William Penn and it was named Pennsylvania after him. The name means 'Penn's Woods.' The grant didn't include the three lower counties on the Delaware—Kent is one of them—but Penn convinced the Duke of York, who did own them, to let him incorporate them in his grant. So, we became part of Pennsylvania and still are, except a long time ago the three counties felt they could look after their interests better if they had their own legislature and so the three counties set up New Castle as their capital."

Her husband, Jemima was pleased to note—and not for the first time—was always interested in learning about things. His daughter, she further noted, seemed to have inherited that same interest.

Polly's concern about Indians made Jemima curious.

"Are you worried about them?" she asked. "What have you heard about Indians?" Haslet had never mentioned Indians in letters home, nor been asked about it in the letters from there. There was almost no contact between Indians and the people in the Three Runs area.

"Well, there were stories in Ireland about settlers in America being attacked and killed by Indians," Polly said. Her face revealed some concern. Travelers to America had brought back stories of fighting between settlers and the Indians, grisly stories of scalping and torture. The Indians came out of the woods wailing like banshees, the travelers assured enraptured listeners.

"Some stories made it seem like there was no place in this country where you were safe from them," Polly said. "Are they really as savage as the stories made it seem?"

"Many are," John responded. He thought about the Indians the Forbes expedition had encountered in the 1758 march to Fort Duquesne and the massacre of Major James Grant's troops in a premature attack on that fort in September, 1758. He remembered also the desecration of the dead and mistreatment of the wounded and captured. He also allowed that the English and Americans could be just as brutal.

"Many are not," he continued. "I have met both friendly and un-friendly Indians in my short time in America. I think it only fair to mention, Polly, that the settlers were capable of savage acts against the Indians, too.

"Just a couple years ago a group from up north in Pennsylvania massacred several friendly Indians in a place north of here called Lancaster."

"Why did they do that?"

"Well, it was a time when Indians along what we call the frontier—that's the place where the plantations end and the real wilderness begins—were attacking the settlers there. Many settlers lived in isolated plantations and whole families were killed." He did not go into the grim details.

"This group of men—I'm ashamed to say they were Presbyterians—were called the Paxton Boys, after the place where they lived. They decided to avenge the killing of the settlers and took out their revenge on a group of friendly Indians that had been taken to a place in Lancaster County where it was expected they would be safe. It is not a very pleasant story. You may also hear from time to time of other such incidents where white settlers and Indians live near each other. But that is not the case here."

Jemima watched her face for reaction. Polly was lost in thought, but it seemed the concern had vanished.

Haslet returned to his plans for the new property, talking about the crops he would be planting, and about selling some of the timber they cleared to local shipbuilders, but both Polly and Jemima were lost in their own thoughts.

"We'll probably take some of it to the sawmill to cut planks for our new home," he said, catching their attention for the moment. "Some of it we'll sell for firewood, ship it up to Dover, I suppose."

There was a good market for firewood in colonial America.

"We'll have wheat and corn and rye. Too bad we won't be ready to plant the rye this fall. And, of course, there'll be horses and sheep and cows and pigs. And we'll need oxen, and a garden for herbs and vegetables."

Jemima could have pointed out that they had all these things now but she realized her husband was happily contemplating his first real home in his new country.

"We'll grow flaxseed," Haslet said, resuming his train of thought and turning to Polly, "and maybe send it home to help them with their linen. Your Uncle James would certainly appreciate it now that he's a seed merchant."

The mention roused a bit of homesickness in Polly.

"Father, does one ever get used to living so far away from home? Of the possibility you'll never see Ireland again?" She couldn't help but notice the wistful look on his face at those times when she told him about happenings at home since he left and she could sense his mind wandered with hers over sweetly familiar ground, remembered pleasantly familiar sounds.

"Well, my darling daughter," he said, finally, "you'll never forget the special things about Ireland. Memories of the land, of the people who reared you from a baby, the sights, the sounds will float into your mind like unforgettable melodies. They'll fill your thoughts at bedtime and sneak up on you when you are working at the loom or scratching at the soil. They'll bring a smile to your face and, perhaps, an occasional tear."

Haslet paused, lost himself for a while in his own memories, before continuing: "I still think of Ireland as home. But we have our hopes and our dreams as well as our memories. And our hopes, our dreams are here in Kent County. And the answer is: you accept that this is your home, this is your new life, and you determine that you will give it the best of what is in you, that you will never hold anything back just because it is not the land of your birth."

Jemima glanced at the young girl beside her, wondering what she was thinking. Ever since John put down the letter from Ireland and told her about the plans for Polly's voyage to America, Jemima had been curious about her stepdaughter. The reality was pleasing. Her mother obviously had been a beautiful woman and John had remarked how Polly reminded him of her mother. Jemima didn't worry about comparisons. She had grown in self-confidence managing the plantation and from her marriage. John's love for her seemed genuine and unreserved and their times together were very happy. There were no indications of any change since Polly arrived.

"We must start planning for the fall when we get home," Jemima said to Polly. "There'll be candles to make, yarn to spin, clothes to make, food to prepare for the winter."

"I'll look forward to that," Polly responded.

"What do you think of America?" Jemima asked her.

"Oh, it's a pretty country," the girl responded. "Different. It's my home now and that's the most important thing for me."

It was an appropriate answer and all three rode silently for a period of time. John thought about the new plantation; Jemima thought about the busy months ahead preparing for the winter and, especially, about the new life stirring inside her. Polly continued to absorb the sights and relationships of her changed life.

It was different from County Derry, certainly, as her father had told her it would be in his letter explaining the arrangements for her arrival at New Castle. He had included a description of the land, partly to help her and her cousin William confirm their route to the plantation, partly to prepare her for the changes from Ireland. Until this trip she hadn't fully appreciated his descriptions.

Three Runs was more sparsely settled than the Roe Valley back in Ulster, but the plantations were much larger. Haslet made it a point to take his daughter around to see the area and its people. Forests were everywhere, stands of many varieties of trees, particularly different kinds of oak. She had heard her father say the oak trees were much in demand by shipbuilders. Shipbuilding along the Mispillion had attracted a variety of artisans—bricklayers, carpenters, saddlers, wheelwrights as well as the shipbuilders and boatmen—and they in turn attracted a few support businesses. One building they passed was identified by her father as both a home and a store. And there was a tavern just to the south on one of the many branches of the Mispillion. There was, of course, a sawmill—the area where they just purchased the land was known as the Sawmill Range—and gristmills for grinding the wheat. The Presbyterians, Anglicans, and Quakers all had their churches or meetinghouses scattered through the woods. There were the rudiments of a village, in fact. It would be more than a dozen years, however, before the locals began to think of Three Runs as a town and not until after the turn of the century was this town incorporated as Milford.

Her father, she was surprised to find, was active in the Presbyterian Church. Back home it was widely believed her mother's death had caused him—as she heard family define it—"to lose his faith." His kin believed that this, more than any other reason, led to his decision to emigrate.

The Mispillion River itself was so different from the Roe. It was deep enough that ships could come up as far as the mill where travelers on the King's Highway forded the Mispillion. That was twenty winding miles from the Delaware River. It seemed every plantation along the river had its own landing where the product of its land could be loaded for shipment to Philadelphia or Wilmington.

Yes, a far different life, but a more peaceful one.

She never heard the adults complain about landlords, or rents, or the influence of the Church of Ireland over their lives, topics that were so much a part of the adults' conversations in the evening back in Ulster. Nor were there mentions of the kinds of violence that occasionally erupted from the resentments these impositions created.

Except for some brief mention one night about problems with something called a stamp tax, conversation in the Haslet household since her arrival mostly had been about things around the plantation. Occasionally her father would relate something about the patients he had seen. From time to time he would tell her stepmother about some of the people who were important in the county. These were unfamiliar names to her, of course.

Adjusting to her new life occupied her every day. In many ways, the household chores were similar to those back home, but the role of the Negro slaves was both intriguing and strange. There also were many immigrant men and women working as servants in the area, but they seemed to have more freedom of movement, more social acceptance than the slaves.

She was pleased to note that many of the immigrants were from Ireland. Often, when she and her father met people around the area, she would close her eyes and listen to the familiar accents, imagining she was back in Ulster.

Polly also was excited at the prospect of a sibling. And curious and concerned about what it would mean to her relationship with her father. She had no doubt of his love for her and she felt a growing closeness with her stepmother. Still, she wished she could have more time to allow the relationship to flourish before she had a rival for their affection.

Autumn had changed the landscape and put a chill in the air when Jemima's time arrived.

Haslet had arranged for a midwife from the neighborhood to attend the birth, the common practice in those days. The obstetrics that Dr. William Shippen Jr. practiced in Philadelphia, that he had learned studying under Dr. William Smellie in London, was a very, very small part of the medical world of 1766.

Haslet waited with Polly in the kitchen as the women attended Jemima upstairs. Besides Mrs. Manlove, the midwife, there was Jemima's favorite servant, Bett, and another Negro slave, Sarah. Bett had lived on the Molleston plantation and had been willed to Jemima by her father. From time to time either Bett or Sarah would come down to fetch something and leave.

Memories of his first wife's death in a similar scene more than a dozen years ago inevitably filled Haslet with concern but he kept it to himself.

Polly busied herself with chores. The colonial household was an industry in itself and Jemima's increasing debilitation meant there was still bread to bake, wool and flax to spin, jars of preserves to prepare. Haslet marveled at his daughter's facility with these household chores. She had learned much in his Uncle Samuel's house, he decided, and Jemima had added to her domestic education.

"The Lord has blessed me with a wonderful daughter," he told her, instinctively realizing she needed reassurance about the impending arrival of a competitor for her father's affection. "You will always be special to me."

After several hours, there was an increase of activity upstairs. Haslet sensed a critical moment had arrived and he bowed his head to pray, the only thing he knew to do.

Shortly, Sarah arrived in the kitchen.

"He's here and he's fine and healthy, Dr. Haslet," she said happily.

"He?" Haslet questioned.

"Yes, a little boy. Mrs. Manlove says you can visit now."

Haslet took Polly by the hand. "Come with me, darling, and meet your brother."

Mrs. Manlove and Bett were busy cleaning up. There was a pile of bedclothes on the floor, which Bett gathered up and took out of the room. Jemima rested among fresh bedclothes, holding the infant in her arms. Haslet knelt by the bed and smiled at them both. He was filled with both love and relief.

"What shall we call him?" she asked.

"Joseph. After my father."

"Polly," Jemima said, "come look at your brother Joseph. Isn't he handsome? Don't you think he'll make the girls giddy when he smiles at them?"

Polly became part of the family tableau at the bedside.

Chapter Eight

Portents

As 1766 came to a close, the furor over the Stamp Act had faded to echoes. But not so faint as to mute the feelings of betrayal nor to quiet the uneasiness over the future.

In Boston, the Massachusetts General Court, the colony's legislature, dallied well over a year before agreeing to Parliament's demands that the colony compensate the victims of the destructive mobs during the protest of the stamp tax. Lieutenant Governor Thomas Hutchinson had been among those victims, his house severely damaged.

The autocratic governor, Francis Bernard, had demanded a quick response on compensation but the likes of James Otis, John Hancock, and Samuel Adams were not about to submit meekly to demands from British authorities. Town meeting democracy prevailed in the New England colonies and they blithely told the governor that the legislature should first sound out public opinion. Thus it was December of 1766 before the legislature finally agreed on compensation for the August 1765 destruction. The legislators included a provision for pardons to those people involved in the vandalism. Parliament considered that an impertinence.

Coincidentally, a little over a week after the Massachusetts action, New York's assemblymen refused to appropriate the full subsistence requested by Parliament for British troops living in that town. It had become the principal barracks in America and the New Yorkers said they couldn't afford all that was demanded. Besides, they reasoned, why should they bear the major cost of supporting troops supposed to protect settlers on a faraway frontier.

John Haslet: A Useful One

Nevertheless, the general good feeling created by the repeal of the Stamp Act muted these discordant notes. Pennsylvania, the southern colonies, and, indeed, most colonies placidly agreed to support the British forces in America.

To the people living in the peninsula between the Chesapeake and Delaware bays, it all had been a storm that blew through their lives and moved on.

For John Haslet, the singular event of early 1767 was the long-delayed purchase of the 250 acres in Mispillion Hundred that he had bid on in July of 1762. The tract was adjacent to the land he purchased from the Bradys in 1766 and it expanded his plantation to 378 acres.

So, he traveled to Philadelphia in March 1767, checked into the Indian King Inn on High Street between Second and Third Streets, a three-story brick building noted for its service to travelers. Once his business was settled, he sent a message to Francis Alison suggesting dinner, apologizing for not telling him sooner about his trip.

The clergyman/educator showed up with a young friend, a man with whom Haslet would be involved at important moments in the coming years.

"John, this is Thomas McKean. I'm sure you've heard of him since he's made a name for himself as a lawyer in your colony as well as here in Philadelphia."

"Of course I've heard of Mr. McKean," Haslet replied, holding out his hand to that offered by McKean. McKean, just turned thirty-three, was believed to have the largest law practice in Pennsylvania and the lower counties. He also was a member of the Delaware Assembly since 1762 and a justice of the peace in New Castle County.

By the time of the Revolution he would distinguish himself in both Pennsylvania and Delaware as a militant patriot. He also tried a bit of soldiering when the Revolutionary War began, but his talent was more with words and pen.

"I was visiting with Dr. Alison," McKean said, "and when he suggested I join the two of you at dinner I welcomed the opportunity. I've heard about you from Caesar Rodney."

Like Haslet, he was well over six feet tall and the two handsome young men drew idle glances from the diners as they stood exchanging greetings.

In colonial Philadelphia, taverns were communal places where social distinctions melted away in the commingling of patrons. People's opinions carried as much influence as their voices could command. This egalitarian spirit made for lively evenings in the taverns.

"I apologize for not contacting you sooner, Francis," Haslet said as they sat down, "but my trip was hastily conceived. As soon as I received word that the Pennsylvania Land Company was ready to close the deal for my land, I gathered my things and headed here."

Alison acknowledged the apology. On previous occasions, Haslet had stayed with him and he had been surprised and a bit hurt when he received the message that Haslet was in town and staying at the Indian King.

Haslet turned his attention back to McKean.

"I was taken by King George's response to the message you and Rodney fashioned at the Stamp Act Congress, thanking him for repealing that iniquitous act. I understand he was so pleased he had his chamberlain read it twice to him."

McKean nodded, the thought spreading a smile across his face.

Haslet's face also showed a trace of a smile when he added: "As I recall you were not quite so gentle with the presiding officer at the Stamp Act Congress."

"Timothy Ruggles was a disagreeable ass, too timid to have presided over such an important event," McKean said, his smile disappearing, his voice rising, and anger flashing across his face. The rumors of his famous temper are true, Haslet thought.

Nearby diners paused to glance their way.

"When I called him out for failing to sign our resolves, he challenged me to a duel. I, of course, promptly accepted, but he left New York rather than face me."

There was a look of triumph in his face. Haslet did not wonder that Ruggles, twice McKean's age, departed for his home in Massachusetts rather than confront the physically imposing young man.

Soon after the congress adjourned, McKean also had a confrontation with another dissident delegate, Robert Ogden of Jersey, a friend of McKean's father-in-law, Joseph Borden of Bordentown. Ogden had pleaded with McKean not to make public his refusal to sign the resolves and asked Borden to intervene on his behalf. McKean pledged to his father-in-law that he would keep quiet only if he wasn't asked about the nonsigners. It so happened that he was asked; he revealed Ogden's name and that of others. Again there was a challenge to a duel, again avoided when the adversary left town.

Not a man to trifle with, this frenetic young spirit, Haslet thought. He could be a formidable ally or a formidable enemy.

The edge of temper quickly disappeared and Alison changed the subject.

"Thomas was one of my best students at the New London Academy."

"Dr. Alison was a demanding teacher," McKean responded. "And an inspirational one. He taught us that public service is a glorious pursuit for a dedicated citizen. He said public servants should have integrity, honesty, and dedication. His words have had a great influence on my conduct in office.

"I well recall his words:"—McKean did his best at impersonating Alison—" 'liberty is a most tender plant that thrives in a very few soils; neglected it soon withers and is lost; but is scarce ever recovered.' "

There was a touch of reverence in his voice.

Alison was obviously pleased at the flattery. "I'm certainly complimented that you remember, Thomas," he said. "Of course, much of my feelings about government and the public obligations came from a very distinguished educator, Francis Hutcheson."

"Hutcheson!" Haslet interjected. "He had just left teaching at Glasgow when I entered the university."

"He was my professor of moral philosophy," Alison recalled. "I learned much from him. You should read his *Short Introduction to Moral Philosophy*, John. Professor Hutcheson had a profound influence on me and I tried to pass along his ideas to my students at New London. Incidentally, I found his principles very relevant to the debate over the stamp tax. Hutcheson taught that government exists to serve mankind, that when it ceases to do so people are justified in resisting. Of course, he had Scottish-English relationships in mind but I think one could apply his principles to our relations with Britain."

Haslet and McKean nodded their approval.

"And now your academy has been moved to Newark," Haslet commented. "Did you have a part in that, Thomas?"

"I favored that location certainly. As did Dr. Alison," he responded. "And not just because it's in my county."

"A good location," Alison agreed.

Newark, Delaware—occasionally referred to as New Ark—was not too many miles down the road from New London, Pennsylvania. The academy had first moved to Elkton, Maryland, from New London, before finding its final home in Newark (where it would eventually transform into the University of Delaware).

There was a lull in the conversation as the men attended to the dinner before them, letting the conversations of the other diners at the long table drift by their ears unnoticed.

Haslet broke the silence, turning to Alison:

"Francis, are you familiar with Charles Tennent? He's a member of my presbytery, a minister at Blackwater church in Maryland."

"I remember him," McKean interjected. "He served in my presbytery for a long time."

"More than a quarter century, in fact," Haslet added. "He transferred to the Lewes Presbytery about four years ago."

"He is a member of a very spiritual family," Alison said, a note of disdain in his voice.

"The talk is that he's a man much possessed with spirits," Haslet said, adding with a laugh, "And I don't mean holy spirits."

Alison laughed, nodding his head to acknowledge he had heard the talk about Charles Tennent's fondness for drink.

"A spiritual family?" Haslet asked.

"His father was William Tennent and his brother Gilbert Tennent, both ministers. They were very much involved in the division that split our church for nearly twenty years. We were on opposite sides and had many bitter words.

"The Tennents and their supporters were inspired by George Whitefield, an Anglican minister who preached many sermons to large groups of people all up and down this continent. He had an extraordinary power to move people. My objection was that Whitefield and the other so-called revivalists addressed the emotions, not the minds of the people. I believed people needed to follow rational forms of behavior in order to experience the grace of God.

"Moreover, these people—called 'New Siders'—disrupted the organization of the church.

"For example, they would appear uninvited in other ministers' areas. The Tennents ran a college in Bucks County, Pennsylvania—Log

College—and ordained graduates without approval of the synod. And, most offensively of all, they challenged the piety of ministers who disagreed with them. Gilbert Tennent disparaged us as 'Pharisee-teachers.'"

Alison's voice reflected the agitation these events recalled.

McKean commented: "It was an interesting and, perhaps unnecessary waste of energy and intellect. Neither party ever accused the other of one fundamental error in doctrine, any imposition on conscience, any gross immoralities or total stagnation of discipline or church government. The disputes were about matters of opinion. It seemed to me there was a want of Christian charity motivating the two sides."

Alison nodded agreement. "It seemed that Satan himself was instigating the debate."

The revival movement known as the "Great Awakening" had split denominations from New England to Georgia. William Tennent and, especially, his son Gilbert, had carried on when Whitefield returned to England. Gilbert was the more influential, preaching extensively through the colonies, including New England, where Jonathan Edwards also was arousing people. Among the Presbyterians the split resulted in creation of a rival presbytery, even a rival synod.

A more subtle effect of those turbulent years was the conviction it gave colonials that their land was divinely endowed and their vision of its opportunities and uses divinely inspired. This spiritual imprimatur validated their concept of their civil rights and strengthened their sense of righteousness when those rights became an issue with the secular powers in London.

"When did the division end?" Haslet asked. "I was not aware of it when I settled in Delaware."

"We made our peace with the Lord and each other in '58," Alison responded.

"Was Charles Tennent part of this?" Haslet asked.

"I don't know," Alison said. "Certainly not as prominently as the rest of his family. Perhaps he doesn't have the intellectual and oratorical powers of his brother and father. Gilbert Tennent died just a couple years ago and the father has been dead, I don't recall how many years."

"Did you happen to see the notices he and his wife inserted in the newspapers recently?" Haslet said, returning to the thought that had prompted him to ask Alison about Tennent.

"Yes. I assume their marriage is an unhappy one. Perhaps the drinking."

"Obviously," Haslet said. "He inserted a notice in January that she had run away and that he would not be responsible for her debts. She responded within the month with a very strongly worded denial, accusing him of abusing her and refusing to let her back in their home. She says in the ad he refused to allow her to use their carriage to go to have a sore tooth drawn. A very sorry situation, I suspect.

"I expect this matter will come before the presbytery before long."

"Will that involve you?" McKean was curious.

"I don't know," Haslet said. "I'm an elder in our Three Runs church and it will depend if the matter comes up when the presbytery meets in July. Our church is cohost of the session."

The men finished their meals and Alison turned to McKean.

"Do you think ill feeling between the colonies and our mother country will abate now that the Stamp Act has been repealed?"

"I don't know. It would appear those feelings have subsided, especially if you judge by the people of Delaware. On the other hand, there is the stubbornness of the Massachusetts and New York colonies. It's possible their behavior reveals a residue of the bad blood stirred by that damnable act, a permanent stain on the fabric of our relationship.

"I also hear there is talk in London of new revenue measures to be directed against the colonies. There is talk of duties on certain imports. It is argued that the government always has regulated trade by the colonies and we've accepted that regulation without complaint. Presumably, these duties would only be an extension of that regulation.

"I'll have to see what the government develops before I can honestly answer your question. I do have an opinion that the government must tread lightly for we have experienced the success of protest in America. It has united the colonies, if only temporarily, and we have developed a new attitude toward British rule. It will depend on whether it becomes an issue of regulating trade or raising revenue."

Haslet listened to the younger man's words with interest. As a member of a dissenting—that is, non-Anglican—church in Ireland he was obviously sensitive to the restrictions imposed by British hegemony.

"The British government has little patience with ideas and practices that upset the institutional nature of its power over its subjects,"

83

he commented. "It will come down harshly on Massachusetts and New York if they persist in their contrariness."

They had capped dinner with glasses of warm punch and that lightened their mood. Now, it was time for parting.

"How long will you be staying, John?" Alison asked as the three men walked through the tavern to the street.

"Just one more night. I will take a boat to Duck Creek in the morning after I arrange to ship some household items I've purchased. There are also a few items I want to pick up for my wife and take with me. I may stay over in Dover tomorrow night, then continue on home."

"I hope now that we've met we'll see more of each other," McKean said.

"I'll make a point of doing that," Haslet responded.

The three men talked briefly outside the tavern, then dispersed, Haslet returning to the Indian King.

McKean's sense of future relations with England were prophetic. Before 1767 came to a close Charles Townshend would turn around the good feelings that followed the repeal of the Stamp Act.

Townshend had emerged as the de facto leader of Parliament in a series of developments dating to the previous summer when King George dismissed the Rockingham ministry and asked William Pitt and the Duke of Grafton to take over.

Pitt was no longer the "Great Commoner," either in fact or in personality, after the king had made him a lord of the realm as the First Earl of Chatham, and his popularity sagged. The people of Bath even burned a copy of his speech against the Stamp Act as a sign of their displeasure over his accepting a peerage. Further, Pitt's health made him ineffective and he soon left Grafton mostly alone to run the government. The latter was an indifferent minister so the leadership vacuum was filled by Townshend, chancellor of the exchequer.

Reporting to the Commons in mid-May 1767 on the last fiscal year, there was a note of triumph in his voice.

"I am pleased to report to you, that not only have we managed to provide support for the army and navy and the entire government this past year, but we have reduced the national debt by £3,900,000. And this despite the reduction in the land tax!"

The members loudly approved. He basked in the applause before continuing.

"It has been said that I have plans for taxing America."

A few cries of "No! No!" came from the benches.

"I declare that to be a libel," he said. "I am not and never was for taxing America. I thought the Stamp Act a very improper measure and used my endeavors for its repeal."

The members smiled at the chancellor's revision of history. Townshend had demonstrated disdain for the North Americans in the earlier debates over the stamp tax and they were sure his attitude had not changed a bit. And it would appear the chancellor's words now were designed to disguise his intentions.

Townshend extended a hand.

"I would cut off that hand," he declared, "before I would vote for taxing America."

He paused for effect, then proceeded matter-of-factly to his main point.

"I will in a few days present to you some proposals for laying duties on our trade with the North American colonies. I promise that if they appear burdensome, I shall not hesitate to remove them. However, it is uncontested that we have the right—in fact an obligation—to regulate the trade within our glorious empire to the benefit of all its inhabitants, both at home and in our colonies. What I shall propose will only be an extension of that obligation and I would hope the members of the Commons and the Lords will recognize the proposals as such."

A few days later, he introduced bills to impose duties on china, paper, glass, and painter's colors shipped from Great Britain to America. Despite the chancellor's defense of these duties as mere extensions of trade regulations, the preamble talked of raising revenue.

Parliament also decided the salaries of governors and judges in the colonies would be provided by the Crown out of revenue from these duties, denying the colonial assemblies that important control over these officers. Moreover, a board of customs would be established in Boston to enforce collection of the duties. It was hoped the colonials' easy avoidance of past regulations would be quickly halted.

As for the two defiant colonies, pardons granted in the Massachusetts bill providing compensation for the 1765 riots were nullified. Only the king had the power to grant pardons, Parliament declared. Included in the package Townshend submitted was a bill denying New York's assembly the power to enact laws until it submitted to the request for supporting the troops.

The immediate reaction in the colonies to this shocking imposition of British rule was not as passionate as the agitation over the Stamp Act. Rather, the reaction reached deeper into the American psyche and with more lasting imprint as the colonists looked more closely at their relationship with England.

Ironically, Townshend would not know his duties exacerbated the disintegrating relationship. He died in September.

Chapter Nine

Marital Stress and Rioting Troops

The Townshend duties nudged the colonies farther down the road to rebellion, but it was still only a gentle slope, not yet a steep descent.

The duties reinforced suspicion that the government cared little for colonial rights. Ostensibly they were designed to regulate trade but the wording plainly said they were designed to raise revenue. Although there seemed little difference from the government's historic exercise of power over trade, the Stamp Act had opened a wound and the word "revenue" in the new duties reopened that wound.

Furthermore, the punishment of New York's legislature for what Parliament considered insubordination signaled that the British government wasn't in a mood to tolerate further resistance from its North American colonies. The colonial reaction was muted, but the colonists were plainly uncomfortable, feeling insecure in their rights as Englishmen.

Americans still professed loyalty to King George III, an expression of belief and pride in Great Britain's preeminent position in the world. They still felt a part of it. But Parliament? That was another matter!

Parliament was an itch in the middle of the back to the colonists and to the members of Parliament the colonists seemed like the neighbor's dog which barks at every movement. Even friends such as William Pitt commented unfavorably about the colonial attitudes toward Parliamentary authority.

There was little obvious revolutionary agitation in 1767, however. Unlike the reaction following the Stamp Act, officials' homes weren't vandalized nor their lives threatened.

For John Haslet, 1767 was a year that brought him increased presence in the lower counties. It was hard to ignore this good-looking man, tall and athletic, articulate, and educated as he made his rounds, waving to farmers, chatting with merchants. Also he was active in his church and that would lead to a larger role in politics since the two institutions fed off each other.

In 1767 he was elected an elder of the Three Runs Presbyterian Church and that involved him in one of the most celebrated problems for the Lewes Presbytery, the marital dispute between the Reverend Charles Tennent and his wife, Jane. It came up at the July 28 session.

It wasn't unusual for the churches to deal with domestic matters in a day when they played such a large role in colonial life and the judiciary system confined itself to more civil matters.

The presbytery rotated its sessions among its churches and it so happened Haslet's own Three Runs church and the Motherkill meetinghouse were cohosts for the summer session of the presbytery, held at the Motherkill church. The Reverend Alexander Huston, minister at both churches, served as moderator.

Haslet attended the session as an elder. Also present were the other ministers of the presbytery (which covered Kent and Sussex counties in Delaware and Worcester, Somerset, Queen Anne, and Kent counties in Maryland) except for Tennent, who was minister at Blackwater in Berlin, Worcester County.

After opening prayer, the members settled in the benches and Huston went directly to the Tennent matter.

"I present for your consideration, a letter from supplicant Jane Tennent, wife to our absent minister Charles Tennent. It contains most serious allegations against Pastor Tennent; first, that he has been frequently in a state of drunkenness; second, that he has treated her cruelly and in a most unChristian manner; third, that he has broken the marriage vow to love and honor her; fourth, that he has treated her most unjustly; and finally, that he has lied about her behavior in conversations with her neighbors and even in advertisements in the newspapers.

"Reverend Tennent is not here to answer these complaints, but Mrs. Tennent is. Mrs. Tennent, please come forward and address the session."

The middle-aged woman stood up and moved to the front of the meetinghouse to stand beside Huston. It was obvious she was uncomfortable, facing the session alone and unsupported, a lone woman wondering if the men in the room held her to blame. Only the sense of needing to have a wrong redeemed gave her enough courage to proceed.

"Reverend clergy, esteemed elders," she began, "I had hoped to present William McKay as a witness to the injustices and indignities inflicted upon me by Charles Tennent. He has suffered his own injustices at the hands of my husband, who has accused him of misbehavior, just as he accused me. However, since Mr. McKay has not appeared, I do not feel I can proceed without him as witness to my charges."

"Very well," Huston responded. "We understand."

He paused to see if she would speak further.

"Since Mr. Tennent is not here to speak for himself and Mrs. Tennent does not feel she can adequately present her complaints," Huston said, "I think it appropriate that I read the notices that Mr. and Mrs. Tennent placed in the newspapers back in January. They state the positions of the parties as well as anything, I suppose."

He picked up a clipping and read aloud:

"'Whereas my wife Jane hath departed from me, without my consent, after having extravagantly laid out large sums of money without my knowledge; has threatened to run me much more in debt than she has already done; and notwithstanding my frequent earnest and tender requests to her, she has refused to return to my house and live with me, according to our solemn obligation. I now hereby give this public notice to all persons not to let her have any money or anything else, on my account, as I will not pay any debt contracted by her in this, or any other province, after the date hereof. I also hereby give notice to all persons who are in any manner indebted to the estate of John Galbreath, deceased, not to pay such debts, or any part thereof, to my wife, as such payments shall not be allowed.'

"Mrs. Tennent responded with her own notice within the month," Huston continued.

He picked up another clipping:

"'Whereas a very extraordinary advertisement hath lately appeared in your paper, signed by Charles Tennent, setting forth that I had departed from him without his consent after having extravagantly laid out large sums of money without his knowledge and had threatened to run him much more in debt than (as he says) I have already done, and that not withstanding his frequent earnest and tender requests to me, have refused to return to his home and live with him according to our solemn obligation. In order to do myself justice and set the matter in a clearer light to the public than what has yet been represented, I do assure the public the matter stands as follows: Mr. Tennent, for reasons which I shall not mention and which would have been but prudent in him not to have mentioned, has used me extremely ill and not treated me like a wife; he has refused me the privilege of my Negro wench to wait on me, refused me the use of my horse and carriage and one day, notwithstanding the extremity I was in with the toothache, he refused me a horse to go and have my tooth drawn; and being under the necessity of going on foot, before I returned, which was the same day that I went, he had posted up advertisements round the neighborhood to the same effect he has done here. I further assure the public I never absconded from him in any other manner, nor extravagantly or otherwise laid out any sum or sums of money since I became his wife but what I paid out of my own estate to answer his debts and for clothes both for himself and his children; not even on my own account, except one suit of clothes which I bought at the same time when I bought a suit for him; that he never entreated me to return and live with him, but on the contrary since I came to town, though I went to his lodgings and desired to see him, he would not see me nor meet me before any gentlemen in town to talk the matter face to face; and I cannot but greatly wonder that such a man—as Mr. Tennent would endeavor to persuade the public he is—would be guilty of putting his hand to such a malicious piece of stuff.'

"There is nothing further at this time," Huston said and stood silently as embarrassed coughing filled the church. The members were obviously distressed at the Tennents' public airing of their problems. Mrs. Tennent stared at the floor throughout the readings.

Haslet spoke up.

"Why is Mr. Tennent not here this morning?"

"No reason has been given," Huston said.

"I would want to hear from him before I reach any decision on such a serious matter," Haslet said. "I would also add that I find it an affront to this presbytery that the reverend has chosen not to respond to his wife's accusations, at least through a note if not in person."

Haslet's annoyance was quite obvious.

"I agree with Dr. Haslet," said Matthew Wilson, minister at the Lewes church. There were sounds of assent from the others.

"Any recommendations, John?" Huston asked.

"I don't see how we can rule on this without his testimony," Haslet said. "I would recommend the presbytery send him a strong note demanding his attendance at a special meeting. We may even go to his church, if necessary, to obtain his compliance."

The meeting gave its assent.

"When do you propose that meeting?" a member asked.

"Probably in early October," Huston responded. "How about October second?"

The gathering again approved and the members made their notations.

(Tennent did attend the October meeting but no decision was reached and the matter dragged on. At a meeting the following month there was testimony from eight witnesses about his drinking. In 1768, the presbytery finally agreed to dissolve the marriage, ordering him to return her clothes but allowing him to keep their furniture as security on her debts. The charge of drunkenness recurred in November of 1769 and he was suspended indefinitely. Tennent died February 25, 1771. At the April 4 meeting that year, the presbytery restored church privileges to Jane Tennent.)

Mrs. Tennent had waited quietly up to this point. Huston now turned to her:

"You pledged to God to be husband and wife, to live in a harmonious, loving relationship with each other and to honor Him through that relationship. That is a pledge we can't easily declare null. It fills the hearts of this presbytery with sorrow that the marriage of one of our ministers and a daughter of God has come to the point that one of you would seek to revoke that pledge."

She shyly bowed her head, unable to comment on Huston's remarks. Now she gestured her thanks to the meeting and walked quietly out of the meetinghouse.

Huston watched her leave and after an appropriate silence proceeded:

"Appropriate to the wishes of this session, we will postpone further discussion of the Tennent matter.

"Next." He paused to look at a paper, "We have been asked for a generous donation to the fund for supporting the families of our deceased ministers."

"I suggest £10," Haslet said.

"That is a considerable amount of money, doctor," observed one of the ministers.

"We are only asked to contribute once a year," he responded. "It has been suggested the money be taken out of our fund for pious uses and I believe there is sufficient monies in that fund."

The fund for pious uses had been created by the Synod of Philadelphia in 1717, intended to support the educational, charitable, and missionary work of the synod.

"I don't disagree, doctor. I was just wondering what other pres-byteries are contributing."

"I think the amount is comparable to the others. We are a large presbytery, with several churches in six counties. I believe it averages out to less than a pound for each church, not an excessive amount for the purpose."

"Well, it is very generous," Wilson commented, "but let that be the reputation of the Lewes Presbytery."

"It is agreed then?" Huston asked. The group indicated its acceptance.

Dr. Alison will be pleased, Haslet thought. It was Alison who in 1755 had created the family welfare fund.

"I would ask the session's prayers," Haslet said, "for a William Clinton. I doubt if you know him since he lived in another presbytery, but he was a brave soldier who served with me during the French and Indian War."

Clinton had been his lieutenant in 1758.

"I learned just recently that he has died," Haslet explained. There had been a notice in the *Pennsylvania Gazette* that Clinton's estate in New London Township, Pennsylvania, was being offered for sale.

The members bowed and Haslet continued:

"Dear Father, our Ultimate Commander, we pray for this brave soldier who served Thee throughout his life as he has served his king, community, and family. We would pray that he marches by Thy side now as he did with this humble supplicant some years ago. William Clinton was as worthy a soldier in the service of God as he was in the service of the Crown."

The short prayer ended the session.

The men lingered outside the church in informal conversational groups, enjoying the warm afternoon sun. John Miller, minister at the Dover church, approached Haslet with a question. The prayer for Clinton had stirred a concern in Miller's mind and Haslet, a well-read man, and one who also had an Irishman's feel for English attitudes towards those outside the establishment, was a logical person to address his concern.

"John, do you think we'll see men marching again? I wonder if the resentments towards the British government that we so painfully witnessed just recently are liable to flare again if the government goes ahead with the plans I hear to impose new revenue measures."

"I don't know," Haslet confessed. "I agree there are remnants of ill feeling in these colonies. The newspapers speak of that almost every week. There also seems a lack of appreciation in the government for the sensitivities of the North American colonists. I read how this lord condemns us as rowdies and that earl condemns us as being ungrateful. The sentiment seems to be not to find accommodation but to impose their will upon us. I read in the newspaper recently a letter from London to Boston asserting that the government would be useless if it tolerated defiance of its authority. Thoughts like these are bad omens."

A recent news item seemed relevant to the issue:

"Perhaps there is a lesson in a story I read in the *Gazette*. It happened in Ireland, in County Kerry. It seems a man named Laughlin Brady was attempting to rob an eagle's nest when the eagle attacked. He fell into the lake and, although a good swimmer, the eagle continued to attack him until he became exhausted and drowned. When his body was recovered, the eyes had been pecked out and the face mangled."

The men shuddered.

"I wonder if there isn't a lesson in that story for England?" Haslet concluded. "Perhaps the American colonies are like eagles which will resent and attack if the government attempts to raid our nest."

"An interesting analogy," Matthew Wilson agreed, "very interesting."

The men reflected privately on the story, then returned to idle conversation until, one by one, they departed for their homes.

Earlier that same day in July soldiers had indeed been marching, with a result that would add to the lore of British insensitivity to colonial rights. It happened in Elizabethtown, Jersey, where British soldiers of the Twenty-eighth Regiment allowed passions to overwhelm discipline.

They had expected a grateful citizenry to support them during their stay, but the citizens had insisted the soldiers pay their own way. Now they were leaving town, headed for Amboy to embark for Europe, their hostility towards what they considered the ungrateful colonials so far unresolved.

The final companies were marching through town just after midnight, drums beating and fifes playing in contempt of the sleeping citizens' peace. It began orderly enough but, for some reason, the soldiers broke ranks and began smashing windows. Their first assault was on the meetinghouse, then the courthouse, then the jail.

The jailer, who also was a constable, had been a principal in the action to collect debts. He thrust a gun out of the window. A British officer grabbed it (officers apparently played a prominent role in the rioting) and they wrestled for control, during which the gun went off, wounding another officer in the legs. The jailer then released his prisoners on condition they assist him against the soldiers, at the same time ringing a bell to alarm the town.

As the sounds of the bell echoed through the village, the soldiers disappeared, only to reappear a short time later with a larger group of soldiers, bayonets fixed. By now many of the town's inhabitants had gathered inside the jail. The local magistrates had also gathered with the citizens and implored the soldiers' captain to bring his men under control. He refused. The soldiers entered the building; there was fighting inside, but when more citizens arrived the soldiers decided it was best to flee. Fortunately, there were no deaths.

The magistrates then proceeded to Amboy to confront Colonel Sir John St. Clair, the regimental commander, with the actions of his troops. The soldiers had already boarded the ships, but after discussion, Sir John ordered as many of the offenders as could be identified brought before the magistrates to publicly apologize. They also agreed to pay £25 for damages.

News of the arrogance of the troops and the assaults on Jersey colonists spread rapidly through the colonies, another nudge down that road to rebellion.

And as the year moved along, as leaves began to spread a carpet of reds and yellows across the landscape and the autumn chill slowed the pace of life, John Dickinson sat down at his desk and began writing what would become known as "Letters from a Pennsylvania Farmer," a series of essays that would stir the pot of colonial opposition to British authoritarianism. The first was published in December of 1767.

Chapter Ten

Letters from a Pennsylvania Farmer

"I am a farmer, settled, after a variety of fortunes, near the banks of the River Delaware, in the province of Pennsylvania. I received a liberal education and have been engaged in the busy scenes of life, but am now convinced that a man may be as happy without bustle as with it. My farm is small; my servants are few and good; I have a little money at interest; I wish for no more; my employment in my own affairs is easy; and with a contented, grateful mind, undisturbed by worldly hopes or fears, relating to myself, I am completing the number of days allotted to me by divine goodness."

Thus began, in the *Pennsylvania Gazette* of December 3, 1767, a series of articles signed, simply, "A Farmer."

In representing his station as modest and his days nearly completed, John Dickinson was disingenuous; at thirty-five he still had well more than half of the years allotted to him remaining. His musings about relations between England and her colonies were to resonate through the colonies following Parliament's passage of the Townshend Duties and its suspension of New York's legislative rights earlier in the year.

It made the author, when his name became known, an instant hero as newspapers up and down North America reprinted his essays. Later, he would prove to be more conservative, opposing independence although he took up a rifle and served in the ranks of the Continental army.

John Haslet read each of the twelve essays avidly, reading what he considered the important paragraphs aloud to Jemima and Polly. He didn't know that the author was John Dickinson.

"Farmer" did not condone New York's action: "In my opinion they acted imprudently, considering all circumstances, in not complying so far as would have given satisfaction as several colonies did."

However: "But my dislike of their conduct in that instance has not blinded me so much that I cannot plainly perceive that they have been punished in a manner pernicious to American freedom and justly alarming to all the colonies."

As the lawyer he was, Dickinson systematically laid out the case for New York and against the parliamentary action. He found it insidious that the government had determined New York had not simply defied the Crown but Parliament as well.

"This gives the suspension a consequence vastly more affecting. It is a parliamentary assertion of the *supreme authority* of the *British* legislature over these colonies in *the point of taxation*.

"It seems to me," Dickinson continued, "to be as much a violation of the liberties of the people of that province and consequently to all the colonies, as if Parliament had sent a number of regiments to be quartered upon them till they would comply."

Ringing the alarm bell, he continued:

"Whoever seriously considers the matter must perceive that a dreadful stroke is aimed at the liberty of these colonies. I say 'of these colonies' for the cause of one is the cause of all. If Parliament may lawfully deprive New York of any of her rights, it may deprive any or all the other colonies of their rights."

A little later in the article:

"He certainly is not a wise man who folds his arms and reposes himself at home, viewing, with unconcern, the flames that have invaded his neighbor's house, without using any endeavors to extinguish them."

He concluded this first article in a more moderate tone, confessing that he was by "no means fond of inflammatory measures; I detest them."

Dickinson's twelve essays were not confined to the New York issue but to the whole range of issues growing between the colonies and the mother country, particularly that of the right of taxation.

He found particularly vexing the law taking control over salaries of colonial officers from the colonial assemblies.

"No free people," he wrote in 'Letter IX' on January 28, "ever existed or can exist without keeping, to use a common expression, 'the purse strings,' in their own hands. Where this is the case, they have a constitutional check upon the administration, which may thereby be brought into order without violence; but where such a power is not lodged in the people oppression proceeds uncontrolled in its career, till the governed, transported into rage, seek redress in the midst of blood and confusion."

John Haslet read this passage to Jemima as they sat after their evening meal. He held the newspaper close to the candlelight in the fading daylight of winter.

"This 'farmer,'" Haslet said, his inflection reflecting his own doubt that the author was a yeoman, "has stated the case far more ably than anyone I've ever read. I don't see how anyone could refute his logic."

Haslet continued reading to himself, then once again to Jemima and Polly:

"He also says: 'Why should all the inhabitants of these colonies be, with the utmost indignity, treated as a herd of despicable, stupid wretches, so utterly void of common sense that they will not even make 'adequate provision' for the 'administration of justice and the support of civil government; among them, or for their own defense?' And he goes on: 'Is it possible to form an idea of slavery more complete, more miserable, more disgraceful, than that of a people where justice is administered, government exercised, and a standing army maintained at the expense of the people and yet without the least dependence upon them?'"

Haslet put down the newspaper.

"God has given this man the gift of insight."

Jemima could tell by the look in his eyes that her husband was profoundly affected by the "Farmer's" arguments. In fact, each of the articles appeared to have that effect and she sensed a distinct increase in the intensity of his feelings about English rule over the colonies. And she at last looked into the Irish psyche about the English government.

"What does it mean, father?" Polly asked, worry wrinkling her brow. She sensed from the ardor in her father's voice as he read the passages that there was something serious in motion, but she could not understand what. Still, her years in Ireland, listening to her uncle and his friends complaining about the government in London, made her apprehensive.

"It means times of trouble I fear, Polly," Haslet said. Hearing him address her as "Polly" made her realize how absorbed her father was in the situation. Normally, he would use more endearing names such as "darling" or "dear."

Haslet continued his explanation:

"The British government has voted duties on some of the more popular items we import—paint colors, paper, glass, tea—under the guise of regulating trade. However, these duties are plainly designed to produce revenue to support the government's troops in this country and whatever other things they need money for. We've objected to this idea in the past and I suspect we'll do so again. The merchants in Massachusetts Bay—that's a colony much north of here—have suggested a boycott on imports. The other colonies, however, while they may be in sympathy with Boston's motives, seem not inclined to take action. Whatever action the colonies take, it's likely that Boston will take the lead. Their passion for resistance to English rule exceeds that of any other colony."

Polly nodded in understanding. Although Jemima had seen to her education in domestic matters appropriate to the colonial woman, her father had undertaken the task of expanding her education and, naturally, his lessons were filled with political matters.

"Do you have any idea who the writer is?" Jemima asked.

"None. However, I'm going to Dover tomorrow. I'll drop in on Caesar Rodney and see if he knows."

Haslet's horse was saddled and ready for him when he finished breakfast the next morning. It was a bright January day, but there was a bite to the air. Haslet's cheeks were bright red by the time he arrived at Rodney's plantation, "Byfield."

One of Rodney's servants took his horse to the barn. From his appearance and accent Haslet suspected the man was an indentured servant from Ireland. Rodney did not own any slaves. In fact, he opposed slavery and had tried unsuccessfully to have the Delaware Assembly ban it.

Rodney welcomed him inside, allowing the visit was a pleasant surprise, and motioned to chairs for them to sit. He had been observing Haslet and his increasing presence in the county's life, wondering if this popular doctor was a potential rival or a potential ally, mindful that the county's most prominent physician, Charles Ridgley, was becoming a rival, this despite the fact Ridgely's father had become Rodney's guardian from age seventeen after Rodney's own father died.

He was tall, slender, of pale complexion, younger than Haslet although only by a matter of months. An otherwise pleasant face was marred by a lump that had developed in recent years on the upper left side of his nose at the eye socket. Haslet wondered if it was a cancer, a term used loosely in colonial times to describe swelling on the body.

Rodney dominated Kent County politics in a quiet, firm manner, holding several county offices—sometimes at the same time—and representing Kent County in the legislature since 1761.

After the usual cordial openings, they began discussing the most recent news from England.

"There are sentiments throughout the colonies for action against these latest developments," Rodney said, Haslet nodding his understanding.

"I can't help but believe we are on a course for another, more serious confrontation over these new duties. Now, some people argue the case that Parliament has every right to regulate our trade and I don't disagree. We've conceded that right for many years, in the interest of trade beneficial to all parts of the empire.

"However, these new duties are quite another matter. They clearly are designed to raise revenue and we have strongly objected to that. What is even more disturbing is that the revenue is going to be used to pay the governors and other royal officers. Thus, we lose whatever influence we have over these officers. I fear the American colonies will become one vast plantation with its people little more than slaves."

The concept of enslaving white Americans took on special meaning coming from Caesar Rodney, considering his ardent opposition to the practice of slavery.

"Further, they have set the customs officers in our midst. Now, that may seem like a positive thing, that we no longer have to wait for rulings to come from England. However, it appears the stated purpose is to keep a closer watch on our commerce. Furthermore, these officers have been given the power to enter our homes or our businesses on any pretense.

"As for its action against New York colony, I find that truly disturbing."

"What do you think is going to happen?" Haslet asked.

"The leaders in Boston are suggesting a boycott of all British trade. So far, however, the idea has not received any significant support from any of the other colonies, despite the feeling something needs to be done.

"I don't doubt New Castle County would support a strong response. Sussex County may vote otherwise. Kent County could be decisive if it comes before the assembly."

"Another idea Boston has put forth," Haslet offered, "is for the colonies to develop their own manufacturing so they may be immunized from British whimsy. We have relied on the British for items we think they produce better than anyone else, but that keeps us too dependent."

Rodney noticed with approval that Haslet obviously followed the news as closely as he did, an effect Haslet had intended. Haslet was of a mind to become more involved in the political life of the county and Rodney was the entry to realizing this ambition.

"I think it's inevitable that we will move away from that dependency," Haslet said. "We're a growing country with ample resources to become self-sufficient. It only takes our determination and hard work."

"And we need to develop the skills," Rodney commented. "Saying we can do something doesn't make it happen."

"We will develop the skills," Haslet answered. "Skilled artisans arrive on every ship from England. They already are employing their skills for the benefit of their families and friends. It wouldn't take much to expand their efforts to service their community, their colony and—who knows?—perhaps other colonies."

"The British merchants certainly wouldn't appreciate that," Rodney said, smiling at the thought.

"I suppose you've been reading the 'Letters from a Pennsylvania Farmer' in the newspaper," Haslet said. "I thought the author has made an excellent summation of the positions we need to take to protect our liberties."

"Very well written, very well argued pieces," Rodney said. "They sound like John Dickinson."

"Dickinson?"

"Quite possibly," Rodney answered. "I have had conversations with Dickinson and the feelings of the 'Pennsylvania Farmer' match his own feelings quite closely."

"I understand there's been favorable reaction all the way to Boston and down to the Carolinas," Haslet said.

"Yes," Rodney agreed, "the man has caught a mood. Perhaps better than he expected."

"Do you know what Pennsylvania is going to do?"

"Pennsylvania is more concerned right now with relations on the frontier with the Indians," Rodney answered. "A few weeks ago a man named Frederick Stump murdered four Indian men and two women at his home in Penn Township, Cumberland County. The very next day he and his servant, a man named John Ironcutter, killed another Indian woman and three children in their cabin. The governor offered a £200 reward for Stump's capture.

"Oddly, the legislators have found in this atrocity a reason for attacking the governor. They say he hasn't showed sufficient sympathy to Indian grievances. It is particularly galling to the legislators that the men involved in that 1763 massacre—the Paxton Boys as they were called—have gone unpunished these years since. And settlers continue to encroach on Indian land in the west and up north in the Wyoming Valley despite the constant proclamations that they are acting illegally.

"What that means is that the influential people in Philadelphia have been preoccupied with those matters rather than considering any issues concerning the colonies. The Boston merchants insist Philadelphia—and New York—must go along if any nonimportation is to be effective. So far, they have not."

"And what about our assembly?" Haslet asked, "will it consider a response to London? A boycott for instance?"

"Possibly. It will have to be carefully nurtured. In the meantime, our first business will be action on the agreement over our boundary with Maryland. We'll have to amend the laws where necessary to reflect the new boundary. That will require study and time.

"I suppose some landowners will be upset at finding they're living in Delaware instead of Maryland. They'll grumble about the paperwork. But that's only minor when you think this should bring an end to the violence that attended the land disputes between us in years past."

"And how did it become so contentious?" Haslet asked.

"In the beginning, Maryland laid claim to the entire peninsula between the two bays. However, the Duke of York claimed what we know as the three lower counties and ceded them to William Penn.

Maryland objected, arguing that the land was theirs by royal grant. Pennsylvania responded that the grant only referred to unsettled territory between the bays and the three lower counties already had been settled. You know how fiercely men can fight over land, even when it's so abundant."

"And how have they settled the boundaries?" Haslet asked.

"It was a very simple solution," Rodney said with a wry smile. "The governments hired those fellows Mason and Dixon—Charles Mason and Jeremiah Dixon—to make a survey. They established a line halfway between Cape Henlopen and Chesapeake Bay as the boundary between our colonies. Next they drew a circle with a twelve-mile radius around New Castle to establish a boundary between Pennsylvania and the lower counties. Then they drew a line northward from the Cape Henlopen–Chesapeake Bay line and where it intersected with the circle—that was the boundary between the three colonies. And from there they surveyed a line due west to mark the boundary between Maryland and Pennsylvania. The lower counties—Sussex County most notably—will profit greatly.

"Remarkably simple. Still, it was not easily accepted. The proprietors had many conversations and, I believe, the Crown finally had to intervene and tell them, in effect, to settle on the plan now agreed to."

Rodney added as an afterthought:

"I sometimes wonder why the Crown doesn't step in and settle the dispute between his government and his colonies just as simply."

"We might not like a solution the king imposes," Haslet responded, memories of the Irish experience suddenly filling his mind. "We can't assume he'd take our side."

That was a startling comment. The colonists all along had clung to the hope Parliament had been acting without royal endorsement, that a benign king eventually would order the members of Parliament to show more sympathy to colonial sensitivities. It was not until they accepted his complicity with Parliament that separation from Great Britain was seriously considered. And that was still some years away. Meanwhile, the colonies' attachment to England would be tested again and again, particularly in Massachusetts Bay.

Chapter Eleven

Massachusetts Stirs the Pot

John Haslet expected all along that the response to the latest English actions would be led by the men of Massachusetts Bay colony. Men like Caesar Rodney and Thomas McKean, he knew, held strong feelings about the rights of British-Americans. But it was men like James Otis and John Hancock and Samuel Adams of Massachusetts Bay who gave fire and passion to such feelings.

The events of 1768 proved him right, although the year started out quietly enough.

The leaders in Boston had been proposing united but peaceful resistance to the trade duties that became effective the previous November, 1767. Their proposals were received with sympathy but little action among the other colonies of British North America.

Then, in February 1768, the Massachusetts Assembly drafted a resolution of colonial rights to circulate among all the colonies, again in hopes of uniting colonial opposition. In marked contrast to the fury that followed passage of the Stamp Act three years earlier, this reflected a rather calm, dispassionate response.

The period of calm in Massachusetts Bay ended in early June 1768.

At the time, British impressment gangs had been active, stirring the resentment of the men who worked along Boston's waterfront.

Toward evening on Sunday, the fifth of June—during a period when the British had been particularly active—a press gang from HMS *Romney* boarded a ship just arriving from Glasgow and informed a number of the crew they were now sailors of the British Royal Navy. But this time the seamen managed to board a boat, row ashore, and escape into the night. The sailors went after them but people at the wharf, out originally to enjoy the cool of the night, turned into an intimidating crowd and prevented them from landing.

Thus waterfront nerves were edgy when Joseph Harrison, chief customs collector in Boston, and Benjamin Hallowell, customs controller, marched on to John Hancock's wharf on Friday, the tenth, and announced they were seizing his ship, the *Liberty,* at its berth.

The British customs service had long suspected that Hancock was one of the more active shippers involved in the smuggling that was endemic in New England (and many other seacoasts).

"This ship is now the property of His Majesty, King George III," Harrison announced.

"Why?" objected one of Hancock's men. "By what perverted reasoning are you seizing this ship?"

"You have been loading oil on board her without obtaining a permit from the customs office," Harrison responded.

"But we are not shipping the oil," the man protested. "We only put it on board for storage because there is no room ashore in Mr. Hancock's store."

"It doesn't matter," Harrison persisted. "Besides, we've had a report that she illegally imported Madeira wine on her last voyage."

"Nonsense!" the clerk shouted. But Harrison motioned to Hallowell, who moved to the rail on the harbor side of the ship and waved towards the *Romney,* anchored a short distance away. Armed sailors immediately embarked in the *Romney's* boats and rowed to the *Liberty.*

Hancock's clerk had followed the customs officers to the rail.

"You can investigate this ship's voyages and cargoes without taking possession of her," he protested. "Mr. Hancock will make the papers available. Why take this ship?"

Several well-dressed men along the shore supported the clerk's protest.

"Certainly, sir," one of them said, "there's no need to do this. This is outrageous!"

A crowd along the wharf grew larger, adding more voices to the chorus of protest.

"Your arguments are unavailing," Harrison declared. "We have our orders. The law has been violated here. We intend to put a stop to smuggling of cargo. We are taking the ship. That will be a lesson to all of you." He swept his arm in the direction of the people on the wharf.

The sailors boarded. The ship's lines were cast free and the *Liberty* was towed alongside the *Romney* and moored there under the shield of the man-of-war's guns.

The customs officers, meanwhile, had left the ship and stood along the wharf while the crowd continued to grow. Men of the waterfront and ordinary workmen had joined the merchants gathered there.

There were angry remarks from the crowd. They closed in on the officials. Someone in the crowd threw a rock; another flailed at Harrison with a club. There was shoving and Hallowell and Harrison's son, who had gone along to bask in his father's power, were knocked down. A couple members of the mob dragged the frightened boy by his hair. The unlucky customs officials and young Harrison broke free, turned and ran, stones showering around them.

The fleeing men and the boy ran up the street to Hallowell's house, hurried inside, and barred the doors. The crowd, still growing, followed. Stones shattered windows.

The noise of breaking glass had a momentarily sobering effect on the crowd; some of the more reasonable among them attempted to dampen the passions.

"Gentlemen, gentlemen!" one yelled. "Enough now. You've made your point. Further injury to person or property would be excessive. Disperse now. Let's dispense with further action until we can get a town meeting."

The respite was brief, for the crowd had become a mob.

"The collector has a boat," someone shouted. "Let's seize it."

The mob, emotions once more stirred, rushed back towards the harbor. By chance the port inspector was headed for his home when the oncoming crowd surrounded him.

"Here! Here!" a person shouted. "Here's the port inspector. Let's show him how we feel!"

With that they set upon the poor man, seized his sword, and snapped it in two, then tore his clothes and sent him fleeing to the safety of his house.

The mob then continued to the harbor where Harrison's pleasure boat was quickly located.

"We'll claim this in payment for the *Liberty!*" someone yelled.

In quick time they hauled the boat onto the wharf and now began tugging it and carrying it to the common.

A torch was lit and applied to the collector's boat. It soon became a bonfire surrounded by a cheering crowd.

"This for liberty and for the *Liberty!*" one man cried out.

As the flames died, the crowd now turned its attention to the nearby homes of Harrison and the inspector general of customs, John Williams. There was another barrage of stones and sounds of shattering glass until Mrs. Williams appeared.

"Please! Please stop!" she pleaded. "We haven't done anything to you. Leave us alone." She was almost hysterical. The stone throwers hesitated, then stopped.

By now it was close to nine o'clock and the night's frenzy had exhausted the crowd. Their passion dissipated, the people dispersed. The pile of smoldering ashes and shards of glass were the only remnants of the night's rioting.

In the aftermath, the customs officials, staffs, and their families—sixty-seven people in all—moved to the warship for protection. They would live in crowded conditions for several weeks. It was an experience many British officials and loyal citizens were to share in the years ahead.

Meanwhile, Hancock, Otis, Samuel Adams, and the other leaders called for a town meeting on the following Tuesday, partly to plan a response to the seizure of the ship, partly to channel the emotions of the townspeople towards a constructive course of action.

The Tuesday meeting group drew up a petition to the governor, Sir Francis Bernard, objecting to the seizure of Hancock's ship and the presence of impressment gangs.

Sir Francis was not renowned for tact or for sensitivity in his relations with the colonials. Rather, his usual attitude was barely disguised contempt. Nevertheless, he received a delegation from the town meeting cordially and promised to do what he could to stop the impressment gangs. But Bernard, a prototypical bureaucrat, also advised them that the *Romney,* a vessel of His Majesty's navy, was outside his jurisdiction. However, he sent a member of his council to meet with the *Romney's* captain and obtain a promise from him to end the impressment of colonists for service in the Royal Navy.

Quiet returned, deceptively, to the town of Boston.

John Haslet learned of the developments a few weeks later when he stopped off to pick up his mail and weekly newspaper in Cullen Town, a small cluster of buildings in the Sawmill Range area of Three Runs.

"The newspaper reports some interesting events in Boston, doctor," William Cullen commented.

Interest showed on Haslet's face as Cullen handed over his packet of papers. There was his usual Philadelphia newspaper along with a letter from his brother James in Ireland and a letter for his daughter Polly from a young man in Philadelphia. He put the letters aside and opened the newspaper to find the Boston dispatch on the front page.

"Those folks up there do seem to have trouble getting along with the British," Cullen chuckled.

"Yes, you're right, William," Haslet responded as he read the dispatch a second time, shaking his head as he imagined the Boston scene.

"What do you think will happen now?" Cullen asked. He was thinking about the rioting that had occurred in Boston after the stamp tax.

"It's curious the customs people picked out John Hancock's ship," Haslet said. "Hancock is one of the most prominent men in that colony and he's been very critical of the British government over the years. It almost seems the officials wanted to make a special point in seizing his ship."

"And what do you think the point is?" Cullen asked.

"Perhaps they wanted to establish that they mean business in enforcing the new trade duties and that they intend to put an end to smuggling. This story quotes the officials as saying they believed Hancock might have smuggled some wine past the customs people.

"People haven't raised much protest over the trade regulations over the years. They weren't a problem because the people simply ignored them."

Both men laughed at the thought.

"Things may be changing," Haslet continued, thinking more aloud than speaking to Cullen. "If that's the case, our period of tranquil relations with the government may be ending." He took his leave and rode off.

Jemima was preparing the evening meal when he arrived. Polly was sitting with little Joseph in a corner, near a window, reading to him. In the prevalent theme of children's literature of the times, the book told Joseph the rewards of being an obedient and faithful child. For Joseph, the joy was the sound of his sister's voice, since he was much too young to appreciate the words. For Polly it was purely an exercise of her reading skills.

She was proud of the fact she could read, an accomplishment not generally achieved by girls in those days.

Her father had started teaching her to read before he left Ireland and she had continued to learn with her Uncle Samuel.

Jemima had been humming along, improvising to the cadence of the text.

Haslet told Jemima about the Boston incident, adding his observation that it may signal a beginning of more significant protests in the colonies over the Townshend duties.

"But Boston seems so far away to have any effect on us," she responded.

"It would seem so," Haslet said, "but protests in one colony seem to spread like a wildfire to other colonies. The good Lord can attest that Boston is as prone to political wildfires as any colony in North America. We must wait to see how London reacts."

"What do you think the government will do?" Jemima asked.

"It's really difficult to say. Dispatches from London say there's growing impatience among the ministry with protests in the colonies. They say the ministry is determined to settle once and for all its authority over us and is prepared to adopt the harshest of measures to do so. You know how they responded to New York. If it's the government's determination to enforce the trade regulations, to put an end to smuggling and to assure that revenue is collected, then it will react very strongly, I fear, to this latest incident in Boston.

"The crowd up there chased the enforcement officers out of town. Their governor isn't going to give in as easily."

Jemima went on with her kitchen chores while she pondered her husband's conclusions.

John turned his attention to his letter from James.

"James says there's been great joy throughout the country. King George finally agreed that the terms of the Irish Parliament in Dublin should be fixed. Our people wanted seven years and he agreed to eight," he said. "James says they rang bells in Dublin, lit bonfires. James adds that many a glass was raised in Ulster as well."

Polly, meanwhile, had turned her attention to the letter from Philadelphia, smiling at the memories the letter raised. She had met the young man some months ago when her father took her with him to Philadelphia.

Haslet was considering sending his daughter to Mary McAllister's boarding school there for the winter months, figuring she needed to expand the education he and Jemima had provided at home. The ad had promised:

"I intend teaching the following branches of literature, viz., the English and French languages, with their proper accent and emphasis; needlework in silks, worsted, and linens; and as a farther accomplishment to the ladies, at particular seasons, shall instruct them in the arts of painting on glass, japanning with prints, wax and shell work, in the newest and most elegant taste . . . I likewise intend, on a certain day in every week, to instruct the ladies in pastry with some other beneficial and amusing articles too tedious to mention . . . For those ladies who incline to be taught writing, arithmetic, music, or dancing, proper masters may be provided, to attend on those days which, in the order of their different exercises, are appointed for them. I shall conclude with this remark, that although the care and education of children is a weighty charge, and the talk more or less laborious and painful, according to the age, capacity, and disposition of children, I say, notwithstanding these difficulties, conscious of the honesty of my intention and relying on the assistance of heaven, with cheerfulness and alacrity I venture on (until now) the untrodden path and pave the way for some person, more capable than myself, to undertake and fully complete the business. It is also necessary to inform you that I intend to take day scholars, at a very reasonable rate, and you may be satisfied I shall not fail to do them all the justice that lies in my power."

He had taken Polly with him to Philadelphia to investigate the school and Polly, a gregarious teenager, had established some friendships in the few days she was there while her father checked out Mrs. McAllister's reputation and tended to his other business.

"Pleasant news?" Jemima asked Polly and smiled. Polly, now fifteen, had confided to her that she had met a nice young man while in Philadelphia and was quite taken with him.

"Very pleasant," Polly agreed.

Jemima turned to John.

"How is the work going on the plantation?" she asked. Her husband and a few of the slaves had been clearing the two tracts he had purchased along the Mispillion, when the needs of the present plantation and his medical work permitted. She knew he was frustrated at the delay in preparing their new home.

"It goes well enough," he replied, unconvincingly. "We've got enough cleared now to think about planting next spring. And we'll get more cleared this summer and fall. Neighbors have given us some help.

I'm also hoping we can get to work on the house. You and I should sit down and discuss the plans more thoroughly."

"Well, I'd want a kitchen comparable to this one, of course," she said. Jemima was quite fond of her kitchen which she had been modeling to her tastes and convenience for these past several years. "We'll want a room for you to do your work and your reading apart from the rest of us. And, of course, bedrooms for all the children."

She slowed as she mentioned the word "children." A glow spread over her face. Now is the time to tell him, she decided. Haslet saw the look, guessed its import.

"It appears we are going to have an addition," she said.

"An addition," he teased. "To this house? Why would we want to make an addition to this house when we're planning to build a new one?"

"I mean I'm going to have a baby," she declared, laughing.

"When?" he asked, pulling her on to his lap and nibbling her ear.

"I would guess about December," she said, shuddering at the pleasant sensation the nibbling caused. "It's been a couple months now since the signs began."

"Well, Polly, did you hear that?" Haslet addressed his daughter.

"Yes, father," she said, smiling. Polly had guessed at the news herself several days earlier and had been considering asking her stepmother about it. "That's wonderful. I'm hoping for a baby sister."

Polly paused, thought about her remark.

"Of course, another baby brother would be fine, too."

The three of them laughed and little Joseph simply smiled because he was happy that the people in his world were happy.

Their mood pushed thoughts of the developing political maelstrom out of their minds. In a day when news of the world took weeks, even months to travel, one's attention did not focus long on the political world. Those events seemed far, far away from Three Runs.

The events, however, continued their momentum, and in that world outside Three Runs, the colonies one by one endorsed Boston's position.

London tried to stifle the movement, telling the colonial governors they should dissolve their assemblies if they tried to vote support for Massachusetts Bay. Many governors did so. However, the opposition grew louder, more strident.

Irish-born Americans like John Haslet had a sixth sense about the inevitable result.

Chapter Twelve

Protest Without Violence

The eighteen men who comprised the legislature of the lower counties on the Delaware—the colony would not officially be Delaware the state until 1776—gathered in New Castle on October 24, 1768, in a mood of apprehension and anticipation.

The annual elections on October 1 had returned most of last year's members. Notable newcomers were Thomas McKean and George Read from New Castle County.

Members milled around the aisles of the statehouse on this fourth Monday in October waiting for the session to begin, exchanging news and political gossip, renewing friendships.

Most gathered around Caesar Rodney, showing the deference that people normally accord a respected leader. This was his first public appearance since surgery in June to remove that ominous lump on the upper part of his nose near his left eye. During the last session, the growth of the lump had alarmed friends and family. A lengthy scar down the nose was an ugly reminder of the painful excision.

"Who was your doctor?" asked one.

"Thomas Bond of Philadelphia. Everyone was urging me to go to England for the surgery. In fact, they said I should leave immediately. Even the governor said he thought I would get better care in London than here. I considered it, but I didn't welcome the thought of a long voyage and an even longer absence from home. Besides, I felt confident about Dr. Bond."

"He did well," commented Charles Ridgely, another member from Kent County and a prominent doctor.

"It's not something I'd care to repeat," Rodney said.

111

The well-wishers nodded in a mix of sympathy, agreement, and the relief people feel at escaping an unpleasant experience. Surgery was even more dreaded in those days of primitive techniques and the absence of anesthesia.

They were interrupted now as the members were called to order and proceeded to the business of the opening session. They began with their oaths of office, ironically swearing their allegiance to government and king. John Vining was reelected speaker, committees were organized.

A committee was appointed, as was customary, to attend Lieutenant Governor John Penn, who was staying at Mrs. Anna Clay's, down the street from the statehouse.

There was a recess to allow time for the committee to go to Mrs. Clay's to advise him they had convened and were ready to receive his message of greeting. At 1 P.M., Vining called the assembly back into session.

There were rumors that Penn would have some sort of message from London; hints were that it would be a warning not only to them but to every colonial legislature. The members gathered in New Castle were anxious to find out if the rumors were true.

As soon as the members settled in their seats and silence settled over the chamber, Vining turned to Chief Clerk David Thompson:

"We have a message from Governor Penn, which I will ask the clerk to read."

Thompson fixed the paper at his comfortable reading distance.

"Gentlemen of the lower counties on the Delaware," the message began. "I am pleased to be in New Castle to attend to whatever business you may place before me and I promise to give every proposal my full consideration. We have had a warm and fruitful relationship during my years as your chief executive and I'm sure that relationship will continue."

Penn, a grandson of William Penn, enjoyed his semiannual trips to New Castle, an escape from the fractious Pennsylvania Assembly.

Thompson, reading ahead of himself, paused to be sure he understood the next part of the text. He slowed a bit and read carefully:

"There is one important instruction I must put before you at the request of Lord Hillsborough, the honorable secretary of state for the American department in the service of his excellency, King George III.

"Lord Hillsborough notes there has been a letter circulating among the colonies from the colony of Massachusetts Bay alleging improper actions of His Royal Majesty's government. The members of that colony's legislative body have asked other colonies to join in this malevolent and libelous epistle. Lord Hillsborough instructs this letter to be ignored by His Majesty's loyal assemblies in America. Any that do not and attempt to endorse the seditious designs of Massachusetts Bay are to be dissolved by the governor."

Thompson looked up from the paper.

"It is signed by John Penn, lieutenant governor of the province of Pennsylvania and of the lower counties on the Delaware."

The lieutenant governor was the nominal governor of the colony, since the real governor—or governors, in this case—were Penn's father and uncle in England.

"The message from the honorable governor is noted on the record," Vining commented dryly. It was sobering to the members to hear the rumors confirmed.

They now turned to the business that all knew would define their work this fall: a message to King George III explaining the position of the lower counties on the exercises of British authority that had the American colonies in turmoil.

Vining appointed McKean, Read, and Rodney to a committee to draft the response. It was a wise choice, for these three men would emerge as the voices of the lower counties in the troubled years ahead, representing them a half-dozen years later when leaders from all thirteen colonies gathered in Philadelphia to consider united action.

The session adjourned for the day.

For the next couple of days the members bided time on routine business, but the problems in the relationships between the colonies and the mother country filled their conversations in the idle moments of the session and at the inns and taverns.

Finally, on Thursday, the twenty-seventh, they took up consideration of the message drafted by McKean, Read, and Rodney, directed to the king, explaining their position on the matters at controversy between the colonies and the mother country.

Light conversation and bantering masked the tension created by the excitement and uneasiness among them as they waited for the session to begin.

"I understand Pennsylvania has hired Henry Fisher to mark the Delaware River channel," commented a member from Sussex County.

"No one knows the river better than Henry," David Hall, another Sussex County member, said. "He's the best river pilot in Lewes."

The men who guided the inbound sailing ships from around the world made Lewes, the southernmost port on the river, their base.

"Can he be trusted to mark the channel so the British men-of-war don't go aground?" asked member Thomas Robinson. They all laughed uneasily, not sure whether Robinson, who tempered his opposition to Parliament's taxes with an unwavering loyalty to the Crown, was serious.

"Certainly," Hall answered. "Henry may have strong feelings about the government in London, but he loves the river and wouldn't tolerate anything happening that might reflect unfavorably on the river's reputation."

Another cluster of members was discussing the punishment of a thief in Wilmington.

"What had he done?" someone asked.

"Stolen from one of the shops," it was explained. "There was a rather large crowd at the 'Cage' [the Wilmington prison] to see the poor wretch. I'll tell you, the markets did a lively business in eggs. The crowd, even the women and children, demonstrated an uncanny accuracy when the constable gave the culprit the order to march forward and the drums began beating. Eggs pelted him from every direction. He was crying for mercy by the time he got free of the crowd and went on his way."

Listeners smiled at the images.

Speaker Vining ended the small talk with the sharp rap of his gavel to bring the session to order.

"Pursuant to the instructions of this House, the committee appointed to prepare a message for his Royal Majesty has presented its draft for the House's consideration, " Vining announced. "The clerk will read the message."

"It is addressed to 'The Most Gracious Sovereign,'" Thompson began.

"We, your Majesty's dutiful and loyal subjects, the representatives of the freemen of the government of the counties of New Castle, Kent, and Sussex upon Delaware, in general assembly met, most humbly beg leave to approach the throne and in our own, and the names of our constituents, to testify and declare our unfeigned and inviolable attachment, by principle and affection, to your royal person and government, and that we glory in being your subjects. We acknowledge, with the utmost sincerity of heart, the tender and indulgent regard you have shown to all your people from the beginning of your reign and that earnest desire to make them easy, safe and happy, under your government, however remote from your royal presence."

No need to offend King George, members agreed silently. The whole point was to win his support.

The message paid perfunctory respect to Parliament.

"We are perfectly satisfied that we lie under all possible obligations to our parent country," Thompson read. "We acknowledge all due subordination to the British Parliament."

"Do you suppose that will win us any friends in Parliament?" a member whispered to a colleague. The colleague shrugged. "I doubt it."

The ritual salutations out of the way, Thompson got down to the point of the assembly message, a list of grievances including suspension of the New York Legislature and the taxes in the form of trade duties.

The message continued:

"If our fellow subjects of Great Britain, who derive no authority from us, who cannot, in our humble opinion, represent us, and to whom we will not yield in loyalty and affection to your Majesty, can, at their will and pleasure, of right give and grant away our property, if they can enforce an implicit obedience to every order or act of theirs for that purpose and deprive all or any of the assemblies on this continent of the power of legislation for differing with them in opinion in matters which intimately affect these rights, interests, and everything that is dear and valuable to Englishmen; we cannot imagine a case more miserable; we cannot think that we shall have even the shadow of liberty left."

Vining allowed the members to test reaction in conversation among themselves before banging his gavel to silence the cacophony of voices filling the chamber.

"Do any members wish to offer amendments or to comment on this message?"

Superficially, there was unanimity among them that the actions of Parliament were offensive. But look in their hearts and you found stark differences in the proper remedies.

Robinson of Sussex County, for instance, opposed the revenue measures passed by Parliament but not Parliament itself and he flushed with anger when he heard disparaging remarks about England and, especially,

115

of King George III. (Eventually he would become the colony's most prominent loyalist and would have to flee for his life.)

On the other hand, people like McKean believed just as passionately in outright opposition to what they considered Parliament's meddling in local matters.

The differences over remedies eventually produced two distinct factions—identified as Whigs or Patriots on one side and Tories or Loyalists on the other—and reasoned argument would give way to violent confrontation. But that ordeal was still in the future. For now, civility marked relationships and persuasion still was the preferred approach to the government in London.

In fact, a person could travel from colony to colony and find similar words being debated in the assemblies.

"Does this message defy Lord Hillsborough's instructions?" McKean was asked. It was assumed this young man was the one who provided the words to express the committee's recommendation (much like Thomas Jefferson in the Declaration of Independence).

"It doesn't mention Massachusetts Bay," McKean answered, "even if our sentiments are common to them. This, however, is to be our independent statement on matters of great concern to us as British subjects and as citizens of one of his Majesty's royal provinces in North America. It is a response to the actions of the government, not a response to the suggestions of our good friends in Massachusetts Bay."

"Certainly something needs to be said," Rodney commented.

He waited to see if anyone else had an opinion, then offered:

"I would move its adoption."

The motion was quickly seconded.

"Any further discussion?" Vining asked. "Hearing none, the chair calls for a voice vote on adoption of this message to His Royal Highness. All those in favor, say 'aye.'"

There was a chorus of "ayes."

"Opposed, 'nay.'"

Silence.

"The message is unanimously adopted. It will lie on the table for the members to sign and I direct the clerk to engross it and see to its proper dispatch."

The business done, the motion was made and seconded to adjourn for the day.

"The House is now adjourned until tomorrow morning at eight o'clock," Vining said, giving his gavel an emphatic thwack on the rostrum.

The members drifted slowly out of the statehouse. They would gather later in various groups in the local taverns to dine and talk about affairs until the late hours.

John Haslet learned about the action a few days later when he stopped at Cullen's for his mail and weekly newspaper. A strong statement, he thought, but how would the king receive it? He had grown up not expecting much sympathy from a British monarch.

These days Haslet spent a large part of his time developing his new plantation along the Mispillion, tending to his rounds as a doctor and caring for his growing family. A second son, John, had been born at the end of 1768, Joseph was now growing past the toddler stage, and Polly had turned into a sixteen-year-old beauty attracting attention from young men of the neighborhood.

But he kept up with the news and the malaise in the political life of North America.

Boston continued protesting, even after Governor Bernard dissolved their assembly. The members met informally when he ignored their pleas to call them back into session. New Hampshire's governor also dissolved his legislature. Jersey Governor William Franklin, Benjamin's illegitimate son, did likewise to his assembly.

Virginia's Burgesses added their voices to the rising clamor in America and it was added to the ranks of the prorogued.

When Maryland's Governor Sharpe told his legislature that the king didn't want them to join the protest movement, they ignored him, telling him it was none of his business.

Pennsylvania's assembly drafted a protest for the government, but Penn did not terminate the session. Throughout the period of growing disaffection with London, Penn seemed to harbor a secret sympathy for his citizens.

The call from Boston merchants for a boycott of British imports picked up the necessary support of merchants in New York and Philadelphia. Their joint support was the sine qua non for a nonimportation agreement in the North American colonies.

The Delaware Assembly rejected the boycott. We don't have enough trade to make a difference was the argument, but merchants in Philadelphia suggested snidely that the merchants in Wilmington and New Castle hoped to benefit from Philadelphia's participation in the boycott movement. The two towns in the lower counties weren't exactly backwater ports and, in fact, were more convenient to many traders in the back country of Pennsylvania.

Massachusetts also was urging the colonies to develop their own manufacturing so they could drop dependence on England for clothing, hardware, and other manufactured items. There were frequent articles in the newspapers about achieving that aim, the "how-to" articles of their day.

Nevertheless, peace seemed to settle over the colonies as 1768 came to an end and held through most of 1769. The grumbling continued, but there was at least relative quiet.

In fact, the major violence among the settlers in America during this period was not created by relations between England and the colonies but over rival claims for the Wyoming Valley of Pennsylvania. Connecticut claimed that northeastern corner of Pennsylvania and settlers from that colony moved in despite protests from Pennsylvania and from the Indians who claimed title to the land. This set off clashes that would recur sporadically over the next several years.

That's not to say there were no confrontations between the colonials and British authority in 1769. In light of past events, "peaceful" can be a relative description.

It is true that soldiers in Boston adopted the annoying habit of stopping citizens on the street for questioning. It is also true there were scuffles. But a superficial civility was preserved.

South Carolina joined the list of colonies dissolved by their governors over support for the colonial protest movement. Virginia's House of Burgesses had been allowed to reconvene but, proving unrepentant, was again dissolved.

Delaware finally joined the nonimporation agreement in August of 1769.

It was peaceful enough, though, that a Boston tavern brawl in September received wide attention. Of course it wasn't an ordinary barroom fight. It involved James Otis, the most articulate of Massachusetts protest leaders, and Customs Commissioner John Robinson.

Oddly, it was precipitated over the matter of loyalty to the Crown, with Otis objecting to statements by Robinson that Otis was disloyal. It was the third time in a few days the two men had confronted each other over this charge and this contact ended with the fiery little colonial leader thoroughly beaten by Robinson and his friends. Otis had the bad judgment to choose a tavern frequented by British officers and sympathizers for his confrontation.

It was a portent of a far more serious confrontation to come in early 1770.

Chapter Thirteen

Massacre in Boston

The most important decade in American history was barely a week old when the relative peacefulness of the past eighteen months began to deteriorate.

In New York, Irish-born merchant Alexander McDougal, thirty-eight years old, father of three, was arrested on January 8, 1770, for distributing around town three weeks earlier a handbill criticizing the idea of supporting British troops. His article was described as "false, seditious libel."

McDougal raised the issue of the freedom of the press, thus becoming one of the earliest journalists to make that defense. He refused bail and demanded a trial. "The cause for which I suffer is capable of converting chains into laurels and transforming a jail into a paradise," he wrote from jail.

His name was linked with that of the English dissident John Wilkes as examples of heroic resistance to authoritarian rule. In McDougal's case, oddly, the plaintiff was the New York Legislature, that very same legislature that had been disciplined by the government in England for insufficient support of the British troops. Its membership had changed, however, since that 1767 incident, and it had become more pliant.

A few days later, British troops attempted to destroy New York's liberty pole, a symbol of colonial resistance to the tyranny of the British Parliament, but were thwarted by a group of citizens, one of whom was slightly wounded by a bayonet before the soldiers withdrew, breaking nearby windows as a parting salute. The soldiers returned four days later and this time were successful in taking down the liberty pole.

A crowd of 3,000 citizens met the next day and declared these incidents showed the troops were not in New York to protect the citizens but to harass them. Meanwhile, citizens in the Jersey counties of Essex and Monmouth rioted over legal fees.

The broad implication of these incidents was the slow unraveling of the restraint that had marked the period since the June 1768 riots in Boston.

They were only a prelude to the event on the evening of March 5 that became known as the Boston Massacre.

Relations between citizens and soldiers in that town had been peaceful enough, even earning praise from local leaders, since the troops arrived in the fall of '68. The chance meetings between citizens and soldiers in that period were often contentious, but fell far short of mayhem. However, the patience on both sides was slowly evaporating in the long, cold, dark days of a second winter of what the locals considered an occupying army. It was equally difficult for soldiers to feel kindly towards people that were plainly hostile. Resentments grew. The confrontations increased in number and violence escalated in the late winter months.

The events leading to the bloody encounter of March 5 began the previous week with fistfights between the locals and the soldiers. There was one fight, then a couple more, then several more. After one such encounter, a soldier returned with several mates armed with bludgeons, swords, and cutlasses, attacking a group braiding rope. A crowd drove them away but they soon returned, augmented by another thirty or forty soldiers. Still the crowd repulsed the soldiers. These skirmishes continued through Saturday evening, March 3, before the peace of the Sabbath restored calm.

The evening of March 5 was a clear winter evening. Many people, including soldiers, were about town. Glistening snow gave an almost festive sparkle to the landscape.

The attention of the townspeople was drawn to several soldiers of the Twenty-ninth Regiment who were parading by the Merchants Exchange, their cutlasses drawn, bayonets fixed to their muskets. These they used to prod citizens out of their path.

A few minutes after nine o'clock, four young men—Edward Archbald, William Merchant, Francis Archbald, and John Leech Jr.— came down Cornhill Street together, making loud and insulting remarks in the manner of hormone-fueled youth. They separated and Edward

Archbald and Merchant continued toward an alley leading to Murray's Sugar House, which was being used as a barracks. Edward glanced down the alley, noticed a soldier playfully striking a large broadsword against the wall, sending sparks flying. There was another soldier with him, a mean looking man, holding a large cudgel.

It had become sport for young Bostonians to taunt the soldiers, even throw stones at them, knowing the soldiers were under strict orders not to fire at civilians unless ordered to do so by an officer. Archbald and Merchant were in a mood for such sport. The soldiers were young men like themselves.

"You take care of the one with the sword," Edward Archbald told Merchant, "I'll get the other one."

"Do you fancy you are slaying dragons or attacking poor, defenseless people?" Edward mocked the soldier, who had not noticed the boys approaching.

Before the sword-wielding soldier could respond, Archbald and Merchant lunged at the young soldiers. The one with the sword turned and struck Archbald on the arm with his sword, then thrust it at Merchant. The sword passed harmlessly through the young man's coat, between his arm and his side.

Merchant swung a stick at the soldier, stunning him. His companion turned and ran to the barracks to summon help. He returned with two more soldiers, one carrying a pair of tongs, the other a shovel.

The one with the tongs chased Archbald through the alley, grabbed him, and struck him over the head.

By now the commotion was attracting other townspeople. John Hicks, another Boston youth, came to Archbald's aid, knocking the soldier down. The soldier got up and, seeing the gathering crowd, ran for the barracks.

The crowd, mostly young people, growing boisterous and taunting, surrounded the building.

Suddenly a dozen soldiers came out, cutlasses drawn, bayonets fixed. Some wielded clubs. It was an unequal match for the unarmed townspeople, who quickly dispersed.

Thirty or forty persons, mostly young men, had meanwhile gathered in King Street, near the customs commissioner's house, where they confronted a sentry, assigned to watch over the customs collections inside the house.

A detachment led by Captain Thomas Preston arrived, their orders to protect the treasury. They began pushing at the crowd with their fixed bayonets. The flickering lights of torches, the bells near and far tolling in the night, the curses shouted across the increasingly narrowing space between the two sides gave a surrealistic touch to the square.

"Make way! Make way!" the soldiers demanded, pushing onward and setting up in a half circle in front of the customs house.

"You are ordered to disperse," Preston commanded. "This is royal property and we are prepared to defend it."

The townspeople, some nursing slight cuts from the bayonets, began yelling at the detachment. Indignation, wounded pride magnified the slight injuries the soldiers had inflicted. Then the people started throwing snowballs at the soldiers.

"Come on you rascals, you bloody backs, you lobster scoundrels; fire if you dare," came from the crowd.

"God damn you, fire and be dammed," shouted someone else. "We know you dare not!"

Testimony later disagreed on the instructions Preston gave his men.

Some citizens insisted they heard him yell to his men: "Damn you, fire, be the consequence what it will!" At his trial and in a written report to London, Preston insisted he told his men: "Don't fire!"

The truth didn't matter, for one soldier did fire. A townsman struck him over the hands with a cudgel, forcing him to drop his firelock. Then the man rushed at Preston, swinging his cudgel at the officer's head. The blow grazed his hat, but landed heavily on Preston's arm.

Then a volley from the soldiers thundered in the night. There was shocked silence before the crowd reacted. Some witnesses claimed people inside the customs house also fired at them from the windows.

Samuel Gray fell dead on the spot, a ball striking him in the head and tearing away a large portion of his skull.

Two shots struck Crispus Attucks in the chest, killing him instantly. Attucks was a Negro from New Providence who was in town to take a ship for North Carolina.

James Caldwell, a sailor from Captain Morton's vessel, was killed by two shots entering his back.

Seventeen-year-old Samuel Maverick was shot in the belly, the ball lodging in his back. He died the next morning.

A ball entered Patrick Carr's body near the hip and went out at his side. Carr, thirty, died nine days later.

Two other seventeen-year-olds, Christopher Monk and John Clark, also fell wounded. Monk was shot in the back, Clark just above the groin.

Merchant Edward Payne was standing in his doorway when a shot shattered bones in his arm. Tailor John Green was just coming up Leverett's Lane when he was shot near his hip. A sailor, Robert Patterson, was shot in the right arm. Young David Parker was shot in the thigh.

As the dead and dying lay in the square, people tried to move in to help them. The soldiers pushed them away at bayonet point.

At this point, an undertaker, Benjamin Leigh, took Preston aside.

"Captain, I suggest you withdraw with your men before the square is awash with more blood. There's been enough mischief this night. Use your command to prevent any more."

Preston looked squarely at Leigh, perceived the wisdom of the man's advice and ordered his men to withdraw. The soldiers retreated slowly towards their barracks, bayonets pointing at the crowd moving toward them. Preston stationed them at the ends of streets to prevent the crowd from moving in on them. He then sent word to the barracks to rouse the rest of the soldiers.

The ringing of bells still filled the night. The sound of drumbeats pounded through the darkness. More and more people were rushing to the scene. There was nothing left for them to do, however, but to care for the casualties. As the townspeople gathered in the square, the soldiers of the Twenty-ninth Regiment were turned out and formed ranks on Kings Street. The crowd stood sullenly staring at the soldiers under arms. There were threats from the crowd but no one undertook to rush the troops.

Now Lieutenant Governor Thomas Hutchinson arrived on the scene and passions began to abate. It had not been easy for Hutchinson to reach the scene. He had been accosted and threatened by angry citizens on the way. He was acting governor now, Sir Francis Bernard having gone to London to explain his contentious relations with the General Court of Massachusetts Bay.

Hutchinson immediately assembled his council members and several civil magistrates in the council chamber. Dozens of citizens also crowded around outside, demanding heatedly that action be taken. Hutchinson appeared on the balcony to address them.

"Please, gentlemen," he said. "Let things quiet down for the night. There's been enough blood shed. I promise you I will do everything in my power to see that justice is done. Let the law prevail and run its course."

Several community leaders endorsed the lieutenant governor's plea.

"Citizens," Samuel Adams implored. "Let's all go home now. Let's not add to the carnage of this awful evening's work. Morning and daylight will be the proper time to pursue redress."

"We won't go until the soldiers leave the square," shouted a member of the crowd.

"That's a reasonable request," Hutchinson said. Lieutenant Colonel Maurice Carr, commander of the Twenty-ninth Regiment, was by his side and nodded agreement.

The citizens then began straggling out of the council chamber. The soldiers marched smartly back to their barracks.

It was 1 A.M. The whole incident had lasted four hours.

At three o'clock, Preston was taken into custody by civil authorities. Two hours later the soldiers identified as responsible also were arrested.

At dawn, evidence of the night's bloody rioting stained the square. Many people came to see the scene, to imagine the events of the night before as the story passed among them. What now? they wondered.

At Cullen's store in Kent County some days later, John Haslet shook his head in disbelief, settling into a chair as he read the story.

"A tragic evening, I say," Cullen remarked. "So many dead. So many wounded. What can all this lead to?"

"If this were the end of it," Haslet finally responded, "I could anticipate the outcome. However, I'm afraid it is only a beginning and no one can foresee where all this will lead us. Blood has been shed and people will feel that blood must be avenged. The people in Massachusetts have such fire; I'm sure they will not defer to the ordinary course of justice. I worry what this will mean to the rest of us. While we may not approve of violent means, we all are united in the effort to protect our liberties from the incursions of Parliament. We rest our hope on the king, on the triumph of reason. Reason, however, doesn't seem to prevail in the current mood of the people, particularly in Boston."

He paused.

"Or in London, for that matter."

Haslet left the store, mounted his horse, and rode slowly home, pondering the events he had just read in the newspaper.

There was a startled look on Jemima's face when he told her about Boston. She kept shaking her head as he read the story to her. Her emotions found their release in a vigorous cleaning of kitchen pots and pans.

"It's just terrible, John," she commented when he finished. "Those poor people. However much they may have antagonized the soldiers, they were unarmed and there was no excuse for the soldiers to fire into the crowd."

"Unfortunately," he said, "most of the soldiers probably are young, Polly's age or even younger. Reason hasn't yet had time to temper blood."

"Well, we can only wait to see what happens next," she said and he agreed.

"I'll be going up to Dover tomorrow and perhaps I'll learn more then," he added.

The next day he stopped in at the courthouse and went to the register of wills office to see Caesar Rodney. Rodney at that time also was serving as recorder of deeds, clerk of the orphans court and justice of the supreme court as well as a member of the legislature.

"I suppose you've read about Boston," Haslet commented.

"Yes. Lamentable," Rodney responded. "Given the temper of the people in Massachusetts, I suppose we shouldn't be surprised blood has been shed. It just shocks me that there was so much of it."

"It's hard to imagine the horror of that evening," Haslet said. "War is one thing. You expect that sort of carnage. But on a city street. Unarmed citizens slaughtered!"

He shook his head, still struggling to comprehend the enormity of the Boston incident. But it was clear feelings of anger and disgust were stirring inside him.

Rodney stood up and looked out a window, composing his thoughts.

How thin he looks in the light by the window, Haslet thought. Perhaps his cancer was more serious than reported, even though almost a year had passed since his surgery.

Rodney turned back to Haslet.

"John, I'd like you to stand for the assembly this October."

"I'm flattered, sir," Haslet responded and he showed his surprise. "You know I've always been ready to serve the public in any capacity the people think I'm fit for."

"There'll be some changes in the county's delegation this year," Rodney said. "Killen will run again and so will John Vining, although I worry about his health. Of course, I intend to run, too. Ridgely will be returning; as you know he didn't serve in the last session. I've discussed it with some of my associates and we all agreed that you and Vincent Loockerman would make a very attractive ticket to present to the voters."

He looked at Haslet to gauge his reaction. He sensed the man wanted to do it.

"Think it over," he said. "It's only April. It's a long time yet to the election. Talk it over with Mrs. Haslet and your family. By the way, how's the baby?"

"John? He's just fine. Seems a happy but quiet little boy. Little Joseph is becoming a test of Jemima's energy. Polly has become quite a young woman and is catching the eyes of the neighborhood boys."

Rodney, a bachelor, smiled. He only had one real love in his life and that was Mary Vining. But she married the Reverend Charles Inglis, rector of Rodney's church in Dover and active in the effort to revive the Anglican church in the lower counties. She died in 1765, soon after the marriage, and Inglis subsequently transferred to the Anglican church in New York. (Later, when Rodney became chief executive of Delaware, Mary Vining Inglis' niece, also named Mary Vining, served as his hostess at official functions.)

"How are things with you?" Rodney asked.

"Very well. I'm gradually clearing the plantation on the Mispillion and hope soon to begin building a home there. My practice also keeps me busy. And I've taken on some charity work for the county. I suppose you had a part in that?"

"Yes, I did," Rodney responded. "There were some people Charles couldn't provide for and I recommended you to fill in for him. He'll of course continue his work with the poor for the county."

Charles Ridgely normally provided care for the poor of Kent County, a service for which the county paid him between £50 and £70 a year.

"I understand," Haslet said. "I was delighted to help relieve his burden."

Their business was done. Haslet took his leave and began the ride back home, thinking about the news he needed to discuss with Jemima.

Ironically, on the very same day of the Boston Massacre, Parliament took the preliminary step to repeal the Townshend Duties. There was little recourse. Income had dropped precariously for British merchants because of the boycott. They sent an urgent petition to Parliament urging repeal.

At first the House of Commons considered repealing all the duties, but a majority of members felt there was a need to assert some authority to tax the colonies and the repeal fell, 204–142. It was then decided to continue the duty on tea while removing the duties on china, glass, and painter's colors. There was no need to count the votes; a loud chorus of "ayes" responded to the speaker's call for a voice vote.

It was a routine matter to complete the revision of the trade duties a little over a month later. Parliament then waited expectantly for expressions of joy from the colonies. Instead they heard catcalls—and worse.

For Haslet, however, the promising news was overwhelmed by family tragedy.

He was reading by the fireplace in the late afternoon in May when he heard a rider dismount outside and hand over his mount to one of the servants. The man entered. It was his brother William. Haslet's joy was arrested at the look on William's face.

They embraced and Haslet held the man at arm's length, stared into his face.

"What's wrong, William?" he said. "Your face tells me that something unpleasant has brought you to my home."

"That's true, John," William said, shedding his coat. "I have truly tragic news about our family. It's Joseph. He's dead!"

William's voice choked, tears filled his eyes. Haslet shook his head in disbelief, tears also appearing in his eyes.

"What happened?" he finally asked.

"He came down with a severe fever several days ago," William said. "He sent one of his servants down to my inn and asked me to come see him. I found him in his bed, his bedclothes soaked with his sweat. He was very pale and coughing constantly. His wife was applying cold cloths to his forehead. There was talk of bleeding him to see if the illness could be drained from his body, but he died before anything could be done."

Joseph had immigrated in late 1763, settling in Queen Anne County, Maryland. Like his older brother, he went to the University of Glasgow, graduating in 1762, and, like John, took up the practice of medicine in America. William, who had emigrated with John, also had settled in Maryland, in Greensboro, Caroline County, where he took over his father-in-law's inn.

Jemima had been some distance away from the house when she saw William arrive. The scene in the kitchen dismayed her. The two men sat at the kitchen table, heads in their hands, doing their best to control their emotions.

"John, what's wrong?" she said, throwing her arms around him.

"My brother Joseph has died," he finally managed to respond. "William was with him and has just brought the news."

"How dreadful!" she said sympathetically. "William, I'm so sorry for you, too. Joseph was such a wonderful man. It's a great loss to this family.

"How about his wife and children?" Jemima asked.

"Her family is taking care of them," William responded. "They'll be all right, I think, but I'm going back to their plantation to check on arrangements for guardianship. Joseph made many friends with his practice as a doctor. He took after you, John. He had great respect and admiration for his oldest brother."

"I appreciate that," Haslet said quietly. "I'll go back to Fishingham with you."

Fishingham was the property Joseph Haslet had purchased the previous year.

"We'll leave in the morning," Haslet added. William nodded.

The family spent the rest of the evening in sad reflections on Joseph Haslet, the men recounting memories of their childhood in Ulster, Jemima adding her own impressions of Joseph from their visits to his plantation and his visits to Three Runs.

In the morning, John and William Haslet rode off together to see to the affairs of their late brother.

Chapter Fourteen

A Public Career Begins

It was October 22, 1770, and John Haslet was beginning a new phase of his life, as a public figure, a member of the assembly for the lower counties on the Delaware.

He already had been a very visible figure, of course, as he moved about his rounds as a physician in the Three Runs area over the past ten years. He also was a voice in church and community affairs. But being a public figure is markedly different from being a visible figure. People's perceptions of public figures are different and less forgiving, for one thing. And there is a much higher demand for accountability.

He would appreciate these differences more and more in the years ahead. For now he mingled with the other members and family and friends at the statehouse in New Castle waiting for the ceremonies to begin. Jemima was there to share in the moment as were Polly and the other children.

Jemima was absorbed in the opening day scene, casually observing the fashion of both men and women. Many garments, she decided, were obviously imported from the better tailors in London for they seemed finer than anyone's Sunday best.

Thomas McKean, as fashionable as any, approached and was introduced to his family by Haslet. A fine looking man, Jemima decided, with a graceful manner, but she also noticed an intensity in his eyes that she suspected betrayed the strong-willed person inside.

Begging Jemima's indulgence, he pulled John Haslet aside. Other members noticed and wondered. Haslet was considered one of Caesar Rodney's men, although, as events would prove, of an independent mind. McKean was a political leader in his own right, an active and effective legislator. He obviously would seek to influence newcomers.

Haslet hadn't seen much of McKean since they were introduced to each other by their mutual friend, Dr. Francis Alison, in Philadelphia in 1767.

Obviously McKean had singled him out for a reason but Haslet would have to await the man's pleasure as McKean began with small talk.

"Did you read about the death of George Whitefield?" McKean asked.

"Yes," Haslet responded. The famed preacher, considered the inspiration for the 1740s revival movement known as the "Great Awakening," had died in Boston on September 30.

"I talked to Dr. Alison about it when I heard the news," McKean said. McKean had been a student under Alison at the school the Presbyterian minister founded in New London, Pennsylvania.

"How did he react?" Haslet asked.

"With some sadness," McKean said. "The revival movement, as you know, led to a dreadful schism in the church and put Dr. Alison on the opposite side of some of Whitefield's disciples. You remember he discussed this at that dinner in Philadelphia when I first met you. Anyhow, it had caused him a great deal of pain. Still, he respected the man's dedication to God and his powerful oratorical skills."

"Had he lost any of that?" Haslet asked. "I read that he was stricken in England some time ago and there were fears for his life. Even when he recovered, there was doubt he would ever be able to preach again."

"He was in Philadelphia in May and delivered a couple of sermons," McKean said. "I attended his sermon at the new Presbyterian church. I thought he retained his command of the language but that the force of his delivery was less than I remembered."

"I'm sorry I never had the opportunity," Haslet commented.

"Here's an interesting bit of history about Philadelphia," McKean continued. "When I was there last month there was a story in the newspaper about a ninety-two-year-old woman named Rebecca Coleman who died. She had been living there since 1683 and was one of the city's first settlers. She remembered there were only three houses in town when she arrived. Everybody else lived in caves!"

"It's difficult to imagine that when you see the city that Philadelphia has become," Haslet said.

"Well, I'm told there were caves along the riverfront and they provided reasonably comfortable living space for the settlers until they could build houses.

"Of course, our counties had been settled well before then." McKean continued. "Wouldn't you think that given our head start, we would have progressed further than Pennsylvania? I suppose the answer is in the leadership. Theirs obviously has been stronger than ours. And I suppose the uncertainty over ownership because of that dispute with Maryland held us back."

"I'm sure," Haslet said, "that William Penn's decision to establish his own plantation near Philadelphia had much to do with it, also."

"True," McKean conceded, "but remember he reserved large tracts in the lower counties for his own use. Much of that land in Sussex County on the other side of the Mispillion from your land had originally been deeded to William Penn."

McKean obviously was leading the conversation in a certain direction. He paused, then confided to Haslet:

"On the subject of Sussex County, John, there's going to be a challenge to seating the county's delegation."

Sussex County, Haslet recalled, seemed to have more fractious politics than any of the other counties in the colony.

"I'm going to support the challenge and hope you might find the cause worthy to join me and the others."

"I'd like to know more details," Haslet answered, his interest picking up now that McKean was finally getting to the point.

"The issue will be raised by John Clowes," McKean explained. "He has, as you may know, been in a long-running feud with the Court Party in Sussex County. The Court Party has tried to prevent the Country Party from winning any seats and has come very near to succeeding. If it weren't for Clowes, they would have succeeded entirely. Clowes tells me the Court Party has stolen this election, that there were more votes cast than eligible freeholders. He'll challenge them when we convene here shortly."

"I'll keep an open mind," Haslet responded.

"That's all I can ask," McKean said, "and hope when you hear the arguments you will find it in your conscience to join us."

Haslet had met Clowes only a few times and knew him more by reputation than from personal acquaintance. The man lived several miles down the Kings Highway from Three Runs. He and his father had developed a successful milling and merchant business at their plantation twelve miles north of Lewes, the Sussex County seat. Haslet recalled that Clowes was known to have a very volatile personality, and a willingness to go to the newspapers in Philadelphia—the only available—with his complaints. On the other hand, he also had demonstrated a willingness to go to the newspapers with an apology when proven wrong.

Haslet had casually followed Clowes' fight with Sussex County Sheriff Boaz Manlove since 1767 when a grand jury headed by Clowes issued a subpoena for Manlove to testify on a complaint he had defrauded a man out of some property.

Manlove had ignored the subpoena until threatened with contempt.

After hearing the sheriff's testimony, the grand jury returned an indictment accusing him of false swearing. The county court threw it out, however, and Clowes' response was to publicly ridicule the court. The court's answer was to cite the grand jurors for contempt and to fine them. When Clowes and eleven others refused to pay the fine, they were jailed.

The case was appealed to the state supreme sourt and heard in a crowded courthouse at Lewes in May 1770. Caesar Rodney, Richard McWilliams, and David Hall Sr. were the justices.

McKean agreed to represent Clowes when local attorneys declined because of their fear of displeasing the court. Despite an eloquent plea from McKean which was applauded by the partisan audience, the court ruled 2–1 to uphold the lower court, with Rodney and McWilliams in the majority. Hall, whose son was a clerk in McKean's law office, issued a stirring dissent that drew cheers from the crowd.

Clowes' supporters hailed him as the "John Wilkes of Sussex County," a reference to the British political leader whose constant opposition to Parliament and Crown going back to 1763 were regularly reported in colonial newspapers and made him as much a hero in the colonies as he was to the many Englishmen who shared his disdain for the British government.

"Do you have any idea how Rodney feels about the issue?" McKean asked.

"None at all," Haslet responded. In fact he himself wondered how Rodney would respond to the challenge to seating the Sussex legislators, in light of his ruling against Clowes as a member of the state supreme court. "He has said nothing to me about it."

McKean reflected silently on Haslet's remark, then excused himself and went off to talk to other members.

The session began, the members were duly sworn, and John Vining was returned to the speaker's chair. Then a committee was sent to Mrs. Ann Clay's home, Lieutenant Governor Penn's residence when he visited New Castle, to receive his message to the assembly.

When the committee returned and the organization of the House was completed, the members waited for the rumored challenge to the Sussex delegation to begin.

The wait was short. Clowes rose from his seat immediately after the clerk finished reading Penn's message.

"Mr. Speaker, members of this honorable body, I present for your consideration petitions from my fellow freeholders in Sussex County complaining of the recent election in our county. They declare there were far more votes counted for certain members of this delegation than there were qualified freeholders. They pray the House to declare the election null and void and to set a date for a new election."

Three of the four members of the Sussex County court that had ruled against Clowes and sent him to jail were members of the Sussex County delegation to the assembly: Levin Crapper, Thomas Robinson, and Benjamin Burton. Crapper and Sheriff Manlove were the leaders of the dominant Court Party in the county.

Crapper stood up.

"Mr. Speaker, members of the House. This petition is absurd on its face. The count reflects the honest opinion of the freeholders of Sussex County as to the men best qualified to serve them in this honorable assembly."

He paused for effect: "With one possible exception."

A smirk was the only indication of Clowes' reaction.

"I would call to the House's attention," Crapper continued, "that the present members from my county have been, with one exception, chosen year after year by the freeholders in my county to serve them in this assembly. They have never been challenged until now. This consistency in their election, I would suggest, indicates the fairness and honesty of the latest election."

It was true that Crapper, Robinson, Burton, and Jacob Kollock had all served in previous legislatures. Clowes was first elected in 1769 but his father had served several terms before his death in 1767. The newcomer in the Sussex delegation this year was Burton Waples, elected in place of David Hall, another member of the Country Party and the minority vote on the state supreme court when Clowes' case was heard back in May. Hall had been elected five times before his 1770 defeat.

Clowes rose again.

"Mr. Speaker, the gentleman is correct that the members he has referred to have been sent to serve in this body several times. Perhaps they began to feel proprietary towards their assembly seats because I maintain that when they perceived their seats were in jeopardy this year, that the citizens of Sussex County had determined they had not served the county's interests effectively, they resorted to fraudulent tactics in order to hold on to their seats."

There were shouts of derision from the Sussex County members as Clowes reached his final point.

"I maintain that an honest vote count would have produced a quite different result," Clowes said, raising his voice to be heard over the clamor in the chamber.

Vining gaveled for order as Clowes sat down.

Haslet was mesmerized by the emotional display.

McKean rose from his seat:

"Mr. Speaker, I move that this House immediately take up consideration of Mr. Clowes' petitions."

Crapper objected.

"Mr. Speaker, there will be time enough for the House to give this matter full consideration without giving it special consideration on this opening day."

"I would differ with the gentlemen from Sussex," McKean countered. "I say it is imperative we resolve this matter immediately. Otherwise, any business of this session might be tainted by any votes the challenged members might cast. Mr. Speaker, I move the previous question."

Under parliamentary rules, moving the previous question ended debate.

"Very well, gentlemen," Vining intoned. "The House will now consider whether to take up the challenge to the seating of the Sussex County delegation as a matter of special business. The clerk will call the roll."

The motion picked up three votes in Kent County, with William Killen and Vincent Loockerman joining Haslet. Surprisingly, Waples voted with Clowes from the Sussex delegates. However, McKean was the only New Castle County member to support it. Seven members in all voted against the motion. Speaker Vining did not vote.

"On the motion by Mr. McKean to take up the challenges to the Sussex County delegation, the vote is six in the affirmative and seven in the negative and the motion is carried in the negative.

"That concludes the business for this session. I direct the chief clerk to notify the absent members to attend tomorrow's session forthwith."

Charles Ridgely of Kent, Jacob Kollock of Sussex, and Benjamin Noxon and Evans Rice of New Castle had missed the opening session.

"What are your plans?" Haslet asked McKean as they left the statehouse.

"I'm not concerned that we didn't prevail today," McKean said, "in fact I suspected we wouldn't. George Read was working against me and he has a great deal of influence. I was pleased Waples voted with us. I was disappointed, if not surprised, that Rodney voted against it. However, we mustn't read too much into today's votes. It was after all, only a procedural issue and some people might have voted against us simply on the principle that consideration on opening day was out of order. We'll push the matter tomorrow and should prevail, at least so far as having the challenge heard. Do you have any idea how Rodney might vote on the challenge itself?"

Haslet shook his head.

"Well, we'll know soon enough," McKean said. "Excuse me now, I'm going off to have dinner with Clowes and discuss our plans for tomorrow."

Haslet and his family had a pleasant dinner with the Killen family. It had been a wonderful day for both families and all so new to Jemima and dazzling to Polly. The wives and children left together the next day for home.

The assembly did accept Clowes' challenge and over the next several days the House heard testimony from the Sussex County members, from Sheriff Manlove and from freeholders on both sides of the issue. Voter lists were presented and examined.

On Friday, November 2, the challenge was brought to a vote. The members of the Sussex County delegation were excluded.

There were two votes: the first on whether to recount the votes, the second on whether to declare the election untrue.

"The clerk will call the roll," Vining ordered on the issue of recounting the votes and Chief Clerk David Thompson went down the list, first New Castle County:

"Mr. (William) Armstrong?"

"Nay."

"Mr. (John) Evans?"

"Nay."

"Mr. McKean?"

"Aye."

"Mr. (Benjamin) Noxon?"

"Nay."

"Mr. Read?"

"Nay."

"Mr. (Evans) Rice?"

"Nay."

The issue is lost, Haslet thought, without the New Castle delegation. Then, Kent County:

"Mr. Haslet?"

"Aye."

"Mr. Killen?"

"Aye."

"Mr. Loockerman?"

"Aye."

"Mr. (Charles) Ridgely?"

"Nay."

"Mr. Rodney?"

"Nay."

Vining, as speaker, did not vote.

"On the motion to ascertain and determine the number of votes cast out at the late election in the County of Sussex," Vining said, "the 'ayes' are four and the 'nays' seven. The motion is carried in the negative."

McKean moved to declare the return untrue, but the outcome was the same.

The session adjourned. Clowes stopped to talk to McKean and Haslet; Killen joined them.

"I thought the evidence that was presented strongly suggested fraud," Haslet assured Clowes and McKean.

"Well, perhaps it wasn't as conclusive as we hoped," Killen added. "There would have to be stronger evidence for the members to upset an entire county's election. It's a very serious step."

"Yes, you're right," Haslet agreed. "Nevertheless, you and I were convinced as was Vincent."

"Too bad Rodney didn't agree with you," Clowes commented. "Others might have gone along if he had supported us and we would have carried the motion."

"He never tried to influence our votes," Haslet responded. "And, I suppose, the matter wasn't important enough for him to try to influence its outcome. I must say he has kept his counsel to himself on this issue."

"Commendable," Clowes said dryly. Haslet ignored what he interpreted as a rebuke.

"Well, how do you feel about your first experience as a legislator?" McKean asked Haslet.

"It's been an interesting experience," Haslet said. "It's quite different from anything I know of the government back home. There is much of the form, but little of the posturing of the parliaments in London and Dublin. More businesslike."

"It has taken a while," Killen said, smiling, "but I believe our Dr. Haslet is becoming Americanized."

The remark drew laughs and the men gathered their papers and departed the chamber.

The session adjourned the next day and Haslet headed back to the quiet of the plantation life in Three Runs.

The year that had begun so tumultuously ended quietly throughout the colonies.

The consequences of the March 5, 1770, Boston Massacre were concluded in the fall with the acquittal of Captain Thomas Preston and six of the eight members of his squad. Two of the soldiers were convicted of manslaughter, branded on one hand, and set free. They were represented by John Adams.

Four civilians accused of firing into the crowd from the customs house were tried for murder and also acquitted.

The colonies' protests over the failure of Parliament to include tea when they repealed the Townshend duties diminished as the year drew to a close. They had decided to continue that item on the non-importation agreements. Some had wanted to continue the total boycott until the tea duty also was repealed and there was widespread denunciation of the merchants of Newport, Rhode Island, when it was discovered they had been violating the boycott. Even merchants in the Delaware ports of Wilmington, New Castle, and Lewes joined in the denunciation, but the resolve among the merchants of North America was weak and the idea of continuing the total boycott was abandoned by all by year's end.

The calm that now settled over British North America would continue almost uninterrupted to the end of 1773.

Chapter Fifteen

Tempest Over Tea

Perhaps it was England's preoccupation with the threat of war with Spain and France, or with unrest in Ireland.

For whatever reason, relations between British Americans and the government in England were less tempestuous from the end of 1770 until Christmas of 1773. In the interlude, the government—through new rules on the handling of tea—turned discontent into renewed defiance, once again demonstrating its incredible ability to miscalculate the feelings of its subjects across the ocean.

War drums had been beating in Great Britain towards the end of 1770 over the seizure of the Falkland Islands in the South Atlantic by Spain's Argentine colonists in June, 1770.

King George III told Parliament in November 1770 that he was negotiating with Spain but would continue war preparations. In fact, roving gangs were busy impressing hapless citizens for duty in the army and navy.

The war threat diminished in 1771 when Spain showed a willingness to negotiate a settlement and agreed to return Port Egmont in the Falklands and its fort to the British. However, the Spanish would not concede sovereignty over the islands and war drums started beating again. Spain finally agreed to pay £500,000 compensation and the furor died down.

John Haslet, meanwhile, was reelected each year to the legislature. He invested much of his effort into bills to transfer the capital from New Castle to Dover, arguing its central location made it more convenient. The majority remained unconvinced. It would take war and the exposure of New Castle, a port town, to the threat of British warships, to effect the transfer. His first legislative success was a bill to repair the causeway leading to Murderkill Creek, which crossed Kent County above the Mispillion River and below Dover.

At home, Jemima gave birth to a daughter in 1771. They named her Ann, after Haslet's mother. Polly was especially grateful to have a little sister no matter how great the difference in their ages.

News from Ireland told Haslet of violence in early 1772 over land rents between a disciplined group of dissidents called the "Hearts of Steel" and British troops. A newspaper report from London in March said the "Hearts of Steel" were "not a raw, undisciplined mob but rather a regular army, being composed chiefly of deserters from different regiments who have fled to the north of Ireland for refuge and are now got together with the country people, headed by discharged veterans, whose experience qualifies them as able commanders."

A letter from his brother James said the dissidents felt that "betwixt landlords and rectors, the very marrow is severed out of their bones, and their lives had even become so burdensome, by these uncharitable and unreasonable men, that they do not care whether they live or die." James reported some 500 British regulars killed, wounded, or captured in a battle at Crumlin, County Antrim, although other estimates gave the figure as fifty.

The letter also expressed disappointment over rejection of a proposal before Parliament to ease the restrictions against religious dissenters imposed during the reign of Elizabeth I. Although Commons approved it, opposition arose in the House of Lords and the proposal eventually failed.

Nothing changes for the better, Haslet mused, when the government values privilege more than people.

There was fighting in the colonies, but it had nothing to do with England. A war, or series of skirmishes, was fought in northeastern Pennsylvania's Wyoming Valley over land claimed by Connecticut settlers.

(That would continue sporadically through the Revolution and beyond until the Congress of the new United States ruled in 1782 the valley belonged to Pennsylvania. Even then fighting continued until Pennsylvania agreed in 1788 to honor the deeds of the settlers from Connecticut.)

The only significant instance of colonials testing British patience was in Rhode Island in mid-1772 when local militants boarded and destroyed HMS *Gaspee* in Narragansett Bay. The warship's mission was to stop smuggling and it was having great success until it ran aground on June 13. That night colonials surrounded the ship, forced their way aboard, wounded the captain and set fire to the *Gaspee,* which burned to the waterline.

Instances like these actually seemed to relieve tensions and periods of quietude followed.

Then the government came up with a plan to help the East India Company with its financial difficulties.

The East India Company was continually operating at a deficit. But its wealthy shareholders included members of Parliament and that body kept approving loans to bail the company out. The debts only accumulated. The company had 16 million pounds of tea in English warehouses, however, and the government decided this precious commodity—valued at £5 million—could help the East India Company out of its problems.

Frederick North, the second Earl of Guilford, had assumed control of the government in 1770 and in 1773 his administration fashioned a solution he believed would make everybody happy: it would eliminate the duty the company paid on the tea imported to England and allow it to ship the commodity on to America, where the company would keep the duty imposed by the Townshend Act of 1767. The government would determine which colonial merchants would be allowed to import the tea. King George signed off on the deal on May 10, 1773.

That applied a match to the tinder of colonial unrest.

The administration assumed this would solve the company's financial problems, appease the colonists by making the popular beverage cheaper, and still preserve the authority of Parliament to levy taxes on the colonies. As usual, it misunderstood colonial feelings, feelings that had been roiled by the colonists' lack of control over the royal governors and officers whose salaries now were being paid directly by the Crown.

The political atmosphere thus was changing when the members of the Delaware Assembly gathered in October for the start of the 1773–74 session.

Communications from other provinces, notably Virginia, quickly focused attention on the revival of troubled relations with the mother country. Virginia, the most populous colony, proposed a course of united action to protect colonial interests against Parliament.

The Virginia House of Burgesses had decided in March 1773 to create a committee of correspondence to sound out feelings in other colonies and to inform them of the sentiments of Virginia's patriot leadership. It then sent copies of this resolution to the other colonies in hopes they would follow Virginia's example.

The resolution was endorsed by Rhode Island on May 7 and by Massachusetts on May 28. It was placed before the Delaware Assembly on Friday, October 22, 1773.

By then, news of the arrangements for the East India Company's tea shipments had added passion to the simmering resentments in the colonies. The merchants were solidly on the side of the dissidents in view of the government's decision to hand out import licenses only to its friends, who could sell the tea cheaper legally than could those merchants who had escaped paying duties by relying on smugglers to supply the product. They were further concerned that the government might extend this licensing idea to other imports.

Caesar Rodney was in the chair as the newly-elected speaker and directed Chief Clerk David Thompson to read the Virginia Resolves to the Delaware legislators.

There were the usual salutations and then came the main point:

"Whereas the minds of His Majesty's faithful subjects in this colony have been much disturbed by various rumors and reports of proceedings tending to deprive them of their ancient, legal, and constitutional rights."

The members leaned forward in their chairs in anticipation.

"And whereas the affairs of this colony are frequently connected with those of Great Britain as well as of the neighboring colonies, which renders a communication of sentiments necessary; in order therefore, to remove the uneasiness and to quiet the minds of the people, as well as for the other good purposes above mentioned, be it resolved that a standing committee of correspondence be appointed, to with . . ."

The resolution went on to name eleven Virginians. Only a few were known to Haslet: "Peyton Randolph . . . (Haslet remembered he was the Virginia speaker) . . .

"Patrick Henry . . . (Virginia's John Clowes, Haslet thought.)

"Thomas Jefferson . . . (He has a reputation as a skilled writer, Haslet recalled, suspecting he had a hand in the Virginia resolves.)"

He noticed that George Washington, whom he remembered from the French and Indian War, was not on the list and wondered why.

The endorsements by Massachusetts and Rhode Island then were read into the record.

Haslet recognized the names of Samuel Adams, John Hancock, and Speaker Thomas Cushing on the Massachusetts committee.

That group should produce some provocative ideas, Haslet thought.

The Rhode Island members were unknown to him. But the whole idea of united action conformed with Haslet's own thinking about the best way to approach an intractable Parliament.

As required by their legislative procedures, the assemblymen put off consideration of the resolves for a second reading on Saturday morning.

McKean entertained Rodney, Haslet, and William Killen at dinner Friday night. It was a subdued gathering and not simply because of the implications of the Virginia resolution. Killen's wife Rebecca, only thirty-seven, had died September 23 and the black band on his waistcoat reminded everyone of that recent tragedy.

The Haslets had been deeply affected by the death since the two families had become so close. Her funeral, and Haslet's moving eulogy, were still fresh in memory.

"Rebecca Killen," Haslet had said, "was possessed of a mild and amiable disposition, which was early cultivated by a virtuous education. She appeared on the stage of life universally respected as she has now retired from it equally lamented. As a wife she excelled in all that is dutiful and affectionate; as a parent was tender and indulgent to an uncommon degree; as a mistress, governed by the laws of kindness and humanity; and as a neighbor was courteous and obliging to all. Nor was she inattentive to the important duties she owed to her God and savior; but manifested the sense she had of religion by assiduous endeavor; to promote it in her family, especially in the minds of her rising offspring, who have reason long to remember her affectionate counsels respecting their eternal interest as well as their discreet and virtuous behavior in the world."

"I was sorry to hear about Rebecca's death," McKean said as the group shared some wine before dinner.

"You've suffered your own loss this year," Killen responded. Mary McKean, twenty-nine, had died in Philadelphia on March 12, two weeks after the birth of their sixth child. Killen did not have the passing of time to lessen his pain; sharing the experience with McKean thus helped him.

"How are your children doing?" Killen added.

"Sadness remains," McKean said, "in the children as well as in myself. The children are resilient, of course, and go about their lives but you can tell they sorely miss their mother."

Killen nodded sadly. There were five children at the Killen plantation to mourn the loss of their mother.

The group sat quietly, each with his own thoughts and memories. Haslet thought about his own loss of his first wife many years ago and said a silent prayer of thanks that he still had Jemima.

After dinner, the men gathered again in McKean's parlor.

"How do you think the House will vote on the Virginia resolves tomorrow?" McKean said.

"I suspect we will endorse them without dissent," Rodney responded. "I'm going to propose that we appoint a five-member committee with representation, of course, from each county. Any suggestions for those five?"

"I think you two certainly should be members," Haslet offered, referring to Rodney and McKean. "I don't know about Sussex. The Court Party appears to have swept that election. It would appear to me that they might be too timid and it seems to me the time for timidity should be put behind us."

"You favor a forceful approach, I gather," McKean observed, roused by the intensity he sensed in Haslet's voice.

Haslet paused to collect his thoughts.

"If we stand together, each of the colonies," Haslet said firmly, "we would have a better chance and I believe this is the possibility created by the initiative from Virginia.

"I read with interest Massachusetts' arguments that it was never intended for Parliament to have any authority over the North American colonies. They noted that James I had asserted America was not part of the realm and, therefore, Parliament should not make laws for the colonies. They further noted that Charles II had asked—asked!— Virginia to act on a revenue proposal in 1679."

"Very good points," Killen commented.

"Yes," Haslet continued, "and they told Governor Hutchinson that to them it was obvious from these precedents that Parliament never had any authority to legislate for the colonies."

"Hutchinson obviously hasn't accepted that argument," Killen said.

"Let's get back to the membership of our committee of correspondence," Rodney said. "John suggested Thomas and me and that seems appropriate since the speakers are serving on the other colonial committees and Thomas is well-known in all the provinces. I think George Read and John McKinly also should serve and, I suppose Thomas Robinson could represent Sussex County as well as anyone. Read and McKinly are very prominent and influential people known in the other colonies as well as our own."

"That would be three members from New Castle County," Haslet noted, hiding his disappointment at not being chosen for a committee he assumed would be in the forefront of the lower counties' opposition to the British government.

"True," Rodney conceded, "but it has far more people than either of the other counties and it would make it easier for the committee to do business if a majority—a quorum—is close at hand. Business needn't be delayed by waiting for people in Kent and Sussex to arrive."

"That makes sense," Haslet conceded. "I would worry about Robinson, but he seems to be the most resolute of the Sussex County people. I know they share our dislike of the revenue measures but I doubt their dedication to any effective solutions. However, Robinson certainly has the force of his convictions and if he can be unanimous with the other members it will be a strong and effective committee."

"Thomas, I'd like you to draft the response of the lower counties," Rodney said. "John and William can stay to help you, if they wish, but I must attend to other matters before I retire for the night."

"We'll stay," Haslet and Killen agreed.

Rodney departed, leaving the other three to work on the resolution.

It was past twilight now and McKean had house servants bring more candles. He spread sheets of parchment on the table and began writing. McKean was a renowned lawyer in both Delaware and Pennsylvania, an early example of the professionals who would in later days be characterized with both admiration and disdain as "Philadelphia lawyers."

"We'll begin, of course, by acknowledging the initiative of the other colonies," McKean said. "Then we'll establish that a quorum can do the work of the committee."

There was silence as McKean put the words to paper. Then he continued:

"We'll state its purpose as 'to obtain the most early and authentic intelligence of all such acts and resolutions of the British Parliament, or proceedings of the administration as may refer to or affect the British colonies of America.'"

McKean was writing as he spoke. "I think it appropriate that we include all the colonies, not just ours."

Haslet and Killen agreed.

"Then we'll state," McKean went on, "that it will be the business of the committee 'to keep up and maintain a correspondence and communication with our sister colonies respecting those important considerations, and the result of such their proceedings, from time to time, to lay before the house.'"

McKean spoke in measured tones, adjusting the pace of his speech to the speed of his penmanship, which, Haslet observed, was quite fast indeed.

"I would suggest," Haslet said, "that we make the matter of the *Gaspee* the first business of this committee. Dispatches from London talk of bringing the perpetrators to England for trial. I don't need to tell either one of you how objectionable it would be to have a free man stand trial before any but his neighbors. To take him to another colony would be unacceptable. To grab him by the neck, put him in irons, and transport him to England to stand trial is an unimaginable blasphemy."

Anger colored Haslet's face.

"Well, it's been a year or more since the incident and they've not made any arrests," Killen observed, "but I agree with you John. At least investigating the incident will give us a chance to express our outrage at the possibility of trials being held in England for American colonists, for any reason."

"A good idea," McKean said, and resumed writing.

"We probably should also find out how the other colonies are dealing with the matter of salaries for the royal officers," Killen said. "I remember that last year Governor Tryon of New York rejected a salary from his assembly because, he said, the Crown already had provided. Massachusetts got a similar response from Governor Hutchinson."

"I read they refused money for repairs to Hutchinson's house," McKean added, smiling.

"Probably figured he should get that money, too, from the Crown," Haslet said.

"And they passed a resolution," McKean noted, "saying that any judge who accepts a salary from the Crown is an enemy of the constitution."

"There's certainly an incendiary spirit among the leaders in Boston," Haslet observed.

"I'll conclude by instructing the committee to communicate our response to the other colonies," McKean said. He wrote silently for a few more minutes, then straightened up and moved aside so his companions could review his work. They had been leaning over his shoulder as he wrote and quickly agreed with the results.

"Looks fine," Killen said.

"I think it is direct and complete," Haslet added.

The men chatted for a while, then Haslet and Killen departed for their quarters in New Castle.

"Mail from home tells of troubled times in our homeland," Haslet said to Killen as they walked through the dark streets to their inn. "My brother writes that the linen trade has collapsed and starvation is widespread."

"Yes," Killen said, "I've read that. It explains the increase in people arriving in New Castle from Ireland. There were some four or five hundred on the *Needham* when it docked there. Many of them debarked there instead of going on to Philadelphia."

But troubles imagined do not have the same control over the mind as troubles experienced. The increasing bitterness in the relations between London and the colonies was overshadowing concerns about their homeland and the news from Ireland was soon lost in reminiscences.

They arrived at the inn and went on to the room they shared.

Chapter Sixteen

The Teapot

The Delaware Assembly endorsed the Virginia resolution on Saturday, October 23, and Rodney then recognized McKean to present the suggested response. It was adopted on a voice vote, without dissent.

The apparent unanimity was not prologue, but epilogue. The ability of men to make common cause against perceived injustices by the English government was coming to an end. The question of loyalty to the concept of empire was not an issue. That loyalty would soon be challenged, however, and would divide citizens irreparably.

Right now, however, the pressing challenge was tea.

"I suppose we should first deal with the tea problem," Rodney commented to McKean at the end of the session. "There's agreement among the colonies to refuse to accept any tea and I'm told there's a ship, the *Polly,* on the way from England with a cargo of tea. My information was that it would leave in late September and, if so, it should be arriving the latter part of November. Its intended port is Philadelphia but the leaders there have met and decided they won't accept the cargo. It's possible the captain will attempt to unload her at New Castle or even Lewes if he learns of the Philadelphia merchants' opposition."

There was a real possibility the captain might hear of the Philadelphia opposition and divert the *Polly,* since it was not unusual for ships passing each other on the ocean to exchange the latest news from their most recent ports.

"We should notify Henry Fisher," Rodney added. Fisher was the principal river pilot at Lewes and an ardent patriot.

The *Polly* arrived in the river in late December and dropped anchor off Chester, Pennsylvania, just below Philadelphia, on Christmas Day. There had been premature reports of her arrival earlier so it was almost with relief that confirmation was delivered in Philadelphia to the special committee of community leaders organized in October to deal with the matter.

That committee already had persuaded the favored merchants in Philadelphia to resign their commissions as exclusive importers.

However, the *Polly*'s shipment was consigned to Gilbert Barclay. He had been in England arranging his deal and thus was unaware of the developments in Philadelphia when he arrived aboard the ship.

He had barely arrived at his store to make arrangements for unloading the cargo when he was confronted by committee members.

"Gilbert," said a member, "the people of Philadelphia have adopted a very firm determination not to admit any of the tea from the East India Company. Not, at least, until Parliament abandons its attempts to force us to accept their arbitrary decisions and despicable efforts to tax us without our consent. They've chosen tea as the means to enforce their will and we, therefore, have chosen tea as the means to express our refusal. We suggest you send it back."

"But, gentlemen," Barclay said. The determination in his visitors' faces made him nervous. These were friends and acquaintances and the change in their attitudes since he last saw them was striking. "I have a great deal of money invested in this cargo. It will ruin me not to unload it and recapture my investment. Please, I'll agree to sell it at cost if only you'll permit me to proceed with my plans. I promise to forego any profit."

"Nonsense," a committee member answered, "you can take your precious cargo to Barbados or some port in the West Indies or anywhere else in this hemisphere if you insist on selling it. I doubt you'll find another port in America willing to do so. We're not going to permit it to be unloaded here."

"I can't do that," Barclay said. "This is my home here and I have been too long away already. I can't wander the world looking for a place to deposit the tea."

"Well, we can always deposit it for you," a committee member commented, "as they did in Boston. In the river."

Barclay hadn't heard of the action by Boston patriots, the Boston Tea Party, on December 16. A member of the Philadelphia committee filled him in quickly.

"If you desire to stay," Barclay was told, "then you'd best resign your commission and send your cargo back to England. Let the government there dispose of it."

"Is that the only choice you give me?" he asked.

"There's always tar and feathers," came a response from someone sitting on the fringe of the meeting.

Barclay fell silent, shocked at the hostility from these men. He nervously fingered his waistcoat as he sat and desperately tried to think of a response.

Finally:

"Very well. I shall resign my commission and return the cargo."

"You're a very wise man and a patriot," a member commented.

As Barclay sat glumly silent, a committee member addressed the others:

"We need to talk to Captain Ayres. We'll send a delegation to Chester to see the captain and set up a meeting."

Three men were appointed to seek out the captain and the merchants rose and departed, leaving the dejected merchant Barclay to absorb this downturn of his fortunes.

Ayres, in the meantime, had moved up the river to anchor off Philadelphia. Word of the ship's movement and its cargo preceded him and a large crowd was gathered on the shore as the *Polly* appeared about two o'clock.

"Hello, the *Polly!*" someone shouted.

Ayres appeared at the rail. He was startled to see the crowds on shore.

"I'm Captain Ayres," he called to the crowd. By now he had been told by an agent that his cargo would be unwelcome and was understandably cautious.

"Come ashore, captain," was the response from the shore, "we need to talk about your cargo. We represent a committee of citizens appointed to deal with the matter of tea."

Ayres reluctantly accepted he had no choice but to meet them. He went to his cabin for his waistcoat and hat, then had a seaman row him ashore.

He eyed the crowd apprehensively as he stepped off the boat.

"Captain Ayres," said one of the crowd, identifying himself as a member of the special committee. "Let's proceed to the London Coffee House. The other members are waiting for us there."

Ayres moved uneasily as the crowd parted, leaving a lane for him and his escort to pass through.

In the upstairs meeting room of the Coffee House, Ayres sat down at a table lined by several citizens. Their dress assured him these were prosperous Philadelphians.

"Captain," someone said, "we understand you are cosigner to this cargo."

"That's correct. Mr. Barclay and I."

"Barclay has resigned his commission to sell the tea in America," he was informed. "You'll find no other in this town to take his place."

Ayres looked around the room.

"No one?"

"That's correct. We've had several meetings on this subject among the merchants of this province and all have agreed not to import any tea owned by the East India Company. We'll not see any colonial money going to those brigands."

"You should be aware," another member advised Ayres, "that this is the position up and down the colonies. In Boston, New York, Charleston—they've all refused to accept shipments of tea and ordered ships carrying such cargo to return."

"And they have complied?" Ayres asked.

"Well, except in Boston," he was told. "Governor Hutchinson intervened on behalf of the importers there. Of course, a member of his family was among those hoping to profit from the tea.

"The governor had ships of His Majesty's navy at his disposal and they were ordered to permit no vessels to leave Boston harbor until their tea had been unloaded."

"How was it resolved?" Ayres asked. "You said the governor and the Royal Navy would not permit the cargo vessels to depart with the tea."

"The tea floated out of the harbor on its own," laughed a committee member.

Ayres looked perplexed.

"It seems several men—some said they were Indians from one of the Massachusetts tribes—savage warriors—boarded the three ships carrying the tea and dumped the bales into the harbor. Of course, the bales first were slit open and they say the harbor became one giant tea cup. That was earlier this month."

"If the governor bothered to read the tea leaves he would have learned that they best leave the tea in India," mocked another member.

Ayres looked shocked.

"And the navy and the governor did nothing?"

"Nothing," was the response. "They were caught by surprise. Besides there were too many people for them to deal with."

Ayres looked around the room. The resolve on the faces of the committee was obvious.

"How does your governor feel about this?" Ayres asked.

"Governor Penn will not take a position. We've already talked to him."

John Penn had returned from England in August and resumed his post as chief executive of Pennsylvania.

"I see," he said. "Then I suppose there is nothing for me to do but seek another port for my cargo."

"Yes."

Ayres rose, made his farewells, and left the coffee house.

A handful of small boys waiting outside pelted him with snowballs but were chased away by the adults.

The next day there was a general meeting at the statehouse.

It was agreed that the *Polly* would sail downriver to Reedy Island, near New Castle, there take on supplies, then depart. A pilot would see the ship from Gloucester Point to Reedy Island. After that, Ayres was on his own but a four-member committee was appointed to see that he lived up to the agreement.

Ayres boarded the pilot boat at 2:30 P.M. the next day and began his return to England.

"That's done and settled," commented a member of the special committee. "We now must wait to see what happens next."

In an unusually swift voyage, the *Polly* arrived in England on January 24, 1774, with the news of Philadelphia's refusal to accept its tea cargo. However, the Boston Tea Party was far more offensive to King George and Parliament. Massachusetts Bay's persistent insubordination had tested their patience too far. It was decided harsh measures were necessary to discourage the colony's impertinence.

Chapter Seventeen

Ominous Signs

John Haslet had returned home following the 1773 legislative session to pick up his role in the intense kitchen industry that kept every colonial household busy preparing for the winter and the new year.

He was too late for the arduous job of candlemaking but he didn't mind that. Besides, it was mostly the work of the women and children. Men usually were busy with outside chores at candlemaking time.

No, it was the imposition on his idle time that bothered him about the candlemaking. The kitchen was his favorite place to relax, sitting by the warm fireplace, catching up on the news, reading and rereading books in his extensive library. That was not possible with the bustle in the kitchen and the organized clutter: poles stretching across chairs and benches, candle rods draped over them with their wicks hanging down waiting to be dipped into the kettles of tallow. Other space would be filled with candles waiting to harden after dipping. The only thing he enjoyed was watching Polly create decorative candles out of the wax the servants had retrieved from beehives.

He was home in time, however, to participate in the annual apple paring. That was a happy chore. The whole family sat around exchanging stories, listening to their father's interpretation of events in the newspapers while everyone busily peeled away the apple skins, tossing the pared apples into the kettle where they would be boiled into a variety of delicious treats for the table. The children, including Polly (who at twenty-two was obviously no longer a child), enjoyed applesauce the most and Jemima was very good at making that.

He also was in time for the annual slaughtering of the livestock, which took him and the slaves from before dawn to mid-day to complete. The meat was allowed to harden in the cold of the morning, then cut up and deposited in tubs for salting and pickling.

The boys, meanwhile, were kept busy shelling corn, scraping the ears across the edge of a shovel. Joseph had come to hate this particular task but little John was still fascinated by one of the few contributions a five-year-old could make to the household. Corn was a mainstay of the colonial diet and the cobs useful for many things. Children used them as toys and the cobs also served as firewood. Jemima favored them to smoke hams.

Joseph was now seven years old and he and his father, weather permitting, went fishing in the Mispillion, where shad was plentiful. Often, they went out in search of game and John taught the boy how to shoot. There was a great variety of animals in the woods and marshlands along the Mispillion but deer was favored for the colonial table.

At other times they walked the woods looking for tree limbs and stones that could be put to use in the household. He explained to his son how twisted limbs could be readily adapted to farm implements such as scythes, yokes for the oxen, or runners for sleds. He would point out to the boy the tree barks, flowers, and leaves that provided the dye for the clothing his mother and sister made for them.

Joseph also was provided his own jackknife, a colonial boy's favorite companion, and his father taught him the art of whittling, both for pleasure and for utilitarian purposes.

So, the time passed; the chores were done; and—if peace be defined as the absence of armed conflict—the Haslet family settled down for what would be the last peaceful year in the relations between the British government and its North American colonies for almost a decade.

Sitting by the fireplace on a cold evening late in the winter, Haslet mused over this long period of tranquility in his life. The comfort of the fireplace was the usual antidote to the cold weather, the dreariness of short days, the views of bleak landscapes, but this winter seemed more blissful than he ever remembered.

"This has been an especially pleasant winter," he commented to Jemima. "Being with you and the children brings me a great deal of contentment."

The children had all gone to bed and Jemima was knitting clothing. She nodded, adding a smile to acknowledge her husband's comments.

"I'm grateful for the blessing of a wife I love deeply and who loves me," Haslet said, "and children who everyday make me proud of them. They're learning to live by God's holy law, to be respectful of His blessings in the land, to respect other people. I believe they're learning these lessons well."

Jemima put down her knitting, leaned over and kissed him. She knew him to be a man of deep feelings, which he rarely tried to hide. On this particular evening, she thought, he was more pensive than usual. A chill ran through Jemima, a premonition, a feeling that this idyll would not be repeated.

"The one thing that disturbs my peace of mind," Haslet said, "is wondering about the future, about what the government is going to do next. Surely, the North ministry is not going to ignore the colonies' defiance of its authority, particularly Boston's destruction of the East India Company's tea. My instincts tell me Lord North is going to react harshly. I've a feeling there are perilous times ahead."

Indeed, the inclinations of the British government already had become apparent in January when Benjamin Franklin was called before the Privy Council in London to explain how he came to obtain letters Governor Thomas Hutchinson and Lieutenant Governor Andrew Oliver of Massachusetts Bay had written to government friends in London. The letters, critical of the colonists in Massachusetts Bay, were being circulated in London and copies fell into the hands of Franklin, agent for that colony as well as Pennsylvania and other colonies.

He sent them on to colonial leaders in Boston, who concluded that Hutchinson had described them in a false, unflattering light; that he had suggested curtailment of their liberties. It was Hutchinson, they concluded, who had turned Parliament and King George against them. Having decided these two men were the root of all their troubles with London, they sent off a petition to have both Hutchinson and Oliver removed from their offices.

Nonsense, said critics, the colonials were just trying to avoid the consequences of their own misbehavior by deflecting the blame. Sympathizers countered that Massachusetts Bay had been subject to a long period of abuse from the autocratic Sir Francis Bernard and that

Hutchinson, who had been Sir Francis' lieutenant governor, wasn't much of an improvement when he succeeded to the governorship.

The public exposure of the letters caused a different furor in London: dismay over a perceived violation of the letter writers' privacy. There even was a duel fought between a man accused of sending the copies to Boston and the man who accused him. The accused man was wounded.

Franklin decided he had better step forward and reveal his role before any one else was blamed.

Appearing before a committee of the council at the meetinghouse in Whitehall (appropriately named "the cockpit"), Franklin presented the petition from Massachusetts Bay to remove Hutchinson and Oliver.

The council had other business in mind, ignored the petition, and asked Franklin about releasing the letters. Franklin's defense was that he considered the letters public since they were written to public officials.

There followed a long interrogation by Solicitor General Alexander Wedderburne, filled with sarcasm directed towards Franklin's character, accomplishments, motives, and native country, delivered before a crowd of thirty-five councilors and other spectators who frequently expressed their delight at the solicitor general's performance.

Franklin, just turned sixty-eight, sat in dignified silence through the long ordeal.

Friends found it incredible that a man who was perhaps the most respected of the colonials both in America and England could have been treated so shabbily by a principal agency of the government.

One Englishman wrote to a friend in America:

"The ministerial people here are outrageously angry with Dr. Franklin. They took occasion, when he was attending the Committee of Council with the petition of Massachusetts Bay, to set the solicitor general upon him, who, leaving the business that was their lordships, in a virulent invective of an hour, abused him personally, to the great entertainment of thirty-five Lords of the privy council who had been purposely invited as to a bull-baiting and not one of them had the sense to reflect on the impropriety and indecency of treating, in so ignominious a manner, a public messenger, whose character in all nations, savage as well as civilized, used to be deemed sacred."

The letter writer said the councilors "appeared much delighted, chuckling, laughing, and sometimes loudly applauding."

That letter was widely reprinted in America. In May, a crowd in Franklin's home town of Philadelphia paraded effigies of Wedderburne and Hutchinson around the streets then hung them from a tree and set them afire.

Franklin himself wrote several days later that the council's treatment of him, an agent of the colonies, left him "at a loss to know how peace and union are to be maintained or restored between the different parts of the empire."

And this was before word of the Boston tea party had reached London.

That word only darkened their mood when members of Parliament met in March to consider an appropriate response to the recent transgressions in the prickly colony centered around the town of Boston.

Lord North already had decided on an appropriate response and been given King George's encouragement. The government's decision was to shut down the port of Boston and reduce the colonial assembly to a shadow council. It wanted more than dependence, it wanted submission.

On March 7, the king urged the members to take whatever action was necessary "for better securing the execution of the laws and the just dependence of the colonies upon the Crown and parliament of Great Britain." The matter was debated in late March.

North rose from his seat to address the House of Commons:

"Honorable gentlemen," he said, "the people at Boston many years ago began to throw off all obedience to this country, yet this is the first time this body has considered an appropriate punishment."

It was more a call to action than admonishment for faint-heartedness.

"It has been suggested the colony be fined or some milder measure than we are considering today. I am by no means an enemy to lenient measures, but I find that resolutions of censure and warning will avail nothing. There was £18,000 worth of tea lost in Boston harbor, a large enough loss on its face to warrant a severe response."

There were murmurs of approval through the chamber. North continued:

"But it is the defiance behind that destruction that we must address and we must proceed to some immediate remedy, a remedy that will affirm the supremacy of this body over its subjects in every part of our glorious empire. Now is our time to stand up, to proceed with firmness and without fear."

North's voice now was almost a shout.

"They will never reform unless we take a measure of this kind!" he said to sounds of approval from many members. "Let this bill produce a conviction to all America that we are now in earnest and that we will proceed with firmness and vigor. Such conviction would be lost if they see us hesitating and doubting. We need to show that Great Britain is in earnest!"

He waited for the applause to subside before proceeding to outline the provisions of the bill.

"This restriction will be continued as long as they persist in their present proceedings," he said, his voice now very calm and businesslike. "It will operate severely or mildly against them, according to their behavior. If they are obstinate, the measure will be severe, if not, it will be mild.

"Some of the honorable gentlemen argue that the Americans will not pay their debts to this country unless we comply with their demands. They threatened us with the same thing if we did not repeal the Stamp Act. We did repeal that act and they still did not pay their debts. If we yield to such a threat again, we may as well take no remedy at all."

He paused to allow that point to sink in, then continued:

"One of the honorable gentleman here describes the act as a waste of paper and says it will take an army to enforce it. Well, I say to him that four or five frigates will do the business without any military force, but, if it is necessary, I should not hesitate a moment to enforce a due obedience to the laws of this country!"

His face showed determination, his voice resonated with triumph.

The threat was applauded heartily although a few members shook their heads in disapproval. North grew calm again.

"The rest of the colonies will not take fire at the proper punishment inflicted on those who have disobeyed your authority," he predicted. "If we exert ourselves with firmness and intrepidity, it is the more likely they will submit to our authority."

Then he came to his conclusion with a flourish, emphasizing each point with emphatic gestures:

"If the consequences of their not obeying this act are likely to produce rebellion, that consequence belongs to them and not to us! It is not what we have brought on but what they alone have occasioned! We are only answerable that our measures are just and equitable!"

He sat down to whistles and clapping.

Colonel Isaac Barre, a retired British soldier known to be sympathetic to the colonists, rose reluctantly from his seat when the chamber quieted down.

"I had not planned to speak on this measure," he said in mild tones, "but for certain remarks I've heard here. To those who suggest we fine the colonists in Boston rather than closing their port, I say that however you describe it, a fine is a tax and as long as I sit here among you I will oppose the taxing of America."

There were hoots of disapproval, which Barre ignored.

"This bill, I am afraid, draws in the fatal doctrine of submitting to taxation. It is also doubtful from a reading of this bill whether the port is ever to be restored to its full extent. Keep your hands out of the pockets of the Americans and they will be obedient subjects."

There were a few hisses of disapproval but most members simply sat silently on their benches, impatient to get on with the vote.

Edmund Burke, another friend of America, spoke bluntly.

"You are placing one town in proscription and the rest in rebellion and that can never be a remedial measure for great disturbances. This is the day that you have decided to go to war with all America in order to conciliate that country to this: to say that America shall be obedient to all the laws of this country!"

Burke's remarks, too, drew shouts of derision from the chamber.

There was really almost no debate as the bill passed overwhelmingly, setting June 1 as the effective date.

Meanwhile, Lieutenant General Thomas Gage, a veteran of service in America during the French and Indian War and commander of all British forces in North America from 1763 to 1772, prepared to go to Boston, having been appointed governor and captain general by King George III. He would be the enforcer.

Gage met with Lord Dartmouth, secretary of state for America, on April 9, as he was preparing to depart for Boston.

"I want you to take whatever steps you deem necessary to carry the Boston port bill into execution," Dartmouth said. "It is the king's wish that you not tolerate any violence or insult to your officers. He also wishes that you seek out and prosecute those responsible for last year's depredations, but if it appears impossible to obtain convictions you are to drop the matter. He does not wish the government's authority to be further embarrassed by futile prosecutions.

"I also want you to move the government out of Boston and locate it in Salem. Take all the customs officers and the port collectors with you along with those from Plymouth and Nantucket. I want you to add collectors at Marblehead. We anticipate Salem and Marblehead will become important ports as alternatives to Boston."

"Have you given thought to the loss of income for these officials when the port of Boston is closed?" Gage asked. Customs officials were paid out of the duties they collected.

Lord North, who attended the meeting, responded:

"We've already decided on compensation for these men to offset such losses."

Gage nodded approval.

"It will be a stern challenge, General," Dartmouth said. "Godspeed."

Lord North added:

"And God bless your efforts."

Before Parliament had finished with Boston and Massachusetts Bay it passed laws that turned over to the governor the power to appoint executive council members, members of the judiciary and sheriffs, jobs previously filled by the assembly. It further ordered that the citizens could be forced to provide quarters for British soldiers. Finally, Parliament passed a law directing that royal officers accused of crimes in Massachusetts Bay be sent to another colony or even to England for trial.

Gage arrived in Boston harbor in mid-May, stayed on board ship for four days, then debarked just two weeks before the port bill would become effective.

Despite the somber atmosphere, the beginning of Gage's rule began auspiciously enough. He was greeted with a grand ceremony, complete with John Hancock's cadet honor guard, companies of local militia, and an artillery salute. He was toasted at dinner that evening at Faneuil Hall by the leading citizens of Boston and the colonial assembly. People observed that he seemed a sociable man, good-humored, dignified, mannerly.

The good will exhibited at his arrival lasted barely a week.

On May 25, the newly-elected Massachusetts Assembly met to organize and chose Thomas Cushing as its speaker and Samuel Adams as its clerk. It then appointed twenty-seven people to the council, not knowing Parliament had voted to take that power away from them.

Gage, although unaware that Parliament had acted to give him the sole power to make these appointments, on the very next day rejected thirteen of their choices, including John Adams. It was then he also told them that hereafter Salem would be the capital and the assembly should meet there.

The cheerful anticipation that the new royal governor, with his long experience in America and his American-born wife, would improve relations between the government and the colonists gave way to gloom.

Chapter Eighteen

Kent County Acts

"Outrageous!" was John Haslet's comment when he read in the newspaper that Boston's port had been ordered closed.

Since water was the main avenue of commerce in colonial times, this was viewed throughout the American colonies as an effort to beggar the defiant province.

Haslet repeated his characterization—more oath than comment—as he discussed the situation with his close friend William Killen at the courthouse in Dover on July 20, 1774, awaiting the start of what Caesar Rodney had called the most important meeting in Kent County's history.

Although some two months had passed since the word of Boston's punishment reached America, Haslet's feelings were no less intense on July 20, particularly since subsequent dispatches told of more punitive measures against the province King George had declared to be in a state of rebellion. These took from the provincial legislature the right to appoint public officers and provided that Crown officers accused of crimes be tried outside the province.

Of course, Haslet had a lot more to say about all this, but "outrageous" summarized his feelings succinctly. Growing up in Ireland, he had suffered under what he considered English oppression and he was determined not to endure it in America. That determination was, in fact, becoming an obsession. He had come to America to escape that oppression.

Now the sounds of the courthouse bell resounded through the open window, urging the people to come in and sit down.

"I believe we'll have a rather full house," Rodney observed to Killen and Haslet, watching the crowd file in.

"Excellent," Haslet commented. "A large crowd will give much more credibility to today's business."

"I only hope the people will get behind the business," Rodney said. He had taken Haslet and a few other associates into his confidence about his agenda for this meeting.

"If our people are influenced by the example of other colonies, I'm sure they will," Killen said. "Anger at Parliament's mistreatment of Boston has spread throughout the colonies. Pennsylvania, Maryland, Virginia, South Carolina, and others have all strongly pledged their support of that unfortunate town."

"There is much talk of boycotting trade with England," Haslet added. "In my opinion that has merit."

Rodney wanted Kent County to echo this wave of protest, to join the many other parts of North America in providing material sustenance to the New England province.

Most importantly, he was seeking endorsement for calling a special session of the assembly for the three lower counties on the Delaware to support united action through a congress of all the colonies. That was a bit more sensitive since the assembly had no session scheduled and, although Rodney was the speaker of the assembly, a call for a special session presumably was a prerogative of the governor. Nevertheless, there was general agreement that the legitimacy of the proposed congress would be suspect unless it appeared it was supported by the chosen representatives of the people in each colony.

"What do you suppose Governor Penn will do?" Haslet said. "Governor Eden dissolved the Maryland Assembly just before he sailed for England and Governor Dunmore dissolved the burgesses for doing what you're going to propose the lower counties do."

"I don't expect the governor to do anything," Rodney answered. "It's my sense of the man that he'll express some mild dissatisfaction, but go no further. I believe that in his heart he agrees with the colonies' position on the punishment of Boston. And, also, he has a little more independence since he's appointed by his own family and not King George."

"Well, Virginia's burgesses ignored Dunmore when he prorogued them," Haslet said, his face showing approval. "They simply went ahead and met in a tavern and chose delegates to this congress. We can be as forceful as they, if need be, I trust."

This last was more challenge than opinion.

By now the room was full. The overflow gathered outside by the windows and door to hear.

Rodney gaveled the meeting to order and called on his pastor, the Reverend Samuel Magaw of Christ Church, Dover, to speak.

Haslet gave Magaw his full attention, curious about what he would say. Although Haslet had met him several times since his arrival at Christ Church in 1766, he had never heard the man preach. And he was, after all, an Anglican and presumably conservative on the issues before this meeting.

He expected Magaw to offer a simple invocation and thus was surprised at the clergyman's remarks.

"As British subjects," Magaw began, "we are ruled by the most excellent constitution on earth. It is a pact—an understanding if you will—between the people and their rulers guaranteeing that the people live as free human beings, free from the whims of despotic monarchs or arrogant nobles, free as God's creatures soaring through the skies and gamboling through the forests.

"These rights did not come easily. Our ancestors shed their blood to win those rights. I believe the Good Lord had His hand in the evolution of these rights. That He intended all men to share equally in His grace."

His voice rose now to full rhetorical volume:

"No mortal can ever take away what God has bestowed on us, no matter how exalted that person's position! The compact that exists is understood to secure freedom for all—all!—subjects of his most bountiful Majesty, King George."

Magaw had caught Haslet's full attention and that of the rest of the crowd. They understood his stress on the word "all" and applauded enthusiastically.

"The ocean does not separate us from our rights as Englishmen," he went on. "That compact is as applicable in North America as it is in Great Britain or any other part of this glorious empire."

Magaw's voice was strong, his tone compelling. The crowd was mostly silent, showing approval only by nodding. A few hushed conversations on the fringe of the crowd outside competed feebly with the clergyman's speech.

"Consider our relationship as that of a family," Magaw continued, "a relationship that brings comfort and security to our lives, to our homes, that allows us to enjoy the bounties of the land and the sea, the results of our hard work, and to pass on those blessings to our posterity. That is the condition I think should exist between the colonies and our parent in England. For any member of the family to subvert that relationship is a heinous act.

"Yet, in the past ten years our parent has chosen mischief over beneficence. In closing the port of Boston, in taking away the powers of their assembly, these men have committed the greatest transgression of all, bringing misery to a people whose only sin has been to assert their privileges of being Englishmen."

Haslet joined in the audible approval that spread through the crowd inside and outside.

Magaw was winding up his speech and chose to finish on a more conciliatory note:

"Citizens, I pray you will be resolute but temperate in your response to the unjust measures I have described. We must join with our neighbors in appropriate action, but we must also be sure that our actions be faithful to our religious teachings. We must practice patience and, above all, we must continue being loyal to our most beneficent monarch, King George III."

He sat down to warm applause.

Rodney, as chairman of the Kent County Committee of Correspondence, took over the meeting. He called on Killen and fellow attorney Richard Basset to define the colonists' historic rights.

When they finished, Rodney resumed:

"I'm in receipt of a series of resolutions adopted last month at a meeting in New Castle. That meeting condemned the actions against Boston and agreed to send delegates to a congress to be held in Philadelphia in September. It also created a committee to promote united action and a relief committee to raise supplies for the oppressed citizens of Boston. I suggest these be a model for the people of Kent County."

There were shouts of approval from the audience. For whatever reason the people had come to this meeting, Magaw had prepared them for action.

Haslet stood up:

"Mr. Chairman, I recommend we resolve that it is the sentiment of Kent County on the Delaware that shutting up the port of Boston is unconstitutional, oppressive to the inhabitants of that town, dangerous to the liberties of the British colonies and, therefore, we consider our brethren in Boston are suffering in the common cause of America."

The crowd applauded loudly and Rodney declared the resolution adopted unanimously, not even bothering for a formal call to vote.

Charles Ridgely then rose to propose the appointment of a thirteen-member local Committee of Correspondence with himself as chairman. Approval for this, too, was shouted by the gathering. Ridgely then offered a list of names including Haslet, Killen, and Caesar and Thomas Rodney. The crowd readily approved this selection. The committee also was charged with raising money for the relief of Boston.

Finally, Killen proposed that the county approve a meeting of the assembly in New Castle on August 1 to elect delegates to a congress.

There was some grumbling in the room.

"Why New Castle?" someone in the crowd demanded. "Why not Dover?"

Rodney was firm in his response, determined not to let this issue sidetrack their resolve:

"New Castle is the seat of our government and the traditional meeting place for the assembly."

There was silence, then Rodney called for a vote. It passed by acclamation and the meeting ended.

Haslet listened as people stood and began filing out. It was his sense there was a great deal of support for the positions enumerated this evening.

"What happens next?" Haslet asked Rodney.

"I've already drafted letters to all the members of the assembly to gather on August 1 in New Castle to consider the general situation in the colonies and to appoint delegates to the congress," he said. "I didn't want to send the notices out until we'd given the people a chance to express their feelings. I wrote to George Read that I felt it important to wait for that expression from the people. I want the people to feel they're part of the process, that it's not something being forced upon them by a handful of men."

"You certainly got that expression this evening," Haslet commented.

"Yes, and I'm very pleased," Rodney responded.

"Rector Magaw was a good choice to open the meeting," Haslet told him. "It was an excellent speech. I think it put the audience in the proper mind for this evening's business."

"He's very passionate in his beliefs," Rodney answered with a smile. "I knew he would set the right mood."

Haslet had developed admiration for Rodney's skill in controlling situations without being overbearing and this meeting bore testimony to that skill.

The room was almost empty now of all but members of the new Committee of Correspondence and Ridgely interrupted.

"Well, let's get to the business of helping the desperate people in Boston."

They discussed ways to solicit donations of supplies and money, then adjourned. (Eventually the committee raised £200 and sent it by messenger to the Committee of Correspondence for Massachusetts Bay.)

Sussex County citizens met at the courthouse in Lewes on July 23 and followed the lead of the other two counties. While reaffirming their allegiance to the king, their resolutions spoke of "the inherent right of British subjects to be taxed by their own consent, or by representatives chosen by themselves only" and declared "that every act of the British Parliament respecting the internal policy of North America is unconstitutional and an invasion of our just rights and liberties."

Sussex County went a step further, calling for a boycott of all trade with England, an idea that was spreading through the colonies but had not yet developed into formal action. The Delaware Committee of Correspondence had urged such a boycott at a meeting in May.

It was a vigorous response from Sussex County, reflecting the strong feelings boiling in that most isolated part of the colony, but it was curious because in another year it also would become the location of the most Loyalist faction in all of the lower counties.

The legislators duly assembled in New Castle on August 1 and 2 and chose Rodney, Thomas McKean, and George Read to represent it in Philadelphia. The delegates were instructed to acknowledge loyalty to King George but to assert the rights of colonial citizens to the freedom of all English citizens. They also were instructed to stress the rights of the assemblies to make laws for each colony and the rights of citizens to be tried in their home counties. The assembly expressed its sympathy and support for Boston and Massachusetts Bay. It added thanks to American supporters in Great Britain and its regard for all the people of Great Britain. It was suggested that petitions be drawn by the Congress to seek redress from King George and the House of Parliament.

Importantly, Rodney, Read, and McKean were instructed to persuade the other colonies "to agree to a nonimportation of goods from and exportation to Great Britain until relief shall be obtained."

Rodney signed the resolutions as "chairman" rather than "speaker," acknowledging that it was an extra-legal session, since it had not been held at the call of the governor.

"Well, they were finely-worded resolutions," Haslet said to Killen as they left the statehouse in New Castle. "I heartily approve of the idea of boycotting all trade with Great Britain. I think if we get the merchants on our side again Parliament will be forced to change its mind, just as it did with the Stamp Act."

They walked into the bright sunlit morning.

"Did you think Dr. Ridgely was a bit aloof in there?" Haslet said, nodding towards the statehouse behind them.

"Not particularly," Killen answered. "I didn't have occasion to talk to him. Why do you ask? What did you notice?"

"Nothing certain. I just felt he went out of his way to avoid me at this session."

The two men fell silent for a while. Haslet felt an uneasiness about Ridgely, a sense that the man was withholding something involving Haslet. This occupied his mind as the two men walked along the streets to their inn.

Killen broke the silence.

"Are you staying here or going home?"

"There are still plenty of daylight hours left," Haslet answered. "I think I'll ride on home. I've already packed."

"Give me enough time to get my things together," Killen said, "and I'll ride with you at least as far as Dover."

"That's fine," Haslet said. "I may stay at Frenchie Battell's inn if it's too late when we reach Dover."

That would be a good place to pick up gossip, Haslet thought.

"No need," Killen commented. "You can stay at my place in town. By the way, how's Battell doing now that he's bought the inn from Loockerman?"

"I've not heard, but his business seemed brisk enough when I've stopped in. When you consider he was running the place for Vincent the last nine years, you'd expect everything to continue as it was. But, perhaps Frenchie has plans for changes now that he has a free hand. We'll see."

In a short time the two men rode together out of town.

Chapter Nineteen

A Political Setback

John Haslet learned soon enough why Dr. Charles Ridgley had seemed aloof at the assembly meeting in New Castle in August 1774. As the October 1 election drew close, Ridgley was organizing his own ticket for Kent County's delegates to the assembly and it did not include Haslet or William Killen.

Thomas Rodney gave him and Killen the details when they went to Caesar Rodney's plantation near Dover on a late September day.

The younger Rodney was taking care of the plantation and looking after political affairs in the county while his brother was attending the meeting in Philadelphia of representatives from all the colonies. The brothers frequently exchanged letters on political matters but Caesar seemed to be more absorbed with the issues before the Philadelphia meeting than with Kent County politics.

Thus it was Thomas' job to face the political challenge from Ridgley, a challenge the elder Rodney might easily have brushed aside if he were home. The younger brother dealt with challenges with a great deal of fervor but he lacked the political skills and the prestige of Caesar Rodney. Too many people considered Thomas shadow and not substance—wrongly so, as he would prove in the coming war.

Haslet and Killen made themselves comfortable in the sitting room while Rodney directed a servant to attend to their thirsts.

"What do you hear from your brother?" Haslet asked.

"He writes that they are working very hard," Rodney answered, "that he's been appointed to a twenty-four-member committee to discuss colonial rights, the infringement of those rights, and possible remedies."

"Hard work, eh?" Killen commented, smiling. "I read in the newspaper that the delegates were treated to a grand feast by the citizens of Philadelphia. Did he mention that? Sounds to me as if it's not all work in Philadelphia."

"He did mention it, said it was intended to be the greatest feast the city ever held and that it could cost at least a thousand pounds," Rodney answered, "but he didn't get into much detail. Like you, most of what I know I read in the newspapers."

"I understand there were some 500 people at the dinner," Killen said.

The conversation lagged as each tried to picture the gathering in Philadelphia's State House on September 16, with the best-known political leaders in all of North America mingling with Philadelphia's aristocrats and their ladies. They had been to the city often enough to imagine the scenes, each creating according to his own tastes.

"The party started out at the City Tavern," Rodney said, "but my brother didn't mention that."

The City Tavern, recently refurbished, advertised itself as the most elegant house in America.

"I suspect they didn't get much work done that day," Haslet said.

"Well, I suppose if the delegates are working as hard as my brother says, they needed the relief," Rodney added. "Did you know, by the way, that Tom McKean got married?

His visitors looked surprised.

"His wife is from New Castle, a half-sister to Francis Alison's wife, a Sarah Armitage," Rodney said. "He's spending his honeymoon in Philadelphia. If the delegates are working as hard as my brother claims, it won't be much of a honeymoon for the new Mrs. McKean."

The men nodded agreement and smiled.

"Incidentally, the delegates in Philadelphia now style themselves as a 'Continental Congress,'" Killen said. "I like that name. It has a unifying effect."

"My brother wrote me," Rodney said, "there'd been an alarm to the delegates from Boston, word that the British ships in Boston harbor were firing on the countryside and the soldiers were marching. Fortunately it proved to be a false rumor. However, what is interesting is that thousands of people are said to have taken up arms before they learned the falsity of the alarm."

"I think General Gage's decision to fortify Boston Neck probably has people very apprehensive," Haslet said. "Apparently British soldiers have been abusing citizens passing through the neck. As I understand it the land is only about 120 yards wide and is the only passage between the town and the rest of the province."

(This, of course, was before landfills changed the contours of Boston.)

"It's significant, I think, that so many people responded under arms to the false alarm. I wonder if Gage was impressed by the turnout and if it made him uneasy."

"I doubt it," Killen commented. "You know the high opinion the British have of their army and the low opinion they have of colonial militia."

"Gage should know better," Haslet responded, with some heat. "He was a lieutenant colonel with Braddock's advance party back in '55 at Fort Duquesne and the Virginia militia, I've been told, performed much better than Gage's regulars when the French and the Indians ambushed them. The regulars panicked when the enemy started firing at them from behind the trees and rocks."

Thoughts about his own service in 1758 drifted through Haslet's mind, but the word "militia" brought him back to the present.

"That reminds me that it's time for us to look at our own militia. The people have been ignoring their obligations. I suppose since we don't have Indians threatening our borders or pirates attacking our port towns they don't see the need.

"But General Gage's behavior in Massachusetts Bay ought to persuade us otherwise. He's been very autocratic since he took control of the colony. He's ordered the arrest of people calling for a boycott of trade, tried to stop a town meeting in Salem . . ."

"Unsuccessfully," Killen interjected.

"Yes, they went ahead and held the meeting anyhow," Haslet continued, "even though he sent two companies of the Fifty-ninth there."

"The people of Massachusetts Bay have a lot of spirit," Rodney commented.

"Indeed," Haslet said. "Gage relieved John Hancock of his command of the Cadet Company and the company promptly returned its standard to the general saying it didn't wish to be the governor's honor guard any longer."

Rodney and Killen nodded approvingly.

"Well, let's get on to the matter of the coming election," Rodney said.

The men, relaxed in their chairs up to this point, straightened up.

"I gather from your message that there are some difficulties ahead," Killen said.

"It's my understanding," Rodney responded, "that Dr. Ridgely is planning to support a ticket that has my brother, himself, Thomas Collins, Jacob Stout, John Clark, and John Banning on it. But not you two.

"I also understand he had planned to run at the head of the ticket himself and leave my brother off but he ran into some warm opposition from my brother's friends. I suppose he also realized that a ticket opposed to Caesar Rodney wouldn't be acceptable to the freeholders. But now that my brother's name is on the Ridgely ticket, it poses a problem for us because we have to convince the voters that it's not the ticket we favor. And I include my brother when I say 'we.'

"We'll support Collins and Banning, along with you two and Vincent Loockerman. My brother on the top of the ticket, of course. Also either John Cook or Philip Barrett for sheriff."

"This would be Cook's third year as sheriff," Killen observed, "and that's the limit."

"But you don't have Ridgely?" Haslet asked.

"Not Ridgely," Rodney answered firmly, his face flushed.

"The doctor heard that I might be promoting a ticket without his name on it and sent Cook to talk to me about it."

"What did you tell him?" Killen asked.

"I told him in quite strong language that Dr. Ridgely's stand on public issues denied him of any support from me. I mentioned my resentment at the doctor's original intent to drop my brother and he seemed surprised to hear that, but offered no comment. I told him the ticket we presented was a compromise."

"And what did Cook say in response?" Haslet asked.

"He said he would not be part of any ticket that didn't have the doctor's name on it and I said I stood by our choices and am prepared to take the matter to the voters on election day."

"You don't think Ridgely is firm enough about Parliament and all the mischief it has done to the colonies, do you?" Haslet asked.

"If you use the word 'firm' in describing his position, it would not—in my opinion—be a fair reflection of his attitude."

"We'll have to work hard to upset his plans," Haslet conceded. "The Ridgely name is old and honored in this county and Charles' work with the poor has added to the family's reputation."

After fourteen years in the colony, Haslet had become mindful of the influence of families who were into the second and third generation in America. Ridgely had a further advantage in his medical services to the poor; the fact he was reimbursed by the county for those services did not diminish their appeal to the beneficiaries.

"I'll do all I can to encourage support for both of you here in St. Jones Hundred and in Duck Creek Hundred," Rodney said. "Duck Creek is of great concern to me. I'll leave it to you to talk to the freeholders in your own hundreds."

"The election may very well be decided in St. Jones Hundred," Killen remarked. "I think I can count on Murderkill Hundred and I'll try to help you where I can in St. Jones since I live so close."

(The county subdivisions known as hundreds were Delaware's equivalent of the townships in other colonies.)

The men all stood up, shook hands, and the two visitors left to return home.

Election day as usual was a festive occasion in the lower counties, in Kent County no less than New Castle or Sussex Counties. The commons was crowded all day, people meeting friends they hadn't seen for a while, perhaps not since last year's election, reunions adding their special aura to the occasion. Wives discussed their families while the men bragged about their crops and livestock. And they exchanged information about the craftsmen working in the county. There was, of course, plenty of food and drink available on Dover Green for all who didn't mind submitting to a little political conversation in return.

The Haslet and Killen families combined to set out an attractive feast. An appetizing selection of cold dishes attested to Jemima's skill with seasonings. Haslet also secretly hoped her connection to the Molleston family—which settled back in the last century—might help

Dover Green—view from state house
Photo by Fred B. Walters

Dover Green—view to state house
Photo by Fred B. Walters

minimize the impact of the Ridgely family name. Besides, she was an attractive addition to the Haslet–Killen table. The Haslet and Killen children were there to suggest family virtues and, of course, help with the servings and beguile visitors. Polly Haslet, at twenty-two, was an eyeful for the young men.

The Ridgely faction set up its own spread on the opposite side of the commons.

There was a surprise in the presence of a third ticket at Dover Green. It was represented by Thomas Hanson and Powell Cox, but seemed to attract little interest. It created some confusion, however, since it had Killen, Haslet, Loockerman, and Banning also on the ticket. They billed themselves as the "Country" party. Ridgely's ticket claimed the title of "Court" party. Thomas Rodney called his ticket of his brother, Haslet, Killen, Loockerman, Banning, and Collins the "Middle" ticket, but he stressed his brother's presence on the list, implying it was his brother's preferred ticket.

They were all set up and ready when young Rodney arrived, his face alive with the promise of important information.

"Ridgely's changed his ticket," Rodney informed them. "He's put Robert Holliday in place of Banning. I'm also told they're pushing the entire ticket, not any single individual, not even my brother or Ridgely. They don't want to take a chance on people picking and choosing from the lists."

"But Banning is Ridgely's brother-in-law," Killen said. "Do you know why Ridgely dropped him?"

"I suspect he was annoyed that Banning agreed to be associated with us," Rodney answered. "I don't know whether this will help us or hurt us. Besides, Holliday is from Duck Creek and that's an uncertain hundred in this election."

Rodney spent the day circling between the table and the door to the courthouse, greeting arriving freeholders, putting in a word for what he described as the "Caesar Rodney" ticket, employing the Rodney name to gather as much support as he could.

Haslet observed him at work, noting the sharp difference between the gregarious young man noted for his passions and quick temper and his brother noted for his calm, dispassionate approach. Despite the contrasting temperaments, there was great affection between the two brothers, the oldest and youngest of eight children. Thomas, at thirty, was sixteen years younger than Caesar and was in awe of him.

Haslet and Killen complemented each other very well: Killen with his more cerebral approach and Haslet with his charm, wit, and good looks, each in his way explaining their positions on issues of the day, particularly their ideas on defending colonial rights. Mostly, the freeholders asked about more local issues—damming creeks for mills, providing for markets, controlling roaming animals (hogs had been annoying people in Dover).

Killen reminded them that he and Haslet had supported moving the capital from New Castle to Dover and promised they would continue to do so. This was a position favored by Kent Countians and it also gave Killen a chance to remind the voters that he and Haslet were incumbents.

As the twilight deepened, the last of the voters straggled in, mostly ignored the campaign tables, and went right inside the courthouse.

As provided by law, Sheriff John Cook presided over the election, assisted by an inspector for each of the five hundreds. On a long table inside there was a designated ballot box for each hundred. One by one, the voters entered the courthouse, waited for one of the two clerks to announce his name, then dropped his ballot into the appropriate box.

Freeholders were white males over twenty-one who were citizens of Great Britain, Pennsylvania, or Kent County and who lived in the county for two years. They also had to own property of fifty acres or more (at least twelve acres cleared) or possess £40 sterling, cash. All were required to vote and the polls stayed open until they did.

Each county chose six members for the legislature and two candidates each for the offices of sheriff and coroner. While the election of the assemblymen was final, it was left to the governor to choose between the two leading candidates in each of the sheriff and coroner races. He usually chose the one that got more votes.

With the last freeholder leaving, the candidates walked into the courthouse, Haslet and Killen joining them while Jemima began preparing to dispose of the food that couldn't be returned home—much of it would be sent to Frenchie Battel to serve as giveaways at his nearby inn—and securing the food and beverages they would take back to Three Runs.

Sheriff Clark read the results and it was bad news for Haslet and Killen. Ridgely's ticket had carried the day.

Haslet offered pro-forma congratulations to the winners. Ridgely was gracious in response.

They bade the people inside the courthouse good night and went into the cool October air. Jemima could read the results in their faces and offered her regrets while giving her husband a warm, reassuring hug. He found solace in her affection, but couldn't help wondering if his political career, his opportunity to be part of the group shaping the future of his adopted home, was over.

Back home, Haslet covered some of his disappointment by concentrating on negotiations with a neighbor, Major Henderson, to buy his 200 acres adjacent to Haslet's land. Henderson already had built on the property and Haslet was particularly interested in the house that sat right by the line between their properties. He saw it as the home he had been dreaming of since his arrival in America nearly twenty years before but hadn't so far found time to build.

Meanwhile, he continued to follow with interest the news from Philadelphia about the Continental Congress.

That meeting concluded on October 20 with the delegates adopting plans to boycott British goods. Starting December 1, 1774, all imports from Great Britain, Ireland, and the West Indies would be banned. To reinforce that ban, they encouraged an austerity program: American colonists, the delegates resolved, should practice "frugality, economy, and industry, promote agriculture, arts and manufactures of this country, especially wool, and discourage every species of extravagance and dissipation, especially all horse racing, and all kinds of gaming, cock fighting, exhibitions of shows, plays, and other expensive diversions and entertainments." They suggested mourning be observed only by a black crepe or ribbon on the arm or hat of the men and a black ribbon or necklace for ladies. They further encouraged the colonists to "discontinue the giving of gloves and scarves at funerals" since these were usually imports.

It was particularly pleasing to Rodney that the boycott included the importation of slaves, something he'd been trying, unsuccessfully, to get his own legislature to do.

The delegates were ready also to ban exports, but not immediately, not until September 10, 1775. They hoped by then the measures they had adopted and the petitions they would send to London would persuade Parliament and King George to reverse their decisions and make that final and most drastic economic step unnecessary.

They assumed, of course, they would find allies in the merchant class of England, a feeling that would be given credibility in early January when London merchants met at King's Arms Tavern in Cornhill and appointed a committee to prepare a petition to Parliament on the "alarming situation with respect to America; the total stoppage of all commerce to those parts; and the present decline of trade and manufactures in this kingdom."

Besides the petitions to Parliament and the king, the Congress sent off letters to the people of America, Great Britain, and Canada, seeking their understanding and support. These letters enumerated the colonies' grievances, among which was mentioned—except in the letter to Canada—the Quebec Bill's support for Roman Catholicism, passed by Parliament in June. It gave official recognition to the religion of the French Canadian settlers, a fact that incensed many Protestants in the colonies to the south, particularly in New England. It also awarded all the land from the Ohio Valley west to the Mississippi to the jurisdiction of Canadian Governor Guy Carleton. Many colonial leaders, including George Washington and Benjamin Franklin, had invested in that land.

One by one, the colonies fell into line with the Congress on the boycott, the Lower Counties in late March of 1775.

Before then, New Castle County's patriots—the most ardent in the lower counties—issued a call before the end of 1774 for all men between the ages of sixteen and fifty to organize militia companies, a move the other two counties would follow.

This movement would provide Haslet with the role that would mark him for history, but that was still several months away.

There was a more immediate concern that revived Haslet's political career.

An anonymous letter, appearing in a Philadelphia newspaper in early 1775, cast doubt on the loyalties of Kent Countians to the so-called patriot faction. The writer identified himself only as a resident of the county. As a member of the county's Committee of Correspondence, Haslet became active in the search for the writer's identity.

That search took several months. By the time the matter was resolved, British troops and colonial militia had clashed in two towns in Massachusetts Bay called Lexington and Concord.

Chapter Twenty

The Letter

A letter in the February 11, 1775 edition of the *Pennsylvania Ledger* suggested that nine out of ten people in Kent County would rally to King George III if his standard were raised in the county.

The letter concentrated John Haslet's attention like a bad habit. Although it had been more than four months since he was defeated for reelection to the Delaware Assembly, resentment lingered and fanned his anger. He grasped the newspaper tightly as he read and reread the letter, almost as if he had the writer by the collar.

Jemima saw the look on his face as he put the newspaper down.

"What's wrong, John?" she said, her concern obvious. "Is there bad news in the newspaper?"

He lowered the newspaper.

"This is a new newspaper," he said, his voice sharp with emotion. "A messenger delivered this to me this morning. There's a letter here, supposedly from a person who lives in Kent County, claiming the great majority of the people here are opposed to any action against the government in England.

"Listen to this."

He raised the newspaper and read to her:

"'The people have not till lately considered the consequences of a civil war with so brave and powerful a nation as that of Great Britain,' this person writes."

He stopped reading. "I wonder if the writer considered the consequences of meekly submitting to the outrages Parliament has inflicted on the colonies."

Haslet picked up the newspaper again:

"The writer goes on: 'the heat and rage of party had not given them'—meaning the people in Kent County—'leisure to reflect on the devastation and havoc it would occasion.' This writer claims nine out of ten people would rally to the Crown if there were a war."

"Is that true?" she said with surprise.

"I don't believe it!" he responded, pounding on the kitchen table. "I believe the reverse would be true: the great majority would rally to the colonial side."

He read silently for a minute or so, then out loud.

"The writer goes on to say we are 'blessed with peace and plenty under the happiest form of government in the world.' He says, 'every branch of business is flourishing; men are secured in their liberty and property; trade is open to foreign ports of the world, which occasioned a ready sale for our produce.' He goes on: 'who could think that a three penny duty on tea could have occasioned all these difficulties, when only a refusal to purchase the article would keep us free.'"

"Nonsense!" Haslet said, folding the paper and throwing it forcefully down on the table. "This man has completely ignored the issue and distorted our present conditions."

"Who is saying this?" she asked.

"It's unsigned," he answered. "Small wonder. If I knew the name of this person I think I might find him and convince him in a short time how mistaken he is."

Jemima looked at her husband and believed he would do exactly as he said.

"What will you do? What will your friends do?" she asked.

"I don't know right now. Something will have to be done to respond to the lies in this letter. Otherwise, I fear it might frighten the faint-hearted from our fight for our freedoms.

"I'm going to ride on up to Dover and talk to Caesar and some of the other members of our Committee of Correspondence. They've certainly read this letter by now and maybe they have some information about the writer."

Joseph was at school at Three Runs Presbyterian Church, but Polly, John and Ann sat entranced and a little fearful at their father's anger. They knew him to be a person open with his feelings, but angry feelings were usually brief and much milder than they were seeing now.

"You should talk to the others," Jemima agreed. She walked discreetly to the children, casually touched them, offering silent reassurance.

"I'll put some things together in case I need to stay overnight," he said, more calmly now. He left the room and she could hear him packing his things. He soon reappeared with his saddle bags over his back, kissed her warmly—she almost welcomed his comings and goings because that's when she could best measure his feelings for her—and left.

A few hours later Haslet found Rodney at his office in the courthouse where he was attending to his dual duties as Recorder of Deeds and Register of Wills.

"Well, John, it's been a few months," Rodney greeted him cheerfully. "Is everything all right with you?"

Haslet's anger had abated in the long ride in the cold winter day.

"I'm fine. I've been busy attending to my two plantations, and, of course, it's been a busy time with my patients for all the fever that's been around this past winter.

"By the way, I expect I'll be in to see you soon to register the deed on that piece of property next to mine at Longfield."

He had chosen that name for his own plantation, suggested by a place in Ulster between Londonderry and his old church at Ballykelly.

"The property is well developed and I expect to make the house there my home."

"That's the Henderson property isn't it?"

Haslet confirmed this and briefly described the buildings Henderson had built there.

"That's wonderful John. Congratulations. I'll look forward to the hospitality of your new home."

When Haslet settled into a chair, Rodney picked up the conversation.

"Christ Church in your area has a new minister. Have you met him?"

"Reverend Thorne, Sydenham Thorne," Haslet answered. "Yes, I have. Your Society for the Propagation of the Gospel sent him. He only arrived in late December and I met him last month. He says he studied at Kings College in New York and also under your former rector, Charles Inglis, at Trinity Church there. He just finished last June and then he went to London to be ordained there by the bishop, no less. Seems like a fine gentlemen. We Presbyterians will be easy on him."

"Inglis had written to me about him," Rodney said, laughing at Haslet's good-natured jibe, "and put in a good word, urging our congregation in Dover to give Reverend Thorne any help he might need from us since we're a larger congregation, which we'll do, of course. I told him so a few weeks ago. He came up to visit with Reverend Magaw and I had a chance to talk to him. In fact, we had dinner together. I don't think Mr. Thorne is as supportive of our position on Parliament as Mr. Magaw is. I suppose that's Inglis' influence. From what the New York delegates to the Congress told me, Charles is opposed to any defiance of the British government, but we'll bring Reverend Thorne around soon enough, I hope."

(As it turned out, Thorne played a passive role in the Revolution but after the war he made his mark in Delaware's history as a leader in developing the town of Milford.)

"Speaking of the Congress," Haslet said, "I was disappointed the assembly didn't endorse their resolutions. Is there a problem?""

Rodney frowned.

"We haven't submitted our report yet. McKean and Read and I felt there weren't votes to support the recommendations. Ridgely and [Thomas] Robinson were opposed. However, we've been working on the members since adjournment. We need some incident to turn around the conservative members."

(HMS *Diana* conveniently provided the incident on March 7 when its crew boarded a shallop on the Delaware River, roughed up the owner, George Taylor of Wilmington, and ransacked the vessel. Eight days later the Delaware Assembly unanimously voted to join the boycott.)

"I would have supported the measures enthusiastically," Haslet commented. Rodney sensed a tone of reproach in Haslet's voice over Rodney's absence from the campaign last fall.

"I'm sure, John." Rodney said soothingly. "I know you're a man I can count on. You're as ardent a patriot as I know in this county."

"Thank you," Haslet said, his mood quickly changing. "Tell me about the Congress. What's your assessment of the feelings in the other colonies?"

"I think the New England colonies are solid. So is Virginia. In fact, I was pleased to find as much spirit among the Virginia delegates as those from Massachusetts. I dined regularly with four of the Virginia delegates—Randolph, Lee, Washington, and Harrison. South Carolina also is solid and I believe Maryland and North Carolina are also sanguine about taking strong action. Pennsylvania will come along although there are some among its leaders who are very moderate, Dickinson among them. Georgia has some very patriotic spirits but not enough to overcome their governor's refusal to allow them to participate. New York is my major concern. There are some very influential men in that colony who favor conciliation, favor it to the point, I fear, of giving away precious rights. I was most encouraged by the intelligence and spirit of the Virginians."

"I think the only one of their delegates I ever met was Washington," Haslet said. "He was an aide to General Forbes—held the rank of colonel in the militia as I recall—when we marched to Fort Duquesne in 1758. We had only a few perfunctory conversations."

"Perfunctory conversation is his style," Rodney commented. "He rarely spoke at the Congress. However, I will admit that when he did, his remarks were thoughtful, forceful. Even at the dinner table, he was reserved, although a fine story teller. There's something about the man that commands respect."

"I felt that, too, during the war," Haslet said. "Of course, I understand he was not as taciturn around the ladies. It was said he was as elegant on the dance floor as he was graceful on a horse."

Haslet remembered hearing that from John McClughan as they chatted at Fort Duquesne one night in 1758. It brought back many memories. McClughan, who died a few years after the war, had a strong influence in his decision to settle in Delaware.

"He did seem to be a favored guest at some of the parties among the wealthier Philadelphians," Rodney agreed and laughed. Soon enough the conversation turned serious.

"We may have more concern over our own people than those in other colonies," Rodney said. "I assume you've read the letter in the *Ledger.*"

"Yes, that's what prompted me to ride up here today. Do you know the author?"

"No, I don't. I can't identify either the style or the sentiments expressed in that letter. I'd like to know whether it was a private correspondence that fell into the newspaper's hands or was intended for publication. I worry that some among us who profess to favor our course are secretly opposed. They could emerge in opposition at an inopportune time. I don't suppose you have any ideas on the author?"

"No. Like you, I don't associate the sentiments in the letter with anyone in particular."

"The person obviously is a learned man," Rodney said. "He must be someone well-known to us."

"Yes, unless he is not from Kent County. Perhaps the author used that to cover his identity."

"Quite possibly," Rodney agreed. "I've asked Dr. Ridgely to send out a letter on behalf of our Committee of Correspondence to the Philadelphia committee to see if it can discover the identity of the writer. When we get an answer we'll meet and decide what should be done. We've assured our friends in Philadelphia that Kent County stands as firm in the cause as any people in any colony."

"When will the committee meet?" Haslet asked.

"That's up to Ridgely, of course. He's the chairman, but from my conversations with him I suspect we won't meet until we hear back from Philadelphia."

Rodney sensed Haslet's distrust of Ridgely and added: "I'll be sure you're notified."

The men chatted on for a few more minutes, then Haslet left to return to his plantation.

The Philadelphia committee reported back in a few days that the publisher did not know the name of the author, only that the letter was delivered to him by a Philadelphia resident, Richard Vaux. Vaux was contacted by the Philadelphia committee, said he was not the author, and deferred the matter back to the publisher.

The controversy soon developed a collateral issue: the freedom of people to express their opinions, however unpopular, on public matters and to have such opinions published. The issue was forcibly stated in a letter to Chairman Ridgely, which he put before the committee at a meeting March 2 at the Capitol Hotel. The correspondence was from Jabez Maud Fisher of Philadelphia advising them he was the one who had received the letter and turned it over to Richard Vaux to deliver to the newspaper. Fisher, however, did not say who sent him the letter.

Ridgely read an excerpt from his letter:

"'At the same time permit me to inform you that any attempts to discover the author will not avail, it being so great a violation of the liberty of the press to demand it. And this liberty of the press has been so warmly recommended by the Congress that I cannot suppress my astonishment that a committee appointed to execute their resolves should appear so active in it. And for my part I am determined never to give him up. In this resolution I am confident I shall be supported by every true friend to liberty.'"

Folding the letter he handed it over to be passed around the committee room.

"Perhaps Fisher himself is the writer," Haslet commented. "Regardless, I don't think this is an issue of free expression or press freedom. I think the author of that letter plainly lied. If he had confined his words to his own feelings about our relations with Britain and the so-called might of the British forces, I might concede his right to express his opinions. But in this letter he feigned to speak for the majority of citizens of Kent County and his declaration about their loyalties is a calumny."

"I don't see there's anything we can do to force the information out of any of the principals in Philadelphia," Ridgely responded, a little uncomfortable with the demonstration of feeling from Haslet.

"Not unless we can bring any one of them to our whipping post," Haslet said.

There was laughter among the committee members but the members knew they were stymied in their search for the mysterious author.

"I'll write another letter to the Philadelphia committee," Ridgely said, "and explain our position."

Haslet caught up with Killen outside the hotel.

"Do you think it's possible that Ridgely himself is the author of that letter?" he asked.

"It's possible, yes," Killen said. "I'd hate to think Charles could be so devious. I'm going to reserve judgment until we know something definite. There's too much rumor going around about who's in favor of decisive action and who's in favor of conciliation. I sense passions growing ever stronger and I don't want to add to them."

Fisher's accusations perhaps embarrassed Ridgely and he sent off a defensive letter to the Philadelphia committee declaring the Kent County committee was no less a supporter of free speech and liberty of the press than anyone else.

"Our fathers protected the press with a jealous eye, considering every attack upon it a prelude to an attack upon the constitution," he wrote. "We who are, or hope we are, animated with the same gener-ous sentiments should be sorry to see the press shut to fair political dis-cussion. We think the great and glorious cause which engages the present attention of America cannot suffer by it. Besides we look upon it as the indubitable right of every English subject to deliver his opinion to the public upon every constitutional question. When this ceases to be the case liberty will be but a name, freedom an empty phantom."

In closing, he hedged his opinion: "But we apprehend on this oc-casion that liberty has been abused."

The response was interpreted—passionately by Haslet—as a no-tice to the Philadelphia committee to stop its search for the author of the letter.

While the controversy ran its course, Haslet busied himself with the deal to purchase the 200 acres adjacent to his Three Runs planta-tion, a purchase that would raise his holdings to nearly 600 acres. Major Henderson had bid on it at the same Pennsylvania Land Com-pany auction in 1762 in which the other parcels of the growing Haslet plantation had been obtained, but he lacked the funds to complete the purchase. When Haslet offered to buy it they worked out a deal whereby Haslet would advance him the money. In turn, Henderson would deed the land over to Haslet with the understanding that should Haslet die, Henderson would have an opportunity to buy it back.

The house Henderson built included three rooms on each floor and there was an adjacent cook house and nearby barn, spring house, and the other outbuildings needed to support a growing family and a grow-ing farming business. There also would be quarters for the Negroes.

An agreement to turn the land over to Haslet was reached on April 18.

(It took until February, 1776, for the Pennsylvania Land Com-pany to accept the deed, so Haslet had to settle in the near term for anticipation.)

His exultation was deflated by news of such great import that in-terest in the home had to be put aside and the unresolved issue of the February 11 letter was almost forgotten.

Haslet was in the kitchen at the old plantation at dusk on April 27, discussing with Jemima plans for moving into the new home when a rider approached down his road at full gallop.

He rose from his chair and stepped outside to see what prompted his haste.

He recognized the rider as a young man from Cullen's store.

"The British have attacked!" the rider shouted as he pulled up at the house. "It's war. Mr. Cullen sent me to tell you and the other plantations around here."

"Stop a moment," Haslet said, grabbing the horse's reins. "Tell me what's happened."

"The British attacked colonial militia at some place called Lexington in Massachusetts colony," the young man responded, still gasping for breath. "It is said that much blood was shed by both sides."

"Do you know this for a fact? How did you learn this?"

"A rider came down from Dover a couple hours ago to Mr. Cullen's. He was going on to Murphy's tavern, then down the King's Highway to Lewes. He said he got the word in New Castle and was spreading the word through the lower counties. He said his information came directly from Massachusetts by a rider who's been alerting colonies all the way down from there. Mr. Cullen figured you would want to know immediately."

"When? Do you know when this attack occurred?" Haslet asked. He was trying to gauge the possible movement of British troops from their other barracks in the colonies.

"I believe it was April 19," the young man answered.

"Eight days ago," Haslet said, almost to himself. Not enough additional information to make any plans, he decided. He looked at the rider.

"Very well. Unless you have other information for me, continue on your rounds. And thank you."

The young man turned his horse and proceeded again at full gallop back down the road to alert Haslet's neighbors.

Haslet could feel the blood racing through his body. He sat down on a piece of farm equipment until his pulse stopped pounding. He looked around and saw Jemima and the children standing in the doorway.

The looks on her face and those of the older children showed they had some appreciation of the news they just heard and a great deal of concern.

"What does it mean, John?" she said.

"I wish I could answer with some assurance," he said, shaking his head slowly.

"I'll have to ride to Dover immediately to see if they have further information. At the least, it's only a skirmish between some British troops and some local citizens, such as occurred in Boston several years ago. That would be bad enough. At the worst, it could be the start of a civil war."

"Come," she said, hiding her own concern. "I'll help you get ready."

They all went inside, Ann holding on to her father's breeches and John grabbing his shirt, both hoping to gain reassurance through his strength. Jemima, Joseph, and Polly walked together, her arms around both young people. Before he left Haslet hugged the children, trying to assure them that all was going to all right.

The details as Haslet learned them in Dover were as bad as he feared.

British troops had marched out of Boston intending to seize the colonial militia's gunpowder at Concord. The countryside had been alerted, however, and they were confronted at Lexington commons by a local militia unit known as Minute Men. Gunfire was exchanged and several militia soldiers fell. The troops continued on to Concord where they were again confronted by another group of Minute Men and growing numbers of other colonial militia.

The British decided to return to Boston but hundreds of colonial militia hid in the woods, behind stone walls and in buildings along the road back, firing on the soldiers, inflicting heavy casualties. The return march threatened to become a rout until a relief force coming out of Boston met the exhausted troops at Lexington and stopped the colonial harassment.

"This won't end with some new laws and a flurry of petitions," Rodney commented to the group of Kent County leaders gathered at the Capital Hotel. "We learned only a week ago that Parliament has found Massachusetts in a state of rebellion. That's serious enough. This could be interpreted as an act of war and the government may try to come down with overwhelming force."

"Word is that thousands of colonial militia have gathered around Boston, that cannon have been brought in and the town is under siege," Vincent Loockerman reported.

"I don't know how far this will spread," Rodney said. "Blood is up in all the colonies because of the way British troops and warships have been overbearing with local citizens. Up until now they have been minor enough to fall short of armed conflict. But this!

"If the other colonies rally to Massachusetts' cause, then we have a war!"

It was a sobering thought for the leaders gathered in the room.

"New Castle County already has begun organizing its militia," Thomas Rodney said, focusing the men's attention on action to be taken. "Don't you think we should do the same?"

"Agreed," his older brother said. He turned to Haslet.

"John, do you have any idea of the state of the militia in this county?"

"Not a very good state, I'm afraid. Most of the militia service and training has been neglected over the years. A few companies have picked up training since last year's developments in Boston. My own Mispillion company is in a reasonable stage of training but I wouldn't dare to lead them off to battle."

Caesar Rodney pondered Haslet's response.

"I'm aware of about twenty companies in the county," he said. "I'll call them to a meeting as soon as possible for the purpose of organizing. That will include election of officers and commanders."

It was agreed there would be a series of small meetings over the next few weeks in the various hundreds with a final organization meeting to take place on May 25.

"John, I'd like you to take charge of this situation," Caesar Rodney said. Haslet nodded agreement. "Now, I recommend we bow our heads and pray for this county, this colony, the whole North American continent."

The men bowed. Haslet led them in prayer:

"Almighty God, commander of our beings, we bow our heads in humble supplication at this most critical moment. We hear the drums of war growing louder, coming closer, filling our minds with apprehension and our hearts with sorrow. We stand at a crossroads, Lord. Please bless us with the wisdom to choose the path that will bring happiness and security to our families, our people, this land we call home. Give us the courage to go down that path with steadfast determination and unwavering fealty to the interests of all those we serve. We pray that you will bless our endeavors and the people so dear to our hearts. Amen."

There was a chorus of "amens."

They were preparing to leave the inn when Charles Ridgely spoke up. "Gentlemen, a moment please before we depart. I am in receipt of information about the unfinished business of the February 11 letter. I think it will put an end to the matter. May we meet here on May 2 to consider this new information?"

"Does it include the name of the author?" Killen asked.

"Yes, it does," Ridgely conceded, "but I prefer to withhold the name until we can meet for a full discussion. I believe the hour is too late now for such a discussion."

"Agreed," Caesar Rodney said, and there was no dissent.

"Then we'll assemble again here on May 2, at eight in the morning," Ridgely announced.

It was near midnight as the men left the room, some to nearby homes, others to seek a room in the hotel. Haslet left to stay with Killen.

When they met five days later, Ridgely produced a letter and began reading it aloud.

"'I acknowledge to have wrote [sic] a piece (but did not sign it), since said to be an extract of a letter from Kent County on Delaware published in Humphrey's Ledger No. 3. It was not dated from any place and is some altered from the original. I folded it up and directed the same to Joshua Fisher and sons. I had no intention to have it published and further let them know the author thought best it should not be published, nor did I think they would. I am sincerely sorry I ever wrote it, as also for its being published, and hope I may be excused for this, my first breach in this way, and I intend it shall be the last.'"

The letter is signed, Ridgely announced, with obvious discomfort, "Robert Holliday." Ridgely had supported him over Haslet and Killen for election to the legislature the previous October.

The son of a Quaker who had served five years in the legislature, Holliday was forty-four, lived in Duck Creek Hundred, north of Dover, and was a former justice of the peace.

There were murmurs of surprise among the committee members. They had assumed all along it would be someone of some reputation in the county, but they didn't expect it to be someone that had been elected to represent them in the colonial legislature.

And this man replaced us in the assembly! Haslet said to himself, glancing at Killen. Killen's return glance indicated he was having the same thought.

"Mr. Chairman," Haslet said, rising from his chair, "I move the committee reject this pathetic apology as being totally insufficient."

"I second it," Killen said.

The other members chose not to speak on the subject, appreciating the feelings motivating these two men. Ridgely called for a vote and the motion carried unanimously. It was then decided to summon Holliday to a meeting to answer personally for his letter. That quickly the meeting ended and the men dispersed.

It was an extremely nervous and humble Holliday who appeared before the committee on May 9.

"Members of the committee, I am sorry and contrite for my weakness and folly. I confess myself the author of the letter, but I do declare it was published without my consent and not without some alterations," he began, his discomfort plain on his face.

The looks from the others told Holliday he needed to express more contrition.

"I am now convinced," he continued, "the political sentiments therein contained were found in the grossest error, more especially that malignant insinuation that 'if the king's standard were now erected, nine out of ten would repair to it.' I could not have suggested it but from the deepest infatuation. True indeed it is, the people of this county have ever shown a zealous attachment to his Majesty's person and government, and whenever he raised his standard in a just cause were ready to flock to it, but let the severe account I now render to an injured people witness to the world that none are more ready to oppose tyranny, or to be first in the causes of liberty, than the inhabitants of Kent County."

The members appeared more approving.

Holliday proceeded with a little more confidence:

"I'm conscious that I can render no satisfaction adequate to the injury done my country, I can only beg the forgiveness of my countrymen upon those principles of humanity which may induce them to consider the frailty of human nature. And I do profess and promise, that I will never again oppose those laudable measures, necessarily adopted by my countrymen for the preservation of American freedom, but will cooperate with them to the utmost of my abilities in their virtuous struggle for liberty, so far as is consistent with my religious principles."

It was a thoroughly humbled man who stood before them now, slowly beginning to appreciate that his period of influence in Kent

County was probably ended, destined to become nothing more than a footnote in history.

"I move we accept Mr. Holliday's apology," Haslet said, to the surprise of the other members. Killen offered the second and the motion was adopted.

"The matter is now closed," Ridgely announced, happy the issue could be resolved without angry words. Holliday came forward to shake his hand and thank him, then turned to thank the others, but Haslet and Killen already had left the inn. Haslet's sleight was more indifference than hostility. He had decided Holliday was no longer important.

Holliday would not be the last to appear before a patriot committee and beg for forgiveness. These shows of contrition became routine in all the colonies as people who openly expressed opposition, or even reservations, about the direction the protest movement was taking were hauled before ad hoc committees to be confronted with their "heresy." Occasionally, people who were only suspected of holding thoughts inimical to the patriot cause were similarly summoned to an accounting.

Chapter Twenty-One

Tories and Patriots

The news that the dispute between Great Britain and its American colonies had evolved into armed conflict did not reach England until late May 1775. By then all the colonies were on alert and arming themselves for any eventuality, including war if that was to come. Many colonial leaders felt it already had started.

Earlier in the year, on February 7, Parliament had declared the New England colonies in a state of rebellion. Then, in a surprise move on February 20, Prime Minister North proposed that any colony whose legislature agreed to raise money for the common defense of British North America would be excused from the laws regulating American trade. Parliament would only decide how much to be raised, not how. This, North asserted, would prove the government's benevolent treatment of its colonial subjects.

North suspected the colonies probably wouldn't go along and he was right. Maybe once that would have been a very good compromise, but now it was too late. Colonial leaders decided it was not for Parliament even to determine how much money they should contribute.

Haslet, meanwhile, was fully rid of the depression following his rejection at the polls in 1774, a depression he had not experienced since his first wife died many years ago in Ireland.

It had started to lift when the Holliday matter revived his political life and now Caesar Rodney had fashioned a role for him that would elevate him to the front ranks of the colony's leaders.

The past several months had been a watershed in Haslet's life as an American, and from it he developed a new appreciation of his adopted homeland, like a treasure lost and then recovered. Surely God watched over this land and blessed it, he thought, a feeling he shared with a great many Americans.

As the year 1775 moved along, the division among the people in the lower counties, as well as in other American colonies, grew from polite disagreement to angry confrontation. Once united in protest over Parliament's autocratic rule, the people now found themselves with sharply opposed ideas on the manner and extent of that protest.

On one side were the people who believed the end result of the protests should be reconciliation with the mother country. The means to that end, they felt, should be respectful petitioning. They became known as "loyalists" or "Tories." On the other side were those who believed the end result should be restoration of what they perceived as their constitutional rights as Englishmen. Their means would be confrontation. They were called "Whigs" or "patriots" (the government in London preferred the term "rebels").

The one common bond offering hope these two sides might once again become peaceful neighbors was loyalty to King George III. But it was a bond that became increasingly threadbare by the end of 1775.

In Delaware, at least, these divisions had not yet reached the stage of a civil war.

The officers of the Kent County militia companies who gathered at the courthouse in Dover on May 25, 1775, were concerned solely with organizing on a county-wide basis, prompted by the incidents at Lexington and Concord, not discord among neighbors.

It had fallen on John Haslet to convert desire into reality. Caesar Rodney had given him that charge on May 2 and he had applied his characteristic energy to the assignment.

When he called the role to begin the May 25 meeting, he recorded more than twenty companies represented by their captains as well as some lieutenants and ensigns. Among them were Rodney and his brother Thomas, both in their militia roles as captains.

The farmers, merchants, craftsmen, boatmen, doctors, lawyers assembled in the courthouse bore no resemblance to a regular army muster. After all, militia were expected to fight Indian incursions on the frontier and pirate raids on the Delaware River ports, not professional soldiers, and frontier warfare relied more on common sense than on military discipline. Nevertheless, many of these men would, in another year, be organized and trained as one of the best regiments in the embryonic continental army and they would prove the equal of British and Hessian regulars on the battlefield.

But that was the future. Haslet's concern was now.

"I think we would be best organized," he said, "if we divided the county into two regiments, one for the upper hundreds, the other for the lower hundreds."

It was duly adopted that there would be an upper regiment and a lower regiment.

"Now, we need to choose regimental level officers," Haslet said, "a colonel, a lieutenant colonel and a major."

"I suggest that my brother Caesar be colonel of the upper regiment and you, John, be the commander for the lower regiment," Thomas Rodney said, voicing the arrangement his brother, Haslet and other county leaders already had agreed on.

"Will you have the time to do this?" one of the officers asked Caesar Rodney.

It was a good question. Rodney was still Recorder of Deeds and Register of Wills for Kent County as well as speaker of the Delaware Assembly. On top of those jobs, he was delegate to the Continental Congress that had reconvened in Philadelphia two weeks earlier.

"Yes, I will," Rodney responded and no one challenged him. Rodney was good at delegating and would depend on his junior officers to attend to the details of organization.

There was no further discussion and Haslet and Rodney were duly confirmed as colonels for the Kent County regiments. Thomas Collins next was chosen as Rodney's lieutenant colonel and French Battell as his major. William Rhodes was picked as lieutenant colonel and Robert Hodgson as major for Haslet's regiment. These six senior officers retained the dual rank as captains of their individual companies, as was customary in the militia organizations of the day. The remainder of the companies were divided among the two regiments.

It was agreed they would gather the first Saturday of each month for drills—Rodney's regiment at Dover Green and Haslet's in Three Runs in the meadows near Cullen's store.

"Will we be dealing with the Tories in this county?" an officer asked, bringing into the open a concern of all in the room. After all, they were thinking about neighbors and friends, not British soldiers.

"No," Haslet responded. "We'll leave that to the committees, probably the Committee on Inspection and Observation or the Council on Safety. It's not a matter for armed force."

"It may come to that," commented another.

"It's very near to that in Sussex," offered another officer.

"Nevertheless," Caesar Rodney interjected, "the appropriate committees are handling the situation in Sussex."

Sussex County Tories, under the leadership of Thomas Robinson, were causing serious disruptions. He was frequently heard to mention to customers at his store near Lewes that the militia movement was led by a "pack of fools." One customer reported to the Sussex County Committee of Inspection and Observation that Robinson had stated the Congress was an unconstitutional body of men and that its leaders were using people for nefarious purposes, ignoring the danger the might of the British army presented to the common people. The Patriot committee made an effort to call him to account but he ignored them, declaring at one point he would not show up unless accompanied by an armed force.

"How about the militia in Sussex?" Thomas Rodney asked.

"General John Dagworthy is active there," Haslet said.

"Yes," Caesar Rodney observed. "Of course, right now he's paying more attention to his land holdings than his militia duties."

After Governor John Penn had announced in April that King George III had approved the boundaries negotiated over several years by the proprietors of the two colonies, large tracts that had been considered part of Maryland were now in Delaware, primarily in Sussex County. They included thousands of acres Maryland had awarded Dagworthy for his service in the French and Indian War.

"The general thinks that land should be a separate county," Rodney continued. "We'll be taking up the issue when the assembly reconvenes."

(The legislature would consider, but reject, splitting Sussex County in two.)

"Does Dagworthy still own the land?" an officer wondered.

"Oh, yes," Caesar Rodney said, "he'll keep the land. The deeds will be properly transferred."

The meeting was breaking up into small pockets of conversation and Haslet called them back to the business of the evening.

"I think it's appropriate before we adjourn that we sign a pledge that we will dedicate ourselves to securing our liberties."

"Have you prepared something?" an officer asked.

"Yes."

"Please read it."

Haslet picked up a paper from the table in front of him.

"'We officers of the Kent County militia, assembled at the court-house on the twenty-fifth day of May in the year of our Lord, one thousand, seven hundred and seventy five, pledge, by the sacred ties of honor and love for our country, that we and each of us will, to the utmost of our abilities, well and faithfully execute the important offices conferred upon us by our fellow subjects, and in our military and every other capacity, at the risk of our lives and fortunes, defend the liberties and privileges of America as well natural as constitutional, against all invaders or such as may attempt the least violation or infringement of them.'"

"I assume that includes dissenters in our own county?" he was asked.

"If necessary, yes," Haslet answered. There again was raised the possibility that these officers would be going to war with friends and neighbors. Haslet continued reading.

"'We will subject ourselves to such pains, penalties, military punishments, and disgrace as courts-martial, to be constituted from time to time of the officers of our own body, shall or may inflict on any of us offending against the rules of military discipline, or contravening in word or deed the true interest of America, or the spirit and principle of this Association.'"

He waited now for reaction.

"Dr. Haslet," one commented. "This pledge speaks of our rights as Americans and of the interests of America. Is that correct?"

"Yes."

"But not as Englishmen?"

"No."

There was a murmur in the room as the officers conferred with their companions. There was a hint of independence in this pledge.

"It's a very bold commitment," one spoke up.

"It's intended to be," Haslet said firmly. "I avoided the term 'Englishmen' because I think whatever the outcome of our present troubles, we'll remain indelibly Americans. Even if it comes to pass that harmony is restored between us and Parliament, I believe they must forevermore recognize us as an individual people. They must understand that although we are subjects of the British empire, the distance between our two lands, our very different conditions, creates special circumstances for governance. Whether that means a separate Parliament for the North American colonies, I can't venture to say. But I equally believe it does NOT mean we continue to submit to an arbitrary, inconsiderate and ill-conceived rule that ignores the special circumstances of our position within that empire."

Each man silently considered Haslet's words and its implications, then, one by one, they filed by the table, affixed their signatures to the paper, and departed.

"A good meeting, John," Caesar Rodney told him when the last signature was added to the paper.

"There's a great deal of enthusiasm here," Haslet said with satisfaction. "I hope it extends to the majority in our county. I still worry there may have been some truth in Robert Holliday's letter about the people who would rally to the king's standard."

"There's some, no doubt," Rodney said, "but I think it's fair to say you could turn his figures around and say a great majority of the people in this county have a genuine love of freedom and a willingness to do whatever is needed to preserve it."

"I trust," was Haslet's simple response.

"Well, I've learned in Philadelphia there is much afoot," Rodney said as he and Haslet walked from the meeting room to Rodney's office for further discussions.

"The Quakers have adopted a stance against us. They hope the king can be persuaded by words to reverse the actions of Parliament."

"A forlorn hope, I think," Haslet said.

"Parliament ignored the petitions from the London merchants and from other cities and chose to accept only a petition from Birmingham merchants calling on them to use force to bring America into subservience," Rodney continued.

"Yes, I read that," Haslet said. "Our best hope for beating Parliament has been pressure from merchants, but obviously those gentlemen in the House of Commons are only going to listen to the echoes of their own voices."

He gave a tart emphasis to the words "gentlemen in the House of Commons."

"I was pleased to read that John Wilkes and the City of London is on our side."

"No surprise," Rodney said, "considering Wilkes and Parliament have been in conflict for all these years. And now, as Lord Mayor, he'll be a member of Parliament again. I wonder if they'll try to expel him again."

Rodney paused as another thought occurred to him.

"I wonder what's going to happen when the City of London officials present themselves to King George?"

"I would really like to be witness to that," Haslet commented, smiling as he formed an image in his mind. "As I understand it, that should have happened last month."

(The newspaper account of the April 10 meeting was published in June and said the king gave Wilkes and the official delegation representing the City of London a very cold reception, expressing his displeasure at their support for what he described as the "rebellious disposition" of the colonies. Wilkes, the account said, observed proper protocol during the visit, bowing an appropriate three times before leaving the king's chamber.)

"South Carolina has approved the resolves of the Congress," Rodney continued after a while, "but New York has not. That's worrisome to us. I've had private conversations with the Massachusetts and Virginia delegates and they are concerned that a colony so well-positioned between our two sections could become a barrier between us and to our united efforts."

"And how united are those efforts?" Haslet asked.

"Becoming more so every day," Rodney said. "Our concentration right now is on the militia besieging Boston. They are a disorganized mob, not a disciplined force and we're talking about how to bring some order to them if they're to effect anything positive there."

"They need a unified command," Haslet said.

"Exactly," Rodney said, with emphasis, "and that's what we've been arguing in Philadelphia. The New Englanders are reluctant. It's not the habit of their militia to submit to the discipline of an organized army. The very spirit of independence that's prompted their opposition to Parliament also motivates their militia units."

"Yes, but without it, the siege will just melt away as time goes on," Haslet said.

"We understand that and I believe the Congress eventually will agree to establish a continental army under a commander-in-chief and a formal organization according to military custom. Now that Franklin is back from England and taken his seat in Congress, I'm hopeful we can negotiate some solution. He's an excellent mediator."

"Do you and your friends have someone in mind?" Haslet asked.

"Each of the major regions has preferences," Rodney said. "If he is to be from New England, I understand John Hancock and Artemas Ward are possibilities. I'd prefer it be someone from the southern colonies and if it is, Colonel Washington is the most likely choice. I've been talking to John Adams and I believe he's beginning to come around to the idea of a commander-in-chief from the south as a unifying figure for all the North American colonies."

"If that's so, then I assume we'll soon be talking about raising forces in each colony to serve in a continental army," Haslet said.

"That's already under consideration. Pennsylvania, Maryland, and Virginia will send rifle companies to Boston."

"And the lower counties?"

"We're hardly ready," Rodney said, "except for New Castle County, which is far ahead of the rest of us.

His next comment surprised Haslet.

"John, if there is a continental regiment raised in the lower counties, I'm going to push you as its commander."

"Me?" Haslet found himself disbelieving. "There are so many men in these counties who've lived here longer, who lay claim to military rank."

"Perhaps," Rodney said firmly, "but you have the experience and I know you to be a student of military history and strategy. I've seen those books in that library of yours. I've seen what you've done to get our county organized. I know the people respect you. I also know you are an ardent supporter of our mission. I'd feel more comfortable with you in command than any man I know in these three counties and I think I know all who might be considered for such an important task."

"I stand ready to serve, of course, if selected," Haslet said, "but it's a heavy responsibility. It's one I haven't considered."

"Many things have to happen before such an appointment," Rodney counseled him. "You'll have plenty of time, I'm sure, to consider your response. I want you to be ready, should it come to that.

Haslet left the courthouse and headed home, his mind full of thoughts that had never occurred to him before. He had been minister, physician, politician. Military commander? That was a role that he hadn't contemplated.

Jemima had another major surprise for him when he walked into the house.

"We're going to have another child," she said after they greeted each other, ignoring the fact that he seemed totally absorbed in his thoughts.

The news was slow to sink in, then all thought of military commands, patriots, and loyalists left his mind in a flash. He held her tight, kissing her hard enough that her cap fell off her head.

"John!" she said delightedly, allowing herself to remain in his strong embrace.

"What wonderful news!" he said. He looked at her figure. It was not yet evident.

"When?"

"I figure this year. In the fall. Late October or November, probably."

The children, seeing their father riding up to the house, had run to the house from scattered parts of the plantation in time to see their parents holding each other closely. They were delighted both in seeing him and seeing the affection between their parents.

"You've told him," Polly said, smiling. She, of course, had known for quite some time.

"Told him what?" Joseph asked.

"Yes, what?" John added his voice.

"Tell us," Ann contributed to the chorus.

"You are going to have a little brother or sister!" Haslet said.

Joseph and John had been through this experience before and quickly lost interest. Ann, however, worried how this would affect her status as the baby of the family.

The family enjoyed sharing the moment of reunion, of happiness, before Jemima asked him:

"How did your meeting go in Dover?"

His face immediately turned serious and Jemima became apprehensive about his reply.

"Let me take care of my things," he said, "then I'll tell you all about it."

A few minutes later he walked back into the kitchen, sat down, and reported on the day's events, including the possibility that a military role might be next in his life. She listened, asked an occasional question, and hid her concern over what she sensed would make a major change in their lives.

203

The change came sooner than they anticipated.

When it became apparent that Congress was determined to create a continental army, the Delaware Assembly on June 7 resolved to support it and appropriated £500 as its contribution, deferring for the time being any commitment of troops.

On June 15, the Congress decided to adopt the militia around Boston as a continental force. Two days later, John Adams moved that George Washington be appointed as its commander-in-chief. His cousin Samuel Adams seconded the motion in a strategy designed to unify the New England and Southern colonies. The delegates applauded the choice and Washington accepted.

On that very day, British forces crossed the Charles River at Boston and attacked the militia positions on Bunker's and Breed's Hills. Major General William Howe, who would be named new commander of British forces in North America later in the year, led the attack. It succeeded but not without heavy casualties to the British troops. Howe lost most of his staff in the assault and it was reported his boots were stained with the blood of his own soldiers.

Action was spreading far beyond Boston, too.

In upper New York, in May, a combined force of New Englanders led by Ethan Allan and Benedict Arnold (in an uneasy alliance of clashing egos) captured the British fort at Ticonderoga.

Virginia Governor John Murray, the Fourth Earl of Dunmore, moved aboard the warship HMS *Fowey* in June and from there directed frequent raids against patriots in the colony. For loyalists in Virginia, Maryland, and Delaware he became their de facto leader, the symbol of resistance to the patriots. They hoped that Lord Dunmore would organize a force that would sweep patriots from the region.

In August, Long Island militia drove a British foraging party away.

In October, British warships shelled the town of Falmouth in Maine (then a part of Massachusetts Bay colony). It was reported that 139 homes and 278 stores were burned and that British warships were under orders to burn every seacoast town between Boston and Halifax.

Through the fall, separate forces led by General Richard Montgomery—from the west by way of New York—and by Benedict Arnold—from the east by way of Maine—advanced through Canada towards Quebec, capturing several towns, including Montreal. They joined forces at Quebec at the end of the year but were beaten off by the defenders. Montgomery was killed and Arnold wounded. The American dead included John McPherson of Delaware, selected to be a major in the new Delaware battalion being organized under authorization of the Congress.

Meanwhile, Lord Dunmore added to his reputation among patriots as an arch-villain by seizing a ship loaded with immigrants from Scotland that had been forced into port at Norfolk by a December storm. Dunmore ordered the passengers dumped ashore and commandeered the ship for his Tory friends in the colony. Local militia took care of the unfortunate immigrants and sent them on to their original destination in North Carolina.

Also in December, a combined force of militia from Virginia and North Carolina defeated a British force at Great Bridge, near Norfolk. The British retaliated in early 1776 by burning Norfolk.

The three lower counties moved slowly in implementing their legislature's vote of June 7 to support a continental army. The task was turned over to a Council of Safety, which began work in September under John McKinly of New Castle County.

The council's first action was to organize three brigades, with McKinly, Caesar Rodney, and John Dagworthy as their commanders with the rank of brigadier general.

It was left to Haslet to see to the drafting of rules and regulations for the militia units.

On September 15, following two days of debate, the council adopted the rules. In justifying its decision to arm, it cited Parliament's punishment of Massachusetts Bay and the battles at Lexington and Concord.

The council also noted that General Thomas Gage, governor-general of Massachusetts Bay and commander of British forces in North America, had declared nearly all the British subjects in America "rebels and traitors."

The council then adjourned until October.

The annual legislative elections were held during the recess and this time Haslet, along with his friend William Killen, were chosen again to represent Kent County. The Charles Ridgely ticket that had unseated them a year earlier had been disbanded. Robert Holliday, of course, had seen his chance of reelection vanquished by his inappropriate letter about loyalist sentiments in Kent County.

Dr. Ridgely won reelection, but his commitment to the patriot cause remained suspect because of the Holliday matter. In fact, he was forced to make an earnest assertion of his patriot credentials when he was called to defend himself at a September meeting of the Council of Safety. Only Chairman Thomas Rodney's intervention saved him from tar and feathers by the more zealous patriots at that meeting.

Thomas Robinson led a slate dominated by loyalists elected from Sussex County, verifying that county as the stronghold of Tory-ism in Delaware.

Haslet had little time for legislative activity, however, as military business now took over his life in the final weeks of 1775.

There were two notable distractions.

A girl was born to Jemima on November 7. They named the baby Jemima after both its mother and maternal grandmother. It turned out to be a difficult delivery for the mother and although she soon returned to her normal household routine, she appeared weakened.

Then, on December 23, William Killen's sixteen-year-old daughter left the house on a bitter cold day to walk to a neighbor's house. It was only a quarter mile but she arrived in distress and fainted. She was carried back home but lived only ten or eleven hours. It was exactly twenty-six months since the death of Killen's wife.

Jemima and John Haslet did their best to console their friend, but the girl's death cast a pall over the season.

This tragic event came a little more than a week after Caesar Rodney inquired through a letter whether Haslet would be interested in commanding the Delaware battalion requested by the Continental Congress for service in the Continental Army.

His heart still filled with sadness over Rebecca Killen's death and his mind filled with uncertainty about the burdens ahead, Haslet responded to Rodney on December 24.

Chapter Twenty-Two
Colonel Haslet

"**W**ere I to consult my private interest or domestic satisfaction, I should be induced to refuse," Haslet wrote to Caesar Rodney on December 24, 1775, accepting the offer of command of the Delaware Continental battalion, "but, sir, I have for some time past thought it my principal business to support the present virtuous opposition and think every wise and good American must sooner or later second the generous struggle. In this view of the matter, it would be infamy to refuse, rather than virtue to accept.

"I feel no uneasiness in being thus explicit, but what arises from a consciousness of being unequal to the task and the apprehension of bringing unmerited censure on the undeserved friendship which has dictated the offer. However, if Congress desires it, I (who look on their resolves as the political bible of liberty and America) will consider appointment as the voice of heaven (of the people, it most certainly will be) and strain every nerve to prove the confidence of my friends has not been misplaced."

Thus Haslet accepted the role for which history would best remember him. As the letter avows, he had become the consummate patriot with an immutable belief in the cause of his adopted homeland and faith in the institution created to pursue that cause, the Continental Congress.

His appointment still had to be endorsed by the Delaware Council of Safety and then ratified by the Congress. There also was a tacit understanding that the principal names would be vetted by George Washington before Congress voted.

Approval was considered a formality, given the endorsements of the officers by the colony's political leadership. However, it turned out to be a formality delayed.

Objections arose from Sussex County when the names of Haslet as colonel, Gunning Bedford Sr. as lieutenant colonel, and John Macpherson as major were placed before the council in a meeting at the courthouse in Dover on Tuesday, January 9, 1776.

(The members were not aware that Macpherson had been killed in the attack on Quebec on December 31.)

The meeting opened with endorsement of Congress' request for support of exports to the West Indies, these exports to be exchanged for much needed military supplies.

When Council President John McKinly of Wilmington put the question of the officers for the Delaware Continentals before the council in late morning, Jacob Moore, an associate of Thomas Robinson and a colonel in the Sussex County militia, rose.

"Mr. President," he said, "I ask that a vote be put off until tomorrow. Three of our county's members—General Dagworthy, Mr. Hall, and Mr. Polke—are absent. I think their views on the formation of a regiment should be heard, if—as I understand—it will serve outside the three lower counties."

"Why?" McKinly said. "Do you perceive a problem? The issue of this colony's participation in an army of the united colonies already has been debated and endorsed by our councils. I don't know that the absence of a few out of twenty-one members should delay our attention to our important business."

McKinly showed the impatience of a presiding officer who knows he has the votes to carry an issue.

"There are serious questions, Mr. President," Moore responded. "There is the issue whether the flower of our youth should be risked in an endeavor of uncertain merit, sacrificed, perhaps, for the political ambitions of other colonies. I have no problem and neither do my associates, of raising a regiment to defend the interests of our three counties. But defending the interests of other colonies is another matter."

"Well, as I have said, sir," McKinly declared impatiently, "that issue was examined and concluded last September, at a meeting, I recall, that you attended. If that is your sole complaint, I suggest we can proceed with this business without waiting for men whose votes won't change the business proposed here."

Moore was persistent.

"Mr. President, our delegation also would like to discuss the officers who will lead this proposed regiment, in particular, the temperament of the man chosen to be commander of our soldiers."

That, of course, caught Haslet's full attention. Except for shifting positions in his seat, he avoided any visible display of his emotions, a remarkable exercise in self-control for a man noted for the passions of his feelings.

"What do you mean?" McKinly frowned. The recommendations, of course, had already been determined in meetings with Caesar Rodney and other leaders of the colony.

"Perhaps the commander should be someone of more moderate temperament," Moore said. "We would not want our men led by someone of such emotion that he might put lives at risk."

Haslet felt the blood rise but continued sitting quietly.

Thomas Rodney rose abruptly to interrupt Moore.

"I think a bit of passion would serve our cause extremely well," he said and sat down. Other delegates smiled at the display of the young Rodney's well-known spirit.

Moore ignored Rodney's comments.

"Mr. President, these are not the reflections of a single individual, even though my opinions have been formed in the bitter experience of battle. There are a few officers of our county militia who also would like to be heard. They, too, are men experienced in the military arts, men who know the importance of skilled, temperate hands holding the reins of the beast of war. I would request a vote be delayed until these officers arrive."

"And when will that be?" McKinly asked.

"I expect them to be here before too much longer."

"Very well," McKinly said. "We'll adjourn until this afternoon."

He brought his gavel down to recess the meeting.

The members left the building in clusters, Haslet departing with Bedford and George Read of New Castle County and Thomas Rodney and Thomas Collins from Kent.

"Well, John, it appears not all the members of this council share our opinions of your qualifications," Rodney said as they walked towards an inn for lunch. He tried to keep the tone light, noting Haslet's dark mood.

"Obviously," Haslet said with as much calm as he could muster.

"Well, it's all talk for the record," Read observed. "The Sussex County people want to show they're not going to be dictated to by Kent and New Castle. Moore will probably speak as though he favors Dagworthy but I really suspect he wants the job himself. When it comes to a vote, our choices will be obvious and nearly unanimous."

Read was one of the prominent leaders of the colony, a lawyer, and a Delaware delegate to the Continental Congress along with Caesar Rodney and Thomas McKean. Like McKean, he had studied at the New London Academy under Francis Alison. Unlike McKean, he was reserved, known more for his elegant dress than for his fellowship. He was tall like Haslet, but slightly built.

When the afternoon session convened, Simon Kollock, who held the rank of major, led off.

A prosperous cooper, he was a member of a distinguished Sussex County family, nephew of the late Jacob Kollock, long-time member of the legislature and its speaker for several years. He was known to be part of the element in his county that insisted that any protests should stop short of disloyalty to the king.

(Simon Kollock's loyalist sentiments would lead him in 1777 to mount an insurrection against the patriots. Soon thereafter, he was forced to flee, along with his two sons, and joined a British–American regiment as a captain. He was one of several Tories whom the state legislature excluded when it granted pardons in 1778.)

"Mr. President, members of the council," he said, "I trust you will consider the important question of the command for the Delaware continental regiment with an open mind.

"There are many worthy men in our county—in all three of our counties—to be considered. Colonel Moore, I understand, already has addressed the question of what type of man—what type of men—we want to lead our soldiers as they go forth to join this so-called 'Continental army.'"

There was note of disdain in Kollock's voice at the mention of the colonial force.

"We certainly don't want someone marching at the head of our soldiers who will have the same disrespect for loyalty and honor, the same reckless disregard for life and property that we have seen in the Boston men."

"Mr. President, I object to the aspersions cast on the noble patriots of the Massachusetts Bay colony," Thomas Rodney shouted, his face flushed. "They have had to bear the most cruel and perverse reprisals from a government which has shown it has no respect for the liberties and rights of Englishmen. Or Americans! They don't deserve calumny from our councils."

He stopped to regain his composure, then continued in a more quiet voice. "We should honor them with our words, not insult them."

"If I have inappropriately characterized the behavior of certain individuals from that colony, I apologize," Kollock said in a mocking tone. "Perhaps I have misread the meaning of their words or the intent of their actions. It may be they did not realize they were firing on the king's troops at Lexington and Concord."

"I think their aim proved they knew their targets very well," Rodney responded smartly.

Kollock flushed at this, but decided to ignore Rodney's remarks. Other council members smiled.

"I think the important point is," he went on, "that these men lack experience and qualifications for the command of an entire battalion. Now, I'd like you to hear from a couple of the officers of the Sussex County militia."

Captains Levi Derickson and John Mitchell addressed the council on the merits of General Dagworthy as well as Kollock and Moore.

Whatever points they might have made were lost to Haslet, who had left the room to confer with Thomas Rodney.

"John, it's best you not answer these men," Rodney said. "My brother has discussed all this with others of influence in this colony, men who are serving on this council. I'm sure you and Gunning and Macpherson will have the council's recommendation when it's all over."

"I have no intention of answering their insults," Haslet told him. "I feel I have the confidence of people who count in this colony and I don't doubt my ability to serve well and to lead well."

Rodney nodded his satisfaction and they reentered the room. The two captains had finished speaking and the session adjourned for the day. The darkening sky was visible through the courthouse windows and the members scattered for dinner with friends or at one of the inns.

Dagworthy, David Hall, and William Polke appeared for the morning session the next day, as did Haslet's close friend William Killen from Kent County, who also had been absent the previous day.

It was left to Killen, a respected lawyer, to present the merits of the chosen officers to the council.

While he spoke, Haslet glanced at Dagworthy, who was wearing the uniform of the British officer he once was. He was reminded of the story that Dagworthy had angered George Washington by asserting his British rank to win preference over Washington during the 1755 Braddock campaign in the French and Indian War. Washington's militia rank was considered inferior.

"I wonder how they would relate if Dagworthy leads the Delaware Continentals into Washington's headquarters," Haslet mused. From what he'd been told about the commander-in-chief, it's not likely Washington would have forgotten. Could Washington have sent word that Dagworthy would be unacceptable as a commander in his continental force?

The council also heard from more of the militia captains from Sussex County, addressing the same points as the others on the previous day. They added praise of their own officers.

The testimony finished, the officers who were not members of the council departed. It quickly became obvious that the outcome of the council deliberations had been settled in advance.

"Mr. President, council members," Dagworthy said, rising to speak after the visitors had left, "I am flattered by the kind things my officers have said about me in this room. I would be honored if the command of the Delaware Continentals were tendered to me. I passionately support the cause for which they are being enlisted.

"At the same time, I am familiar with the qualifications of Dr. Haslet and of Mr. Bedford. I further note that Mr. Macpherson already is serving as aide-de-camp to General Montgomery who is leading a force that we are confident will establish support for our cause in all the province of Canada. Whatever the decision of this council, I believe the colony, the Continental army, the cause of freedom will be well served by these three men."

"Well spoken," Killen whispered to Haslet. Dagworthy obviously had been convinced by Caesar Rodney and possibly others not to dispute the selections.

Dagworthy then asked permission to withdraw from the meeting. It was granted. When he had left, Read rose.

"Mr. President, I move that we recommend the name of John Haslet to the Continental Congress for appointment as colonel to command the Delaware Continental battalion under the command of General Washington and I further move that we recommend Gunning Bedford Sr. as lieutenant colonel and John Macpherson as major for that same battalion."

(Bedford called himself "senior" to distinguish himself from his prominent cousin Gunning Bedford Jr.)

"Seconded," Thomas Rodney quickly offered.

"I move the previous question," Read said and was seconded by Thomas Collins.

"It has been moved and seconded," McKinly intoned, "that we proceed to vote on the recommendations to the Continental Congress of John Haslet, for appointment as colonel; Gunning Bedford Sr., for appointment as lieutenant colonel, and John Macpherson, for appointment as major, for the Delaware battalion the Congress has requested to serve in the Continental army under General George Washington of Virginia.

"All those in favor?"

There was a loud chorus of ayes.

"Opposed?"

There was one nay, forcibly and bitterly delivered, by Moore.

"The motion is carried," McKinly announced. "This meeting now stands adjourned."

Before the week ended, the council approved captains, first and second lieutenants, and ensigns for each of the eight companies. It closed its organization of the battalion by choosing Reverend Joseph Montgomery as chaplain; Dr. James Tilton as surgeon; Robert Ball as quartermaster; and Thomas Holland as adjutant, appointments which did not need congressional approval.

On Saturday, the thirteenth, the committee settled some important basics: the battalion was not to enlist apprentices, indentured servants or applicants under five feet five inches or over fifty years of age; each recruit was to receive a felt hat, a pair of yarn stockings, a pair of shoes, and $1 a week for subsistence until he joined the battalion; each recruit was expected to provide his own arms, or to have the cost of providing one taken out of his pay; and he was to bring his own blanket for which he would receive $2. The pay of privates was set at $5.

Enlistment would be until the last day of December, 1776, an unfortunate limitation, as it turned out.

213

On this final day, the weekly Philadelphia newspapers added a somber tone to their discussions. The dispatches reported that King George had opened the session of Parliament in October by denouncing the patriot leaders for rejecting Parliament's "conciliatory propositions" and carrying on what he described as a "rebellious war." It is time, he told Parliament, "to put a speedy end to these disorders by the most decisive exertions."

"For this purpose," he was quoted, "I have increased my naval establishment and greatly augmented my land forces; but in such a manner as may be the least burthensome to my kingdom. I also have the satisfaction to inform you that I have received the most friendly offers of foreign assistance and if I shall make any treaties of consequence thereof, they shall be laid before you."

The king, the dispatches disclosed, had arranged with the German states of Brunswick and Hesse-Cassell to supply 17,000 troops to augment the British forces in America.

The prospect that a beneficent king would intervene to restore the happy relationship with the mother country now seemed forlorn.

Coincidentally, there arrived with the newspapers some fresh and powerful words from the pen of a twenty-nine-year-old English essayist named Thomas Paine, who worked for one of the Philadelphia newspapers.

On January 10, he published a fifty-page pamphlet called *Common Sense*. In those fifty pages, Paine systematically dismissed the reasons for the colonies' loyalty to Great Britain and to the British Crown and said that "common sense" dictated the colonies declare their independence of king and country. It became a sensation as it circulated through the colonies. The king's words to Parliament the previous October had done much to extinguish the affection for him among his North American subjects and Paine's words snuffed the last flicker of that affection.

(Paine had met Benjamin Franklin in London a few years earlier and impressed the elder statesmen with his philosophies of government. When he arrived in Philadelphia in 1774, he carried written letters of recommendation from the city's most distinguished citizen.)

With the council meeting over and the leadership and regulations of the First Delaware Continentals decided, Haslet turned his attention to the business of recruiting. At the same time, his purchase of land and a house ten months earlier from Major Handerson became final on February 10 and he mixed his military duties with frequent trips to his plantation to supervise the move into the home. Thus, these winter months were an exceptionally busy time.

Recruitment moved briskly in those months and he met frequently with his officers to plan for the regiment's organization and training. One of his first, and most significant decisions, was the role assigned to Adjutant Holland.

The two men talked shortly after the Council of Safety had completed its selection of officers for the regiment.

Haslet, seated at the desk in his makeshift office in the courthouse, eyed the middle-aged man before him. He has the lean, fit look of a professional soldier, Haslet noted.

"You're new to this country, Mr. Holland? English I suppose?"

"Yes, sir," Holland responded.

"And you've had service with the British army?"

"Yes, Colonel, I served as a captain with Lord Montague in Germany."

"You saw battle?"

"At Dettingen and Fontenoy."

"That was a long time ago."

"Yes, sir, it was. More than twenty years."

"Why did you leave the army and immigrate?"

"I accused two nephews of Colonel Montague of assaulting a young woman in London. They were acquitted of charges and Colonel Montague suggested I resign my commission. It was that or a court martial. So I promptly resigned and left for America. That was last year."

"The young woman was a friend of yours?"

"A friend and nothing more," Holland responded. "She also was a friend of my wife. We knew her as the daughter of our pastor in England. She was an impetuous young girl and ran away to London. At the parson's request I looked for her and finally found her living with a family there. But she was dying."

Holland paused, lost in memory. Haslet waited in silence for him to resume.

"She told me that she had been assaulted by these two men, a fact attested to by other members of the household. I brought charges against them. But, as I've already said, the court did not believe her story. They believed the perjury of the two gentlemen."

He said the word "gentlemen" in a mocking tone.

The story was finished. Holland now waited for Haslet.

"You mentioned a wife. Is she here? Are there children?"

"My wife is dead," Holland answered without elaboration. "I left two sons living with a friend in England."

Haslet looked off into the distance, remembering his own family tragedy in Ireland many years ago, then returned his gaze to Holland.

"Ensign Holland, you are familiar with the British manual of arms, I understand."

"Yes, Colonel, I am."

"Do you feel you can train men to fight your former comrades-in-arms without any reservations? Can you oppose the king and country you've served all these years?"

Holland took time to collect his thoughts and choose his response.

"Sir, I consider myself a professional soldier and a loyal citizen. I was committed to my country when I wore the uniforms of the regiments I served. Eventually, I found myself serving a system that rewards men without regard to merit, men of influence, while it puts the heels of its boots on the necks of ordinary, deserving people. I found that system not worthy of defending. That was not my England, not my country of free men and dedicated officeholders. It's not a question of serving one country or another but of serving a nobler cause."

Haslet nodded his satisfaction.

"I will trust you then to turn our recruits into proper soldiers, fit and able to do battle. You know as well as anyone in the regiment what they will face and I know you will prepare them well."

"I will do my best, Colonel."

"I believe your best will be very effective, indeed," Haslet said, rising and walking around his desk. He put his arm around the man's shoulders and escorted him to the door.

Holland departed and Haslet stared after him for a long while, then turned, retrieved his hat and great coat and departed the courthouse. The anticipation of relaxing by the fire in his new home, with his family, lifted his spirits.

It was a weary John Haslet who arrived home a few hours later.

"Sit by the fire, John, and warm yourself," Jemima said solicitously. He shed his coat and hat and a servant placed them on pegs along one wall of the kitchen. She poured hot cider into a tankard and handed it to him.

"How are the plans for the regiment going?"

"Well enough," he said. "Recruiting has been brisk. It is my hope we'll fill the ranks by the end of February or the middle of March. I think we will have a fine corps of officers to lead the men. I had a long talk today with the man I hope will make soldiers of our citizens. A man with an interesting story."

He recounted the story of Thomas Holland. Jemima listened with interest and sympathy for the man.

"It's a very sad story," she commented, "but I'm pleased you've found him a worthy addition to your staff."

A possible impediment occurred to her.

"He's so new to this country and served so long with the British army are you sure he will be loyal?" Betrayal was a worrisome thought to her because of its implications for the safety of her husband.

"We discussed that," Haslet answered, "and I'm satisfied he is trustworthy."

After a pause to let the cider warm him, Haslet continued:

"And how are things here?"

It had been some months—months marked by his frequent absences—since the family began moving from its longtime home to the new plantation Haslet now called Longfield.

"We've moved everything over," she said. "The only thing left at the Marsh plantation are things we need to continue farming there. Dollar and Tobias will continue to live there and look after things along with Toby's wife Ruth and their two children."

Jemima had saved the most interesting development for the end.

"Polly thinks she would like to stay there and manage the plantation. It's a wonderful opportunity for her to learn to be mistress of her own plantation someday. She's kept bedding, one of our spinning wheels, and the other things that should take care of her needs. She even says she'll have us over for dinner soon."

She paused for her husband's reaction. He smiled and nodded his approval, thinking with satisfaction about the twenty-three-year-old Polly's growth to womanhood and her adaptation to America.

"Where are the other children?" he asked, looking around the vacant room.

"Jemima's asleep in her cradle. Joseph and William are at school, should be home very soon. Ann is with Polly. They'll be here for dinner."

"I've missed the children. I've missed you. I've missed the whole family," Haslet said wistfully.

She sat on his lap and put her head on his shoulder.

"We've missed you, too. I've missed you terribly. But we all understand what you have to do. We just hope this war never comes to the lower counties and that you don't have to go away."

War still seemed far away, mostly focused on the town of Boston where the fledgling American army and a smaller British force had faced each other in a standoff for nearly a year.

However, the British had new strategies in mind, movements that would broaden the war to the entire settled parts of the continent. The Delaware Continentals would become involved and stay involved for the duration of the war.

Even before then, chance encounters brought the war near to Three Runs and to Longfield.

Chapter Twenty-Three

HMS *Roebuck*

His Majesty's Ship *Roebuck* brought the war to the Delaware River in the spring of 1776.

The warship made its appearance in the very month the British abandoned Boston. Her series of menacing maneuvers towards Philadelphia, then both the political and cultural center of North America, tempered the joy at the news from Boston

The British vacated that incubator of rebellion on March 17. The fact that their position was untenable, surrounded as they were by a numerically superior American force, was motivation enough. But there were also broader considerations of strategy.

Rather than launch an offensive against the Massachusetts Bay colony, the British had decided on a series of alternatives. They would send one large force through Canada and down New York's Hudson Valley, another through Charleston, South Carolina, and thence northward, and a third through the town of New York. That, the British were sure, would swiftly bring the Americans to their senses and end the "rebellion."

Accordingly, Major General William Howe, commander of all British forces in North America, took his troops from Boston to Halifax, Nova Scotia, for the eighteenth century version of rest and rehabilitation. The long months cooped up in Boston had left his corps debilitated. At Halifax he also would await the reinforcements to carry out the new strategy.

Washington contemplated possible British moves and decided—correctly as it turned out—that New York would be Howe's next objective.

The commander-in-chief had sent Major General Charles Lee to New York in January to begin fortifying both the town and nearby Brooklyn Heights on Long Island. In March he moved Lee to South Carolina and placed Brigadier General William Alexander, better known as Lord Sterling, in charge at New York. As soon as the British troops departed Boston, Washington began moving substantial forces towards New York, following them himself to take command in New York on April 13. He left behind only enough troops to watch the British fleet that hovered around Boston harbor until June.

In light of the grand British strategy, the contacts with the *Roebuck* and its escorts on the Delaware River were only minor incidents. Unless, of course, you lived along the river. And, at the time, it was conceivable the British would choose Philadelphia for the next campaign and that could bring great numbers of British forces up the Delaware. If that was Howe's plan, then the *Roebuck* could be a prelude to an advance of a larger British force.

The *Roebuck* was not just one of many British warships. It was the pride of Lord Sandwich, British Lord of the Admiralty, named after the ship commanded by the famed explorer William Dampier before it sank off Ascension Island in 1701. It had been built at Lord Sandwich's direction the previous summer and then sailed in September to Halifax where it remained through the winter.

A harbinger of its arrival in the Delaware Bay was the capture on March 17 of the American sloop *Grace*. She went to the aid of a small ship signaling it was in distress, which proved to be a ruse. The ship was one of the *Roebuck*'s escorts.

In the last week of March the warship itself appeared with the rest of its squadron.

On March 27, river pilot Henry Fisher, the leading patriot in Sussex County, anxiously sent word to Philadelphia of the warship's appearance off the lighthouse near Lewes, adding that it was accompanied by the frigate *Liverpool* and several tenders.

The *Roebuck* seized Fisher's pilot boat, the *Alarm,* intending to add it to her squadron, but one of the four British sailors placed on board the pilot boat fell asleep at the helm early next morning and it ran aground. Local patriots took the officer and his crew of three sailors prisoner and sent them to Lewes to be placed in custody of the Delaware Continentals.

The next prey of the British squadron was a schooner owned by Nehemiah Field, a Lewes merchant. On April 7 he was returning from St. Eustatius in the Dutch West Indies, but decided against making port at Lewes after he had been warned by a passing ship of the man-of-war's presence in Delaware Bay. Field opted to anchor a few miles south of the Cape Henlopen lighthouse, marking the entrance to the bay, but the approach of a British tender changed his mind and he moved a few miles farther south, towards Indian River. However, fearing he would be overtaken, he beached his boat before he could make the river. Then he sent word to Lewes that he would need assistance.

It happened that John Haslet was in Lewes at the time to pick up the captured seamen for transfer to more secure quarters in Dover and also to assess loyalist activity in that area. He had assigned two companies to Lewes, primarily to monitor and, if necessary, counter Tory activity. He was meeting with their captains, David Hall and Charles Pope, and with Fisher when the word arrived from Field.

"That's Nehemiah Field's sloop," Fisher said. "He told me he was going to St. Eustatius to pick up a cargo of cloth."

"We certainly need that," Haslet remarked, remembering that a good many of his soldiers still lacked uniforms. He turned to Hall.

"Captain, take some men from your company and see to Mr. Field's cargo."

"Yes, Colonel," Hall replied.

Haslet paused, curiosity and a sense of adventure intruding on his thoughts.

"In fact, I'll go with you."

He turned to Pope as Hall hurried out of the house.

"Captain, see to the security of our prisoners until I return."

"Certainly, Colonel," Pope responded.

Drums were beating Hall's company to order as Haslet went outside. And, he was pleased to note, the soldiers assembled smartly. They formed a column and marched out in quick time, Haslet riding on ahead.

Field and his crew, in the process of unloading the schooner, viewed his approach warily. They saw a man in uniform, rare for colonial militia, wearing the distinctive blue coat of his regiment, with red and white facings, white waistcoat, buff breeches, high-peaked, round hat. The epaulettes on his shoulders suggested he was an officer. But,

Field wondered, an officer in whose service? Was this officer really an advance of the help he sought?

Haslet sensed the man's unease.

"Mr. Field?" he asked.

"Yes."

"I'm Colonel John Haslet of the Delaware battalion in service to the army of the United Colonies of America. I have a company of men coming to help unload your ship."

Field relaxed slightly.

"I'm very glad you've come, colonel. I tried to make Indian River after a British tender approached me at my first anchorage. When I saw I couldn't make it, I beached my ship here, near this other boat, which I recognized as Henry Fisher's pilot boat."

"I left Mr. Fisher awhile ago," Haslet commented. "He told me his pilot boat had been seized by the British and pressed into service as a tender for the *Roebuck* squadron. He said it had run aground when the helmsman fell asleep. This must be it, then. I have the British crew in custody at Lewes and plan to take them with me to Dover as soon as I can finish my business down here."

Field felt more at ease now.

"A company of my soldiers will be along soon," Haslet said, dismounting.

He was helping carry bundles away from the water's edge when Hall's company arrived. Just as they prepared to join in unloading the cargo they were interrupted by a warning shouted by Field.

"Colonel! That tender is back, just a few hundred yards off shore."

The tender had dropped anchor and was preparing to fire on the party on shore.

"Take cover," Haslet directed and the shore party positioned themselves on the deck of the schooner and along the beach as the tender's guns opened fire. Musket fire from the shore was answered by musket fire from the ship and the air filled with the thunder of the ship's cannons and the popping of the muskets.

It was soon obvious that they were out of each other's range.

"Tell your men to cease firing," Haslet told Hall. "We're just wasting precious powder. Let them waste theirs. We need to get this ship unloaded. That tender and its crew isn't doing us any harm."

The tender obviously came to the same conclusion and its crew also ceased firing. Ominously, however, it retrieved its anchor and there were signs it intended to move in closer to shore.

"I have two swivels on my schooner," Field said to Haslet as they watched the ship maneuver. "Perhaps we can make them keep a respectable distance."

Haslet smiled. He hadn't figured his first combat would be a naval engagement. "Very well, then, Mr. Field. Let's give them something to worry about if they come in range."

Field's sailors scrambled onto his deck, loaded the guns and turned them towards the tender. Once again the Delaware soldiers took up positions and prepared for firing.

Field watched intently and when he deemed the tender within range he gave the order for his men to fire their two swivels.

The tender's crew was caught by surprise. It dropped anchor and prepared to resume firing, but before it could get ready, there was a crash as its mainsail fell to the deck, its halyards cut by the grape shot from Field's guns. Two sailors fell to the deck, hit by musket fire from the soldiers on shore.

There were shouts of triumph from the Delaware soldiers.

Movement on the tender's deck told Haslet her captain was now more concerned with extricating himself from the engagement than continuing to exchange fire with the Americans. Its crew began to retrieve its anchor, an action made hazardous by the fire from the shore. Now it was the tender that was in peril, rendered nearly immobile by the loss of its sails and under fire from Field's ship and the soldiers on shore. Finally, two boats were lowered, crews boarded them, grabbed lines and, bending to the oars, towed the tender out of range. Before its escape, however, two oarsmen were seen to fall from the musket fire of the Americans.

Cheers spread through the American ranks as the tender moved away.

"Congratulations, Colonel," Field said, "your soldiers have performed very well."

"They performed with spirit and valor," Haslet agreed. "I'm extremely proud of them all. You and your seamen proved to be quite formidable as well."

He turned to Hall.

"Captain, let's get Mr. Field's cargo to its destination. And please draw an extra ration of rum for your company when they've finished. I'll return to Lewes Town now and wait for you there. Your company has made us all proud today."

Haslet mounted and rode off, leaving a happy group of soldiers to complete their task. They had confronted the British navy and came off with a victory, a victory achieved without any casualties. He exulted in the results of this first test of his soldiers' mettle.

Haslet had one more mission in Lewes before he headed north to home and to Dover. That task was to test the Tory sentiment in Sussex County. Lewes was reputed to be the center of that sentiment and that pointed to Thomas Robinson.

Haslet rode out to Robinson's store near Lewes the next morning.

Robinson, a short, portly man, dark complexioned, frowned as his visitor entered his store.

"Good morning, Thomas," Haslet greeted him, attempting a friendly demeanor.

"You're not welcome here, Dr. Haslet," Robinson responded gruffly.

They had served in the legislature together and had been on a first name basis then, but Robinson made it obvious now there would be no familiarity between them.

"I'm sorry to hear you say that," Haslet said, dropping the cheerful tone. "I come as a friend, with no malice towards you and I'm distressed that you're showing malice towards me."

"I don't welcome that uniform," Robinson said. "It is a uniform that says you're an enemy of the king and of our mother country that have nurtured us these many years, made it possible for us to enjoy the bounty of a free land and to live under the protection of the finest army and navy in the world. I can't show respect for a uniform that denies our allegiances and our obligations."

"I find the land less free than when I came here two decades ago," Haslet said, an edge to his voice, "but I'm not here to debate our relationship with England. I'm here seeking information."

"I'm not kindly disposed to your rabble," Robinson said. "It's only been a short time since I was accosted by young Rodney and his highwaymen on my way to perform my service to this colony as a member of the legislature. Young Rodney has neither the wisdom nor the temperament of his brother. It's criminal to turn him loose with a gang of armed men to harass respectable citizens, particularly those chosen by the citizens of this colony to serve in the legislature. That was outrageous behavior."

Haslet had heard the story of Thomas Rodney's troop of light horse stopping Robinson and Jacob Moore on their way to the legislature in March and placing them in custody as enemies of the people. Moore had drawn his sword and attempted to defend himself but was disarmed. Members of the Kent County delegation, including Thomas's older brother Caesar, had prevailed upon young Rodney to release the two men, pleading their service was needed in the assembly.

Haslet was inclined to agree that it was improper to interfere with members of the legislature in performance of their offices, thinking about the efforts by royal officers to interfere with colonial office-holders, but he kept his opinion to himself. Besides, the image of a discomfited Robinson pleased him.

"I had no role in that," Haslet said.

"But aren't you their commander?" Robinson demanded.

"That's not a company under my command," Haslet responded.

Robinson considered the response and decided not to continue discussing the incident. Obviously it still rankled after all these weeks.

"I'm here because I've been told that there has been communication between citizens of this county and the British warship *Roebuck*," Haslet said. "I wondered if you could tell me anything about it? If you know anything of its purpose? Or the identity of the participants? We are concerned about the trepidations committed by the *Roebuck* on innocent commerce and we wonder if this communication had any connection with the warship's activities."

Fisher had told Haslet that three men rowed out to the *Roebuck* on two consecutive nights while it was anchored off Lewes. They had been entertained by the captain, Fisher had learned, and escorted back to shore by one of the squadron's tenders. On the second night, Fisher was told, the three men handed over some papers to the captain.

Robinson managed a half smile at Haslet's questions. The rebels, he thought, know about the visit to the *Roebuck* but they don't know who was involved or what the visit accomplished. That was some satisfaction for the harassment from the so-called patriots.

"I'm sorry Dr. Haslet," he said, "but I have no information to give you about that."

"Do you mean you know nothing of the incident or choose not to tell what you know?" Haslet asked.

Again that smirk on Robinson's face.

"Choose whichever interpretation you wish," Robinson responded.

There were a handful of men in the store enjoying Robinson's treatment of the uniformed visitor. Whatever inclination they might have had to join in, however, they were dissuaded by Haslet's size.

Robinson's defiance to patriot inquiries by now had become well-known throughout the colony and made him a hero and leader among the loyalists. It was further known that he had a substantial following in lower Sussex County and that dictated care on Haslet's part in making his inquiry. When Robinson had been summoned in 1775 to appear before the Sussex County Committee of Inspection to answer for his denigration of the patriot cause, he declared he would not honor the summons unless accompanied by a large, armed guard and no one who knew the situation doubted he could organize such a following. In fact, he would give further proof of it within weeks of Haslet's visit.

Haslet knew he was stymied in his inquiry, but he was not surprised.

"Very well, Mr. Robinson," he said, responding in the same cold voice Robinson had used to greet him. "Oh, by the way, some of our troops had an engagement yesterday with a tender from the *Roebuck* squadron and acquitted themselves quite well. They chased the tender away and inflicted several casualties."

"Congratulations," Robinson said sarcastically, "on your great victory."

He started to add a comment, then thought better of it.

"Goodbye, Mr. Robinson," Haslet said.

"Goodbye, Dr. Haslet."

Haslet departed, mounted, and rode off towards home.

He was in a good mood when he arrived at Longfield. It always lifted his spirits to see Jemima and the children and he embraced them all warmly.

"You seem very happy, John," Jemima observed.

"I am, dear. I am. I had a most wonderful experience with my troops near Lewes Town yesterday, an encouraging experience."

He told the story of the engagement to the delight of his children. Jemima also showed pleasure, but with a mixture of relief and concern. She had hoped his service in the army would not place him in harm's way. That now seemed unlikely.

The *Roebuck* soon imposed itself again on the colony's consciousness. In early May, its captain, Andrew Hammond, decided to sail up the river to explore the defenses guarding the river approach to Philadelphia. He had been told there were only chevaux-de-frise (an obstacle just below the surface composed of tree trunks facing downstream, their butt ends trimmed to a point) and an insignificant navy protecting the town. That navy was actually only a dozen or so row galleys, each manned by twenty oarsmen and carrying one, nine-pound cannon in its bow. That was hardly intimidating to a British navy captain whose *Roebuck* had forty-four guns. Its escort HMS *Liverpool* had twenty-eight.

What the *Roebuck* did lack as it sailed boldly up the river was a pilot familiar with the river's shoals. Nevertheless, the squadron leisurely cruised the Delaware, sending out crews to forage for cattle and fresh produce on the Jersey side of the river, a bounty that did much to improve the spirits of the crews among the two warships and their escorts. Occasionally they fired at passing small craft, more to intimidate than to harm.

It had been a pleasure cruise for the British squadron until it arrived north of New Castle, near Wilmington, on the afternoon of May 8. There the two warships in the lead were confronted by the American "fleet" of row galleys.

The British were amused by the Americans' audacity. Foolhardy was the descriptive word that came to their minds.

The galleys fired first and the *Roebuck* responded, neither with much effectiveness. William Barry, an American seaman taken prisoner when the *Grace* was captured, from his cell below deck could hear the officers mocking the American effort.

But two of the galleys got in close enough to do some damage to the warship's rigging. The annoyed captain maneuvered for a broadside on the tiny craft buzzing around her like insects.

The ship shuddered. The sound of her keel scraping the river bottom startled the *Roebuck* captain and crew. The ship came to an abrupt stop and heeled sharply to one side. The warship was held fast on a shoal, its guns pointed uselessly towards the sky and water. River pilot John Emmes, who also was a prisoner aboard the ship, noticed the crews hastily closing portholes on the low side of the ship to keep the water from flooding it.

As night was falling, the *Liverpool* moved in closer to protect the sister ship. Boats were sent out to circle the warship, its armed crews ordered to fight off any effort by the row galleys to come in close enough to finish off the crippled vessel. Meantime, her captain tried desperately to free his ship, manipulating the anchor and stream cables without success. He fretted over the possibility that fireships would be floated into the helpless ship, a tactic Americans had used effectively in similar situations. Barry heard the crew even making plans to flee to the *Liverpool*.

The situation was relieved just before dawn when the *Liverpool* was able to pull the *Roebuck* free on the rising tide. The British spent the morning of the ninth repairing the damage from the brief encounter.

In the afternoon, the row galleys came on again, this time joined by the schooner *Wasp* commanded by Charles Alexander. His ship had been chased up the Christiana Creek earlier in the week and he was delighted at the chance to add his six guns to the renewed assault on the enemy squadron.

The American fire from the schooner and row galleys was devastating. Barry and Emmes could hear the balls striking the hull. They counted at least seven hits. One member of a gun crew was killed by a ball that came through the rail while his crew was preparing to fire its cannon. The misfortunes of the *Roebuck* continued when a barrel of gunpowder exploded, injuring six crewmen.

The British fire killed one American and wounded a few others but the *Roebuck* was much the worse for the engagement. Emmes later reported "one mizzen shroud, one of the foretopmast shrouds and two of the back-stays were cut off, the mainstay cut as far as a strand and a half and much running rigging broken; the mizzen yard twice wounded so that the lower end was obliged to be cut off, the main yard wounded so that it could not be depended upon, the sails pierced several times, not easy to be numbered."

Meantime, people gathered on shore to watch the spectacle and cheer their tiny fleet's success. Only two days earlier they had been fleeing New Castle in panic on the approach of the British fleet.

By nightfall of this second day, the British had had enough. Captain Hammond headed the *Roebuck* and its escorts downriver towards Reedy Island, several miles south of New Castle, to anchor for the night.

By now the British had abandoned plans to bombard the town of New Castle, but the *Roebuck* captain was reluctant to leave without claiming some honors. He decided they would bombard Fort Penn on the Delaware shore opposite Reedy Island and reduce it to rubble.

The *Liverpool* was sent to the channel between the island and shore, but reported back that the channel was too shallow. Rather than risk another grounding and further damage to Lord Sandwich's beloved warship, Hammond decided to withdraw.

That disappointed a 150–member detachment of the Delaware battalion, which had been waiting on shore since 4 A.M., expecting a fight. Haslet had led them there, accompanied by Thomas Rodney with his light infantry company of sixty-eight men. Haslet and Rodney left to attend to other business, leaving Lieutenant Colonel Gunning Bedford in charge, along with Captain Jonathan Caldwell of the Continentals. Now they could only watch the *Roebuck* squadron's sails disappear downriver.

The warship spent a few weeks in Delaware Bay repairing damage, then headed to Norfolk, Virginia. The *Liverpool* sailed to join the main fleet at Halifax in Nova Scotia.

Meanwhile, the Continental Congress on May 15 adopted a resolution written by John Adams and Virginia's Richard Henry Lee recommending that provinces "adopt such government as shall, in the opinion of the representatives of the people, best conduce to the happiness and safety of their constituents in particular and America in general."

The resolution, Caesar Rodney wrote to his brother, "amounted to a declaration of independence."

It would not find easy acceptance in the three lower counties, Haslet informed Rodney, declaring that "Congress must either disarm a large part of Kent and Sussex or see their recommendation treated with contempt."

It very quickly exacerbated the division between loyalists and patriots.

Chapter Twenty-Four

Neighbors Divided

A light, warm breeze off Delaware Bay, scented with the wildflowers sprinkled among the fields and forests, greeted the visitors to Haslet's Longfield plantation on an afternoon in late May 1776.

The breeze was an antidote to spring's chilling rains, an affirmation that cold weather was behind them. The effect was to revive the body's energy and stimulate the mind. Such a pleasant spring day, Haslet thought, that the serious business that brought his visitors to Longfield seemed an intrusion. Or, perhaps it was heaven sent, designed to invigorate their discussions.

Last to arrive was Dr. James Tilton, the Dover physician, youngest of the four men gathering to plan Kent County's role in the accelerating movement towards a break with England. He also was surgeon to the Delaware Continentals.

He was thirty-one, barely a year younger than Thomas Rodney, who would turn thirty-two on June 4. The oldest, at fifty-four, was William Killen, six years older than Haslet.

The meeting had been suggested by Thomas' brother Caesar Rodney. The elder Rodney, in Philadelphia to attend the Continental Congress, had written to Haslet on May 17 that it might be best to act preemptively on Congress' May 15 resolution suggesting each colony adopt a new government.

Anticipating that the Delaware Assembly might hesitate to act on the resolution since it amounted to an act of independence from England, Rodney suggested the public be encouraged to support the congressional recommendation, thus overcoming any legislative resistance.

Rodney was concerned about delay, fearing that a martial government might take over while civil authority dithered over its source of legitimacy. Officeholders swore allegiance to the king, therefore could they now act in defiance of that oath? Pennsylvania was wrestling with just such a dilemma over whether its assembly should act on Congress' resolution or convene a special convention to act. It chose the latter course.

Rodney figured that Kent County held the key to the course chosen by the three lower counties on the Delaware. New Castle County probably would go along willingly, even eagerly in support of a new government. Sussex County was doubtful and no one would be surprised if a majority of its political leaders lined up in opposition.

He suggested that Haslet, Killen, Tilton, and Rodney's brother Thomas develop a plan of action, perhaps drafting a petition for the public to show the legislators how people felt.

So it was that Haslet invited the four men to Longfield.

Haslet's two sons and daughter Ann were sent off to visit with their half-sister Polly, who had remained to manage the old plantation after the family moved to Longfield. Seven-month-old baby Jemima stayed home, of course, and had been put in her cradle where she already was fast asleep.

Haslet watched regretfully as the ox-drawn cart bearing the children moved down the road, led by one of the servants. It seemed there was so little time for family anymore. But he knew the children enjoyed visiting with their big sister and the freedom from the rules at home.

The invitation had included dinner, and Jemima, bustling around the hearth in the kitchen, advised the men: "Dinner will be ready in a little while."

"I am filled with anticipation," Tilton commented, a mischievous look in his eye. "It's said your cooking could enchant the gods on Mount Olympus."

Jemima blushed at the hyperbole but appreciated the underlying compliment. She had met the young doctor casually in Dover on a visit with her husband. She remembered her husband telling her that Tilton was a graduate of the medical school at the College of Philadelphia, a rare education in those colonial times where preparation for the practice of medicine consisted of studying under an established practitioner, or, as in Haslet's case, a college degree of any kind. The Philadelphia medical school, first in North America, had opened in 1765.

"Well, if the food disagrees with you," Jemima responded wryly, "I'm sure my husband can find a remedy."

They all laughed and Jemima returned to the hearth to tend to her pots. The servants Jinn and Bett were there to help, as they usually did when there were guests for dinner.

The men moved into the front room and sat down. Haslet brought out a bottle of peach brandy and filled their cups. There was a brief exchange of neighborhood news, then they got down to the business of the meeting.

Haslet picked up Rodney's letter from his desk.

"Caesar has been concerned about the military taking control of government unless a civil government is formed," Haslet said and, referring to the letter, quoted Rodney that military rule would be "'fatal, perhaps to the liberty and safety of the people.'"

He put down the letter.

"He's worried that the assembly might hesitate to act without some expression from the people and, therefore, he suggests we circulate a petition among the freeholders ahead of time seeking support for the Congressional resolution. He believes that's the best way to persuade the assembly when it meets."

"What do we say in this petition?" Killen asked.

"I'd suggest it ask that the Kent County members support formation of a new government and beseech the other members to do the same," Haslet said. "Failing that, then they should propose a convention be held for the same purpose."

"That will require a demonstration of courage that I fear is beyond that body," Tilton said. "There are far too many in the assembly who are uncomfortable with any action that even hints at a final breach with the mother country. Suppose the assembly refuses to do either?"

"Then our members should vote to dissolve the assembly," Thomas Rodney said firmly.

"The question has been asked whether the assembly can act in obvious transgression of its oaths of office," Killen commented.

"They could perhaps do what Rhode Island has done and authorize commissions for public officials be issued in the name of the governor rather than the king," Rodney said.

"I wonder how many governors would agree to that?" Killen asked. "Not many I'd wager. Few colonies have sympathetic governors like Rhode Island and Connecticut."

"Maryland held a convention," Haslet noted, "and that convention assumed the powers of government. It authorized public officials to perform their duties without taking oaths of allegiance to the king."

"They also assumed control of the militia, which is a good thing," Tilton added.

"But they also expressed the hope their actions will lead to a reconciliation," Killen pointed out.

"I don't know about reconciliation," Rodney commented. "I ran into John Dickinson in Dover the other day. He knew about Congress's resolution and allowed that it was a good thing. He said he thought that if proper governments are organized in the colonies that will be a step towards ending hostilities and restoring relations with England."

Since his "Letters from a Pennsylvania Farmer" had won fame as a definitive justification of colonial rights, Dickinson had displayed a more conservative approach to the political developments.

"What did you say?" Tilton asked.

"I kept my counsel out of respect for his exalted intellect," Rodney said, with a touch of sarcasm, "but as far as I'm concerned I never want to see the government of the lower counties in any way mixed with that of England. Reconciliation is beyond my consideration. This also is an opportunity for us to complete our separation from the province of Pennsylvania."

His voice made it clear his feelings on the subject were passionately held. The others nodded silently. Haslet, in fact, shared in the intensity of young Rodney's feelings.

"Now, do we present a petition to the assembly requesting action?" Haslet asked. The faces of Tilton and Rodney indicated agreement, but Killen had reservations.

"I doubt we could circulate it widely enough to carry any weight," Killen suggested. "Signatures collected in just a couple of the hundreds would not be persuasive, I fear."

"I think we must try," Haslet said, somewhat impatiently. "I would begin with members of the militia. Thomas, you certainly could present it to your men at this Saturday's muster. I'll do the same at the Mispillion muster. I just wish my own soldiers were available, but most are now either in Wilmington or Lewes."

Jemima interrupted at that point to announce dinner and they all retired to the front dining room where dishes had been set on a fine walnut table, covered by a white, embroidered, linen tablecloth, with matching napkins at each place. Haslet proudly informed them that his daughter Polly had made both the tablecloth and the napkins.

"Polly always has been very quick at learning how to do things and learning to do them well," Jemima commented, taking her place at the table while Jinn and Bett served the food. She said it with obvious approval and Haslet felt warmth towards her for the way she had so completely accepted Polly as her own.

Haslet offered a blessing and they commenced the meal, passing on idle talk about people and events in their parts of the county.

When dinner was finished, the servants cleared the table and Jemima left the room to see to the baby.

The men resumed their discussion, refining their plans, assessing the opposition, until twilight shadows deepened on the fields and forests. Haslet brought the meeting to a quick conclusion.

"Well, let's draw up the petition and put it into circulation quickly."

Turning to Killen, the lawyer: "William, could you see to its preparation? I think it should begin with mention of the congressional resolution and then go on to suggest the response we've agreed on: the assembly should either organize a new government or turn the matter over to a special convention."

Tilton and Rodney nodded agreement.

Killen seemed reluctant, but finally agreed and the men left for home, a bright moon illuminating the roads. An omen, the men thought, that God looked favorably on their labors.

The petition met a great deal of resistance among the freeholders, however. When Rodney presented it to his militia company on June 1, only twenty-eight of the sixty-eight soldiers agreed to sign it. He tried to put a positive face on the result in his letter to his brother, writing that "all the officers and principal persons in my company signed our instructions." He did not include a count, noting only that "a few of the inconsiderable ignorant ones declined it, but I hope we shall obtain sufficient, upon which to ground a compliance with the resolution of Congress."

Haslet reported to Caesar Rodney in a letter June 5 that counterpetitions were being circulated around the county. In fact, he was chagrined that they were even presented at the June 1 militia muster by his neighbor John Clark.

His letter also was filled with concern about conditions in Lewes. In fact, the chairman of the Sussex County Committee of Safety, David Hall (father of the Delaware battalion captain), had sent an alarm to Congress. Such was the situation that the messenger had to slip up the river by boat because it was too dangerous for him to attempt the roads out of Lewes. Haslet informed Rodney that he had left Major Thomas McDonough in command of the detachment at Lewes and directed him to secure all the ammunition and arms there.

(McDonough had been chosen in place of John Macpherson who had died December 31 in the assault on Quebec before he ever had a chance to even know, let alone accept, his appointment to the Delaware Continentals.)

Haslet added that he had sent orders to McDonough that if the uprising among the loyalists "assumes a still more serious appearance, he is to seize the most suspected of the ringleaders as hostages for the good behavior of their dependents." He conceded that Tories were very active in Kent County as well, particularly in his own Mispillion Hundred, where two of the most active loyalists, Clark and Thomas White, lived.

That was the political atmosphere as the twenty-five members of the Kent County Committee of Inspection and Observation met in the courthouse on June 8 to consider the response to Congress. A large number of interested people crowded into the chamber, some sharing in the sentiment for a break with England, some just as adamantly opposed to such a step, the remainder trying to avoid the divisions among their neighbors.

Dr. Thomas Miller, minister of the Dover Presbyterian Church since 1749, sat as chairman. Like most Presbyterians in the colony, he was an ardent patriot.

As soon as the opening prayer was finished, Haslet, although not a member of the committee, asked for recognition.

"Mr. Chairman, I come before your committee in the role of an ordinary freeholder of Kent County to lay before you for examination a charge of disloyalty against one of our citizens who also happens to be a member of this committee."

"Who is that?" Miller asked.

"John Clark," Haslet announced, turning to point at his neighbor in the front of the room. The members stirred uncomfortably in their chairs. A few rose to protest. Clark sat silently and did not look at his accuser, but his mouth betrayed his agitation as he pressed his lips together as if to block any outcry.

"Mr. Chairman, it was my understanding that the business of this meeting was to be our county's response to the May 15 resolution of the Continental Congress," declared George Manlove. "Dr. Haslet's motion is out of order."

"Mr. Chairman," Haslet hastily added, "it is my understanding that the regular business of this committee is to examine charges against any citizen accused of actions contrary to the best interests of this county and destructive of the effort to secure our constitutional rights."

"What is the basis of your complaint?" Miller asked.

"Mr. Chairman," Joseph Oliver interrupted. "I support Mr. Manlove's objection that Dr. Haslet's motion is out of order."

Loyalists were not going to recognize Haslet's military role and thus used the word "doctor" pejoratively.

Miller would not play the game.

"We'll be at ease," Miller announced. "Colonel Haslet, may I talk to you in private?" The word "colonel" was uttered firmly.

He rose from his chair, motioned Haslet to follow him, and together they went into a small adjacent office.

Miller was several years older than Haslet and the poor health that plagued him for a good part of his adult life added even more years to his appearance. However, it affected neither his spirit nor his energy.

"Well, John," he said, "you have certainly put a stick into a beehive."

Haslet smiled. "I intended to. Clark is going to fight us in that room, try to prevent any meaningful action. I fear he may influence many members of your committee. I simply wanted to give those inclined to his side to think about possible consequences."

"Well, it may work, John. I don't know. I've been totally unable to find out what the majority is thinking. I believe, however, that fighting over Clark now will divert attention from our main business."

"I have no problem withdrawing my request. I mostly wanted to make a statement for whatever effect it may have, beneficial effect I hope."

"Let's pray that it works, John. Now, let's return to the room and you can put aside your request."

They reentered the meeting room. Haslet returned to his seat along a side wall and, still standing, announced:

"Mr. Chairman, in view of the important business before this committee at this time, I will withdraw my request to consider my complaints against Mr. Clark, although I feel they should be heard at some time."

"Very well, Colonel, and thank you," Miller said. He recognized Thomas Rodney.

"Mr. Chairman," Rodney announced, "I have a petition signed by many of the citizens of this county asking that we support the Continental Congress' call for a new government in this colony."

Rodney placed several sheets of paper on the table in front of Miller.

White, one of the largest landowners in Mispillion Hundred, rose.

"Mr. Chairman, I, too, have petitions signed by citizens in this county who have opinions on this issue that are counter to the suggestion in Mr. Rodney's petitions."

White walked up and deposited what appeared to be a considerably larger number of papers.

Miller recognized Rodney.

"Mr. Chairman, it has been customary for the freeholders of Kent County to instruct their delegates to the assembly in New Castle on the important issues that concern them. There certainly is no more important issue than the stability of the government for the lower counties. It is clear to everyone that the actions of the government in London have left this colony—indeed every colony on the continent of North America—nearly helpless. The very authenticity of our government is in doubt. At this time, the legitimacy of government is based on oaths of allegiance to a government thousands of miles from hence, a government whose actions have made those oaths mere murmurs in the wind. Many colonies have, in fact, eliminated allegiance to the king in the oaths of office. Without a legitimate government to enforce our laws, to conduct our civil business, we are reduced to the state of savages. I urge this petition be honored, that this meeting support the Continental Congress and instruct its representatives in the assembly to move immediately to restore stability to the government for New Castle, Kent, and Sussex Counties."

There were some voices of approval, some murmurs of dissent in the room. Clark rose to speak.

"Mr. Chairman, I strongly disagree with the action suggested by Mr. Rodney. Many of us do not believe our government is in the condition Mr. Rodney describes. As I understand it, the Congress resolution was directed at those colonies—and I quote from the resolution—'where no government sufficient to the exigencies of their affairs has been hitherto established.' Mr. Chairman, that does not describe the government of the three lower counties. I disagree strongly with Mr. Rodney's characterization of our present government. Therefore, I speak for many of our freeholders who oppose what amounts to a declaration of independence from the protection and beneficence of our king and government in London. I believe, in fact, that far more people signed our petition than the opposition's presentation."

There were mutterings among some of the people gathered in the room, a restless stirring.

"Let's vote," Rodney suggested.

"On what?" asked Manlove.

"On whether to support the Continental Congress' call for the colonies to form new governments," Rodney said.

"Is there any further discussion?" Miller asked. He waited a few moments, then had the roll called. The committee voted fifteen to ten to support the Continental Congress. Haslet noted glumly that all seven members from Mispillion Hundred voted against the motion. Nevertheless, he was encouraged that the motion carried.

The business was not done, however.

"The next question," Miller said after announcing the vote, "is the instruction we give to our members in the assembly."

"Mr. Chairman," Rodney said, "I move that we instruct our delegates to work with the delegates from the other counties to create a new government for the Delaware colony, the method of achieving that commendable outcome to be determined by the majority of the assembly. If that is not possible, then we should instruct our delegates to call for a convention to attempt the same objective."

"Mr. Chairman," White said, "I reiterate Mr. Clark's position that the government of Delaware is functioning quite ably and should not be subject to the tinkering of a group of disaffected rebels."

Protests came from several people. Haslet was barely able to stop himself from adding his voice to the protests and Miller's face clearly indicated his disapproval of White's characterization of the patriot faction.

"We shall proceed to vote," he finally announced.

Stunningly, four of the members who had voted to support the Congress now voted against action to implement that support. The fourteen to eleven vote left the meeting in disarray.

"What do we do now?" asked one member.

"I think this committee has clearly indicated its preference to do nothing," White announced, a note of triumph in his voice. "Clearly, it is the sentiment of this committee that it is appropriate that governments be reformed in those colonies where the misguided actions of a certain faction have unsettled the colonial government but that such action is not necessary in the three lower counties on the Delaware. I think a great majority of our citizens agree that our government remains intact as long as the present allegiances are continued."

There were jeers from some of the spectators as White sat down. It appeared many uncommitted spectators were siding with the patriot faction.

Someone shouted: "Tars and feathers for the damned Tories!" That brought cheers from many in the crowd. There was increasing restlessness in the room, voices growing more strident as neighbor confronted neighbor.

Miller conferred with Rodney, Killen, White, and Clark.

"I think nothing further is going to be accomplished tonight," he said. "I think we should adjourn before this crowd gets out of control."

"Agreed," Killen said and the others nodded approval.

Killen returned to his place, turned to face the chair and moved for adjournment. White seconded and Miller declared the meeting ended. Spectators already had begun moving out of the courthouse, but there was an obviously angry mood growing among them.

Killen and Rodney lingered to talk to Miller, and Haslet joined them.

Outside, Clark and his friends found themselves surrounded by angry faces as they moved into the growing darkness and walked towards their horses. A few torches flickered around Dover Green, particularly around the platform containing the village pillory.

"Let's show them what kind of rebels we are," a voice shouted out of the darkness. Several voices echoed agreement.

Clark found movement through the crowd more and more difficult. Suddenly a large man whom he did not recognize seized him around the waist. Clark struggled but was lifted off his feet. Two other men grabbed his legs. He found himself being dragged towards the pillory. Someone lifted the top board; Clark's head and arms were thrust into the recesses and held firmly by his captors until the board was secured.

An egg splattered near enough to his face to stain one cheek. More eggs and garbage were thrown his way, with more accuracy. Clark struggled to turn his head as best he could away from the missiles but he was quickly smothered in egg yolk and other garbage.

People in the crowd were yelling and laughing like school children at play.

The growing commotion attracted the attention of those lingering inside the courthouse. "Wonder what's happening outside?" Miller commented.

White suddenly hurried through the door, his clothing in disarray, his wig gone. His face was flush with anger.

"The crowd has seized John Clark. They've placed him in the pillory," White announced, pausing to catch his breath after each sentence. "They're pelting him with garbage. This is a horrible outrage. You must stop them!"

A handful of the Delaware Continentals had been in attendance at the meeting and Miller turned to Haslet: "John, why don't you take your soldiers and put a stop to this? This isn't a proper thing to do. Besides, I fear it may turn many people against us."

"I wouldn't think it appropriate for soldiers to interfere with the people's exercise of their free speech," Haslet responded, leaning casually on a chair. He had a satisfied look on his face, seemed almost transfixed. "They're only expressing their displeasure at the speeches they heard here tonight."

Rodney, realizing Haslet's feud with Clark had reached the point that it had overwhelmed his judgment, slipped out of the courthouse and headed for the pillory.

Clark's face and clothing dripped with the residue of garbage as he sagged in the pillory, helpless to fend off the barrage. His angry command that the crowd stop had become a plaintive request.

Rodney quickly stepped up on the platform. The crowd paused in its attack.

"Enough!" Rodney said firmly. "This man has done nothing to warrant this treatment. He was only speaking his mind. The freedom to do so is exactly why we've become estranged from the British government."

This was a surprising request from the man generally considered among the most fervent of the patriots.

"He deserves it," an unidentified man in the crowd called out, "for calling us 'damned rebels,' for refusing to allow us to form a proper and free government."

"I believe the term he used was 'disaffected rebels,'" Rodney said, working to free Clark from the pillory, while he addressed the crowd. "Nevertheless, this is not proper behavior. I'm freeing Mr. Clark and I suggest you all go home."

Rodney's unexpected intervention had the effect of quieting the crowd. It began dispersing.

Clark stepped down from the pillory, wiping his face and clothing with a cloth someone had handed him.

"Thank you, Thomas," he said, his anger at his treatment barely contained. "This is a terrible time in Kent County. You see what happens when the orderly state of affairs has been disrupted by disrespect for the king and government."

"You know I strongly disagree with you, John," Rodney answered, "but I didn't think this was the proper way for people to express their disagreement. I'm sorry for the treatment."

"Someone will have to answer for this," Clark insisted. "I notice Haslet and his soldiers did nothing to maintain order. Is it their intention to allow the rabble to roam at will and attack whomever they please? Is freedom to exist only for those who agree with them?"

Friends gathered around him to offer their sympathy and assistance and together they walked off towards their horses.

Haslet, Killen, and Miller stood on the steps watching.

"I think you should have intervened, John," Killen said. Miller agreed with him.

"Perhaps you're right," Haslet said after a while. "The man has so offended me over the past several months with his criticism of our cause that his remarks tonight disarmed my sense of responsibility. I'll take it as a lesson learned should a similar instant occur again."

He reflected for a moment, then added: "And I suspect it will."

The incident spurred Clark and White to plot revenge and also would have repercussions in Sussex County.

Chapter Twenty-Five

Revenge

Thomas Rodney was asleep at home when barking dogs awakened him. His wife Elizabeth rose out of bed and went to a window. He sat up and, half awake, watched her.

"Thomas, there's a man riding at great speed down our road," she said.

In these troubled times the Rodney household often was disturbed at odd hours since her husband served as adjutant to his often-absent brother Caesar, commanding general of the Kent County militia.

"See to the child," Thomas said, getting out of bed. He lit a candle and held it over his watch. It was a little after midnight. He took his pistol off the bureau and headed downstairs as Elizabeth picked up four-year-old Caesar Augustus and sheltered him in her arms.

A servant already was at the door with a lantern to greet the arriving stranger.

"I need to speak to Captain Rodney," the man said, not seeing Rodney back in the shadows.

Rodney stepped forward.

"I'm Captain Rodney," Thomas acknowledged.

"I come from Captain Pope," the visitor began, referring to the Delaware battalion's Fifth Company, commanded by Charles Pope.

"The captain told me to tell you there's a plan to attack and burn Dover."

"Burn Dover?" Rodney found it hard to believe.

"Yes, sir. Captain Pope told me to tell you that Thomas White and John Clark are behind it because of the attack on Mr. Clark the other night at the meeting in Dover. Captain Pope says Captain Basset has joined the plan."

Richard Basset commanded a militia company of light horse.

"Captain Pope says they also plan to burn Colonel Haslet's home."

Rodney shook his head, partly because of the extraordinary tale, partly to clear the last traces of sleepiness from his mind.

"How do you know this?" he demanded.

"One of Basset's company told Captain Pope. He said Basset's cavalry is to attack the town from the north and an infantry company will attack from the south, from Puncheon Run."

"What infantry company?" Rodney demanded.

"We don't know that, sir."

Patriots worried about the militia's loyalty and Rodney wondered if this might be alarming evidence of defections. He made some quick decisions.

He turned to the servant.

"I want you to ride to William Killen's plantation. Tell him what is happening and tell him I'd like him to meet me at the courthouse, as soon as possible. I'm going there right now."

"Yes, sir."

Rodney turned to the visitor. "Tell Captain Pope to meet me at the courthouse as quickly as he can get there."

The man returned to his horse, mounted, and dashed away. Rodney hurried upstairs.

Other servants had gathered out of curiosity at this midnight intrusion when Rodney came back, fully dressed, carrying his musket. He turned at the door, kissed his wife, who was still holding their child.

"Be careful, Thomas," she said.

"I will, dear," he responded and rode off quickly into the night, stopping en route to rouse Lieutenant Mark McCall and Ensign Simon Wilson of his own company.

Dawn was still a couple hours away when Killen arrived at Rodney's justice of the peace office near the courthouse. Charles Pope followed shortly afterwards.

"What monstrous plot are these men conceiving?" Killen asked as he settled into a chair. The servant had given Killen the barest of details, mentioning White and Clark.

Rodney pointed to Pope.

"Charles, would you please tell us all that you know?"

Pope did, repeating the information Rodney had learned from his midnight visitor.

Killen shook his head angrily. "Damn!" was his only comment.

"I assume Haslet is in Lewes," he said.

"Yes, he is," Pope interjected. "I've sent a message to him as well but I don't know that there'll be time to wait for his response. Some of the plotters are already at Puncheon Run."

Rodney reflected on the situation. He turned to McCall.

"Lieutenant, I want you to muster our company on the green as quickly as they can be assembled." McCall hurried out of the room.

"We must see to Longfield," Killen added, referring to Haslet's plantation.

"Yes," Rodney agreed. "Charles, I'll leave that to you. Assemble your company and march there as fast as you can."

"My soldiers are encamped near here," Pope said. "I'll have them on the road before dawn."

"Simon," Rodney said to young Wilson, "I want you to get Sergeant McNett and Corporal Dawson here immediately."

The meeting broke up, the various participants leaving to carry out their instructions. Killen lingered.

"What is your plan?" he asked Rodney.

"Why, I think I'll confront the conspirators immediately, surprise them before the sun is over the courthouse, and put an end to their nefarious scheme."

"Then I'll ride on to Longfield," Killen said, "and look after things until Pope's soldiers arrive."

"Very well," Rodney answered.

The sky had only suggestions of dawn when Rodney, accompanied by Ensign Wilson, Sergeant McNett, and Corporal Dawson and a few other soldiers arrived at Basset's plantation.

Basset's servants were just rising. Assuming the visitors were part of Basset's own company, the servants ignored them. There had been a frequency of such visits the past couple of days.

Basset was still in bed when his visitors forced their way into his home.

"Mr. Basset," Rodney announced, "I'm taking you into custody."

"For what reason?" the startled man demanded, struggling out of his bed.

"For breach of the peace," Rodney answered. "As a justice of the peace I'm exercising the powers of my office to arrest you."

"Nonsense!"

"We've learned of your plot to burn Dover," Rodney said "and intend there'll be no such harm done to our town."

"That's preposterous!"

"Time enough to defend yourself when we hold a hearing," Rodney said. "Now, get dressed, or we'll take you off to jail in your night clothes."

A flustered Basset complied and soon was off to Dover, escorted by Rodney and his soldiers, leaving a perplexed family and household entourage staring at the riders disappearing down the road.

At Longfield, Jemima Haslet drew a deep breath as she saw Killen approach the house. Would he be the bearer of bad news, she wondered.

"Good morning, William," she greeted him. "You're up and about early this morning. Nothing wrong I hope."

The last was as much prayer as statement.

"No, no," and, sensing her concern, he added: "put your mind at ease. I'm not here about John, I'm here because there's some talk among the discontented elements to make mischief and Longfield might be in their plans."

"Oh. And what might those plans be?"

"To seek revenge for the rough treatment your neighbor John Clark received at the meeting the other night. He and Thomas White and Richard Basset have devised some heinous endeavor to satisfy their anger."

He paused to judge Jemima's reaction, then continued.

"You shouldn't worry. Thomas Rodney and his troop are acting now to stop the miscreants before they get started and Charles Pope is coming down here with his company to make sure they don't decide to carry out any evil designs on Longfield. So, there's really nothing to worry about."

"I'm sure, William," she feigned relief. "Why don't you come in. I'm about to feed the family and you're certainly family to us."

"Thank you, Jemima. I am hungry. I've been up for a few hours."

He went inside and seated himself. He and Jemima chatted idly while she served him and the children, curious about the reasons for "Uncle William's" visit. Early morning visits of friends weren't unusual but there was a seriousness in Killen's and their mother's faces that made the children wonder.

In a couple of hours, Pope and his company could be seen encamping just down the road. Pope rode up to the house.

"Mrs. Haslet," he said, "I just wanted you to know that my men will be camping around your plantation. We'll discourage any attempts by the malcontents around here to do mischief around here."

"Thank you, captain," she said. "Are your men properly supplied with food? If not, I have ample here and I can put the servants to work preparing it."

"That won't be necessary, ma'am," Pope responded. "We're setting up our own mess."

Killen noted that Pope had set up pickets around the perimeter of the plantation. Satisfied that all was secure, he bade goodbye to Jemima and the children and rode off.

By noon, Rodney also had several associates of Basset in custody and turned his attention to the infantry company south of town.

The first move came from them.

A disparate collection of militia had gathered at Puncheon Run, under Clark's command, awaiting instructions for the attack on the town, when word of the arrests reached them. Clark realized the plans obviously had been seriously compromised. He decided to send a messenger to Dover, asking for a conference with Rodney.

Rodney turned him down. A frustrated Clark instructed the messenger to return to Rodney and insist on a meeting.

"Tell him," Clark said to the messenger, "that we will not disperse until the men responsible for the outrage against me are arrested and hanged."

It was almost dark when the messenger returned with word that Rodney not only had refused but said he was preparing to march on their position with his own militia company.

Clark looked at his disorganized assortment of soldiers. He considered that Rodney had a trained, disciplined core of soldiers at his command, that his group would be overmatched. The best course, he decided, was for his men and himself to disperse just as quickly as they could.

That ended the plot as far as it was directed at Kent County, but word of the June 8 assault on Clark fed the festering discontent among Tories in Sussex County, where they were more numerous and better organized.

Men sympathetic to Thomas Robinson had been gathering near his store, anticipating some movement to deal with the patriots, now emboldened by the presence of Haslet's soldiers. It was the ominous implications of this developing Tory presence that had prompted Henry Fisher on June 11 to send a messenger to Philadelphia to ask Congress for help. Fully mobilized, Fisher suspected, the Tories might overwhelm the patriots in Sussex.

There were further concerns about the intentions of Virginia Governor Lord Dunmore, reported to be assembling loyal forces that might sweep the entire area between the Chesapeake and Delaware Bays.

Haslet, meanwhile, had set up camp at Fisher's house, contemplating how to deal with Tory activity. Rumors seemed to arrive at his headquarters almost hourly. He was concerned that the two companies at his disposal could eventually be outnumbered by the Tory militia. Except for Pope's company at Longfield, the rest of his battalion was north, encamped in New Castle County. He had to consider the possibility of adding reinforcements.

He sent for Second Lieutenant Enoch Anderson of the First Company, then camped at New Castle, to come down and help out. He liked the twenty-year-old officer, found him to be very intelligent, physically fit, and dependable; one who could be counted on to help organize assistance if Haslet determined a need.

Used to the friendly environment of New Castle County where the sentiment was overwhelmingly in favor of the patriot cause, Anderson was shocked by the feelings he encountered as he rode south.

His uniform, of course, revealed his service and he found passing horsemen glancing disapprovingly at him. (A rarity among the regiments being assembled for the Continental Army, the Delaware Continentals were mostly all uniformed.) He passed a group working on the King's Highway (the main road between New Castle and Lewes) and heard someone refer to him as "one of the damned Haslet's men." He prodded his horse and moved on.

Farther down the highway he stopped at a wayside inn.

"There's one of the rebels," a person standing nearby hollered out.

He was pulled roughly off his horse by two other men.

"I mean you no harm," Anderson said, pulling himself free. "I'm on business of my regiment and that business doesn't concern you."

"And what might that business be?" asked one of the three men.

"I'm not free to say," Anderson responded.

"I doubt that business would please us," commented one.

Anderson looked at the group around him, his posture defiant, his stare intimidating. The men backed off a bit. This had started out to them as a mere diversion but Anderson's reaction took the fun out of it.

"Oh, let him proceed," suggested one. "He's only one man. He's no threat to us."

The tension of the encounter had broken.

Anderson's saddle bags had fallen to the ground when he was pulled off his saddle and as he reached for them a couple of the men picked them up. His concern they might try to take their contents disappeared as they helped him place the bags over the saddle.

"Thank you," Anderson said as politely as he could, springing on to his horse. He trotted slowly off towards Lewes, feigning indifference to the scene behind him.

He went straight to Fisher's house overlooking the Delaware Bay when he arrived in Lewes. Haslet, Major Thomas McDonough, and Adjutant Thomas Holland, recently promoted to second lieutenant, were discussing tactics as he walked in.

"Lieutenant Anderson," Haslet gave him a warm greeting and handshake. "Glad you made it safely. Did you have any trouble?"

"Well, Colonel, I've found the atmosphere down here much different from New Castle County. There certainly are a lot more Tories down here than up north."

Anderson recounted the experience at the inn up the road.

Haslet smiled. "That's why we're here."

"Well, what do you wish of me, Colonel?" Anderson asked.

"Before we talk, I have some business to finish here, so why don't you look around town and get a sense of things."

"Be careful," McDonough warned him. "You're not in New Castle County anymore.

"Yes, sir," Anderson responded and departed.

A tavern is always a good source of news, Anderson thought, so he stopped at the first place he found. Not only could he learn what was on people's minds but a little refreshment would wash away the effects of his long ride from New Castle.

It happened to be Thomas Evans' tavern and Anderson knew as soon as he entered that the environment was hostile. Dislike was on almost every face. He ordered a large bowl of rum and sat down at a table, listening to the pieces of conversation around the room. "Rebel" and "Haslet's soldier" were clear in the babel of talk. Enough time spent here, he thought, and stood up, feigned nonchalance and headed toward the door.

"Just a minute" shouted a large, rough-looking man in the room. Anderson ignored him and quickened his pace.

"Grab him," someone else shouted. "Grab that damned rebel. He's one of that damned Haslet's men. Don't let him get away."

Anderson made it outside before anyone could reach him. Curious bystanders gathered to investigate the commotion and a few men, cradling muskets in their arms, came to Anderson's side. His pursuers stopped in the doorway, mindful that the armed bystanders might be members of Haslet's forces.

"Is there a problem?" one of the bystanders asked. "Are you with Colonel Haslet?"

"Yes," Anderson responded, identifying himself, "and everything is fine."

The group from the inn turned and went back inside. Anderson returned to Fisher's home.

Haslet listened while Anderson told of his encounter at the inn.

"I should have warned you that the inn is a known Tory den," Haslet said. "We may have to put that place out of business."

Anderson nodded vigorously.

"Sir, what do you think is going to happen?"

"I don't really know. Thomas Robinson is the leader of the local Tories and he's been gathering a group of men at his store for a few days now. I doubt their feelings towards us are friendly. We know Robinson has sent messengers out to the warships in the bay. We can only assume they've asked for help from that quarter. Mr. Fisher has got people keeping an eye for any indication of a landing party."

"How many warships are there?"

"About eight, as far as we can tell," Haslet said. "They're keeping a respectful distance from shore, however. I think the lesson our gunboats gave them up the river last month has made the British more cautious.

"Anyhow, stay a couple more days, get a sense of things here. I've ordered the rest of the battalion to come down and I'll count on you to brief the commanders."

Anderson left to observe security at Fisher's barn where Haslet had arranged to store arms and ammunition.

As tension increased with the growing number of armed men gathering in and about Lewes, Haslet decided to seek a meeting of the two sides, hoping for an agreement that would avoid bloodshed. He wasn't afraid of a fight, but he felt that it would be better to establish respect for each side's point of view than to risk a bloody divide within the lower counties.

The meeting duly took place in mid-June at the home of William Bradley, a local political leader acceptable to both sides. The patriots denied any plan to harm the loyalists. The latter, on their part, said they had no plans to start an insurrection, that feelings had been stirred only by the mistreatment of John Clark earlier in the month.

The mutual assurances seemed to relieve tensions. There were even some friendly exchanges between the locals and the uniformed visitors in the next few days.

Arrival of the remainder of Haslet's battalion on June 19 and of Colonel Samuel Mile's Pennsylvania riflemen the day after—sent by Congress—provided the overwhelming numbers that forced loyalists to forego any thought of regaining the upper hand in Sussex County. They would have to wait for a better opportunity.

Two days later, the twenty-second, Caesar Rodney and John Evans (New Castle County) arrived to evaluate the situation for an official report to the Delaware Assembly.

"You'll be cheered by the news I bring you, John," Rodney said on greeting Haslet at Fisher's house. "Our assembly agreed last Saturday to form a new government. All the present officeholders will continue in office, only now their allegiance is to our government, not the Crown."

Rodney's enthusiasm was obvious in the contrast to his normally reserved manner.

"That date, June 15, will be one we'll celebrate forever in the lower counties!"

"It's truly a memorable event," Haslet agreed. "Will that be a permanent arrangement?"

"No, only until we can determine how we'll go about creating a new framework of government for the colony. I suspect we'll call for a convention to do that business."

He smiled broadly.

"But, John. Think of it! Delaware has decided to govern itself! We've practically declared ourselves an independent colony!"

"It's what we've hoped for these many months," Haslet said, matching Rodney's enthusiasm, "ever since it became clear that scrambling group of monkeys in London would never honor our rights.

"By the way, what about Governor Penn?"

"For now," Rodney said, "I'll be the chief executive as speaker of the House. A permanent arrangement is one of those things we'll have to take up when we decide on the final form of government. I don't know what will happen to Governor Penn. I suppose he'll have the choice of living quietly in Pennsylvania or elsewhere or going to England."

"I'm sure the colony will be in capable hands," Haslet said. It came as a simple statement of fact, not flattery, but Rodney obviously appreciated it.

"What's the Congress up to?" Haslet asked.

"I haven't been to Philadelphia since our assembly session convened," Rodney responded. "I understand Richard Henry Lee of Virginia introduced a resolution declaring all the colonies independent of England. A committee has been formed to write a resolution to that effect, but it hasn't been brought to a vote yet."

"That's a long reach. Will it succeed?"

"I don't know, John. It's one thing to say we're going to run our own lives. To some that holds out the possibility that some relationship with Parliament and the king may be resumed under new terms. But to declare ourselves completely independent, no longer loyal to the Crown, no longer a part of the empire . . ."

Rodney paused for a long moment.

"That step terrifies many of the delegates."

"Of course, England is not going to simply accept such a declaration," Haslet commented.

"No. No. It won't. I suspect considerable blood will have to be shed before it is accomplished."

"Well, I'm prepared to shed mine," Haslet said, reaching deep into his feelings for the appropriate words. "I believe in this country. It's been good to me. There's promise here that never existed for me in Ireland, nor for any of my people. Promise there was only for the privileged and the sycophants."

Rodney observed him appreciatively. He shared Haslet's dreams and was just as passionate about them, but his ardor was an inner fire that he kept hidden from others.

"One other thing you should know, John," Rodney continued after a while. "General Washington has asked that a flying camp be established at Perth Amboy in the Jersey colony. He's asked that 10,000 continental soldiers be sent there to be at his disposal as he sees fit. Congress has agreed and I expect your battalion will get its marching orders in due time."

"I hope we'll be ready when the order comes," Haslet said. "My men are still not fully equipped. We're also waiting for more uniforms. However, we're working to resolve these problems. I hope we'll be ready to march before too long."

Four days later, Rodney left for home, deciding to rest before returning to the business in Philadelphia. He suspected that business would demand a considerable expenditure of his energy and his health had long been fragile.

He wondered what the committee on independence would present to the Congress. With Benjamin Franklin and John Adams on it he was sure they would present a strong case. They also had on the committee young Thomas Jefferson, a Virginian who had been active in the patriot cause in that colony's House of Burgesses, and Roger Sherman of Connecticut and Robert Livingston of New York.

A distinguished group, Rodney thought, a good cross section of the talent assembled in Philadelphia to plot the future of the North American colonies. But would the Congress vote for independence? Should that be the committee's recommendation, Rodney decided, he would certainly support it.

Meanwhile the advance ships and personnel of what would become an enormous British military and naval force had arrived in New York harbor. Sir William Howe, the army commander-in-chief, was with them and set up headquarters on Staten Island.

Chapter Twenty-Six

Independence

It was late evening of July 1, 1776, and Caesar Rodney was already into a deep sleep when a knock on his bedroom door stirred him. He raised his head, listened, decided it was only a dream, and let his head fall to the pillow again.

A frail man, he still didn't feel fully rested from the last busy weeks. First in Philadelphia, as a delegate to the Continental Congress, then to New Castle for the session of the Delaware Assembly which he served as speaker, then on to Lewes in Sussex County to find out first hand about Tory activity down there. He had returned to Dover only a few days previously.

The assembly session was especially notable as he maneuvered that body into a decision to form a new government over the objections of loyalist members.

There. No mistake. Someone had knocked discreetly on his bedroom door.

"What is it?" he called out.

"It's Samuel, Mr. Rodney. There's a gentleman downstairs who says he has an urgent message for you from Mr. McKean in Philadelphia."

Rodney became fully awake now. He got out of bed, opened his door, and followed his servant down the stairs, the light from Samuel's lantern dimly defining the stair treads.

A man stood in the shadow of the front door, his hat showing he had recently ridden in the rain. In fact, lightning flashed off in the distance, but too far away for its thunder to be heard here.

"Mr. Rodney, I'm Jonathan Gray. I've just come from Philadelphia with a message of such urgency I've not stopped once along the way but to refresh my horse and myself."

"And what is your message?" Rodney asked.

"Mr. McKean told me to tell you that the Congress is about to vote on a resolution for independence and that you must come to vote if Delaware is to support that resolution."

"Isn't Mr. Read also there?" Rodney asked. "His vote should carry our colony's vote with Mr. McKean."

Rodney, however, had had enough conversations with Read to anticipate the messenger's answer.

"No, sir. Mr. McKean says Mr. Read is opposed and if Delaware is going to vote for the resolution, you must cast the deciding vote. Mr. McKean said to tell you that it is very important that Delaware vote favorably because the Congress wishes the vote of all the colonies to be unanimous. He also says a couple of other states are waiting to see what Delaware does."

"I see," Rodney said. "Very well. Samuel, prepare my things and my horse for travel."

He turned to his visitor.

"Thank you very much Mr. Gray. I suspect you've done your country a very great favor tonight."

"Your country." Rodney realized that was the first time he had spontaneously thought of North America as one country. It is true the delegates to the Congress talked of the united colonies of America, or the united states of America, but that was not quite the same as thinking of them as one country.

It was a thrilling thought and spurred his preparations to leave for Philadelphia. There was indeed important business awaiting him in that city.

Dark clouds almost totally obscured the moon as he mounted his horse. Off in the distance he could see flashes of lightning and the horizon appeared to be a wall of gray, suggesting a rainstorm.

Well, he was dressed for it. He secured his hat to his head, tightened his cloak around his neck, reined his horse towards the King's Highway, and was off. Philadelphia was more than eighty miles away.

He was a frail specter as he rode through the night, often silhouetted against the dark sky by the brilliant white flashes of lightning. Rain ran off his hat and down his cloak.

He moved as rapidly as he could, slowing only where pools had formed in the road from the downpour, stopping to rouse a ferryman where he had to cross streams too wide and too deep to ford and to change horses at a wayside inn. At more than one inn the owner provided him with a drink and a bit of cold meat while the fresh horse was being saddled.

Through the ride, his excitement sustained him, making him oblivious to the elements. If his spirits sagged, he would quickly remind himself that he was about to experience a unique political event when he reached Philadelphia, certainly the most momentous event in his life if not in the history of the North American colonies.

Dawn eased the difficulty of the ride and also saw the rain ease. There was a hint of a better day in patches of blue on the western horizon. Eventually those patches grew bigger, the clouds lessened, and sun began shining on the rain-drenched land. The relief was only temporary, however. Intermittent showers appeared by early afternoon when Rodney reined up outside the State House on Chestnut Street in Philadelphia. McKean quickly appeared from inside.

"Caesar," he exclaimed, "I knew I could count on you."

"If the business is what I anticipate, it will be well worth the journey," Rodney responded.

"Well, we're very close to voting. I persuaded the delegates to delay to allow time for you to arrive."

"What are the prospects?"

"Well, yesterday it appeared South Carolina, Pennsylvania, and New York would oppose. John Adams has argued eloquently in favor of the resolution. It comes down to this: if Delaware supports the resolution, South Carolina will go along and John Dickinson and Robert Morris will absent themselves so Pennsylvania will also have a majority in support. We're divided. Read thinks we're premature in acting for independence and will not support it. New York's delegation lacks a quorum so they won't participate."

He waited for Rodney to indicate he understood, then continued.

"So, with Delaware's vote there'll be no opposition."

"Let's proceed then," Rodney said and the two men walked inside to the chamber where the delegates milled around the room, waiting for Rodney's arrival. They all turned to look at the sight of the muddy, rain-soaked figure as he walked into the room and moved to welcome him. His purposeful demeanor made it unnecessary to ask him about his intentions on the issue before them.

Rodney's entrance was a signal to President John Hancock to gavel the session to order.

"Gentlemen of the Congress," he announced, "we have before us on the table a resolution of the delegate from Virginia, Richard Henry Lee, that the united colonies of North America ought to be free and independent states."

There was a great degree of the stage actor in Hancock's voice for this occasion.

"The clerk will call the roll of the states."

One by one the delegations declared for the resolution and even the knowledge it would pass did not diminish the excitement, which increased as the roll proceeded.

Clerk Charles Thompson handed over the tally to Hancock.

"The resolution is unanimously adopted and this Congress hereby has declared that these colonies are free and independent states!"

The pronouncement rang through the suddenly silent room, then there was a burst of applause and the members milled around congratulating each other.

Hancock waited for the members to enjoy the moment, then called them back to order.

"Gentlemen, the next and equally important order of business is the declaration drafted by the select committee to explain the action we have just taken. It is equally important for our citizens—indeed for the whole world—to understand why we have voted as we just did. The clerk will proceed to read the declaration."

Thompson began to read from the paper before him.

"When, in the course of human events, it becomes necessary for one people to dissolve the political bonds which have connected them with another, and to assume among the powers of the earth the separate and equal station to which the laws of nature and of nature's God entitle them, a decent respect to the opinions of mankind requires that they should declare the causes which impel them to the separation."

"Ah, the poetry and style are Jefferson," Rodney thought as the reading continued, "but the arguments speak of John Adams and the common touch is Benjamin Franklin."

Adams, McKean had said, carried the debate the day before on behalf of Lee's resolution and would also lead the debate on the Declaration of Independence.

Franklin, at age seventy, had little to say at any time in the Congress but when he did speak up, it was to summarize the debate in simple terms and thereby hasten its end.

Rodney's attention returned to Thompson as the clerk came to the conclusion of the declaration.

"We, therefore, the representatives of the United States of America, in general congress assembled, appealing to the Supreme Judge of the World for the rectitude of our intentions, do, in the name and authority of the good people of these colonies, solemnly publish and declare, that these united colonies are, and of right ought to be, free and independent states, that they are absolved from all allegiances to the British Crown, and that all political connections between them and the state of Great Britain is and ought to be totally dissolved, and that as free and independent states they have full power to levy war, conclude peace, contract alliances, establish commerce and to do all other acts and things which independent states may of right do. And for the support of this declaration, with a firm reliance on the protection of divine providence, we mutually pledge to each other our lives, our fortunes and our sacred honor."

Once more there was a hush in the room. Many eyes glistened as the import of the words filled them with pride—pride in their work, pride in their colonies, pride in their colleagues. It was a moment of bonding among the delegates, even those opposed to independence.

After an interval of time to allow the mood to run its course, the debate began. There would be few changes—the most notable being a decision to delete a whole section that impugned the institution of slavery and placed the stigma of its origins and survival on the Crown—before the Declaration was adopted two days later, on July 4. It would be another month, however, before the delegates affixed their signatures to the document. Read would be among the signers.

Word of the Congressional action reached Dover on July 5, as the Council of Safety met to vote on changes in the roster of officers for the Delaware battalion. Haslet was there, both as a member of the council and, of course, as commanding officer.

The meeting was interrupted by the breathless intrusion of a man who announced he had just ridden from Philadelphia.

"The Congress has declared us free and independent states!" he exclaimed.

The man was so excited he had to parcel out the information, pausing frequently to catch his breath.

"On Tuesday.

"They also approved a Declaration of Independence yesterday."

He handed the paper to Chairman John McKinly.

"I also have a message for Colonel Haslet."

He looked around the room and a tall man in a military uniform approached him.

"I'm Colonel Haslet."

Haslet took an enveloped, sealed, addressed to: "Colonel John Haslet, Commander, Delaware Continentals."

'This is momentous," McKinly declared, reading the paper in his hand. It was a copy of Lee's resolution, approved on July 2.

"I think we should march over to the courthouse and read that to the people," Thomas Rodney said.

"Splendid idea," McKinly agreed. "Gentlemen, let's assemble and march in a body."

Haslet, meanwhile, had opened his message. It was the long-awaited marching orders for his regiment. He reread it, then lowered it to his side and looked off into the distance.

"What's the message?" William Killen asked. Haslet hesitated, then turned to his friend.

"The Congress wants me to move the battalion to Wilmington and await further orders."

A pleased look spread over his face, but his eyes said something more. Killen knew that look by now. Haslet has learned that he will finally be able to act on his convictions. His friend was never satisfied at idleness when he felt action was demanded.

"So. It appears you are soon to join the Continental army," was Killen's only comment.

"I suspect you're right, William. Well, let's take care of the more important news first."

They joined the members filing out of the meetinghouse. Outside, they assembled in a column of twos. Someone had found a drummer to beat time as they circled Dover Green.

The obvious glee on the council members' faces, the drum beat—always a summons in colonial times—began attracting a crowd.

"What is it? What's happened?" people in the crowd asked the marching column.

"Join us at the courthouse and we'll tell you," was the answer.

When the column finished circling the green, the council assembled by the steps of the courthouse, surrounded by a growing crowd of passersby. People stood on doorsteps of nearby homes and at the windows and doorways of the courthouse, curious to find out the meaning of this almost boyish behavior of the distinguished members of the Council of Safety.

McKinly walked up to the top step.

"I have a message from Philadelphia," he began. "It informs us that the Congress has declared the colonies of North America free and independent states!"

Loud cheers filled the air, overwhelming the few sounds of disappointment, a disappointment that was shared, but silently, by some members of the Council.

"There should be a celebration," someone shouted.

"There must be a feast," another agreed.

"This is the most magnificent moment in our lives," a third added.

"It will be done," McKinly announced. Noticing innkeeper French Battell in front of the crowd, he addressed him:

"Frenchie, get some people to help you and take charge of the preparations. This day won't be complete until we've feasted the independent State of Delaware and the United Colonies of America."

"We have some fine turtles brought up from the bay just this morning," Battell announced. "They'll make a proper soup."

With that the innkeeper grabbed a few others and began issuing instructions to light a few fires, assemble cooking kettles, gather torches, solicit refreshments.

Satisfied, McKinly turned to his council members.

"Let's return to our business, gentlemen. Then we can celebrate."

When they emerged from the meeting a few hours later, there were several roaring fires on Dover Green. Kettles suspended over the fires sent out an aroma of fine turtle meat. Tables were filled with an assortment of breads, fruits, and sweet treats.

The council members once again assembled in a column. This time, Thomas Rodney had summoned his light infantry troop to the green. When the council was ready, McKinly, cradling a painting of King George III, stepped out, preceded by a drummer. Behind the council members rode Rodney's soldiers, followed by drummers and fifers playing martial airs. They circled the green then marched to the middle where one fire burned alone.

McKinly stepped forward, took the painting from the drummer and solemnly proclaimed:

"Compelled by strong necessity, thus we destroy even the shadow of that king who refused to reign over a free people."

With that he pitched the painting into the flames.

The crowd's cheers resonated across the green as the portrait of their once beloved sovereign was consumed.

Frenchie Battell's Tavern on Dover Green
Photo by Fred B. Walters

"Well, it's done," Killen commented to Haslet, who stared at the flames gradually spreading over the painting. The face of the now reviled king was the last bit of the painting to blacken, then disappear.

"I would have expected a more rousing reaction from you," Killen continued. Haslet turned away from the fire.

"I am excited about this, William, as you know I would be. I'm simply reflecting on the events this declaration has put in motion. We all know our independence won't be a fact until the British government accepts it. We all know they won't accept it easily. That's not the character of the present government.

"Now I have orders from the Congress to march my regiment to Wilmington, but I don't expect us to stay there too long. Congress has also indicated it will want us to move on to join Washington. My assumption is we'll be in a good position at Philadelphia to go wherever we're needed. To New York, if that's where the issue is to be joined. Or, if the British decide to make an attempt on Philadelphia, they may come from the Chesapeake or up the Delaware. We'll be prepared to march in any direction. We'll soon test how firm our resolve is to be independent."

He looked around at the preparations for the feast.

"I'm sorry to have to miss this feast," he said, wistfully. "It certainly appears it's going to be a memorable night. But I must join my regiment in Lewes."

"Do you plan to stop at Longfield?" Killen asked.

"Yes, I'll stop overnight to be with the family and tell them the plans. I fear I won't be seeing much of them in the months ahead."

Killen walked with Haslet to the stable, bade him "God speed" and watched as he mounted and rode off in the deepening twilight.

Haslet could see the light from the kitchen fireplace in Longfield as he rode down his road. There was nearly a full moon and the night was cloudless. Shortly after he turned off the King's Highway several deer dashed across the road in front of him. It all reminded him of how precious this land had become to him and he felt some sorrow at the thought he would be seeing so little of it and his family as he went off to face the British.

Jemima was sitting by the fireplace knitting clothing for the baby when she heard him arrive outside and turn his horse over to one of the servants. She met him at the door and he grabbed her firmly in his strong arms and held her head against his shoulder. She could sense there was a touch of sadness in him and with her uncanny sense of events that touched their lives she suspected he was going away. But she would let him break the news.

He stood silently by the door, grabbed her hand, and led her towards a bench by the little garden she had fashioned around the front door. They sat and he put his arms around her again.

"Well," he began, "I've been ordered by the Continental Congress to take my regiment north to Wilmington and then on to Philadelphia. I don't know what will happen after that. Washington has his main force encamped at New York. He also has a force attempting to take Quebec and another force in the south. I have no idea what plans he may have for me. There's talk the British may try a direct assault on Philadelphia, either coming up the river or from the Chesapeake. No one really knows. General Howe has had his army at Halifax and the reports are that as soon as he receives reinforcements he'll move on Washington. I've heard from my family that several thousand soldiers have been ordered from Ireland to join Howe. That's also in the newspapers. We've also been told that Howe sent General Henry Clinton to attack South Carolina."

"But, John, is there no more effort to get the government to change its mind, now that they've given up on Boston? Is it possible to restore peace between us and England?"

"I've forgotten to tell you the most important news of the day," he said, and he knew from what she just said that this news would be very disappointing.

"Three days ago the Congress passed a resolution declaring the colonies free and independent of British rule. We no longer hold any allegiances to Parliament or King George, nor do we consider ourselves part of the British Empire. We are the United Colonies of North America."

She knew that pleased him, but she could not help but worry about its impact on their lives.

"I suppose there was no recourse," she finally responded. "I just wish it could stop at that and we could go on enjoying our lives, raising our children, making Longfield all that we dream for it. I suppose, however, the British won't just go away and leave us in peace."

"No, I'm afraid they won't," he admitted. "The men in London seem determined that we shall live according to their designs and they are determined to crush us, it seems, unless we submit. We won't, of course, but they can't see that.

"Certainly, those among them who have visited here, seen this land, mingled with the American people, sense their spirit, know better. However, there are precious few of them. The rest just see America as a resource to be exploited."

"Strange," she said, "to hear you refer to this land as 'America.' That's something I'll have to get used to. America."

"It's on everybody's tongue now," he told her.

They sat for a long time on the bench, discussing the children, making plans for the management of the plantation while he was gone, but he remembered she already had proven herself quite capable of that.

After a time they went inside and to bed and enjoyed their love of each other.

Before the month ended newspaper dispatches confirmed the British buildup in New York, reporting New York harbor was filled with the sails of British warships and transports and that thousands of British soldiers had been landed at Staten Island.

Chapter Twenty-Seven

Off to War

Patches of light were widening over Delaware Bay as Haslet said goodbye to Jemima and the children on the morning of July 6, 1776.

He held each of them tightly, lastly Jemima. She clung to him for a long time in silence before she finally released him.

Then he was on his horse and headed towards the crossing of the Mispillion and south towards Lewes. His head was still filled with the news from the day before about the Continental Congress' vote for independence and as he journeyed south he pondered the implications for the colonies, for his battalion, for his family, for himself.

But there was much to be done in Lewes, preparing the battalion to march north to Wilmington and—who knows where from there. And, of course, there was the Tory activity in Sussex County to be considered. He had been directed by Congress to leave one company behind to deal with the Tories and had decided it would be Henry Darby's Fourth Company.

On his arrival, Haslet immediately summoned his officers to a meeting at his headquarters by Henry Fisher's house. He first told them the news about independence, news that was greeted with cheers and backslapping. He allowed the feelings to run their course before he spoke again.

"Gentlemen, the purpose of the Delaware battalion from this point will be to help secure that independence. We've been ordered north, to Wilmington. From there I expect we'll be ordered to take our place in the ranks of the Continental army, probably in New York."

There were expressions of approval. His officers were ready to put their military skills to the test and believed the rank-and-file was, too.

"We're ready, Colonel," Adjutant Thomas Holland said. "The men are in fine spirits. We've not had one soldier desert in four months."

(About a dozen men had deserted in the first three months after the battalion was organized.)

"We're going to keep one company down here to deal with the dissidents," Haslet said. "Captain Darby, that will be you and your company. I hope it won't be necessary to keep you here very long."

Darby was a solid officer, with a staff that included a future leader of the battalion, First Lieutenant Robert Kirkwood.

(Kirkwood remained with the battalion to the end of the war, leading it with distinction in several southern battles. After the war he moved west and served on the western frontier. He was killed on November 4, 1791, his thirty-third battle in the service of the new United States.)

"I'll be meeting with Colonel Hall in a short while for a briefing," Haslet said, then turned to Darby. "Henry, I want you and your officers to remain for that meeting. The rest of you go back to your companies now. You may tell them about independence, but please keep our orders to yourselves until we have a chance to plan the movement."

Colonel Hall, commander of the Sussex County militia, arrived as the meeting broke up, stopped to chat with his son David, commander of the battalion's First Company, then proceeded inside, greeted Haslet, and sat down. His face spoke of serious business on his mind.

"Well, David," Haslet began "tell me what the Tories are up to in Sussex County."

"I've written a report for the Congress about the situation," Hall began. "I've witnessed some of it, the rest comes from a number of patriots in the Broad Creek and Wicomico areas. I'd like you to see that it's delivered."

Haslet nodded.

He handed his report to Haslet. It included testimony from the Broad Creek area gathered by several patriots.

"I'm sure you know that a large majority of the people in the lower part of this county appear disaffected," Hall said. "That's lately been fully demonstrated by their hostile appearances.

"The most alarming circumstance is that Lord Dunmore is recruiting with success among them. I am told they repair to him without reserve and supply him with the produce of the country."

Haslet frowned but allowed Hall to continue uninterrupted.

"The warship *Fowey* has been operating in the Nanticoke River in Maryland and we're told that they're being provided with cattle and provisions. Furthermore, vast numbers of the people in Somerset and Dorchester Counties (in Maryland) and Sussex County have enlisted to serve on those British ships and I'm told they're trading, enlisting, even taking an oath of allegiance, and only the Good Lord knows what other treasonous acts."

"That is most alarming," Haslet agreed.

"Of course," Hall said. "These people are far more dangerous to us than the British because they know our country well and can guide the ships to the heads of our rivers.

"Your soldiers and our militia took up some of the most insolent and put them in confinement. They disarmed the offenders of lesser concern. But I'm sorry to say this has not improved the attitude of these people. I had hoped they would have worn a face much more in favor of our country than they now show."

"How large a force are we talking about?" Haslet asked.

"I would say they outnumber us by six to one."

Haslet pondered that for a long time and his face revealed his concern. The thought occurred to him that he might be endangering the lower counties—and his family—by withdrawing his battalion to march north.

Hall intruded on the silence.

"I believe, John, that with three or four companies of soldiers we'll be able to defend ourselves against any force the Tories can muster."

"I'll be leaving only Henry Darby and his company here," Haslet said and waited for Hall to consider the result.

"Well, John, I think we can assemble enough dependable militia to keep things under control."

"I pray that you're right, David. I believe a few hundred men dedicated to freedom can prevail over a disaffected mob of people whose only dedication is to their own selfish interests. Surely God is on our side."

The two men rose to their feet and the others present also rose.

"Thank you for your report, David," Haslet said. "Did you ever dream, when we served together in the assembly, that some day we'd be fighting for Delaware's independence? Or the independence of the entire continent?"

"I truly believe in it," Hall responded. "By the way, my son tells me that you and the battalion are headed north, perhaps to join Washington. I feel comfortable knowing his life will be in your hands."

Haslet accepted the compliment in silence but squeezed the older man's hands in appreciation and understanding. Hall strode out of the tent.

Haslet rode out the next day to meet with John Dagworthy, the militia general for Sussex County. Seven years older than Haslet, he also had served in the French and Indian War. In fact, he had held a commission in the British army, a rarity among colonials.

Haslet remembered that many had favored Dagworthy to command the Delaware battalion, but there was no obvious animosity as the general received him graciously at his plantation. He owned more than 20,000 acres of land, a reward to him from the colony of Maryland for his service in the French and Indian War. At the time the land was part of that colony but when Charles Mason and Jeremiah Dixon completed their survey settling the boundaries between Pennsylvania and Maryland, the new boundaries put Dagworthy's land in Delaware. His title was promptly accepted by Governor John Penn in 1769.

"Colonel Haslet, so glad to see you," Dagworthy said. "Your messenger advised me that you wanted to discuss the political situation in Sussex."

"Greetings, General," Haslet responded. "Yes, I wanted to discuss the disaffected here. Colonel Hall tells me they are numerous, but poorly organized."

"True. True," Dagworthy conceded. "They listen only to that rascal Thomas Robinson. Fortunately, there's not a military sense among the lot of them or we'd be truly troubled."

"What about Dunmore? I hear he's active in this area."

"There have been incursions along the Nanticoke," Dagworthy conceded, "but he seems to be more concerned about the Virginia colony. Governor Eden of Maryland has fled to the *Fowey*. That warship has been active in the Chesapeake and the Nanticoke but he's not the leader Dunmore is and the people in his colony seem to look to

Dunmore. As long as Dunmore worries more about Virginia, they're not a threat to us."

"Do you think your militia can contain them?"

"Most certainly, colonel. My soldiers are loyal to the Delaware colony, not the king or that damned Parliament."

"That's very good news, General. You know I can't keep my battalion here much longer. There's a larger cause to be served and General Washington has asked Congress for reinforcements from the colonies. My soldiers are anxious to go."

Mention of Washington brought a smile to Dagworthy's face. During the French and Indian War Washington had objected strenuously when General Braddock, because of Dagworthy's royal commission, had granted him preference over Washington's colonial rank.

"I understand, Colonel," Dagworthy commented. "My only wish is that I could join you to fight in our common cause. Until then, however, you can depend on my militia to control the poor disaffected Tories."

Dagworthy's confidence was reassuring. The conversation turned to more mundane matters. He shared some of Dagworthy's brandy and after awhile stood to leave.

"How soon will you march, Colonel?" Dagworthy asked.

"Soon. Very soon," Haslet responded. He was reluctant to give any more information than that, even to Dagworthy. A few more words were exchanged and he left for Lewes. It was time to prepare to march.

Haslet spent the next few days with his officers, completing plans for the move north.

The next challenge to Haslet was to reinforce the dedication and enthusiasm among his soldiers for the task ahead. Securing liberty in the three lower counties was a cause easily understood, but the need to secure that right for people in other colonies was much more difficult to accept. There was no flag to wave, no patriotic songs to sing to rally a collective purpose. Somehow individual motivations had to be woven into a passion for a broader community.

The Declaration of Independence offered the opportunity.

On the tenth, Haslet directed his officers to assemble the battalion. A copy of the Congressional declaration had arrived, along with confirmation of the battalion's orders from Congress, and he wanted it read to them and to add a few words of his own.

267

Haslet was mounted as he watched the troops assemble. As line upon line of blue-coated soldiers stood at attention he felt pride in the military appearance of his troops, especially now that they all were uniformed. They looked the match of any army in the world.

"Adjutant Holland," he said to Thomas Holland, "you and the other officers have done a remarkable job in bringing this battalion to its present condition. I'm extremely proud to be their commander. And honored, too. Have them stand at ease."

Haslet's appreciation of his troops would be shared by many, including Washington, after they were tested in battle.

He turned to Major Thomas McDonough and handed him a sheet of paper.

"Soldiers," Haslet announced. "As you well know, the Continental Congress has declared Delaware and all its sister colonies free and independent states."

There were cheers from the ranks.

"We've received a copy of what is called the Declaration of Independence. Major McDonough will read it to you."

McDonough moved to the front of the ranks and read from the paper Haslet had handed him.

"When in the course of human events," McDonough began, "it becomes necessary for one people to dissolve the political bonds which had connected them with another and to assume among the powers of the earth the separate and equal station to which the laws of nature and of nature's God entitle them, a decent respect to the opinion of mankind requires that they should declare the causes which impel them to separation."

Haslet noticed the soldiers were giving McDonough their full attention, a good sign.

McDonough read the litany of complaints against the king that had led to the decision to sever the ties between him and his colonies in America. Then the conclusion:

"We, therefore, the representatives of the United States of America, in General Congress assembled, appealing to the Supreme Judge of the World for the rectitude of our intentions, do, in the name and by authority of the good people of these colonies, solemnly publish and declare that these united colonies are and of right ought to be, free and independent states . . ."

Cheers interrupted McDonough at this point and he stopped to let them fade away. He repeated the last phrase as he continued:

" . . . Free and independent states; that they are absolved from all allegiance to the British Crown, and that all political connection between them and the state of Great Britain is and ought to be totally dissolved; and that as free and independent states they have full power to levy war, conclude peace, contract alliances, establish commerce and to do all other acts and things which independent states may of right do.

"And for the support of this declaration, with a firm reliance on the protection of divine providence, we mutually pledge to each other our lives, our fortunes and our sacred honor."

McDonough finished almost in a whisper. There was an almost reverent silence in the ranks, then someone shouted: "We pledge our lives and honor as well."

Approval spread through the ranks in a wave of nodded heads, audible "yeas," and handshakes, backslapping.

Now it was time for their commander to spell out their mission.

Haslet waited for the echoes to fade away, then began speaking. There was a mix of the pulpit and the parade grounds in his delivery and a touch of bedside manner in his attitude as this erstwhile preacher turned doctor turned soldier spoke firmly to his troops.

"Men of the Delaware battalion, you've heard the declaration of the Congress of the United Colonies of America. It says we are no longer vassals of Great Britain. We are now Americans, an independent people."

Everything he expected of them, hoped from them, depended upon their acceptance of that fact.

"For many years we lived as free men, developing our plantations, raising our families, pursuing our businesses and we gave our allegiance to the Crown of England because it was a beneficent Ruler. We shipped the fruits of our labors to England and people on both sides of the ocean prospered from it.

"When a foreign power threatened our frontiers, which were the frontiers of the Empire of Great Britain as well as the frontiers of America, we left our plantations and our businesses to fight under the flag of Great Britain. And we fought to plant that flag permanently in the promised land of that frontier.

"The government has proved ungrateful!

"Somehow greed has poisoned the relationship between us. The government in Britain has chosen not to treat us as a treasured partner but as mere servants, toiling for their benefit alone and subject to the whimsy of insensitive public officials. In their rapacious designs they have even chosen to deny us our rights to the property we obtained from our own hard work, to deny us our birthright as free men.

"We tried to reason with the government and the king, to affirm our dedication to the king, to the empire. They turned their faces from us, refused to listen to us. We were ridiculed rather than respected. The more earnest our pleas, the more severe their treatment of us. They have invaded our villages, even our homes, and confiscated the fruits of our labors, even cut off our commerce."

Haslet paused, then his voice rose.

"They, therefore, have forfeited their right to our allegiance."

There were nods of understanding and agreement in the ranks.

"Now our Continental Congress has voted to sever all relationships with England. That action has opened the gate of opportunity for all of us. It is a gate we will pass through now, not as fiefs of a cruel and unappreciative sovereign and government but as free and independent Americans. God has blessed this land and I believe He will bless our cause."

Haslet paused, searching the sky as he thought of the words needed to prepare his troops for the coming events.

"At the beginning of the year, you pledged your service to a noble cause. It is to the cause of people from New England to the Carolinas who cherish their freedoms just as we do and who already have sacrificed in great measure for that cause. It is a common cause of people in Massachusetts Bay, in Maryland, in Virginia, as well as the people in the three lower counties on the Delaware. Just as the members of the Continental Congress pledged their lives, their fortunes, and their sacred honor, you have pledged yourselves to the cause of America.

"We are now members of the Continental army, united as Americans."

He emphasized "continental" and "Americans" so his next words would be clearly understood.

"The Continental Congress has ordered our battalion to move to Wilmington, except for Captain Darby's company, which will remain to keep the peace in Sussex County. The rest, I expect, will be ordered on from Wilmington to Philadelphia and, eventually, to join the command of General Washington.

"Until now, we have only been asked to secure the welfare of our families and neighbors. Now we have been asked to serve a much larger community. I can't promise you gold or silver as your reward, but something far more precious—the right to live as free men as God made us.

"We humbly ask that He look with favor on our cause. We ask His blessing on our endeavors, that He watch over our lives, over our families, over our land, over America."

Now he assumed the tone of the commander:

"Soldiers of the Continental army, let us march to secure this independence for the United Colonies of America."

The soldiers seemed to stand a bit straighter, their faces determined.

"Adjutant Holland. Bring the battalion to order. Have Captain Darby and his company return to their encampment. The rest of the battalion will march for Wilmington."

Holland turned to the captains and gave the order.

Haslet felt proud as the soldiers came to attention smartly, turned, and marched in perfect step to the King's Highway and headed north, Lieutenant Colonel Gunning Bedford riding at the head of the line, fifers and drummers providing the cadence. Darby's company remained at attention until the rest of the battalion was underway, then was dismissed.

Haslet remained behind to brief Darby and his officers on the mission to watch over the Tories in Sussex County.

He also met with Fisher, the river pilot whose workplace was the Delaware River and Bay, and who had a better sense of the politics of the area than anyone; knew his people as well as he knew his river and bay.

He held the rank of major in the militia and Haslet addressed him as such:

"Major, tell me of the British presence in the bay."

"I've spotted about eight vessels," Fisher responded. "The *Roebuck* is among them, but the fleet seems to be concerned only with stopping river traffic, not with events on the land. I'm told that some of the local disaffected asked the captain to supply them with arms and ammunition and he refused them."

"Good. Good," Haslet commented. "I trust the *Roebuck's* captain remembers the lesson our fellows gave him and his ship a couple months ago."

Fisher nodded and smiled.

"What's your opinion of Tory strength in Sussex?"

"I think they're capable of mischief," Fisher said. "There are many so-called loyalists here, far more than patriots."

"Is that going to be a problem if the battalion leaves?"

"Well, I think the militia can handle the situation, Colonel. Although the disloyal are many in number, they are few in heart. Except for Thomas Robinson and a few others, I doubt they would have stomach for a stiff fight."

"That's good to hear," Haslet said. He rose now and the two men exchanged small talk for a bit then Fisher left.

On the thirteenth, his business in Lewes concluded, Haslet took passage on a schooner headed for Wilmington.

A week later, on the twentieth, as Haslet had expected, orders from the Congress came to his headquarters at Wilmington to move his battalion to Philadelphia.

Dispatches in the newspapers made it clear to him that Philadelphia was only a temporary encampment.

The British forces had encamped on Staten Island and their numbers constantly increased. General William Howe, commander of all the British forces in North America, established his headquarters there.

Ships of the Royal Navy dotted the lower harbor: transports, warships, tenders. The Americans had nothing to challenge them except shore batteries at Brooklyn Heights and on Manhattan Island so they moved freely around the harbor. Some even ventured unimpeded up the Hudson River, known then as the North River.

Their presence became even more imposing on July 12 when it was augmented by an armada of 150 ships under the command of Admiral Richard Viscount Howe, the general's older brother.

Lord Howe's arrival touched off a celebration among the British forces. Sailors cheered; ships at anchor fired salutes, loyalist batteries on Staten Island joined in, even spectators lining the shores joined in hailing the fleet.

Settled at anchor, the assembled fleet was an awesome sight. Sails filled the bay and it seemed one could cross the harbor by walking from deck to deck.

(Not so grand an entrance was the arrival of a smaller fleet under the command of Commodore Peter Parker soon after. Splintered wood and tattered sails attested to a recent battle and suggested Parker's ships had not fared well. Newspaper accounts in late July confirmed it. On June 28, Parker's fleet had supported a landing force led by Lieutenant General Henry Clinton in an assault on Charleston, South Carolina, the largest town in the South. The American defense commanded by Major General Charles Lee and stirred by the leadership of Colonel Henry Moultrie of the South Carolina militia had mauled the British invaders, driving them off with heavy casualties. It was said a cannon ball had landed on the deck of Parker's flagship, the *Bristol*, setting the commodore's pants afire.)

Lord Howe quickly turned his attention to what he considered his primary mission to America. King George III had designated the Howe brothers as peace commissioners, so the admiral sent off messages to colonial authorities even while Sir William and his staff were planning to confront and demolish the American army.

The peace effort was badly handled. Lord Howe twice sent a message to Washington, addressed to "George Washington, Esquire," without mention of rank. Washington, who could be as imperious as any British peer, returned it unopened each time, insisting he would only receive mail that included his military rank in the address. The Americans were clearly offended by this offhand treatment of their commander-in-chief and the Congress concurred in his position.

In a half-hearted effort to make amends, the Howes sent General Howe's adjutant general, Colonel Patterson, to meet with Washington on July 20 at his headquarters in New York. Patterson attempted to explain that no slight was meant in the letters to Washington.

Patterson also carried with him copies of a message Lord Howe had sent to the colonial governors explaining his role as a peace commissioner with authority to offer pardons to any colonials and de facto colonial governments who would reaffirm their allegiance to the king and Parliament.

The meeting began with a discussion of Washington's complaints about treatment of Americans captured in the Canadian campaign.

Patterson explained that Howe had no jurisdiction over the British forces in Canada.

"Colonel, I have forwarded my complaints also to General Burgoyne," Washington replied. Major General John Burgoyne commanded the British forces in Canada.

"I have not had the courtesy of a reply as yet," he added coldly.

Patterson in turn, pressed Howe's own complaints about treatment of British General Richard Prescott, taken prisoner by the Americans at Montreal.

"I have no knowledge of General Prescott," Washington replied, "but be assured, Colonel, that it is my practice to treat such prisoners with kindness and the customary courtesies. I have no idea where General Prescott is being held but I feel confident he is being treated as I have directed all prisoners be treated."

Washington, it seemed, had a better sense of British military courtesies than the British themselves, contempt having replaced courtesy as the prevailing attitude towards the colonials.

But this discussion of prisoners seemed a mere preliminary to the purpose of Patterson's visit.

"Is this the intent of your mission?" Washington finally asked. "General Prescott and this message you wish me to forward to Philadelphia?"

"Lord Howe and Sir William asked that I present the essence of that message for your own consideration," Patterson responded, with some discomfort. He already perceived that the contents would be harshly considered by these rebellious colonials.

He went on to explain the offer the Howes were making to the colonists and their newly-formed governments.

Washington considered his answer at some length before speaking up.

"Colonel, you may inform Lord Howe and Sir William that I've no powers to accept such offer as they are so graciously making." Patterson detected some sarcasm in Washington's pronunciation of the word "graciously."

"I derive my power from the people of the United States of America through their representatives in Congress and, therefore, I must defer to the Congress on this matter."

Washington obviously was elevating Congress to the same rank as Parliament in his considerations. And it was pointed that he perceived that power came from the people, not a monarch.

"I might observe that their excellencies are offering only pardons. I feel quite strongly that those who have committed no wrong, have, therefore, no obligation to ask for any pardons for their behavior."

At this point, Washington stood straight as a ramrod in the room. He was exceptionally tall to begin with, but he had an ability to maximize the effect of his height. At those times he was a truly intimidating presence.

"We are only defending what we consider our rights as free men," he declared. "That action, I'm sure all free men would agree, does not warrant our asking for forgiveness."

"That, General, opens a very wide field for argument," Patterson responded. "I regret that your adherence to form would obstruct business of great moment and concern."

The frown forming on Washington's face portended a storm raging inside and Patterson realized his mission had been concluded. It was time for courtesies.

"We have prepared a small collation for you, Colonel. Please share our simple table. May I offer you some colonial brandy?"

Patterson, good staff officer that he was, subdued his impatience with this arrogant colonial. There would soon enough be time for meting out the appropriate response, he decided.

"You're very kind, General, but I had a very late breakfast with Sir William and don't have the appetite to give full appreciation to your collation."

"I understand, Colonel."

"I'll take my leave then, General."

"Very well, Colonel. Give my regards to Lord Howe and Sir William. I'm sure we will meet again somewhere."

"Yes, General, I'm sure we will. Soon, perhaps."

Both men smiled at the implication in Patterson's words. Washington was perfectly aware of the British force assembling on Staten Island and understood its intentions.

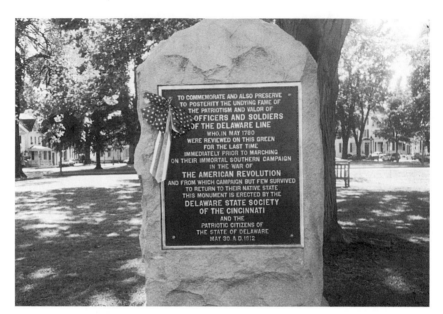

Memorial on Dover Green

Chapter Twenty-Eight

Loose Ends

Perhaps it was a premonition, maybe just an exercise of common sense. Whatever the reason, John Haslet decided he should draft his will before he led his regiment off to war.

So he remained behind when the Delaware Continentals marched north to Philadelphia from Wilmington at the end of July 1776.

The departure concluded an eventful period for the colony of Delaware.

The assembly had convened in special session on July 22 to advance the business of organizing a new government, given preliminary approval on June 15. On July 27 the assembly adopted a resolution for a constitutional convention starting August 27. Delegates would be elected August 19: ten from each of the three counties. In a key victory for the patriots, the assembly agreed that each delegate would be required to swear to "support and maintain the independence of the government as declared by the Continental Congress."

That done, Speaker Caesar Rodney turned his considerable powers of persuasion to help Haslet obtain the assembly's consent for the battalion to take the arms provided by the assembly and the three counties out of the colony. There had been a reluctance on the assembly's part to permit this, reflecting a tradition of self-interest common to all the not-yet-united colonies of America. Permission was granted mostly on the understanding the arms would either be returned or replaced by the Congress. They assumed, with some trepidation, that Rodney would be in a position to see that understanding honored when he returned to Philadelphia as one of the colony's delegates to Congress.

It was now cleared for Haslet to order the battalion to break camp and head for Philadelphia. After seeing his soldiers off, he turned his horse and rode off to Longfield. He had much to do in a short time to arrange affairs for what he expected would be a long absence.

On the first morning he rode over to the Marsh Plantation to discuss its management with his daughter. At her own request, she had remained behind to run it when the family moved to Longfield.

Polly rushed to greet him.

"Father! Father!" she said, throwing her arms around him.

"Polly. Darling daughter," he responded with equal joy, then backed off and looked admiringly at her. "You're such a beautiful young lady."

He thought about the little girl he had left behind in Ireland and the apprehensive teenager he had greeted at this same place a decade ago. Now she was twenty-three, a fully grown woman. After a moment:

"I understand you're doing a wonderful job of looking after things here."

She was more pleased at his compliment for her management than his remarks about her beauty. While she still had doubts about her management skills, she was confident in her appearance. The young men of Mispillion Hundred and Dover had assured that. She, her father, and the slaves Dollar and Tobias walked to a small rise where they had a panoramic view of the plantation while Polly proudly filled him in on the status of the crops, the health of the animals.

"Miss Polly is looking over things very well," Dollar commented.

"I'm pleased," Haslet said. "Thank you for all you've done to help her in my absence."

Haslet glanced around the plantation. It had been his home for so many years and it held memories of children, successes and failures, and his full life with Jemima. Longfield was the home he dreamed for, prayed for when he immigrated but it was too soon for Longfield to accumulate such memories.

After a while he turned to Polly:

"I'm going back over to Longfield now. Are you coming for dinner, Polly?"

"Yes, father. I'll be along shortly."

Haslet mounted and rode off.

The family had a happy meal together that evening and it was like it had always been, before the political situation had grown grim and talk of war tainted conversation. There was no talk of war at the dinner table, but Haslet's uniform hung on pegs on one wall, a silent reminder should anyone forget the events that were taking shape beyond Three Runs.

In his few precious days at home, he also found time to work out a plan to help his friends John and Amelia Rovell straighten out their claim to their plantation in Kent County.

Amelia was the widow of Sothby Brinckle, who owned several hundred acres in lower Kent County at the time of his death. John Rovell had bought a piece of the Brinckle property from Amelia in March 1770 after her husband's death, but the sale of the remainder had been held up by the matter of a debt hanging over the estate. That litigation was still pending when she married Rovell in November 1773. Later, the Kent County Orphans Court ruled the remaining property should be sold at auction to satisfy the debt.

The Rovells turned to John Haslet as the influential neighbor in the Three Runs area most likely to help them out. And so, on August 5, John and Jemima Haslet bought the entire package of land—the 450 acres Rovell had purchased in 1770 and the remaining 350 acres of the Brinckle plantation. The next day he sold it all to the Rovells for the same price, a little over £1074. The effect was to clean up the title to the 800 acres for the Rovells.

That same day, August 6, he filed his will with the Register of Wills. It was witnessed by friends Vincent Loockerman, Robert McGarment, and Peter Torbert.

(McGarment would marry his daughter Mary "Polly" Haslet on November 13, 1783.)

His will began with the bequest of Longfield to his son, Joseph, along with £100 and the slave Solomon. To his other son, John, he left the adjacent land purchased from Major Handerson in February of 1776—or the value of the land should Handerson exercise an option to buy it back within the year (which he did, except for eighteen acres that included the Haslet home). John also was to receive £200, the slave named Will, and two boys, George and Jonathan. He left Polly £200 and the girl Jude. Ann and baby Jemima were each to receive £400; the slave girl Ratchel was left to Ann and Miriam to baby Jemima. The balance of his estate was to be distributed equally among the five children.

The will bequeathed £400, the male slaves Dollar and Tobias, and the female slaves Jinn and Bett to Jemima, who also was named executrix. William Killen was named as the alternate executor.

It was midday on the sixth when the business was completed. The family had accompanied him to Dover (Jemima as a party to the land deal with the Rovells) and now they all gathered outside the courthouse as Haslet prepared to depart.

He tried to make it appear as just another business trip, but the children sensed their mother's concern. In the past, his trips were short, whether making the rounds to see his patients or attending to legislative business in New Castle. Even his trips on battalion business this year ended happily with his return home. Despite their mother's brave efforts to dismiss this as just another trip, the children sensed his absence this time would be a long one.

Five-year-old Ann clung to his leg. The boys traced patterns in the dirt beside them. Polly stood back, but stared long at her father, creating an indelible memory.

One by one he called them to his arms and gave them hugs and kisses.

Jemima was last and their embrace lingered.

"I love you, John," she said. "You are the most important person in our lives. Please take care. Don't take foolish chances. Come back to us."

It was a simple plea, delivered with great feeling.

"I will, dear wife. Know that I love you deeply. You also are the most important person in my life. You and the children are most dear to me. I will place my life in the hands of the Lord. I know He will make sure my life will serve Him and the cause of these united colonies."

There was one more lingering kiss. Then Haslet mounted his horse, turned it towards the north, and rode slowly away.

His family watched until he was out of sight, then sadly climbed into the carriage for the trip home to Longfield.

Haslet arrived in Philadelphia on the eighth of August and found the battalion, which had arrived five days earlier, encamped by the Delaware River, about a mile north of the city.

Gunning Bedford greeted him when he checked in at the house being used as headquarters.

"How are the men?" was his first question.

"Eager, John. Eager. Congress provided us with arms three days ago and now we're ready to march with Washington. We've been drilling regularly and I must say we've attracted quite a few spectators from the town. From the comments I would say the men have made a very great impression."

"Fine," Haslet responded. "I hope the city hasn't corrupted their morals." He smiled at the thought.

"Caldwell has been exhibiting his fighting cocks quite regularly and drawing a crowd," Bedford reported.

Jonathan Caldwell, commander of the Second Company, had a ferocious group of fighting cocks, swift and lethal in the pit. He claimed they had been bred by a blue hen and when the soldiers of the Delaware battalion, clad in blue uniforms, demonstrated the same ferocious fighting spirit, other units in the Continental Army likened them to the blue hen's offspring, committing the appellation "Blue Hens" to posterity.

"I suspect Jonathan has done quite well in his off-time," Haslet commented.

"Quite well," Bedford agreed, smiling.

Adjutant Thomas Holland provided him with a report of the day's muster, showing all present and none on the sick list.

"Colonel, the Congress has ordered Captain Darby's company to join us and we've dispatched a messenger to Lewes."

When the battalion left Lewes in early July Darby's company had been left in that southern Delaware port town to help counter activity by the Tories in the area.

"I would guess that's a sign we'll soon be moving on," Haslet commented. Bedford and Holland nodded agreement.

"Oh," Bedford said, "I'm reminded that Caesar Rodney has asked that you come to the State House when you arrive. I think he may have word about the battalion's orders."

"I'll tend to that as soon as I take care of my things," Haslet said. Most of his gear had been sent ahead on the wagons with other battalion baggage and he only had brought along a few books and incidental clothing.

He was soon riding to the State House, a two-story brick building whose bell tower was the most noteworthy landmark in a city dotted with landmarks.

In the Name of God Amen, I John Haslet of Mispilion Hundred in the County of Kent on Delaware, Sensible of the Uncertainty of Human Life in General, & my own in Particular; tho' in Good Health, think it my Duty, while of Sound & disposing Mind and Memory, to distribute that Portion of Worldly Estate, which the divine Goodness hath bestowed upon me in Manner & form following Viz

Imprimis I give and bequeath to my Wife Jemima Four hundred Pounds, two Negro Men, named Dollar & Tobias, & two Negro Women, named Din & Bett —

Item I give and bequeath to my Son Joseph Haslet the Plantation whereon I now live, with the eighteen acres before my door Purchased of Major Henderson, to him, his Heirs & Assigns for ever, I give also to my Son Joseph a Negro fellow named Solomon & One hundred Pounds in Cash, when he comes of Age, or is married —

Item I give and bequeath to my Son John Haslet the Plantation whereon Major Henderson now lives, bought of him at three hundred and fifty Pounds, the Ballance to be paid him out of my Estate; or I give & bequeath the said three hundred and fifty Pounds to my Son John Haslet, in case the said Major Henderson shall pay back the Purchase Money within one year next after my Decease & take the Plantation; if not my Will is, that the said Plantation be & remain to my Son John & his Heirs for ever — I also give and bequeath to my Son John a Negro Man, named Will, & two Boys named Jonathan & George, and also two hundred Pounds in Cash, when he is of Age or married, & my Will is further, that if either of my Sons die before Heirs of Age, & without Issue, the above Bequeathments shall be to the Survivor of them

Haslet will

Item I give & bequeath to my Daughter Mary Haslet two hundred Pounds, when she is of Age, or marries, I also give & bequeath unto Nor a Negro Girl named Inde —

Item I give & bequeath to my Daughter Ann Haslet four hundred Pounds, when she is of Age, or married, also a Negro Girl, named Natchel,

Item I give and bequeath to my Daughter Jemima Haslet the Sum of four hundred Pounds when she is of Age or married, I also give to her a Negro Girl, named Miriam — my Will farther is, that the above bequeathments shall be to the use of my Children immediately after my Decease —

Item My Will is, that the residuary Part of my Estate, shall be divided equally among my five Children, share & share alike — And I do hereby constitute & appoint my Wife Jemima Haslet, in whose discretion & Wisdom, I very much confide, to be the Sole Executrix of this my Last will & Testament, so long as she continues Mistress of her Self & in her own Power; & when she ceases to be so, I do then appoint my Esteemed Friend William Killen Esquire Executor of my Will, & Guardian of my Children — & finally I do hereby revoke all Wills of Date prior to this, & they are hereby disannulled, & do publish, pronounce & declare this to be my Last will and Testament. Witness my hand & seal this 6th Day of first 1766

Executed & done
in the Presence of
Vincent Luckerman
Robert Mcgerman
Peter Torbit

John Haslet

Haslet will

283

LAST WILL AND TESTAMENT[1]
Dated August 6, 1776   Probate March 6, 1777

In the name of God Amen. I, John Haslet of Mispillion Hundred in the county of Kent on Delaware, sensible of the uncertainty of human life in general and my own in particular, though in good health, think it my duty, while of sound and disposing mind and memory to distribute that portion of worldly estate which the divine Goodness hath bestowed upon me in manner and form following, viz.:

I give and bequeath to my wife Jemima four hundred pounds, two Negro men named Dollar and Tobias and two Negro women, named Jin and Bett.*

I give and bequeath to my son Joseph Haslet the plantation whereon I now live, with the eighteen acres before my door purchased of Major Henderson, to him, his heirs and assigns forever. I give also to my son Joseph a Negro fellow named Solomon & one hundred pounds in cash, when he becomes of age or is married.

I give and bequeath to my son John Haslet the plantation whereon Major Henderson now lives, bought of him at three hundred and fifty pounds, the balance to be paid him out of my estate; or I give and bequeath the said three hundred and fifty pounds to my son John Haslet in case the said Major Henderson shall pay back the purchase money within one year next after my decease and take the plantation; if not, my will is that the said plantation be and remain to my son John and his heirs forever—I also give and bequeath to my son John a Negro man named Will and two boys named Jonathan & George and also two hundred pounds in cash, when he is of age or married and my will is further that if either of my sons die before he is of age and without issue the above bequeathments shall be to the survivor of them.

I give and bequeath to my daughter Mary Haslet two hundred pounds, when she is of age or marries. I also give & bequeath unto her a Negro girl named Jude.

I give and bequeath to my daughter Ann Haslet four hundred pounds when she is of age or married, also a Negro girl named Ratchel.

I give and bequeath to my daughter Jemima Haslet the sum of four hundred pounds when she is of age or married. I also give to her a Negro girl named Miriam. My will farther is that the above bequeathments shall be to the use of my children immediately after my decease.

---

[1] From Delaware Archives, Volume A22, pages 225–230; Jemima's will is same volume, pages 223–224, with comment by William Killen that she died intestate.

* Jemima was left a Negro woman slave named Bett in her father's will.

(continued)

LAST WILL AND TESTAMENT (*continued*)

My will is that the residual part of my estate shall be divided equally among my five children, share and share alike and I do hereby constitute and appoint my wife Jemima Haslet, in whose discretion and wisdom I very much confide, to be the sole executrix of this my last will & testament, so long as she continues mistress of herself and in her own power; & when she ceases to be so, I do then appoint my esteemed friend William Killen Esquire executor of my will and guardian of my children & finally I do hereby revoke all wills of date prior to this & they are hereby disannuled, & do publish, pronounce and declare this to be my last will and testament. Witness my hand and seal this 6th day of August, 1776.

(Signed John Haslet)
Witnesses:
Vincent Loockerman
Robert McGarment
Peter Torbert

Personally appeared before me, Caesar Rodney Esquire, Register for the Probate of Wills & Granting Letters of Administration in & for Kent County on Delaware, Vincent Loockerman, Esquire, Robert McGarment and Peter Torbert, all of the town of Dover in the county of Kent on Delaware. And being sworn on the Holy Evangelists of Almighty God, depose and say to wit, that they the afore-mentioned Vincent Loockerman and Robert McGarment saw and heard John Haslet the testator, sign, seal publish pronounce and declare the foregoing instrument of writing entered on this sheet of paper as and for his last will and testament, that at the time of so doing and say he was, to the best of their belief, in perfect health and of sound and disposing mind and memory, that they at the instance and request of the testator and in his presence, signed and saw each other sign their names in witness to the said writing. And the said Peter Torbert, another of the subscribing witnesses to this said testament deposeth and saith that he was called upon to sign his name as a witness to the said instrument of writing, that he did sign his name to it as a witness and said Vincent Loockerman and Robert McGarment at the same time signed as the two other witnesses to the same paper. But that we neither know nor asked what the contracts were. In testimony whereof I have hereunto put my hand this 6th day of March anno Domini 1777.

A final accounting of the estate was filed by Killen in May, 1791 and approved May 28. It showed a balance of £3787:8:6 after payments of debts amounting to £4353:12:8. Killen filed a separate accounting for the education and maintenance of the children, showing expenditures of £1315:10:4. There are separate accountings of distributions to the children, handling of Jemima's estate.

Haslet entered through the center hall and stood at the door to the room where the Congress held its sessions. Delegates were standing around the desks in clusters, talking, their business for the day ended. Rodney almost immediately came out to meet him and a few other delegates, curious about this tall, handsome stranger in the blue-coated uniform and high-peaked cap of the Delaware Continentals, followed him.

"John, so good to see you've come," Rodney greeted him. "I've important news. We'll dine together. Give you a chance to get acquainted with the City Tavern, the finest inn in all of North America."

A portly, elderly man moved in and thrust out his hand.

"I see you're a colonel," the man said, "and by your uniform I judge you must be the commanding officer of that fine group of soldiers from the lower counties that arrived a few days ago."

"Yes, I am," Haslet said, shaking the man's hand. He strained for recognition.

"Oh, forgive me. I'm Ben Franklin, one of the Pennsylvania members of this Congress," the elderly man said.

"My goodness, yes," Haslet said enthusiastically at meeting the most famous person in all of North America. "Your compliments on my battalion are valued above all others, Dr. Franklin."

"I see you've not lost your Irish charm," Franklin observed, "even if your accent is beginning to wear at the edges."

"I've been twenty years in this country, Doctor," Haslet said, "I suppose I've become somewhat Americanized."

"Fine," Franklin said, "we'll need all the colonies to become 'Americanized' and we'll count on you and your soldiers to keep them from becoming 'Anglicized.'"

"Let me add my compliments about your regiment," offered a newcomer to the growing crowd around Haslet, "I saw them drill the other day and I was very impressed."

The stranger was short and stout with a New England accent.

"I'm John Adams," the man said.

"Sir, I'm so glad to meet you and to get a chance to offer my compliments for the role Massachusetts Bay and its statesmen have played in leading us to claim our rightful liberties," Haslet responded warmly.

"Well, spoken, Colonel," Adams said.

"Hear, hear," Franklin added.

"I second that sentiment," said another and Haslet recognized the accent of a Virginian.

"I'm Tom Jefferson," the man explained. The man was nearly as tall as Haslet, with red hair and a slender build. Haslet was surprised at the softness of his voice. All he had heard of the man had led him to anticipate a more forceful speaker.

"Mr. Jefferson, of course," Haslet said and, turning to Rodney: "Squire, we're indebted to you and these men for providing the vision and leadership on which to build our nation of free men. Meeting them reinforces my belief that the Almighty sees fit to bless this country."

He spoke with a warmth and sincerity that impressed the gathering.

"Many people have had a hand in shaping that vision," Jefferson said and the others nodded.

"Well, come, John," Rodney interrupted, "let's get on to the City Tavern. I have some instructions for the battalion from the Congress and I want to discuss Kent County politics with you. Excuse us, gentlemen."

More people had joined the gathering in the hallway, offering their compliments on the battalion and Haslet warmly shook hands. The other two Delaware delegates, Thomas McKean and George Read, caught up with him just before he left and they had a brief exchange before he and Rodney departed through a door onto the common.

The tavern was a few blocks away and as they walked along the cobblestoned streets Rodney filled in some of the color of Philadelphia, the most cosmopolitan of the North American cities. Of course, Haslet had sampled the Philadelphia life several times over the years, but not in the depth related by Rodney, who added political insight to his descriptions.

The tall officer drew glances from the patrons as he and Rodney walked through the tavern and took a seat at a table. Rodney arranged for some wine and when they had sipped a little, got to business.

"The Declaration of Independence was laid out for our signatures last Friday," Rodney began, "and Read signed it."

Haslet acknowledged the information with a smile. Read, although a firm patriot, had declined to vote for independence in July, precipitating Rodney's famous ride to cast the tie-breaking vote to place Delaware in support of the resolution.

When they were comfortable, Rodney outlined his concerns about the forthcoming elections to the Delaware Convention.

"I'm confident New Castle County will send a strong delegation of patriots. I accept that Sussex County will have more than a few dissidents among its ten delegates. It's Kent County that I'm worried about.

"I've written to my brother Tommy to be very careful about how he presents a ticket to the voters of our county. I know that Tommy tends to be passionate in his politics and I've warned him about that. I've cautioned him to emphasize devotion to independence rather than to party.

"If he presses the ticket as a party, he'll lose. He's formed a committee to screen candidates and I've told him to be sure the members are men devoted to liberty, that they'll make that the only issue for the candidates. I've sent him a statement of principles to put before the people in support of this approach.

"I would fear that if the Tories control the convention, we'll get a government that would be susceptible to the peace overtures we're hearing from the Howes."

By now the Congress had heard about the offer from the Howe brothers to grant pardons to any who renewed their allegiance to the Crown and government.

Haslet sensed a rare display of emotion gathering in his friend.

"Forgiveness and pardon if we surrender our rights!" he said angrily. "What arrogance!"

"Agreed," Haslet said. He stared intently at Rodney, who rarely lost control of his emotions.

"General Washington's response was very appropriate, I think," Rodney said, growing calm again. "We've done nothing to seek forgiveness."

Rodney let the anger ebb and the two men silently examined their concerns.

"I almost forgot my important news for you, John," Rodney finally spoke up. "The Congress decided today that the Delawares should march forthwith to the flying camp at Amboy in the Jersey Colony. I'm sorry I got so involved in the elections that I put off telling you."

"My men and I are eager to march north," Haslet said. "They are in a proper frame of mind for whatever role the general has in mind for us."

He paused and smiled.

"Provided it's a fighting role."

"At least we've finally provided you the means to fight," Rodney said. "The Congress made our battalion a priority. The arms they voted to give you arrived just last Friday on a French ship. There were a thousand stand of arms aboard and the Delaware Continentals account for most of them. They're fine English-made muskets, with bayonets."

"Yes, Gunning told me. I stopped at our headquarters before coming to meet you."

"The battalion has made a fine impression here in Philadelphia," Rodney said.

"I hope they make an even better impression on the British," Haslet said.

The two men raised their glasses in a toast to the battalion's success.

They were joined at that point by Dr. Francis Alison. Haslet had sent word to Alison that he was in town and his old friend found him at the City Tavern in time to join them for dinner.

Rodney already had met the distinguished educator and clergyman, another committed patriot.

Alison grasped Haslet's hands.

"John, it's been a long time. How are you? And your uniform confirms what I've heard about your new role as a military leader. The Delaware Continentals, I hear."

"I'm fine, Francis and what you've heard is true."

"They've made a wonderful impression here," Alison said.

"They make me proud," Haslet said.

"They do you proud," Alison added. "How long will you be in the city?"

"Not long," Haslet said. "We've orders to join Washington and we'll depart soon."

"I pray for the army's success," Alison said. "Our cause offers the best hope in this world for men to live free."

"I remember you saying," Haslet commented, "that if a mother country should seek to change its relationship to its colonies by force, or if what had begun as a safe, mild union should degenerate into a 'severe and absolute one,' resistance on the part of the colonies was justified."

"I was only quoting Francis Hutcheson, who taught me at Glasgow. He was speaking about Scotland, but his remark is certainly applicable to our current situation.

"May God march with you, my friend."

They turned to their dinners and spent the rest of the evening in idle conversation, from time to time interrupted by other congressional delegates who stopped at the table to meet Haslet and talk with Rodney and Alison. Occasionally one sat down and shared a glass with them.

The battalion moved out a few days later, Haslet and the senior officers riding ahead of the columns as they headed north to the point where they would cross the Delaware and march through the Jerseys to Amboy, site of the flying camp.

Chapter Twenty-Nine
The Flying Camp

War had transformed the village of Amboy in the Jersey colony. Located along the Arthur Kill, a channel separating the colony from Staten Island at the mouth of the Raritan River, it was an important transit point between New York and Philadelphia. It also alternated with Burlington in the southern part of the colony as Jersey's capital (a reminder that Jersey was once two colonies). It was a logical place for the Continental Congress to establish a flying camp, a base to assemble troops for deployment with the Continental Army across New York Harbor and, consequently, it approved the camp on June 3, 1776.

When the Delaware battalion arrived in mid-August, the camp was swelling with soldiers arriving from the several colonies. Thousands of tents and other improvised shelters, clusters of supply wagons, grazing horses and mules, spread across the meadows.

In charge of it all was Brigadier General Hugh Mercer, a Scot who had fought with the Scottish Highlanders against the British in the 1746 battle of Culloden Moor. After the British routed the Highlanders, Mercer fled to America. Less than a decade later he was fighting alongside British soldiers in the ill-fated Braddock expedition of 1755 in the French and Indian War. He marched again with the Forbes expedition of 1758. When Fort Duquesne fell, Mercer was placed in charge of the fort (renamed Fort Pitt) and held that key frontier post for several months. Forbes' second-in-command, Colonel Henry Bouquet, had written of Mercer's "zeal and attachment to the king's service."

Now, Mercer—once again fighting against the British—strode out of his headquarters as the blue-coated Delawareans marched in to camp, Haslet riding at their head.

They exchanged salutes and Haslet dismounted.

"I'm Colonel John Haslet," he introduced himself, "commander of the Delaware regiment of the Continental army."

"Fine-looking soldiers," Mercer said. He searched his memory for further recognition:

"There was a John Haslet who served with the Pennsylvania militia during the French and Indian War," he finally spoke up. "Held the rank of captain, I recall. Could you be him?"

"I did serve with James Burd's second regiment, General," he responded. "And I do remember you from the '58 campaign." Mercer had commanded the Third Pennsylvania Regiment, with the rank of colonel.

"Well, Burd's was a fighting regiment," Mercer said, "and, Lord knows, we'll need fighters when we meet the British. Which I suspect will be soon. I hope your men fight as well as they look."

"Better," was Haslet's simple response.

The two men walked towards the headquarters as Mercer briefed Haslet on the situation.

"General Washington will want your battalion to move to New York, probably to Brooklyn Heights overlooking New York harbor. We've been fortifying that place, and also Manhattan Island, since February.

"General Sullivan is in command there now. General Greene had the command but he's come down with a fever and is quite ill. Too bad. He supervised the preparations on Long Island and no one knows the terrain better. General Washington depends on him."

Major General Nathanael (sic) Greene, a native of Rhode Island, was thirty-four years old, smart, energetic, and considered one of Washington's staunchest supporters. Major General John Sullivan was thirty-six, born in New Hampshire and, like Greene, had served at Boston. Both men had been approved for their second star by Congress on August 9.

"The British are not far from here," Mercer went on. "Thousands of them on Staten Island, just across that channel there. In fact you'll probably hear occasional gunfire across the channel. On the other side of the island you'll find what looks like the whole damned British navy. The lower bay is a forest of masts and rigging. I swear you could walk across the harbor from deck to deck without getting your boots even damp.

"More ships arrived just the other day. Transports as well as warships. Our spies tell us there were several thousand Hessians on them, landed at Staten Island."

"How many of the enemy would you suppose are there now?" Haslet asked.

"Including the Hessians, our guess is about 30,000."

"And our strength?"

"We have about 28,000 on Manhattan Island. About 10,000 here. I'm not sure. Soldiers come and go every day."

"How many trained soldiers?"

Mercer smiled at the question. It was obvious Haslet had some suspicions about the army being assembled. Mercer did not answer his question directly.

"Well, Colonel Smallwood's Marylanders look competent to give the enemy a good battle. Your regiment the same. There are some dependable troops among the Pennsylvanians. Perhaps a few thousand here."

William Smallwood was commander of an elite regiment recruited from professionals in the Baltimore area.

"And on Manhattan?"

"They have militia from Massachusetts Bay. Connecticut. Rhode Island colony. New York, of course. The general has them drilling every day. Skirmishing. Target practice.

"I notice, Colonel, your men seem well equipped."

"The Congress provided us with English-made muskets before we left Philadelphia."

"I see they also have bayonets. Not too many of our soldiers have bayonets. And, if you remember, the British make good use of bayonet charges. They've been known to intimidate and scatter many a skirmish line with the bayonet."

"My men have been training to use that weapon," Haslet responded.

He observed the camp commander closely and although they had had very little contact during the war, he did remember stories about him.

Most interesting was the story that Mercer was separated from his regiment during a battle and had to hide in the hollow of a tree from pursuing Indians. After they stopped looking for him, Mercer made his way over 100 miles through the frontier, living on roots and rattlesnakes, to rejoin his unit.

He still looked fit, Haslet thought. At fifty-two, he was about three years older than Haslet.

"What did you do after the war?" Haslet asked.

"Washington suggested I move to Virginia," Mercer answered. "We had become quite friendly during the war. So, I moved to Fredericksburg and took up medicine. I opened an apothecary."

"You had your own shop?"

"Yes. I didn't feel like splitting fees with an apothecary. Besides, there was no shop in Fredericksburg, nor anyone interested in establishing one."

(In early colonial times physicians and apothecaries sometimes competed in treatment of patients. Eventually they learned to cooperate, with apothecaries paying fees to doctors for referrals, recouping their fee through the charges for the remedies they dispensed.)

"That's what I was doing when I was called by the general to join the Continental army. And you?"

"I decided to settle in Delaware, along the Mispillion in Kent County. I also became a doctor. I did some preaching, too. Later I served in the assembly."

"Preaching?"

"Yes. Presbyterian. I studied at Glasgow and was ordained in Ulster, but I gave that all up when I came to America. I'm still active in the church but I don't do much preaching any more. I did that at first, when there were more congregations than ministers, but medicine has kept me busy for several years."

"Well, after you see to your encampment come join me here for dinner," Mercer said. The two men parted and Haslet rejoined his soldiers, already in the process of setting up camp.

The orders for them to move on came a few days later.

The Delawareans broke camp and marched on up the North River to a point where they could safely cross without worrying about British warships, which moved freely in New York harbor, little concerned about the shore batteries.

The crossing completed without incident, they marched down Manhattan Island to New York.

Chapter Thirty

New York

In August of 1776, New York—with close to 30,000 people—was second only to Philadelphia in population. The town covered about a square mile of the southern tip of Manhattan Island. Fort George marked the southernmost point of the island and the town fanned out from there, its streets mostly laid out in a grill pattern, intersecting each other at right angles. The exception was the road known as Broadway, which bisected the town running diagonally from north to south.

On the nearby park known as Bowling Green, there had been a lead statue of King George III. It was there a crowd gathered on July 9 to hear the Declaration of Independence read to the troops and other spectators on Washington's orders. Roused by the spirit of the occasion, the crowd pulled down the statue, shipping the parts off to Connecticut to be melted down and cast into bullets. They expressed the hope the statue would be returned to the British one bullet at a time.

There were many among New York's citizens, however, who maintained their allegiance to the Crown. It was, in fact, reckoned to be the most loyal among the American colonies. Fear among the Tories of harassment from the patriots and fear among others of bombardment from the huge British fleet at anchor only a few miles away in the lower bay had driven many to seek the safety of the countryside.

Their departure and the growing numbers of Continental army soldiers had almost obscured New York's basic character as a sailor's town, a busy seaport.

The soldiers' mock battles and target practice, ordered by General Washington, provided the main daily entertainment.

There were many fine houses in the town, Haslet noted. Not as many as Philadelphia, of course, but just as fine, nevertheless. Washington had taken over one of them, the home of Tory Abraham Mortier, paymaster for the royal forces and thus an absentee and unwilling host.

It was there Haslet and his regiment reported in the middle of the third week of August.

An officer on horseback watched their arrival, carefully observing their uniforms and weapons. Haslet was struck how the man sat tall in the saddle the entire time. As the regiment came to a halt and was put at ease, the horseman effortlessly dismounted and approached Haslet.

The man's epaulets indicated he was a high-ranking general and recognition came quickly to Haslet. The resemblance to the young Virginia colonel he remembered from almost twenty years ago was obvious. This man was George Washington, the commander-in-chief, now forty-four years old.

Haslet saluted and had his salute returned.

"This is the Delaware battalion," he said, "and I'm their commanding officer, John Haslet."

Washington turned to the troops.

"Welcome to my command. I'm General Washington, commander-in-chief of the Continental Army of the United States of America."

That was meant to impress upon the new arrivals that they were now part of a movement that embraced much more than the three lower counties on the Delaware.

"I've heard many fine reports about you. You impressed the delegates to our Congress when you drilled for them in Philadelphia. I have been looking forward to your arrival."

Turning to Haslet:

"A fine-looking group of soldiers, Colonel. I see they have bayonets. How many?"

"All my men have bayonets, General."

"Do they know how to use them?"

"Only on British soldiers, General."

A smile crossed Washington's face.

"They may soon enough find an occasion to try their skills," he said. He turned to another officer who had come out of a nearby building and stood by Washington.

"Colonel Moylan," Washington commanded, "see to the arrangements for these men."

Irish-born Stephen Moylan, thirty-nine, a wealthy shipping merchant with businesses both in Lisbon and Philadelphia, was serving as quartermaster general. He had been in the country only seven years, but his outgoing personality quickly made him popular and he had been elected first president of the Friendly Sons of Saint Patrick in 1771.

"Colonel Haslet," Washington said, "you'll camp just north of town. My staff will show you where."

Haslet saluted. Washington returned his salute, turned, and went inside the building.

The battalion had encamped only two days when Haslet and the battalion's senior officers were summoned to Washington's headquarters.

Washington was standing at a table with a map of nearby Long Island spread out. Icons indicated the deployment of forces and the locations of fortified positions.

"I'm sure you'll be glad to know that I'm moving your men," Washington began. "With all the sickness around here you'll be better off getting away from this place before your troops, too, are infected."

Smallpox and an ailment known as the "bloody flux" (marked by dysentery and bloody stools) had sent between a quarter and a third of the American forces to hospitals by late August of 1776. So many, in fact, that houses, barns, and stables had to be used as dispensaries. Even then, some of the ill were laid out along fences and bushes. Haslet had spotted them on the march down the island and quickly identified their illness, hoping his own soldiers might escape the disease.

Washington moved his hand across the map and pointed to an area east of the American positions.

"General Howe has moved substantial forces from Staten Island to Long Island. There've been several skirmishes over the past couple of days."

He traced a line between two points that pinched Brooklyn Heights about a mile inland from New York harbor, identifying the points as Wallabout Bay on the north and Gowanus Cove on the south.

"I've set up our lines between these two points. General Putnam is in overall command with Generals Heath and Sullivan as division commanders.

"You'll be serving in General Sullivan's division, in Lord Stirling's brigade," Washington continued.

"He also has Smallwood's Maryland Regiment, Miles' Pennsylvania riflemen, Atlee's Pennsylvania battalion, and some small militia units from Pennsylvania.

"We have to anticipate Howe will be moving soon."

Haslet observed Washington as the general outlined the commands and positions. Washington was very tall, as Haslet remembered, and although Haslet was about the same height, the general seemed to stand above everyone in the room. His command presence was almost mesmerizing.

The general turned to another officer in the room and beckoned him to come forward.

"This is Colonel Glover" Washington explained. "He'll see to your movement to Brooklyn Heights."

John Glover, forty-three years old, was a short, stocky New Englander, commander of a regiment from the Marblehead area of Massachusetts Bay, men more comfortable as sailors than soldiers. (The regiment is generally considered the predecessor of today's United States Marine Corps.)

"I'll make the arrangements," Glover said. "How soon?"

"Tomorrow won't be too soon," Washington responded.

Glover nodded and departed.

"What military experience have you had, Colonel?" Washington said to Haslet.

"I served as a captain with Colonel James Burd's Second Pennsylvania Regiment in the Forbes expedition in 1758," Haslet responded. "I've been active with the Delaware militia for several years and formed this battalion last winter. We've had some contact with the British—with their warships, really—this year on the Delaware.

"Also, I do quite a bit of reading of military history and tactics."

"You're attracted to war?" Washington asked, eyeing Haslet closely.

"I wouldn't say I'm attracted to it," Haslet said. "I am intrigued by its strategies, however, and by the character of military leaders. It takes a fine mind to plan and execute on the battlefield."

"That's true," Washington commented. "Good instincts also help."

"Instincts are even better when they've been sharpened by the lessons of history," Haslet responded and Washington looked at him with appreciation.

There was a long pause in the conversation. Washington seemed to be searching his memory.

"I remember the Pennsylvania regiment. Good soldiers, good fighting men, I recall."

Haslet accepted the compliment with a nod. He also was re-membering how angry Washington had been during that war when the British command chose a route through the frontier favored by Pennsylvania over the road favored by Virginians. Washington had protested loudly, advocating the Virginia road used three years earlier by the Braddock expedition. However, the Forbes command felt the Pennsylvania route, although only partly completed, offered a more di-rect and more favorable route for movement of supplies.

Haslet decided he wouldn't bring up that bit of history.

Washington picked up a piece of paper and frowned as he glanced at its contents.

"One other thing, Colonel. I'll want you and Lieutenant Colonel Bedford to serve on a court martial board that I'm convening tomorrow. It will hear charges against an officer with the New York Continentals.

"It has been called to my attention just today," Washington con-tinued, waving the paper, "that he may have offered to spy for the British." A redness in his cheeks and the edge to his voice suggested the anger within him.

"As you wish, General," Haslet responded. He saluted and he and his staff left the house to rejoin the battalion. It was Saturday, August 24.

The Delaware battalion moved over to Brooklyn Heights the next day, the twenty-fifth, and was placed in position on the right flank of the American line. With 750 soldiers it was the largest regiment in the army. Next to them on the line were the 600 soldiers of the Mary-land regiment, all men of means. Their love of soldiering was not di-minished by the easy life made possible by their wealth. And they would prove their mettle in a few days.

The court martial also convened that Sabbath day—indicating the importance Washington placed on it—at the headquarters about a mile up the North River side of Manhattan Island. Washington had ap-pointed Brigadier General James Wadsworth of Connecticut to pre-side over the court martial and twelve officers, mostly colonels, to hear the case. Smallwood and his lieutenant colonel were among them.

It was Haslet's first chance to meet the man whose military ca-reer would intertwine with his over the next few months. Smallwood, forty-four, son of a leading Maryland merchant and planter, had been educated in England and, like Haslet, fought in the French and Indian War. He, too, had served in his colony's legislature. He was tall like

Haslet but considerably heavier. Haslet found him an agreeable and pleasant colleague.

The defendant was Lieutenant Colonel Herman Zedwitz, commander of the First New York Continentals. The evidence against him was a letter written to New York Governor William Tryon, offering to provide details of the Continental army's strength.

Zedwitz, German-born, had emigrated to America after service with the British army in Germany during the Seven Years War. He enlisted (under duress, he claimed in his letter to Tryon) in the American militia and had served on the ill-fated Canadian expedition in 1775 where he was injured falling from a wall. On April 11, the Continental Congress awarded him $255 as compensation and for reimbursement of his expenses to come to Philadelphia.

Immediately after the formal opening, Zedwitz pleaded for an extra day to prepare his defense and the court adjourned until 10 A.M. on Monday, the twenty-sixth.

At that hour, Judge Advocate William Tudor presented to the court an affidavit from an Augustus Stein attesting that Zedwitz had spent three days the previous week recruiting him as a messenger to Governor Tryon, now living aboard a British warship in the harbor. On Thursday, the twenty-second, he said, Zedwitz produced a letter for him to give to the governor. Instead, Stein turned it over to a Captain Bowman who forwarded it to Captain Alexander Hamilton, a Washington aide.

That was the paper Washington had displayed at his headquarters two days earlier.

The letter, which the defendant acknowledged as his, was then presented to the court martial. It was evident he had barely learned the language as he outlined, in broken English, his plans. He claimed that he had access to weekly reports on the status of the American army, which he would supply to Tryon in return for £4000 sterling. Zedwitz said he expected to split the money with his contact in Washington's headquarters. That contact, he said, came when Washington had asked him to prepare a pamphlet to be sent to the Hessian camp, offering any who came over to the American army 200 acres of land in America.

The letter was handed over to the court martial board. The members passed it around slowly as they tried to make sense out of the misspellings and irregular syntax. It was still in circulation when Zedwitz began his defense.

Zedwitz claimed that it was only a scheme to get reimbursed for recruiting soldiers in late 1770 for the English army which was preparing for a prospective war with Spain over the Falkland Islands.

(The Spanish colony of Argentina had seized control of the islands earlier in the year and war had seemed imminent.)

He testified that he had served with the British army in Prussia during the Seven Years War but declined further service until the Marquis of Granby, under whom he had served, invited him to serve again and to recruit a thousand riflemen among his German countrymen. The bounty would be £24 sterling per man, Zedwitz said.

He said he recruited twenty men and arrived with them in London where the Marquis promised to pay the bounty and recruiting expenses. However, Zedwitz went on, the Marquis died before the deal could be consummated. Zedwitz said he solicited reimbursement from British officials, including Lord North, without success. His only reward, he said, was letters of recommendation from the prime minister to Canadian Governor Guy Carleton and to Tryon.

After arriving in North America two years later, he said, he enlisted in the New York militia and almost immediately began scheming to be paid the money promised by the Marquis of Granby. He said he saw the growing dispute between the colonies and the government in London as an opportunity.

"I wrote the letter to Governor Tryon," he said, "such stories as he might believe without any intention on my part of performing."

The stories he told Tryon included a claim he had been involved in the so-called Life Guards conspiracy in June.

That was a reference to a plan by members of Washington's bodyguards to help the British capture New York. It was discovered accidentally during an investigation of counterfeiting activities. One of the alleged counterfeiters, Gilbert Forbes, a gunsmith, confessed to recruiting men for the British and identified one of them as Thomas Hickey of Washington's Life Guards. Brought to trial, Hickey claimed it all was a ruse to fool the Tories. His explanation was rejected and on June 28 he was hanged in full view of some 20,000 Continental soldiers. New York Mayor David Matthews also was mentioned as a member of the conspiracy and was jailed.

Zedwitz said in his letter that he was one of the alleged conspirators identified by Forbes, but testified he brought that up only to convince Governor Tryon "that he might expect great service from me."

The board was obviously struggling to understand the witness, but otherwise displayed no reaction to his testimony.

At the conclusion, Wadsworth turned the case over to the court martial board and adjourned for the day. The board retired to consider a verdict.

Haslet had not liked Zedwitz. He thought him shifty and pretentious. His mangling of the English language added to the poor impression.

Opinions varied among the other board members.

"I think he planned to cooperate with the British," commented one officer, firmly.

"Probably," agreed another, "but he has fashioned a reasonable explanation."

"It's intriguing," said a third, "if, in truth, he devised such an elaborate plan to get the money he says the British owe him."

"He served in Canada and was wounded in our cause there," said a fourth.

"But he wasn't shot, he fell off a wall," interrupted another board member.

"It's difficult to tell where truth ends and deception begins," Haslet offered. "His story is plausible but the scheme casts no honor on him, even if it is true that he was only trying to deceive the governor."

"I don't understand why he brought up possible involvement in the Life Guards plot," said one. "I'm surprised he would even mention that, considering the disapprobation that sorry episode cast on the participants."

The board finally concluded that Zedwitz was guilty.

The next morning, General Wadsworth read the court martial board's decision:

"The court, being cleared, are of opinion that the prisoner is guilty of concerting a plan and attempting to treacherously correspond with and give intelligence to the enemy; and the court sentence and adjudge the prisoner be cashiered and rendered incapable and he is hereby cashiered and rendered incapable of ever holding a commission in the service of the United American States."

(On November 22, the Continental Congress ordered him transferred to Philadelphia to be placed in a state prison. At the same time it voted some $130 in payment to his wife, Julianna, representing services rendered by her husband before his conviction.)

As the court martial sat, British troops on Long Island were preparing to march on the American lines at Brooklyn Heights.

Chapter Thirty-One

Foul Weather
Most Fair

But for fortuitous breaks in the weather, the War of the Revolution might have ended at Long Island in August 1776. Wind, rain, and fog in turn formed tactical alliances with the American army, confounding the British command.

The first break came with a shift of winds on the twenty-sixth as the British mobilized their superior, more experienced army, augmented by the Hessian mercenaries, to assault the American position on Brooklyn Heights.

The strategy developed in concert with General William Howe, commander-in-chief of British forces in North America, called for Admiral Lord Richard Howe, the general's older brother and commander of the naval forces, to send five warships into the upper harbor where they could dominate the water route between New York and Brooklyn Heights and also add their firepower to that of the British artillery.

However, a shift of winds kept the huge British navy out of the action.

Lord Howe felt the narrows between Staten Island and Long Island too treacherous to risk the warships in an unfavorable wind. Only one made it, HMS *Roebuck* (a ship well-known to the Delaware Continentals) and its forty-four guns contributed mostly noise in the battle that followed.

The main land attack was against the American left flank. Howe assigned Lieutenant General Henry Clinton to command the advance column, appropriately, since the plan of attack was mostly Clinton's. Major General Earl George Cornwallis and the reserves would march behind him followed by the main force under Lieutenant General Hugh Earl Percy. Howe would march with Percy.

Britain's use of the military to enforce its position as a preeminent world power ensured that all were men of considerable experience. Howe, himself, at age forty-seven had thirty years experience.

Although only thirty-eight, Clinton had been in the army since he was thirteen. He was born in 1738 in Newfoundland, where his father, George Clinton, served as governor (1732–41). In 1741, his father was moved to New York where he served as governor until 1751, the same year his son joined the army. Young Clinton moved quickly up the ranks, becoming lieutenant colonel in 1758, when he was only twenty, and major general in 1772. He was anxious to redeem himself after the failed assault at Charleston, South Carolina, in June.

Cornwallis was an authentic aristocrat, scion of an ancient British family. He was slightly younger than Clinton, being born on New Year's Eve, 1738. His service began at age eighteen and like Clinton, included duty in Germany during the Seven Years War.

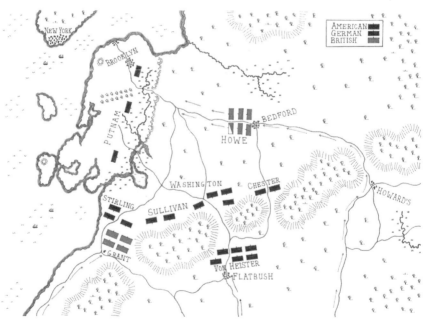

Position of forces at Battle of Long Island
Map by John Mackenzie of britishbattles.com

Percy was another young, experienced officer whose confidence in the superiority of the British military had not been diminished by his involvement in the bloody retreat from Concord in 1775 nor his experience at Bunker's Hill a couple months later.

In command of the British left flank was fifty-six-year-old Major General James Grant, with thirty-six years of experience. His troops would give the Delaware battalion its first exposure to the British regulars.

This was the same Grant who had been defeated at Fort Duquesne in 1758 in an ill-advised test of the French and Indian defenses. Intended as a reconnaissance mission, it turned into a general engagement in which the British force was mauled by the defenders. Only two months later the fort fell to the British-American force without a battle. The 1758 expedition included in its ranks such future American leaders as George Washington and, of course, John Haslet.

Grant was probably the most anti-American among the senior British officers. He had dismissed the Americans lightly, claiming they could not fight and bragging that he could conquer the colonies with only 5,000 men, which was, by coincidence, the approximate number under his command for this battle. It was the same attitude toward American militia that he had exhibited back in the French and Indian War and it was in sharp contrast to that of Cornwallis and William Howe, who had shown sympathy to the American cause during the debates in Parliament, where both served.

The Hessians were assigned the center of the assault, under the command of Lieutenant General Leopold Philipp von Heister.

Washington, who divided his time between New York and Brooklyn Heights, placed Israel Putnam in command of the American lines.

Putnam, sixty-eight, grew up in Massachusetts before moving to Connecticut and taking up farming. He also had served in the French and Indian War. His military credentials included time with the well-known Rogers Rangers. A colorful figure, his role in the heroic defense of Bunker's Hill in Massachusetts made him a legend. He was remembered for the celebrated line: "Don't fire until you see the whites of their eyes." Although the British won that battle, the stout patriot defense had cost them many casualties, something Howe, who had been involved, did not forget. In the coming engagement, however, Putnam would be overmatched as a field tactician.

In addition to the overall command, Putnam was responsible for the left flank. In command of the center was Major General John Sullivan, thirty-six. William Alexander, more commonly known as Lord Stirling, commanded the right flank, which included the Delaware battalion. None of them were professional soldiers and, of course, did not match the British command in experience.

Lord Stirling was a native of Jersey, but claimed his title to a Scottish earldom through his family. His claim had been recognized by the Scots but denied by the British House of Lords. Nevertheless, he continued to use the title. He was fifty years old, burly, rumored to have a weakness for drink, but considered a good field commander. He was another veteran of the French and Indian War. Both he and Sullivan had only recently been promoted to brigadier general by the Congress.

The British plan called for Grant and the Hessian troops to make feints against the American right and center while the main force would attack the American left. When the main attack was well underway, a cannon would be fired from the nearby town of Bedford as a signal for Grant and von Heister's troops to attack in full force.

In all, the British and Hessians had assembled about 20,000 soldiers, but Washington's intelligence contacts had led him to believe there were only about 8,000 enemy soldiers disembarked on Long Island. That's about how many American soldiers he had dispersed in and around Brooklyn Heights. As it turned out, only about half of the Americans, including the Delaware battalion, would be involved in the actual fighting. Almost all of the 20,000 British and Hessians participated.

At 100 feet, Brooklyn Heights had a commanding position over New York harbor. Brooklyn itself—sometimes referred to as "Brookland"—was a village of only about a dozen houses. All of Brooklyn Heights was about a mile wide and three miles long. Where Wallabout Bay on the north and Gowanus Cove on the south pinched in the land, that three miles was reduced to approximately two-and-a-half miles. The Americans had set up a necklace of redoubts and entrenchments, concentrated in the northern half of this neck, nearer to Wallabout Bay. Tidal waters flowing into the Gowanus Creek from the cove had turned the southern half of the neck into a marshland, providing a natural defense.

From this defensive line, the land sloped downward to the Gowanus Road, which ran parallel to the neck.

Beyond the Gowanus Road, the island stretched out in a series of heavily wooded and rolling hills. Three roads converged on the heights. Northernmost was the Jamaica Road running along the hills from the easternmost (Jamaica) pass directly to the American left flank. About halfway there it was joined by the Bedford Road, running through the middle of the line of hills. Southernmost was the Flatbush Road, splitting off from the Bedford Road just before the Bedford Pass and running diagonally through the hills to meet the Jamaica Road at its intersection with the northern end of the Gowanus Road.

Several hundred American soldiers had been deployed in the woods to defend the passes at Flatbush and Bedford, but only five soldiers had been posted at the Jamaica Pass, farthest from the American lines.

So, the Americans waited, unknowing, while the British assembled in the open plains below the Jamaica pass. At nine o'clock in the evening of the twenty-sixth they began their march.

The British easily overwhelmed the small patriot patrol at Jamaica Pass. This initial success, although insignificant in terms of forces involved, filled the British command with optimism and they sought fulfillment in the nearby tavern of William Howard.

It was about 2 A.M. when a group of strangers entered the tavern and asked for drinks.

These obviously aren't country people, Howard thought. The one who seemed to be their leader was tall, on the heavy side. Despite the plain hat and cloak, Howard caught a glimpse of a military uniform. The man's speech and demeanor suggested a man of rank among the citizens. This was Howe. Clinton and two aides were with him.

"Tavernkeeper," Howe said, "are you a member of the association?" It was a reference to the patriot organizations.

"Why do you ask?" Howard responded, apprehensively.

"Just curious," Howe said.

"Well, I am," Howard confessed, his courage fed by the man's seemingly benign attitude.

"Very well," Howe said, growing stern. "I applaud your integrity, but I must inform you that you are now my prisoner. I'll grant you parole if you direct me to the village of Bedford."

The Jamaica Road met the road through Bedford Pass in that village.

Howard's shoulders slumped briefly, then he stood erect again.

"As you command," he said with as much defiance as his nerve could muster.

Howe, who had never identified himself to the tavernkeeper, finished off his drink then exited with the others pushing Howard ahead of them. They all mounted and rode a short distance where a line of British soldiers stretched on into the darkness, waiting for the order to resume marching. The startled Howard gave them directions to Bedford and watched with concern as that long column disappeared in the night.

Meanwhile, Grant, moving north up the Gowanus Road, had made his feint at the American right about 1 A.M., driving a small party of Americans back to the Brooklyn Heights line. That was enough to alarm Putnam, who ordered Stirling to send two regiments across the marsh to take up positions on the Gowanus Road near the Red Lion Inn, a few miles south of the intersection with the Jamaica Road.

Stirling sent the Delaware and Maryland Regiments. Since the commanders were in New York for the Zedwitz court martial, Major Thomas McDonough was in command of the Delaware battalion and Major Mordecai Gist of the Maryland Continentals. Stirling arrayed them in a v-shaped column, with the Delawareans on the left as they faced the British.

They were reinforced by Colonel Samuel Atlee's Pennsylvania Musketry, Colonel Jedidiah Huntington's Connecticut Continentals and Lieutenant Colonel Peter Kachlein's Pennsylvania Associators. So they waited—some 2,100 soldiers—through the night, listening to the sounds of sporadic gunfire in the distant woods.

Dawn arrived with wet, gray skies. Brisk, northerly winds chilled the air.

Looking over his deployment just before the battle began, Stirling addressed the soldiers, recalling Grant's boast that he would conquer America with just 5,000 men.

"He may have 5,000 men with him now," Stirling said. Then, pointing to the millpond behind them between the Gowanus Creek and the Gowanus Road. "We are not so many, but I think we are enough to prevent him advancing further than that mill pond."

The troops cheered the general's remarks.

The main British force on the Jamaica Road engaged in a brief but sharp battle with a patriot force after dawn and marched on, unimpeded, to the Gowanus Road. There they stopped and prepared to dig in. Cornwallis was detached down the road to flank the American center and right.

Although there had been constant skirmishing through the night and in the early hours after dawn, Grant and von Heister up this point had only done enough to worry the Americans, to distract them from the main attack to the north, while they waited for the signal to attack

As a preliminary, Grant ordered an artillery barrage, expecting to unnerve the Americans, sapping their will before he sent his soldiers against them. Stirling responded in kind and for two hours, the din of the artillery was echoed by the exchange of cannon fire between HMS *Roebuck* and the American shore battery at Red Hook, a mile away. The inexperienced American troops remained calm despite the cacophony of cannon fire. Their courage was the resolve of soldiers whose sense of mission was clear and unequivocal.

(Writing to Caesar Rodney on the weekend following the battle, Haslet boasted that the Delaware battalion "stood unmoved in firm array four hours exposed to the fire of the enemy.")

At 9 A.M., two cannons were fired from Bedford, a signal for Grant and von Heister to launch a full-scale assault.

For some reason, Grant delayed. Von Heister, however, moved his Hessians forward to engage the American center. Cornwallis' forces swung down on its flank. Additional British soldiers moved forward from the Bedford camp to swell the numbers of attackers.

The fighting in the center was swift and decisive; the Americans were soon scrambling back to their fortified lines. Sullivan, attempting to rally resistance, was taken prisoner. Hessian soldiers, told by the British that the Americans would show no quarter to "foreigners," bayoneted Americans offering to surrender. In the propaganda that was later spread through the colonies, it was described as a massacre of helpless men.

Cornwallis arrived too late to be of material assistance and moved on towards the sounds of battle down the Gowanus Road.

Grant had finally advanced, his forces formed into two columns: a double column to the left and a single column on the right. Atlee and his Pennsylvania frontiersmen, positioned in an orchard, exchanged the first shots with Grant's advance. Stirling then ordered Atlee and Huntington to move their forces behind hedges at the foot of a nearby hill. Some of Kachlein's Pennsylvanians were sent to join them.

As word of the British sweeping down from the Jamaica Road reached him, Stirling again moved Atlee's, Huntington's, and Kachlein's units, this time into the woods, under command of Brigadier General Samuel Holden Parsons, adding two companies from the Delaware battalion under command of the senior captain, Joseph Stidham.

Grant moved some of his forces to the right in an effort to link with Hessian troops coming from the center.

That turned attention to a hill offering a commanding position over this sector of the battlefield. Parsons advanced to occupy it, but the British had the same idea and beat him to it. Parsons' troops were repulsed.

During the lull that followed, Stidham withdrew a majority of his soldiers and some of Atlee's men went with him, an action that brought strong criticism later from Atlee. In response, Stidham explained that he understood his mission was to feel out the enemy, then return to the lines, and that is what he did.

Parsons decided on another attack on the hill, this time instructing his troops to withhold their fire until the last possible moment. This strategy was very effective and in a half-hour fight the British were sent fleeing from the hill, both sides suffering heavy casualties.

The American success was short-lived. Twenty minutes later the British returned in greater force and this time it was the Americans who had to withdraw, after a fifteen-minute battle.

By now, British and Hessians were converging on Stirling's position from several directions. Stirling, realizing the overwhelming numbers of the British and Hessians, ordered a retreat back to the lines on Brooklyn Heights.

As the Delaware battalion prepared to withdraw, the Second Grenadier battalion under Lieutenant Colonel Henry Moncton moved towards them through an orchard. Moncton assumed the blue-jacketed soldiers ahead of him were Hessians and sent two companies ahead to contact them.

McDonough watched their casual, friendly approach with surprise. He had no misconceptions, however, about their identity. They were the enemy, he knew, but he waited until they were almost upon him before ordering his troops to fire. The Grenadier companies reeled in complete surprise. Their leader, a Lieutenant Wagg, and a sergeant and twenty-one soldiers were taken prisoner. Now McDonough ordered the Delaware battalion to join the retreat, taking captives along.

It was a difficult but orderly withdrawal. The retreating soldiers had to march a quarter of a mile, fighting the enemy part of the way, before it reached the marsh. The enemy occupied every dry land route and a retreating New England militia unit had destroyed the only bridge across the millpond. The escape had to be across the marsh, now rising from incoming tidal waters.

Grant's artillery played upon the marshland, adding to the tension of the retreat.

Lieutenant Wagg hesitated when the firing began, perhaps hoping to be rescued, but Lieutenant William Popham of Captain Henry Darby's Fourth Company, in charge of the prisoners, pointed his gun at the British officer.

"Come along," he said, "or you will die on this spot."

So the soldiers, British and American alike, struggled through the swamp, often having to swim, some grasping at anything that would float. At least one of the prisoners and one of Haslet's soldiers drowned in the marsh.

Stirling had ordered Smallwood's regiment under Major Gist to cover the retreat and they focused on a large, two-story stone house on the Gowanus Road where artillery and musket fire poured forth from the windows at the Americans struggling through the marsh.

There followed an epic struggle as occupation of the house changed six different times before the British forces overwhelmed the Continentals. The heroic effort cost Maryland more than 250 casualties (out of 400 engaged), but it made it possible for most of the Americans to reach the relative safety of the lines on the Brooklyn Heights. Stirling had remained behind to fight with the Marylanders—"fighting like a wolf," according to Gist—and had to surrender.

Washington, watching the action from the Heights, was heard to comment: "Good God! What brave fellows I must lose today." He would later report to Congress that the Maryland and Delaware soldiers "behaved with great bravery and resolution" that day on Long Island.

Parsons and Atlee, retreating from the loss of the strategic hill, also had joined the fighting at the stone house. Most of Atlee's men were taken prisoner but he and a few other frontiersmen eluded capture in the familiar environment of the dense woods. This wasn't the frontier, though, and by late afternoon they had to give up and surrendered. Parsons and seven others managed to evade British patrols all day, hid overnight, and made their way back to the American lines the next morning.

While the battle raged, Haslet and Smallwood were still in New York, waiting impatiently for the opportunity to cross the harbor with New England militia ordered to reinforce Brooklyn Heights. The battle was in its final phase when they arrived on the Heights.

Smallwood asked Washington to put him in command of a force to help the Maryland regiment at the stone house but the commander-in-chief declined, fearing he would only add to the American casualty list. Instead he put Smallwood in charge of the reinforcements just arrived from New York with orders to cover the soldiers coming through the marshland. Smallwood promptly brought their fire to bear on Grant's artillery that was harassing the retreating mass in the marshland, forcing the cannoneers to move back and thereby reducing their effectiveness.

Haslet hurried over to be with his soldiers straggling out of the marsh, wading part way into the muck to help the weariest of his troops make it through.

It was all over by 12:30 P.M. with the British now in possession of the field.

Seemingly, it remained only for them to advance on the line to overwhelm the remaining defenders. Expecting an attack at any moment, a worried Washington walked up and down the line, issuing instructions, encouraging the soldiers, threatening any who showed an inclination to run away. He ordered the soldiers to withhold their fire until they had a sure shot at the enemy.

Clinton, in fact, wanted to launch an immediate assault. Major General John Henry Vaughan agreed with him and made no effort to disguise his anger at the delay.

"With your permission, sir," he declared to Howe, "I am confident I can march my men up the slopes and end this rebellion once and for all. I doubt the rebels have stomach for any further fight. I think we will find them quite submissive when we confront them with our bayonets."

Perhaps the fact that the grenadiers captured by Haslet's regiment had been part of his command stirred the general's blood.

But the memory of Bunker Hill was still too fresh in Howe's mind, nearly fifteen months after that savage battle. Every one of his personal staff of twelve had been a casualty in the assault on that hill and he could not forget their blood covering his boots. He was determined to avoid any repeat of that costly victory. Instead, the British would settle on an old-fashioned siege, advancing trench by trench until he was able to bring all his firepower to bear on the American line.

Thus the field before Brooklyn Heights fell relatively quiet as night fell on August 27. As did the rain.

Campfires appeared across the landscape on both sides of the line, at least for those who could find enough dry wood and shelter from the pelting rain. The British, feeling confident about their position, went under tent. For the Americans, however, the sound of tools digging away on the other side of the line kept them in constant vigilance and few were able to provide themselves with shelter. The British truly were in control of the situation.

The weather continued damp and chilly on the twenty-eighth.

Washington brought over more reinforcements from New York as Howe's troops continued to inch their entrenchments towards the Heights. He changed his mind and now ordered his troops to fire at random at the enemy lines and although that had little impact, it did bolster morale within the American ranks, perhaps the commander-in-chief's principal reason for allowing it. The Americans by now were beginning to realize they might be in a trap: caught between overwhelming numbers on land and the British warships just waiting for a break in the weather to come up behind them and cut off any retreat.

The next day, the twenty-ninth, as rain continued to drench the scene, Washington called his generals to a meeting. Although he usually relied on his own judgment and instincts in making his final decisions, he liked to consult with them on the conduct of the war. (In that same democratic spirit, he sent almost daily reports to the Continental Congress.)

This time, however, the commander-in-chief had his next move already in mind. In a memorandum he distributed to the council, Washington outlined eight reasons for abandoning Brooklyn Heights. He pointed out the perilous condition of the troops suffering from fatigue, weather, and defeat; he noted the inadequacy of the defenses erected along the Heights. There also was a report that the British navy had moved into Long Island Sound, raising the possibility the British would land at the northern end of Manhattan Island, isolating the Americans both on Long Island and in New York.

After presenting his reasons, Washington told the officers:

"I have ordered General Heath and General Hughes (assistant quartermaster) to gather every available boat. I told them to have them at the Brooklyn ferry wharf tonight. We will evacuate our troops under cover of night."

Between his order and its execution serious peril faced the Americans. There was a mighty army in front of them and a mile of water, perhaps filled with British warships, between them and the relative safety of Manhattan Island. The reaction of his officers was a mixture of relief at the decision for action and concern over the logistics of carrying out Washington's bold plan.

"Colonel Glover's regiment will carry out the transport of the troops," Washington continued. "He'll also have Colonel Hutchinson and his men from Salem. They're experienced sailors, too. General McDougal, you'll supervise the loading at the ferry.

"Pass the word down to your staffs. We will move the troops one regiment at a time, starting with the volunteers and militia. The Delaware and Maryland troops will remain until last. Shee and Magaw's regiments and what's left of Chester's men will stay 'til near the last."

A sadness came over the general's face at the implication of the phrase "what's left." The Sixth Connecticut troops under Colonel John Chester had suffered heavy casualties in the fighting with the Hessians and British on the twenty-seventh. The Pennsylvania regiments of Colonel John Shee and Colonel Robert Magaw were intact, having come over on the twenty-eighth as reinforcements.

"It is imperative the soldiers move as quietly as possible from their positions to the ferry," Washington continued. "Keep the campfires burning. Create every impression that our army is standing fast.

"I'll issue an order to the troops that we're going to move the sick and wounded over to New York tonight and say that replacements will fill their ranks. That may deceive any traitorous minds within our ranks who would betray our movement to the British."

He paused, then concluded: "Pray that the rain and wind keep the enemy away."

The meeting dispersed. It was a solemn group that moved out of the headquarters. The task of moving some 9,500 soldiers across the harbor before dawn without arousing the suspicion of the British and Hessians was daunting. Clearly, the success of the evacuation would determine whether the Continental army would continue to exist.

Brigadier General Thomas Mifflin, whom Washington had placed in charge of Stirling's brigade, immediately went to inform Haslet and the other officers now under his command.

Mifflin was a thirty-two-year-old Philadelphian, active in the Sons of Liberty, who went against his Quaker faith to join the army. He had first served on Washington's staff as his aide-de-camp and subsequently was made quartermaster general. The duties did nothing to satisfy his craving for action and he was given his own command.

Haslet was walking among his soldiers, chatting with individuals, looking for sickness, checking the state of their arms, giving them encouragement. They had gotten soaked in the retreat across the marshland and the incessant rain provided no opportunity to dry out. A lot of the gunpowder also was soaked. They had been unable to set up tents and had to take whatever cover they could find from the trees and brush. Some of them waited in trenches in water up to their waists.

By now some doubt had grown within him about the quality of leadership on the American side. Washington was a person one could respect, Haslet thought. Clearly the fate of the army and the promise of independence depended on this man's strong will, self-discipline, and determination. But why, Haslet asked himself, would he choose to put his army in such a vulnerable position? If it was true that Washington depended on the advice of his generals, Haslet decided, then the commander-in-chief was not getting the best of advice.

(In that weekend letter to Rodney, Haslet said he feared that "General Washington has too heavy a task, assisted mostly by beardless boys.")

His regiment had suffered two dead in the battle. Twenty-five others were missing, including First Lieutenant Jonathan Harney from the Third Company and Second Lieutenant Alexander Stewart from the Fifth Company. They had gone with Stidham to the hill contested by Parsons and had stayed to fight with Atlee after Stidham withdrew. McDonough was slightly wounded in the knee and Second Lieutenant Enoch Anderson of the First Company had a superficial throat wound. Both would quickly recover.

Haslet was talking to Captain Jonathan Caldwell of the Second Company, which had been recruited from Kent County, when Mifflin found him.

Caldwell had fought in the French and Indian War and, so, was one of Haslet's more experienced company commanders. But he was best known for the brood of gamecocks he had brought with him on the march north. They had provided a great deal of entertainment in the encampments and their success brought Caldwell many rewards.

Caldwell had found shelter for their pens under a wagon and was providing his birds some feed when Haslet stopped by.

"Jonathan, some of the officers in other regiments are saying our soldiers fought the other day like your cock birds," Haslet said, smiling. "I was quite proud to hear that. I only wish I had been here for the fighting."

"We did do well, Colonel," Caldwell replied. "And I do believe the blue hen's fighting spirit is in our men."

Haslet nodded, patted the soldier on the shoulder and turned to greet Mifflin.

At the general's request Haslet summoned his officers to the scene.

"General Washington has decided to evacuate," Mifflin informed them. "It's a very delicate procedure, as I'm sure you're all aware. The general will issue an order to evacuate all the sick and wounded to New York, starting tonight. He will say we're bringing in replacements, but that's intended merely to deceive the British, should there be spies in our ranks.

"Your men will stay to the last, doing your best to convince the enemy that our lines remain fully manned. The enemy must believe there are thousands of Americans along our lines even as the actual number dwindles to your few hundred."

A bold plan, Haslet thought. And one with great possibilities for disaster, particularly for his own soldiers. But any plan was better than waiting for the British and Hessians to breach the line and take the whole army prisoner. That seemed inevitable under present conditions.

Haslet's and the remnants of Smallwood's battalions were placed at the northern end of the line, by the fortification dubbed "Fort Putnam," facing the main British force.

The evacuation began after nine o'clock, starting with the volunteers and militia, equipment strapped to their backs. They marched silently through the rainy night towards the ferry wharf, whispering orders down the line. Brigadier General Alexander McDougal of New York supervised the loading of the waiting boats but Washington constantly checked the progress.

(There was some grumbling among soldiers from outside New England about the presence of Negroes in Glover's Marblehead regiment.)

In the early part of the evacuation the tide ran against them and the wind became becalmed. For those boats with only sails, the crews improvised oarlocks so they could row the boats. There was near panic among soldiers anxious to get across the harbor to the safety of New York as the evacuation slowed. Nevertheless, the withdrawal continued hour by hour, boats disappearing into the night, loaded with men and their equipment, to return in due time to repeat the process. After a couple of anxious hours, the tide changed and the wind blew up, making the passage more swift. And so the withdrawal continued through the cold, wet night.

Early in the pre-dawn morning of the twenty-ninth, Major Alexander Scammel, aide-de-camp of the day for Washington, told Mifflin to begin withdrawing the Pennsylvania elements in the final phase.

They were packed and moving when Washington rode up and confronted Colonel Edward Hand of the First Pennsylvania Continentals.

"My God, Colonel Hand!" he exclaimed. "Why have you abandoned your post? I am very surprised. Why are these men not on the lines?"

"We're not abandoning our post. I am only following orders from my commanding officer," Hand responded.

"That's not possible," Washington said, barely controlling his anger. "Where is General Mifflin?"

Mifflin rode up at this point.

"General Mifflin," the commander-in-chief said stoutly, "I fear you have ruined us by so unseasonably withdrawing your troops from the lines."

Mifflin responded with a mixture of embarrassment and anger. "General, I did it by your order. Is not Scammel your aide?" Washington conceded he was.

"Well, he brought me the order to begin withdrawing these men and I can only assume it came from you."

"There's been a mistake," Washington said with some contrition. "Have the men return to the lines."

This they did, with considerable reluctance.

The Delaware battalion awaited its turn anxiously. All through the night they could hear the enemy working with picks and shovels to move their assault positions closer. As dawn approached, the line was so thinly manned that a British soldier probing to find the reason why the Americans seemed so much quieter would surely discover the truth.

When the order to retreat finally came, Haslet had his officers quietly pass the word to the men to gather whatever they could carry and fall in.

He worried about the lightening skies. How could it be possible for the enemy not to discover what was happening?

Once more the weather became a fateful ally. A dense fog spread across the harbor and over Long Island. The enemy could not even see the American line, let alone discover it was being abandoned.

The final defenders vanished in the thick fog.

Washington was waiting when Haslet marched his battalion smartly to the wharf. He nodded his appreciation as the soldiers marched by and boarded the waiting boats.

When the last man was loaded, he turned to Haslet.

"Well, Colonel," he said with unaccustomed lightheartedness, "shall we go to town?" Washington dismounted from his gray charger, and both man and beast boarded that last boat. It was quickly lost in the fog as it headed safely to New York.

By now British patrols had discovered why the line had fallen so quiet and as quickly as they could spread the word, the British began occupying the abandoned positions. But the American army—all 9,500 men, their guns, baggage, provisions, horses, and equipment (and Caldwell's birds)—was gone, vanished in the night!

Chapter Thirty-Two

The Rogers Rangers Affair

John Haslet fell seriously ill in mid-September of 1776. Fever, diarrhea, ennui left him prostrated, unable to get out of bed, and wondering if the "putrid fever" would do to him what the British so far hadn't. ("Putrid fever" was similar to dysentery.)

The Delaware battalion's performance at Brooklyn Heights had won it praise that raised the pride of the folks back home. In camp talk, they had become known respectfully as the "Blue Hen's Chickens," a reference to Jonathan Caldwell's fighting brood.

And now there was a question whether the man credited with establishing the discipline and training in which this fighting spirit thrived might live long enough to enjoy the accolades afforded his fighting continentals.

It would be a few weeks before he would rise from his sickbed and subsequently prove himself one of the most able commanders in the Continental army.

A congressional committee that visited the American encampments in late September reported about 25,000 soldiers on roster but nearly a third of them out sick. It reported arrangements for treating the sick were dismal, with a shortage of hospitals and even surgeons to treat the sick and wounded. According to roll calls on September 21, one-third of the American soldiers were too ill to stand duty. More Americans died from the illness than from British fire at Brooklyn Heights.

The battalion surgeon, Dr. James Tilton of Dover, and the second-in-command, Lieutenant Colonel Gunning Bedford Sr., were shocked when they first saw Haslet.

"I'm sorry I don't have a warm glass to offer you," he said weakly. It was the practice in colonial homes to greet the family doctor at the door with a glass whose contents were designed to stir the spirits as well as warm the body.

"I understand," Tilton responded, smiling. "It's hardly necessary in this weather. And I suspect warmth is not something you're in need of right now. You seem to have an excess."

Haslet nodded, too spent to speak.

Tilton, thirty-seven, had had formal training in medicine in the new medical school in Philadelphia set up by John Morgan and William Shippen Jr. He had been a member of the school's seventh class, graduating in 1771. For this patient, he decided, pragmatic ministrations were necessary.

"I've prepared some tea for you, John," he said, placing a cup carefully in Haslet's hands and raising his head so he could sip. This herbal tea was designed to stimulate bowel movements as a start of treatment that would subsequently include castor oil, sunflower seeds, rum, and water—mixed together in various combinations but not all at the same time—intended to purge the system of whatever infection was causing the illness.

As Haslet sipped the tea, Bedford brought him the news.

The battalion had moved to Kingsbridge on the northern tip of Manhattan Island, assigned to Mifflin's brigade, in a division commanded by Major General William Heath of Massachusetts. Its specific task was to guard Washington's headquarters.

Washington kept five brigades under General Israel Putnam in the city and part way up the East River. Major General Joseph Spencer of Connecticut was given six brigades to guard the balance of the East River shoreline as far as Harlem.

British General William Howe, meanwhile, had moved his headquarters to Newtown, on the Long Island side of the East River. Brooklyn Heights was left to von Heister's Hessians.

During this interlude, his brother, Admiral Richard Howe, made one more effort at ending the conflict. He released the captured General John Sullivan with a message to Congress inviting that body to send representatives—as "private citizens" since the government refused to recognize the legitimacy of the Congress—to discuss a settlement.

On September 11 Benjamin Franklin, John Adams, and Edward Rutledge arrived on Staten Island to meet with the admiral.

Franklin had previously met Lord Howe in London, on Christmas Day, 1774, a meeting arranged by Howe's sister Caroline, with whom Franklin had developed a friendly relationship over the chess board. Their discussions that day, and subsequently, failed to close the chasm between the colonies and the mother country despite Lord Howe's apparent eagerness to intermediate.

Their effort now at reviving the friendly aura of those earlier meetings was strained and the admiral's opening remarks added further chill to the room. There was bantering over the status of the delegation and Howe began his presentation by stating he would hate to see the Americans defeated.

Haslet smiled as Bedford repeated Franklin's riposte:

"I can assure you, my lord, that we will do everything in our power to spare you that pain."

Haslet could imagine a sparkle in Franklin's eye when he responded.

The meeting was fruitless. There was nothing that hadn't been presented before and rejected by both Washington and the Congress. All the admiral had to offer was forgiveness if the colonies' reaffirmed allegiance to the British government. Upon that, the admiral said, the government would do everything to ease the actions that had offended the colonies.

"I would point out to his lordship," Adams interjected, "that the colonies have repeatedly sent petitions to the government explaining our grievances and in every instance our petitions have been ignored. The colonies now have declared their independence. The government is going to have to deal with them individually. The Congress which we represent does not have powers to deal on their behalf."

Howe considered the response, then commented:

"In that case, gentlemen, I guess there is nothing further to discuss."

The three Americans bade their good-byes and left.

And what about New York, Haslet wondered?

Washington had vacillated over the future of New York town. He valued it as a key point between New England and the rest of the colonies. On the other hand, it was a precarious holding. There was the real possibility Howe could throw his forces across the northern end of Manhattan and his brother's fleet could surround the lower end of the island, trapping the Continental army.

He had attended a war council meeting with Washington on September 7 (shortly before he fell ill) which advised Washington to abandon the town and put it to the torch. Haslet was among those urging, in his words, that the town be "laid to ashes." Even the prominent New Yorker and patriot John Jay supported the idea of abandoning the town and reducing it to embers.

There was little debate over abandoning the town, but setting it afire was another matter. Congress, on September 3, had passed a resolution that the town be spared, expressing the opinion that even if the British occupied it, the Americans would recapture it in due time. Washington always hesitated to impose his will over Congress.

On September 12, Bedford told Haslet, Washington decided to withdraw to a better defensive position on Harlem Heights, but he spared the town.

The next move was Howe's. On September 15, he loaded eighty-four boats on the Long Island side of the East River, filled them with soldiers and sent them off to land at Kip's Bay (present day Murray Hill), as a prelude to occupying New York.

The sight of the boats filled with soldiers, bayonet at the ready, was too much for the American defenders. Cannon fire from seven British warships that had sailed up the river added to the effect. It was more fearful than the poorly trained Americans could bear. They broke and ran.

Washington was in the area and tried to rally them, riding head-on at the fleeing ranks, whacking some of the fleeing soldiers with the broad end of his sword, snapping his pistols at others.

"Stand and fight, damn you!" he shouted at them, throwing his hat on the ground. "Turn around, for God's sake. You're soldiers. Defend your country. Good God! Are these the men with whom I'm supposed to defend America?"

Privates and officers felt the general's wrath. Bedford said he had been told that Washington used his whip on some, including—according to some reports—a brigadier general and a colonel.

The fleeing men were oblivious to this angry figure astride a great white horse and simply dashed pell mell for the countryside, putting as much distance between themselves and the landing place as their legs could manage. Washington ignored his own danger until he finally turned his horse around and rode after them, continuing his diatribe against the panicked men.

His force safely ashore, Howe, always comfortable with the social perquisites of his position, chose to stop off at the home of a Tory merchant, Robert Murray, rather than chase the Americans.

"General Howe seems not too sanguine at pursuing his advantages," Haslet commented. "Thank the Lord for that."

He lapsed into sleep and his visitors departed.

On the night of September 20, renegade Americans did to New York what Washington had been reluctant to do. A succession of fires were started in buildings near Whitehall Street. Fanned by high winds, it swept up the west side of Broad Street to Velattenberg Hill. They were so intense the harbor lit up like daylight.

The British dispatched boatloads of sailors and marines from their ships to help fight the fire and deal with the incendiaries. They found men running through town with torches, tossing them into buildings. While some sailors attempted to squelch the flames, the marines moved to stop the torchbearers. Several were bayoneted. One was tossed into a flaming building. But the fire was too far along for them to do anything but hope fate would spare the town. When it finally subsided after dawn, nearly a quarter of the town had been razed.

Washington's dry remark when word of the fire reached him was: "Providence or some good honest fellow has done more for us than we were disposed to do for ourselves."

By October 5, Haslet felt well enough to answer a September 12 letter from Caesar Rodney. Haslet blamed his affliction on the damp conditions in which he lived those last couple of days on Brooklyn Heights. He was distressed to find that he had been reported killed in action at Brooklyn Heights and thanked Rodney for assuring his stricken family that he was all right.

In a long letter to Mayor Nicholas VanDyke of New Castle on October 8, Haslet noted that elections to the legislature under the new constitution had been set to coincide with Fair Day, October 21, in an apparent attempt to distract attention from the issues. Haslet said he counted on the ladies to concentrate the men's attention on the election.

"In this I speak assuredly," he wrote, "because, so far as I know, the ladies are ten to one on the right side, and their inspiring virtue is sufficient to save the colonies."

In an October 10 letter to Caesar Rodney, Haslet expressed his concern about a festering sectional conflict within the army, between the "northern" (i.e., New England) troops and "southern" (i.e., colonies from Pennsylvania south) troops. It had been exacerbated by the incident at Kip's Bay where the Connecticut militia fled in panic at the sight of the British invasion force.

"Some officers have poured much contempt upon the (northern) troops and great animosity subsists just now among them," Haslet wrote. "(I) have used my small influence to discourage it. 'Tis likely to have most dangerous consequences."

Caesar Rodney's brother Thomas was among those complaining about the behavior of the New England troops.

Finally, on October 11, Haslet returned to duty, once again under Lord Stirling, for whom Haslet had developed great respect. Stirling had been released by the British and returned to his command on October 7. Mifflin was reassigned as quartermaster, where his talents and previous experience were much needed. Meantime, the Delaware Continentals had shrunk below 600 men. The roster report of October 4 listed 569 men, with about 450 present and fit for duty. Haslet, of course, was counted among those sick and absent at the time.

On October 12, General Howe stirred from his lethargy and moved his forces to Throg's Neck on the southeast corner of Westchester County, just off Long Island Sound to the east of Washington's position at Harlem Heights. The British landing was unopposed but when Howe moved up a causeway towards the bridge leading to the mainland he was met with a twenty-five-member detachment of riflemen under Colonel Edward Hand of Pennsylvania. They had torn up the planking on the bridge and hid behind a long pile of cord wood. When the advance guard came within range they rose up and unleashed well-aimed fire. The British withdrew in confusion.

Four days later, Washington decided to move his forces north of the Harlem River, into Westchester County, leaving behind 2,800 men to hold Fort Washington, a decision with tragic consequences.

The move to Westchester County was slow going. Because of the lack of horses and wagons, the available wagons had to make more than one trip to complete the move.

By the eighteenth of October the two armies were marching northwards in parallel routes, the Americans headed along the Bronx River towards White Plains; the British along the Boston Post Road to New Rochelle.

Howe decided to establish his new headquarters at New Rochelle and threw out a line from New Rochelle to Mamaroneck.

The Americans were now based at White Plains, except for the Fort Washington garrison and Stirling's brigade, still at Washington's former headquarters on Harlem Heights.

At 2 A.M. on October 21 Stirling received orders to bring his brigade to White Plains. The soldiers, including the Delaware Continentals, were on the march before daylight, leaving their baggage train to catch up as best it could, and at 9 A.M. reported to Washington's new headquarters.

The new line established at White Plains was on slightly rising ground and Washington had a double line of entrenchments dug. His right flank rested on the Bronx River, his left on a swamp. The flanks were drawn back slightly to form a modified horseshoe.

It was Washington, not Howe, who decided on the next move.

Haslet was summoned to the headquarters on the twenty-second and Washington, who had been chatting with staff officers and his commanders, including Stirling, seemed suddenly more animated as the Delaware officer arrived.

"Good afternoon, Colonel," he greeted him. "I trust your men are well settled now. I hope you are finally well. I was concerned about you."

"Yes, General, thank you."

When Washington said he was concerned about you, you felt privileged.

"We've set up camp as best we can since our baggage train is straggling in from Harlem Heights."

"Well, no matter. We've decided on a diversion for your men. It will occupy them while they wait for your supplies. Lord Stirling will explain."

Stirling stood up from his chair.

"You've heard of Rogers' Rangers, I assume," Stirling began.

"Of course," Haslet responded.

It was a name that had acquired almost legendary status from its frontier exploits in the French and Indian War. It had been led by a youthful and audacious Robert Rogers, a native of Massachusetts Bay and a descendant of Scotch-Irish ancestors. The Howes' brother George had fought with the Rangers during the French and Indian War and was killed at Ticonderoga in 1758.

Rogers had gone to England after that war, returning when the Revolutionary War began. He applied to Washington for a commission but was turned down. He then was granted a commission in the British army and formed the Queen's American Rangers (although few of his former compatriots joined him).

Now in late October of 1776, Rogers, approaching his forty-fifth birthday anniversary, and his rangers were stationed at Mamaroneck on Long Island Sound on the extreme right of the British line.

"Rogers has about 500 men in his command," Stirling was telling Haslet. "They're stationed in a field near the woods there. He's set up headquarters in the village schoolhouse.

"His men are somewhat detached from the rest of the British line. We feel they're vulnerable."

"Rogers is a vexatious man," Washington interjected. "His men have been committing heinous assault on local militia."

A pause while Washington brought his emotions under control:

"I can't forgive him for young Nathan Hale." His voice faded as he lost himself in thought about the personable young school teacher.

Hale, just twenty-one, was a captain in the Connecticut Rangers whom Washington had sent to Long Island to find out what he could about the British plans to invade New York. When Washington abandoned that town and the British moved in, Hale crossed over to the town and continued his efforts to ascertain British plans.

He was trying to return to the American lines when he was stopped and questioned. When intelligence information revealed his role as a spy he was hanged on September 22.

"It was Rogers' men who captured him," Washington said and once again grew silent.

Stirling resumed:

"You'll march tonight. Besides your own men you'll have soldiers from Maryland and Virginia, about 750 men in all. I must caution you that you'll be marching very close to the enemy lines to reach Rogers' position.

"He's set out pickets on the roads leading to his position, but he's left his rear unprotected, assuming it's covered by the nearby British. That's where you should attack him."

Stirling had been pointing to roads and positions on a map as he outlined the plan. Haslet studied it closely.

"So we're to march out of sight and sound of Rogers' pickets and the rest of the British army, sneak around behind him and . . ."

"Destroy the Queen's American Rangers and bring Rogers to me," Washington said vehemently, finishing Haslet's statement, then, more calmly, adding:

"Incidentally, I commend to your attention one of the Virginia officers to be assigned to this task, Major John Green. You'll find him most able for any important assignment of your choosing."

"I'm sure we'll find something worthy of your confidence in him, General," Haslet responded. Washington seemed satisfied and withdrew from the table, leaving Stirling and Haslet to continue their planning.

Later, Haslet gathered with his captains and the officers from Maryland and Virginia, including Green. He repeated the strategy discussed earlier and made assignments.

Green would lead the advance party.

So, they set out in a nearly moonless night, 750 men, marching silently, communicating only in whispers. At a crossroads near Mamaroneck they took the road towards New Rochelle. Scouts from Green's detachment reported back they could see British soldiers silhouetted against their campfires.

Haslet's expedition followed a road that would pass them between Rogers and the rest of the British force and eased by, nervously watching the dozens of campfires blazing in the distance.

Thus they arrived in the woods opposite the Queen's Rangers' camp and proceeded to crawl towards the sleeping enemy.

They were told that a single sentry guarded this approach and that information proved correct. The sentry was an Indian, a reminder of the Rangers' frontier origins. One of Green's men grabbed the sentry, muzzled him to prevent an alarm, then ended a brief struggle with a sword thrust. The Ranger camp remained quiet.

Green's company continued to crawl forward through the woods and brush, the main force right behind. It was Haslet's expectation that the attackers would now burst upon the sleeping enemy, subdue them, capture Rogers, and escape. What they didn't know was that Rogers had decided that night to set up an outpost with sixty men between his encampment and the lone sentry.

Green's advance stumbled upon them in the darkness.

The Rangers, rousing from their sleep, ignored demands for their surrender and hand-to-hand combat followed. Haslet, close behind Green's advance, called for the rest of his force to join the attack. Hundreds of Americans jumped up and swarmed over the outpost.

Demands for "Surrender you Tory dogs!" resounded in the darkness but it was as often uttered by a Ranger as an American and it was hard to tell friend from foe. After a brief skirmish, the overwhelmed outpost was subdued.

By now the Rangers in the main camp had been awakened and were scrambling for their weapons. They formed a line and faced it towards the sounds of combat and the dark shapes moving in the field in front of them. Rogers, it was later learned, fled the scene at the first sound of gunfire.

Haslet ordered his men to move forward, only to be stopped by a volley from the camp.

The area was thoroughly alarmed now. Soldiers in the other British encampments were rushing from their tents, grabbing weapons, waiting for orders.

Haslet considered the situation.

"I believe it best we take our prisoners and prizes and return to White Plains," he said calmly to his officers.

The drummer was ordered to sound retreat. Accordingly, the Americans assembled and marched off in the darkness in quick time, pleased with their night's work. They had in custody thirty-six prisoners, a pair of colors, sixty weapons, and many highly-prized blankets. Haslet suffered three men killed and about twelve wounded, including Major Green and Captain Charles Pope of the Delawares.

Toward dawn, well away from Mamaroneck and the British line, the Americans had relaxed and were trudging along toward White Plains in the fading darkness when there was a sudden volley from the woods. Several of the marching Americans fell mortally wounded. The remainder scattered into the woods on the opposite side of the road and returned the fire.

As the morning light grew brighter, the firing ceased. The bodies of the dead and wounded were quite visible on the road.

Someone in the woods across the road cried out to his comrades: "Hold your fire! I think they're Americans."

"We are Americans," Haslet shouted towards the voice. "And who are you?"

"We're Americans, too," the voice responded. "I'm coming out."

Haslet ordered his soldiers to cease firing while a couple of men emerged from the woods, dressed in the hunting shirts that were the common uniform of the Continental army.

"These are some of the Blue Hens Chickens," one said, examining one of the fallen soldiers.

Haslet stepped out of his hiding place and walked warily to meet them.

"And who are you?" he demanded.

"We're from Colonel Samuel Miles' Pennsylvania State Riflemen," the soldier responded. "We thought you were Hessians."

The man obviously was distressed.

"I'm Colonel Haslet of the Delaware battalion returning from a secret mission for General Washington," Haslet said angrily. "And you've done more harm to my men in these past few minutes than the enemy was able to accomplish at Brooklyn Heights."

"I can't tell you how terribly sorry we are, Colonel," the Pennsylvanian responded. "Colonel Miles is not with us but I'm sure he would share your grief at this blunder on the part of his men. We did not expect Americans to be marching at this hour, on this road."

"You will have to ask God to forgive you," Haslet said. "I don't have it in my heart to do so."

He looked at the road where nine Delaware soldiers lay dead; six Pennsylvanians had died in the woods.

Haslet ordered the drummer to sound assembly and the solemn task force now resumed its march to White Plains, its feeling of triumph drained by the tragedy of the early morning.

Later that day Stirling ordered his brigades to muster on the parade grounds and there publicly praised Haslet and his troops for the night's work. They barely had time to settle down and begun making camp as comfortable as possible when the army was alerted of the approaching enemy.

Chapter Thirty-Three

Chatterton Hill

The attack on Rogers' Rangers not only annoyed General Howe, it chased away his languor. Two days later, the twenty-fifth of October, the British and Hessians were on the move toward White Plains.

Washington had spread his forces across both sides of the Bronx River, meanwhile sending an advance force of about 1,600 soldiers under General Spencer to meet the advancing British at Scarsdale.

Howe's forces arrived at this point on the morning of the twenty-eighth. Spencer's Connecticut troops, stationed behind walls and fences, twice turned back the British and Hessian troops. At one point, fleeing Hessian soldiers threw down their arms and supplies to escape the American volley. The Americans rushed out, retrieved the discarded weapons, and drank amply from abandoned flagons of rum before the British forced them to retreat. Outnumbered and in danger of being outflanked, Spencer's troops withdrew back to the lines at White Plains.

Howe now gave White Plains his full attention.

The American right rested across the Bronx River, on Chatterton Hill, an elevation of about 180 feet which ran for about three-quarters of a mile from north to south. The hill sloped steeply towards the river and was densely wooded. The hilltop, however, had been cleared for farming.

Washington, fearing the British might gain the hill and thus enfilade his main line, sent Colonels Rufus Putnam, Eleazer Brooks, and Joseph Graham with their Massachusetts militia to this hill to begin some entrenchments.

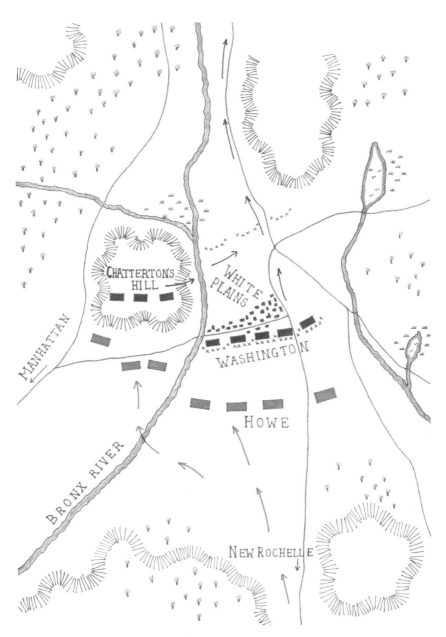

Deployment for Battle of White Plains and direction of retreat
Map by John Mackenzie of britishbattles.com

Then he ordered Haslet's regiment to augment the defense. The regiment by now counted fewer than 300 fit and able, including Haslet, Bedford, McDonough, three captains, three second lieutenants, and three ensigns.

Washington put Brigadier General Alexander McDougal in charge of Chatterton Hill with his First New York Regiment, Colonel Rudolphus Ritzema's Third New York, and Colonel Samuel Webb's Connecticut unit. Washington also sent Smallwood's Maryland line, which had been replenished after its heavy losses at Brooklyn Heights, and it and the Delaware Continentals were placed in the center of the line. The force guarding Chatterton Hill had grown to about 1,600.

The British assembling in the plain across the river presented a breathtaking spectacle: thousands of red-coated British soldiers and blue-coated Hessians formed in perfect columns, the sun reflecting off their rifles and diamond-like flashes of light sparkling on their bayonets, suggesting they had been freshly cleaned for the grisly work to come. Officers on horseback gathered together in front of the line, obviously conferring about the attack.

A little after 10 A.M., the officers' conference ended, a portion of the British force faced left, and in one long column marched to the river, their movement partly obscured from the Americans' view by the dense woods. The remaining soldiers, some 10,000 of them, settled down to be mere spectators to the upcoming battle.

Fallen trees and hard-working beavers had dammed the river and it was so swollen the Hessians refused to cross until a bridge had been improvised. While their engineers proceeded to nail fence posts to some of the fallen trees to form a bridge, the impatient British marched downstream, found a fordable crossing and took it, the soldiers cheering at the top of their lungs, as much to razz the reluctant Hessians as to frighten the waiting Americans. There were 4,000 soldiers and a dozen artillery pieces.

McDougal, an inexperienced officer, seemed a bit uncertain and hesitant when Haslet approached him with news of the enemy movement.

"I'd suggest, General," Haslet commented, with all the deference his anxiety would permit, "that you post those Massachusetts and Connecticut men on our right, on the south slope. There are stone walls there to provide cover."

"Yes," McDougal agreed and the order was given. There were about 430 men, approximately a fourth of his force, involved.

"Perhaps Smallwood, Ritzema, and Webb could hold our left flank," Haslet added. That suggestion, too, was quickly implemented.

As usual, the assault began with the thunder of artillery.

The first American casualty was a Connecticut soldier, struck in the thigh by a cannon ball. At that the whole contingent began to run. It took the yeoman efforts of the officers to turn them around.

The wooded slopes soon filled with smoke from the guns and fires started by the cannon balls. It was impossible to make out the movement of the enemy troops below.

Noticing two field pieces and their crews standing idly on the hill, Haslet suggested to McDougal: "General, I think it's time to bring these pieces into play."

The gun crews resisted McDougal's command and Haslet strode to one of the guns, grabbed a tow rope and began dragging it forward. Suddenly, a ball struck near the gun, scattering shot and setting ablaze the sponges used to clean the gun. The artillerymen fled towards the woods.

"Hold your positions," Haslet shouted at the retreating men. The commanding presence in his voice caused them to hesitate a moment. One returned. The others resumed flight but then two of them stopped and returned to help prepare the field piece for firing.

Their courage held for only two salvos. Apparently satisfied they had performed their duty, they dragged their field piece off the battlefield. Haslet could only shake his head in wonderment.

Meanwhile, Smallwood's and Ritzema's soldiers opened fire on the Hessian bridge builders below them, sending them running in disorder.

By now the British force, led by Brigadier General Alexander Leslie, had crossed and Leslie ordered a bayonet charge.

Smallwood and Ritzema moved down the hill to meet them. The British infantry faltered under the heavy fire from the Americans.

The remaining British forces and the Hessians had meanwhile crossed the river, formed into a column and marched along the base of the hill, then turned up the slope. Again, Ritzema and Smallwood contested the advance. When a detachment of British light infantry tried to turn the left flank, Webb's Connecticut troops drove them back.

While the American left flank thus seemed to have turned back the enemy advance, attention turned to the American right where Hessian troops under Colonel Rall lay hidden on a wooded elevation south of Chatterton Hill. His 250 dragoons—mounted soldiers—suddenly rose up and swept down the slope, across a little valley, and charged against Brooks' and Putnam's militia. At first the militia resisted stoutly. Then Birch's British light dragoons appeared. The sound of the kettledrums and trumpets followed by the galloping horses and flashing sabers, terrorized the militia. They broke and fled. The dragoons over-took them, cut off their retreat, and killed or wounded many. After a half-mile of this chaotic retreat, some of the militia stopped to resist but again were routed. Some fled; the others surrendered.

The Delaware regiment's right flank now was exposed. Haslet drew the men back toward the north. Rall sent his full force against the Delaware battalion.

Uncharacteristically, a part of the first three companies broke and were driven from the field. Haslet kept the others together, lined them up behind a fence, and twice stopped the advancing enemy. Bedford, Captain Jonathan Caldwell (keeper of the Blue Hens chickens), and Ensign Cord Hazzard fell wounded. Captain Nathan Adams of the Sixth Company was killed.

Meanwhile, the Marylanders and Ritzema's New Yorkers on the left were being driven back by the steady pressure from the superior British numbers. Smallwood was wounded twice. McDougal retreated with the Maryland and New York soldiers to a road leading to the main lines, then ordered his troops to halt and protect Haslet's withdrawal.

Haslet stood alone on the battlefield. The dragoons were return-ing from their chase after the militia and formed for a charge. The rest of the attacking force also was preparing an assault.

"We seem to have been deserted by all hands," Haslet said to his commanders. "We have no choice but to retire."

This they did in good order, taking the artillery along, pausing oc-casionally to discourage any enemy soldiers who came within musket range. A captain in Webb's regiment defended the bridge across the Bronx River, holding off a British force twice the size of his force.

Belatedly, more American troops were arriving to help out, sent from the main force, but they were too late. Now out of harm's way, Haslet formed his men and marched smartly back into camp.

The British took possession of Chatterton Hill, formed at the top of the hill, and dressed their line but made no attempt at pursuit.

The battle for Chatterton Hill was brief, but violent. Washington's secretary, Colonel Robert Harrison, reported it lasted about fifteen minutes. Delaware lost fifteen who were killed and as many wounded. Estimates of the total American losses ranged from less than 100 killed and wounded to 313. British/Hessian losses were consistently estimated at 229.

There was one more battle between the two sides before the day ended, this time on the left flank of the American line, across the Bronx River, employing those enemy soldiers who had been spectators to the earlier assault on Chatterton Hill. Although there was much troop movement, the battle never got beyond the artillery stage.

Washington, meanwhile, became concerned that the British might outflank him on both sides and decided to move north. He told Stirling to hold the White Plains position temporarily as a rear guard while the sick and wounded were moved to a safer distance, followed by the baggage and equipment. Thus, when Haslet and his battalion arrived at camp they found all their baggage, artillery, and supplies gone.

The night of October 28 they were forced to sleep without tents or blankets, warmed only by whatever fires they could maintain. (Lieutenant Enoch Anderson recalled years later that they slept comfortably even though it snowed all night.)

Washington now established a new position at North Castle, across the Croton River. His forces now occupied hills only twenty to thirty feet higher, but steeper. He ordered his soldiers to burn several barns and a house which contained forage and stores that couldn't be moved.

Howe at this point decided he needed reinforcements and broke off contact. It was two more days before Lord Hugh Percy arrived with the reinforcements, but now heavy rains made Howe feel he should wait still longer. By noon of the thirty-first, the storm stopped but Howe now decided it was too muddy for an attack. So, once again, the British commander-in-chief dictated his army wait.

Finally, on Friday, November 1, the British attacked—not once, but twice—starting at 9 A.M.

These attacks never got beyond the stage of artillery duels. In both cases the American artillery silenced the British guns and scattered assembling enemy troops before they could ever get into battle.

Howe decided once again to rest his army, the two forces only a long cannon shot apart.

The weather was cold and fires dotted the hills and fields as soldiers tried to warm themselves against the chill of both weather and inaction.

And then, on the night of November 3, the Americans could hear the sounds of British supply wagons on the move and, surprisingly, growing fainter. Howe had decided to withdraw to the town of New York for the winter! By the fifth they were all gone!

American Colonel Gold Silliman of Connecticut later commented to a Tory judge that Howe had the whole American army within his grasp in Westchester County. Only divine providence, he concluded, saved the Americans. If so, God used Howe as the instrument of divine intervention.

On November 6, Washington called a council of his senior officers to discuss the situation. He decided to take 5,000 troops and cross over to Jersey. Heath was assigned 3,000 Connecticut and Massachusetts troops and told to guard the Highlands at Peekskill.

He ordered General Charles Lee, with 7,500 soldiers, to remain at North Castle, until Howe's intentions became clear.

Lee only recently had rejoined the main army after his victory at Charleston, South Carolina. En route he had stopped at Philadelphia to hear himself hailed by the Congress, which also voted a $30,000 loan to enable him to buy an estate in Virginia.

The acclaim fed Lee's feeling that the fate of the nation would be more secure if this British-born son of privilege were the commander-in-chief and not the provincial Virginian who lacked Lee's education and military experience. Lee, only sixteen days older than Washington, was sharp of pen and tongue and missed no opportunity to undermine Washington's command. He would follow his own strategic sense for the next several weeks, ignoring requests from Washington to reinforce the pathetic group of continental soldiers wending their way through Jersey to Pennsylvania.

Chapter Thirty-Four

The Fox and the Hounds

As 1776 neared its end, the British turned the War of the Revolution into a game of the "Fox and the Hounds." The Americans, naturally, played the role of the fox.

It began with the American move across the North River at Peekskill on November 9, led by Haslet's Delaware battalion. The remainder of Lord Stirling's brigade followed in the next two days. Washington crossed on November 12 with the balance of his army. A week had passed since Howe seemingly had abandoned the contest for the winter.

The Americans were 5,000 in number, but a tattered, bedraggled bunch, their numbers diminishing day by day. Many of them had rags wrapped around their feet in place of shoes. Blankets served as coats against the chill. Even the Delawares' smart blue coats and buckskin breeches showed the wear of four months in the field.

Frequent rainstorms turning roads into quagmires would add to the misery of this pitiful corps as it marched south, sometimes just ahead of pursuing British and Hessian soldiers, whom Howe had kept in the field to harass the retreating troops.

Stirling's brigade first stopped briefly at Hackensack, then moved on to Brunswick on November 17. There they waited almost two weeks for the rest of the army.

During that time, Haslet was visited by Thomas Collins and Samuel West, sent by the Delaware Assembly on a mission to determine how best to raise the new Delaware battalion requested by Congress.

Both men were from Kent County and Haslet greeted his visitors warmly, anticipating not only news of Delaware but also of family and home. Collins had been sheriff of Kent County and now was active in Caesar Rodney's militia unit, rising to the rank of lieutenant colonel (and soon, brigadier general). Both had served in Delaware's Constitutional Convention.

"John, I heard you were quite ill," Collins greeted him, "but you look very well now."

"I've been well for more than a month now," Haslet responded, "although I'm a little tired of running from the British.

"Have you any news of my family?"

"I visited Longfield just last week," Collins responded, "and Jemima and the children all were well and managing things. William Killen visits the plantation from time to time just to be sure."

"Caesar Rodney assures me all is well," Haslet said, the concern of the absent husband and father strong in him.

"The news of the battalion's performance in battle has filled the lower counties with pride," West said.

"For good reason," Haslet said. "Our soldiers showed at Brooklyn Heights and at Chatterton Hill that they are men of courage with a fighting spirit to match."

A smile crossed his face: "And we sent the celebrated Major Robert Rogers running for the woods when we attacked his rangers at Mamaroneck."

They all laughed as Haslet recounted the experience, not mentioning the unfortunate "friendly fire" incident with the Pennsylvanians on the way back to camp.

"Are you ready for another campaign?" Collins asked. "The Congress has asked us to raise a new battalion, to serve for the duration of the war. We—and I mean the members of the assembly—feel you should command it. We also need your help with recruiting. There seems to be great resistance among our people to serve, specially since we want them to commit for the duration."

Their instructions were to give preference to filling Haslet's battalion and they carried blank commissions with them, empowered by the assembly to sign officers on the spot.

Haslet pondered the offer. Thoughts of Jemima and his children, of Longfield, filled his mind and stirred his heart. He also was harboring some resentment that the Congress had chosen William Small-wood of Maryland over him when it voted promotions to brigadier general on October 23. There had been some discussion with Washington over preferences in rank and Haslet had believed Washington favored him.

"I confess that home and family are exerting a powerful influence on me," Haslet finally answered. "At the same time, I realize home and family are never secure when tyranny rules unchallenged over our towns and countryside.

"My mind is conflicted. I must weigh these considerations before I give you answers."

They all sat silently until Haslet spoke up again.

"Tell me of the three lower counties, particularly Kent."

"The convention has created a government that is moving reluctantly in support of the cause," Collins said. "There are many who consider the situation an evil, who would prefer to see us restored to England and King George III. But even they have to admit the reality of the British government's unwillingness to deal with us fairly. Given time, I think all but the most adamant Tories will come around."

The mention of Tories prompted a question.

"How is the situation in Sussex?"

"Very bad," West conceded. "They run unchecked through Lewes. Last month they put fear in the hearts of our friends on election day for the assembly. They stood at the courthouse door and demanded all those arriving to vote to swear allegiance to the king. Henry Fisher's liberty pole was chopped down and destroyed. They even threatened to tar and feather him."

"And they have been recruiting for the British army," Collins added.

"What about the militia?" Haslet asked.

"It is difficult to find men to face them," Collins said. "Our best men are here with you and with Sam Patterson over at Amboy. Some of those still at home are suspect in their loyalties. The best we can do now is contain the Tories, but we can't control them."

Haslet shook his head.

"It's different in New Castle County," West said, attempting a cheering note. "The Reverend Reading has closed the door to his church at Appoquinimink."

Episcopalian Philip Reading had remained courageously committed to the Church of England through the turmoil of the time, standing as an inspiration to those who opposed the break with England. It was a difficult position in a county as passionate about independence as New Castle.

Reading had insisted on including prayers for the Crown and government in his services, but had conceded in a letter in March of 1776: "Threats have been used to deter me from reading the prayers for the king but hitherto I have stood firm and my answers to these representations is that having taken the oath of allegiance to his present majesty, having vowed canonical obedience at my ordination and when I was licensed by the bishop, and subscribed to the liturgy of our church, I do not think myself at liberty to dispense with these solemn obligations but shall persevere by God's grace in complying with them."

He vowed he would continue to comply but on July 28 he gave up the effort, declaring it was impossible for him to honor his vows.

"I suppose we should admire his courage," Haslet said, "but religion and its litany should not be an excuse to submit to injustices. I'm grateful that my church has stood almost solidly behind our cause.

"What about that fellow Asbury—Francis Asbury? Has he returned to the colony? I contemplated him as inimical to our side, using religion to encourage the disaffected. I confess to concern about his ability to persuade people."

"He's not been seen for a long time," Collins answered.

Francis Asbury, a follower of John Wesley, had arrived in America in 1771, preaching Wesley's particular style of worship that came to be known as Methodism. He had made several visits to Delaware early in his time in America and attracted a great deal of attention, but in recent years he had concentrated his mission in the more southern colonies and on the frontier. Since Wesley had abandoned his earlier support of the American cause and opposed independence, his followers were suspected as Tories.

(Asbury returned to Delaware in the late '70s and settled in Dover. When he refused to swear allegiance to the new nation, he went into seclusion, protected by friends. After the war he made Dover his base when he spread the Methodist faith throughout Delaware and other colonies. It enjoyed phenomenal growth, eclipsing rival sects, and Kent County became known as the "Cradle of Methodism.")

"The man wasn't much at sermons, but he could pray better than any minister I ever met," Haslet recollected. "But, Magaw has spoken well of Asbury and that says something for the man."

Samuel Magaw was the Anglican rector in Dover, but a strong supporter of the patriot cause.

The visitors thought about these matters silently and the conversation lagged.

Their visit had fulfilled its purpose and it was time for Collins and West to leave. They stood up.

"Please let us know of your decision concerning the new battalion as quickly as you decide," Collins said.

"I will," Haslet agreed. The three exchanged farewells and Haslet accompanied them outside where Collins and West mounted their horses and left for the flying camp at Amboy to see Patterson, who commanded a newly-recruited regiment of Delaware militia. Haslet knew, however, what his answer would be and on November 19 he wrote to Rodney that he would accept the command, despite "tender charities of the father and husband which draw me by the heart strings to revisit Kent."

Washington, meanwhile, had made Fort Lee his first stop. There he witnessed the unfortunate consequences of the decision to hold on to Fort Washington, directly opposite on Manhattan Island. (Fort Lee had been renamed from Fort Constitution in commemoration of Charles Lee's victory in South Carolina.)

Congress felt Fort Washington and Fort Lee would block passage of the British fleet up the river, a vital link in the passageway to Canada. Washington acquiesced.

Twenty-eight hundred men had been assigned to Fort Washington under command of the able Pennsylvanian, Colonel Robert Magaw. The general command felt, and Magaw agreed, that they had enough supplies to withstand an indefinite siege.

Magaw confidently assured everyone that he could hold out through December and then, and only then, would safely withdraw if pressed.

It was a tragic miscalculation.

Howe, marching south from White Plains, arrived on November 15 and called on Magaw to surrender. The Pennsylvanian declined. Howe waited until the next day, then launched four attacks on the fort, driving in the outposts. HMS *Pearl* supported from the river side.

The Americans now all crowded into the fort. It was easy to anticipate what artillery would do to these crowded masses. Magaw sadly conceded that holding out would only result in carnage. He offered his sword. Twenty-eight hundred American soldiers were marched off to fill prisons in and around New York.

Washington and his staff watched the brief encounter through binoculars, in disbelief.

Beyond the loss of men and equipment, the debacle made Washington's leadership ever more questionable and General Lee seemed always to find time to encourage the critics in Congress and the army.

Lee had come to America in 1773. When Congress created the American army in 1775, Artemas Ward and Lee were ranked second and third to Washington. The aging Ward declined service, however, and Lee thus became second on the seniority list.

In Lee's mind, the rankings should have been reversed. There were some officers and politicians who agreed.

Washington was under no illusions about Lee's attitude. A November 24 letter Lee had written to Colonel Joseph Reed, Washington's adjutant, fell into Washington's hands. The thirty-five-year-old Reed had written to Lee praising his work back in the spring when Lee was in charge of the fortifications at Long Island before heading to Charleston to direct the defense of that South Carolina port. Lee's response was critical of Washington's leadership. It also was obvious that Reed had made some unflattering remarks about his commander-in-chief.

Reed was on a mission when the letter arrived, so Washington opened it.

"I opened it thinking it was an official communiqué," Washington later explained to Reed, but it was more accusation than explanation. Washington masked the feelings at this betrayal from a man he considered both a confidante and valued aide.

Washington delayed at Fort Lee until the twenty-second, then moved out on word that the energetic Cornwallis had crossed the river about five miles to the north two days earlier. Obviously the British had changed their minds about a winter hiatus. The fort's commander, Nathanael Greene, tarried—longer than prudent—and then departed in so much haste he had to abandon his supplies. One hundred tardy American soldiers were taken prisoner.

The next move was to Newark, where once again Washington moved out barely ahead of the pursuing Cornwallis.

Washington arrived at Brunswick with his forces on November 28, joining up with Stirling's brigade. A large part of the army, however, was missing, lingering in New York under Lee's command.

It was Lee's hope and expectation that the British hounds would catch the American fox—Washington—before long and Lee would become the commander-in-chief, thus he kept making excuses for not catching up.

There were more troop arrivals in Brunswick on November 29 when Patterson marched his Delaware battalion in to join Stirling's brigade. Haslet was in the greeting party, looking for familiar faces. What he saw was embarrassing.

The new arrivals were an unruly bunch of soldiers, nowhere near the Delaware Continentals in discipline or spirit. At Philadelphia in September, Haslet learned, 300 of them had threatened to go home unless they were paid a bounty. Patterson called in regulars from the Continental army to disarm and arrest the ringleaders. He had to force them at bayonet point to board boats for crossing the Delaware. At the flying camp he attempted to instill discipline, but without much success.

"Are your soldiers ready to fight?" Stirling asked Patterson. It was more hope than question.

"I'm sorry to say, General, that my men are not fit for fatigue duty, have no constitutions, and are always dissatisfied."

Stirling frowned. He had been expecting—hoping, really—to have men of the quality of the Delaware Continentals. This news was discouraging. Washington, who had been standing by, now spoke up.

"How long are their enlistments?"

"They expire in two days, General."

"Can they be persuaded to stay two weeks?"

Patterson shook his head. Washington, whose opinion of the militia grew more negative each day, turned to stare out a window, struggling to disguise his disgust.

True enough, the very next day the Delaware militia left for home. They had plenty of company. The enlistments of more than 2,000 soldiers from the Pennsylvania, Jersey, and Maryland battalions also expired on November 30. So, they, too, went home.

In fact, the whole army, including the 3,000 remaining, were in motion on that same day because Cornwallis, who had marched twenty miles in a single day, was almost upon them.

Receiving the alarm, Haslet ordered his men to burn their tents as they prepared to move out.

"We have no wagons to carry them," he explained, "and no time to find some."

The lack of time was soon proven. The rear of the Delaware battalion exchanged fire with the British advance before hastening south.

But once more the enemy cut off pursuit. Howe had told Cornwallis to wait for him at Brunswick while he returned to New York to take care of business.

When Washington realized he was not being pursued, he halted Stirling's brigade at Princeton while he continued on to Trenton, intending to make that his new base.

Princeton was a pleasant interlude for the Delaware battalion. The College of New Jersey had been closed by its president, a strong supporter of independence, and the soldiers moved into the college buildings. For the first time in weeks the soldiers were warm and sheltered.

"These are very comfortable lodgings," Lieutenant Enoch Anderson of First Company commented to Haslet.

"They certainly are," Haslet agreed. "I hope the men enjoy it. Of course, that depends on how long the British will permit us to lodge here."

It was longer than they had any right to expect.

It was December 5 before Howe returned to Brunswick and the chase resumed.

Washington was riding toward Princeton that same day and was met on the road by Stirling and his soldiers.

"General, the British are on the move again," Stirling said. "We thought it best to leave Princeton, for they badly outnumber us."

Heading toward the Americans were Howe with 5,000 British and Hessians, and Cornwallis following a parallel road, with 3,000.

Washington was reluctant to give up another colony, but the reality of his situation left him no choice. "I think it is time we retire to Pennsylvania," he said and rode off to Trenton to order the evacuation.

He had had the foresight to have boats collected from a seventy-mile stretch above and below Trenton. Now, his retreating soldiers were loaded as quickly as they arrived at the river bank at Trenton and were ferried across to Pennsylvania.

Once again, the Delaware battalion brought up the rear, as Stirling's brigade abandoned Princeton. A handful of soldiers was assigned to tear up bridges and fell trees across the road to impede the enemy advance. The ubiquitous Washington rode with them, personally directing their efforts.

The Delaware River crossing dragged on through the night into the next morning. Campfires lit up both banks as boats crossed and recrossed the river ferrying the able-bodied and the ailing soldiers, along with their horses and equipment.

The thirty-five-year-old artist Charles Wilson Peale, a first lieutenant with a Pennsylvania militia unit, described it as a scene of desolation, driven home with shocking force when a bedraggled, nearly naked, bearded soldier walked up to him. He didn't recognize the man as his brother until the man spoke to him.

It was an anxious night for the remnants of the American army, including the Delaware battalion, still on the Jersey side of the river.

But once again Howe had given them time, halting at Princeton for seventeen hours, perhaps taking advantage of the relative comfort of the college just as the Americans had done for the previous several days.

The last of the Americans were just disappearing on the Pennsylvania shore when the pursuing force finally arrived at Trenton, led by Major General James Grant, the Delaware battalion's adversary at Brooklyn Heights. A thousand Hessians followed, their brass band pompously blaring their arrival, banners flying. The Americans responded with a different kind of music, firing their cannons at the enemy position, forcing them to back off to a safe distance from the river.

It was now December 8. As the two armies watched each other warily, the question in the American ranks and in the city of Philadelphia was: how long before the enemy moves on what was, in effect, the capital of the new United States of America?

Howe had that objective in mind but his challenge first was to find a way to cross the river safely. The capture of Philadelphia, he was sure, would bring the rebellion to an end. However, the Americans had successfully commandeered everything that would float for miles along the river.

The first night, the exhausted Americans made the best of their new situation as they could. Enoch Anderson noted "we lay amongst the leaves without tents or blankets, laying down with our feet to the fire. We had nothing to cook with, but our ramrods, which we run through a piece of meat and roasted it over the fire and to hungry soldiers it tasted sweet."

Stirling's brigade was dispersed along positions to the north of Washington's headquarters in Morrisville. In the days following, Haslet put them to work building huts for quarters. They proved so adept that other soldiers came to learn from them. Haslet also had Adjutant Thomas Holland resume regular drills to prevent deterioration of discipline.

Washington, meantime, pondered his desperate situation. The steady Continentals had dwindled to a handful and he had lost all confidence in the militia. Morale matched the scarcity of supplies.

His needs were great and not all of the needs were material. Washington had to find some way to erase the gloom, to hearten his soldiers, indeed, give heart to the whole fledgling nation.

Stories of atrocities committed by enemy soldiers in the pursuit across Jersey served some propaganda value.

Tories and patriots alike suffered from this inhumane side of war.

It had been reported that a Woodbridge man found a Hessian officer raping his daughter and instantly killed the officer only to be mortally wounded by other Hessian soldiers, who then plundered his home. A Hopewell man reported the enemy made off with all his furniture, personal effects, and horses after destroying his personal papers. It was said his neighbor was beaten.

Three women who sought refuge with the Americans reported they had been ravished by a British officer. It was reported that a number of young women who sought refuge in the mountains were discovered by enemy soldiers and brought to their camp and held captive ever since.

The enemy was reported to have ravaged the communities of Maidenhead and Hopewell, carrying away whatever was portable, seizing livestock, leaving inhabitants without shelter or clothing in the winter season.

Soldiers paroled from British captivity brought back tales of mistreatment of prisoners, particularly by the most notorious of the British prison supervisors, Captain William Cunningham, provost at New York. The stories told of cruel treatment, contaminated water, lack of heat, short provisions, overcrowding, and lack of proper clothing. Many prisoners died under these conditions and were dumped into common graves. It was claimed Cunningham hanged several prisoners.

Dispatches from London reported that Americans had been confined to the hold of a ship that brought them from America, denied adequate food, and given barely enough space to breathe. It had aroused protests among sympathetic Londoners.

346

(The American cause enjoyed considerable support among the middle and lower classes in London.)

These stories certainly stirred the passions of the patriots who read them in their newspapers or heard them in the stories passed from village to village. But Washington was looking for inspiration to season the passion and, so, summoned Thomas Paine.

The man whose pamphlet *Common Sense* had stirred colonial fervor the previous January had joined the army at Fort Lee, shouldering a musket just like an ordinary soldier in the march south.

"Mr. Paine," Washington greeted Paine when he arrived at the headquarters. "I noticed you've been doing a lot of scribbling these nights we've been on the march."

"Yes, I have, General. I've been trying to find words to tell our country about our situation, not to discourage them, but to hearten them, to inspire them to your support."

Washington looked squarely at his visitor. Paine was a bit shorter than Washington, trim, broad-shouldered, but slightly stooped. The general was pleased at his steady, determined gaze. There is fire behind those eyes, the general thought, the fire of a mind devoted to liberty, a creative fire. On the march Washington had found him a quiet but knowledgeable and agreeable companion, with manners that would have fit well in Virginia society.

"Our soldiers need words as much as deeds, words that will inspire them, words that will reinforce a sense of duty right now," Washington said. "I count on you to provide those words."

"I'll certainly strive for that, General," Paine responded.

"What do you need from me?"

"Nothing more, General, than a place to write. The phrases already are in my head."

"Please. By all means go to your work and may God bless your effort."

Paine returned to his tent and, using a drum head as a desk, resumed the writing he had begun at Fort Lee, from time to time scratching out some of his copy, inserting new phrases.

"These are the times that try men's souls," he wrote. "The summer soldier and the sunshine patriot will, in this crisis, shrink from the service of their country; but he that stands it now, deserves the love and thanks of man and woman. Tyranny, like hell, is not easily conquered; yet we have this consolation with us, that the harder the conflict, the more glorious the triumph."

The words felt proper and he worked long at phrasing and rephrasing.

The next day, December 9, he showed them to Washington, who nodded approval. Then Paine left for Philadelphia to seek a printer, accompanying Israel Putnam, whom Washington had assigned to command the defense of that city.

Lee, meantime, on December 2 had finally crossed the North River, at Haverstraw, New York, and was wending his leisurely way south, staying well west of the enemy's line of march. He had some 7,000 soldiers with him, plus another 3,000 that he had intercepted en route from the command of General Philip Schuyler at Albany to join Washington.

By the twelfth of December Lee only had advanced as far as Vealtown (present day Bernardsville) still hanging far behind Washington's position. He decided to spend that night at Widow White's inn in Basking Ridge, three miles away, taking a small entourage along.

He did not rise for breakfast on the thirteenth until late morning

Major James Wilkinson of General Horatio Gates' staff was sent to pick up dispatches from Lee, a friend of Gates, and was chatting with Lee as the general prepared for breakfast, penning his letter to Gates while he awaited the food service. As he wrote, Lee expounded to Wilkinson on what he considered the deficiencies of the American command, obviously meaning Washington.

They were thus engaged when Wilkinson looked out a window to the lane leading to the inn and saw a small party of British cavalrymen advancing.

It was a five-member party of the Queen's Light Dragoons with a twenty-two-year-old officer named Banastre Tarleton leading them.

(Tarleton, son of a wealthy Liverpool merchant, had squandered the money left him by his father and decided to seek service in the British army, persuading his mother to buy him a commission as coronet. Before the war was over, he would achieve fame as a commander but infamy as a ruthless officer showing no quarter to Americans he subdued.)

Tarleton's men quickly chased two sentries posted at the front door, then began firing into the building through its windows. There was a response of gunfire from inside for a few minutes, then silence.

An elderly woman crawled out the door, begging for mercy.

"You don't want to hurt me," she cried. "You want the general, General Lee, he's in the inn."

Tarleton was aware of Lee's presence, tipped by the capture of an American soldier carrying a message from Lee to General John Sullivan, whom Lee had left in charge at Bernardsville.

"General Lee," Tarleton called out. "Surrender and we will spare you and your party. Resist and we will put you all to the sword."

"Colonel," one of his men interrupted, "they're escaping out the back door."

Tarleton spurred his horse around the inn, his dragoons following. There were, indeed, some figures fleeing towards the woods. The pursuers ended the escape abruptly, killing a couple, wounding others, and taking the remainder prisoner. None was Lee.

Tarleton rode back to the front of the inn, where the rest of the detachment, commanded by Colonel William Harcourt, had arrived. A disheveled Lee appeared, wearing only his night shirt and slippers. He was a subdued man, the celebrated wit and oratory silenced by this ignominious event. Harcourt ordered him seated on a horse and they all rode off to the British post at Pennington, thirty miles away.

The raiding party did not bother to search the inn so Wilkinson, hiding in a closet, pistols in hand and cocked, emerged when they left. He grabbed the letter Lee was writing to Gates and other papers, saddled his horse, and rode back to the American lines to report the shocking news.

(Lee, in his letter, confided to Gates: "Entre nous, a certain great man is most damnedly deficient. He has thrown me into a situation where I have my choice of difficulties." He would spend a year in captivity, his ambitions to reap the glory of leading the American army to victory over his former compatriots forever lost. In fact, when he finally returned to service with the American army, his performance in battle was such that Washington had him discharged in disgrace.)

News of Lee's capture was viewed as just one more stunning setback to America's hopes for a successful conclusion of this war for independence. Many politicians felt the cause was lost without Lee's presence to guide it.

Panic among civilians matched the low morale of the soldiers.

Congress already had adjourned on December 12 and moved to Baltimore. The streets of Philadelphia now filled with carts loaded with furniture and other personal possessions as its citizens headed to seek safety elsewhere. Even the local newspapers ceased publication and left town.

John Haslet: A Useful One

Thomas Rodney, arriving in Philadelphia on the eighteenth with his troop of light horse, was shocked at the exodus. He found the streets deserted and the city looking like it had been plundered.

Haslet, meanwhile, began thinking about recruiting the new battalion. On December 12 he called his officers to his quarters for dinner.

"Gentlemen," he announced, "the battalion has covered itself with honors these past few months. But the enlistments soon run out and it will cease to exist.

"You know that the Congress has asked our colony to raise a new battalion of 800 soldiers. You also probably know that we are having much difficulty recruiting even a company, let alone a whole battalion.

"Word of our deeds has spread throughout the three lower counties. I believe we can use that to rally the citizens to serve. I'll allow a few of you to return home—take along your soldiers to parade before the people—to win their hearts to the service. You'll be returning home as heroes and that can be useful to encourage the dedication to our cause that is at present lacking.

"I'll give you each $100 to offer as bounties."

Four officers chose to take the assignment.

"May the Supreme Power bless your efforts," Haslet said to them, "and speed you home safely. When you arrive, pass along the love for family and friends of those who will remain behind. I hope we'll soon all gather at Dover Green and march out to bring further glory to our state of Delaware."

State of Delaware. Haslet liked that term. It emphasized that the three lower counties were no longer a colony of Great Britain nor an adjunct to Pennsylvania.

Howe, meanwhile, lingered for a week, then—rather than take time to build or import his own transport—he decided on December 13 to abandon the campaign for the winter, after all. He dispersed the Hessians along the Delaware at Bordentown, Trenton, and Burlington and assigned the British troops to Staten Island, Amboy, Brunswick, and Princeton.

Howe returned to the comfort of New York and the company of Mrs. Elizabeth Loring, whose companionship he had first enjoyed back in Boston. Her husband, Joshua, also had moved to New York, but Howe mollified him with an appointment to care for the growing number of prisoners of war.

As Judge Thomas Jones, a New York loyalist, viewed the arrangement in a letter to a friend: "In this appointment there was reciprocity. He (Loring) fingered the cash; the General enjoyed Madam."

Loring's prison commission certainly offered reward. There were an estimated 5,000 American prisoners, counting the 2,800 from Fort Washington and about 1,000 taken at the Battle of Long Island, plus political prisoners and others. The British used the Brick Church, the Middle Dutch, and the North Dutch Churches plus Columbia College, the Sugar House, the New Jail, the new Bridewell, and the old City Hall. They were all filled to capacity. The excess was transferred to prison ships.

The campaign apparently over for several months, Cornwallis made plans to sail back to England to join his family. His wife (also named Jemima) had been ill for some time.

Washington learned of Lee's capture on the fifteenth of December and felt free now, relieved that his critics could no longer invoke Lee's supposedly superior tactical skills to undermine the commander-in-chief. He turned to a plan he hoped would revive the flagging American spirit.

A man known to the camp only as that butcher from Trenton provided information for the plan.

His name was John Honeyman and he had been denouncing the patriot cause all over the Trenton countryside, complaining that American troops had chased him from his home. He had moved to Griggstown, near Trenton, and moved freely in and out of the town, now occupied by Hessian soldiers.

Washington issued orders to arrest him on sight and sent two scouts across the river to take him into custody.

They were hiding in the bushes when Honeyman walked towards them, chasing a cow that had strayed from his herd.

Jumping from their hiding place, the soldiers confronted Honeyman: "Surrender, traitor, or your days on earth will end right here."

Honeyman turned and ran, but clumsily slipped on the ice. The soldiers quickly pounced on his chest, tied him, and roughly shoved him towards a boat hidden along the river bank. Minutes later they were across the river and headed for Washington's headquarters, now moved ten miles north, to the home of a local tax collector, William Keith.

"General," one of the soldiers announced as they arrived, "here is that Tory scoundrel you've wanted."

"Excellent," Washington responded. "Leave him with me."

Turning to a sentry, Washington added: "If he tries to escape, shoot him!"

Washington and the prisoner disappeared inside.

When the door closed behind them, Washington smiled: "Well, Mr. Honeyman, may I offer you a brandy?"

"That would be appreciated, General," the man responded, "it's been a cold day and a chilly trip across the river."

Washington poured. Honeyman took a deep drink from his glass, then put it down.

"I hope my soldiers weren't too rough on you," Washington commented, solicitously.

"They were as gentle as the circumstances would allow," Honeyman said, laughing.

"Now, Mr. Honeyman, tell me what you know about the enemy disposition in Trenton."

Honeyman then explained in detail what he knew.

As it happened, the so-called butcher had been a bodyguard to British General James Wolfe at Quebec during the French and Indian War. He and Washington had met in Philadelphia when the Continental Congress was in session and before Washington left to take command of the forces at Boston. Out of the shared experience of the French and Indian War and a common dislike of British indignities to the colonies a role evolved for Honeyman: moving around enemy locations pretending to be a disaffected American in order to learn what he could about enemy troop deployments and strategies.

He finished briefing Washington and the general stood up and warmly grasped his hands. Then he opened his door. There was a stern look on his face as he dissembled for the benefit of the guard.

"See this man is put in custody," Washington commanded. He turned his back on Honeyman as the guard took the visitor out of the headquarters and escorted him to an improvised prison in a nearby log cabin.

That night there was a mysterious fire near the cabin and while the guards were thus distracted, Honeyman sneaked out of the cabin and disappeared into the darkness. Washington was now ready to reveal his plan.

Chapter Thirty-Five

Trenton: Hope Renewed

On December 22 Washington discussed his plan with his general officers at Lord Stirling's quarters. Two days later he summoned his principal commanders to assign their roles.

They were aware he had been considering such an attack for he had freely discussed with several of them over the past few days the idea of a surprise assault on the enemy positions in Jersey.

Now, they gathered around a map on a table as he spelled out the plan of attack.

Haslet nodded approvingly when the commander-in-chief informed the meeting of the target: the Hessian regiments at Trenton. They would embark on Christmas night. They realized as well as he that the survival of the American cause could very well depend on their success.

It will be a difficult crossing, Haslet thought, but it might turn out to be a mere inconvenience compared to the task facing them on the other side.

It seemed an ambitious plan, particularly in light of the reverses of the past several months. Cross the ice-filled Delaware. March to Trenton in terrible weather. Defeat the Hessian garrison there. Sweep the enemy out of Jersey.

It was bitterly cold this Christmas Day in 1776. The Hessians in Trenton would be celebrating the festival; Washington was counting on it. The Americans, on the other hand, would spend the day preparing for a long night's march to Trenton. First, however, was the matter of getting over to Jersey from Pennsylvania.

Ice was spreading out from the Delaware River banks, slowly choking the river. Chunks of ice floated swiftly down the open water. It was a formidable risk for the bedraggled American army.

No matter. Washington was determined on his gamble to surprise the Hessians at Trenton. Surprise was the key. The general had no faith in the steadfastness of his soldiers should they be confronted by an army of professional soldiers who were ready for them. There were too many inexperienced and undependable militia in the American army, not enough experienced and proven soldiers like the Delaware battalion.

Nevertheless, the Americans were a spirited group when they assembled at three P.M. on Christmas Day and marched to the McKonkey's Ferry landing for the crossing. When they landed on the other side they would be about ten miles north of their objective.

To inspire the soldiers, Washington ordered Thomas Paine's latest essay, *The American Crisis*, read aloud to the assembled troops. A man of few words himself, Washington counted on Paine's prose to instill a spirit that would carry them through the ordeal ahead.

And the essay that began "Now is the time that tries men's souls" had the desired effect. Although the ranks were a mixture of boys and young and middle-aged men, they all felt young and boyish as they marched off to the ferry.

Once again John Glover's Marblehead regiment would handle the difficult transport.

A fleet of Durham boats had been assembled for the crossing. Designed to carry iron ore, they could easily carry horses and artillery as well as soldiers. The boats were forty to sixty feet long, eight feet wide, two feet deep with keels, and drew only thirty inches of water when fully loaded. They could be propelled by sail or by manpower, two members of the five-man crew walking back and forth along the running boards on each side, pushing the boat forward by sticking eighteen-foot poles into the river bottom. The fifth crewman served as helmsman.

A Virginia brigade was the first to embark. Next came Connecticut, Maryland, and Massachusetts troops, followed by Brigadier General Lord Stirling with the remnants of Haslet's regiment.

(The roll call of the Delaware Continentals on December 22 had shown three captains, one first lieutenant, two ensigns, one adjutant, one quartermaster, one mate, five sergeants, one drummer and fifer and 124 rank and file left of the 750 who had marched off to war last August. Only ninety-two of those 124 were reported fit for duty.)

Next came two regiments of Virginia Continentals, a Pennsylvania rifle regiment, two Pennsylvania regiments—one of them made up of German settlers—and, finally, troops from New Hampshire, Massachusetts, Connecticut, and New York.

The river was less than a quarter mile wide at this point, but the boat crews labored to keep on course amidst the drifting ice. The ice looked harmless enough until it thumped against the sides of the boats in the swift current, nudging them downstream.

It had been dark for a few hours as they started across the Delaware under a full moon. Soon storm clouds obscured the moon and snow and sleet added to the soldiers' misery. Occupants of the boats peered anxiously through the storm for a glimpse of the Jersey shore and escape from the threatening ice.

Washington waited until the last, crossing with Colonel Henry Knox and his artillery. He was in high spirits, joshing with the twenty-five-year-old Knox, despite a voice that was almost hoarse from shouting instructions as the troops embarked. The commander-in-chief also had earlier caught a cold and had a cloth wrapped around his neck.

The whole enterprise took nine hours, much longer than Washington had anticipated. It was no longer possible to attack Trenton before dawn.

The crossing completed, Washington divided his 2,400-member corps into two divisions for the ten-mile march to Trenton. One, under Major General John Sullivan, would march along the river road, entering Trenton on the lower end of town. The other division, under Major General Nathanael Greene, would follow the parallel, Pennington road into the upper part of town. Stirling's brigade and the Delaware Continentals were with Greene. Washington also decided to ride with this division.

Sullivan's principal commanders were Brigadier General Arthur St. Clair, forty-six, of Pennsylvania; the forty-four-year-old Glover, a colonel; and thirty-one-year-old Colonel Paul Dudley Sargent of Massachusetts.

Under Greene were Stirling, Brigadier General Hugh Mercer, and Brigadier General Adam Stephen of Virginia, all men in their fifties, with Stephen the oldest at fifty-eight.

They were barely on the way before a messenger arrived from Sullivan expressing concern that the snow and sleet had wet the firing pans and would likely make it difficult, perhaps impossible, for his soldiers to fire their rifles.

"In that case General Sullivan is to tell his men use their bayonets," Washington snapped at the messenger. "I am determined to take Trenton!"

That determination seemed to have spread to the whole force. The soldiers, many of them still wearing summer-weight clothing, some lacking shoes, plodded on in the wet, cold night. Major James Wilkinson observed the bloody footprints in the snow-covered road and his heart filled with appreciation for these men.

After four miles, the column halted for a hasty meal, then continued towards Trenton.

As the column marched along, Washington rode up and down the lines giving encouragement to his troops, advising them to listen to their officers. He feared the kind of confusion leading to panic when troops ignored their orders.

At one point his horse's rear legs started to slip down a bank. He nonchalantly grabbed its mane and encouraged it back to more solid footing, a display of horsemanship that impressed the soldiers, adding to their confidence in his command.

Then came one of those little vignettes that soldiers in later years remember with more clarity than the battles they fought. As Greene's column neared Trenton, barking dogs appeared and an elderly man rushed out of a nearby house. He clearly was angry.

"Be gone! Get off my land!" he shouted, adding some profanity to emphasize his agitated feelings. "I'm tired of your pillaging. You've left almost nothing for a man and his family to live off. I'll not tolerate it again. Get away from my land."

Eighteen-year-old Lieutenant James Monroe, an artillery officer with one of the Virginia regiments, confronted him.

"Sir," Monroe responded with as much patience as he could manage, "we are American soldiers under the command of his Excellency, General George Washington. We will do you no harm if you return to your home and be quiet."

The man's rage vanished in a moment.

"Americans! General Washington!" the man exclaimed and repeated his remarks.

"You shouldn't be out on a night like this," he said. "Please. Please. Tell the general to come inside. I'll have some food prepared."

"Thank you," Monroe answered, "but there's no time. We are on our way to reclaim Trenton for the United States of America."

"I'll go with you," the man said. "I'm a doctor and I'm sure I can be of service."

"As you wish," Monroe said. The man disappeared inside and after a while reappeared carrying his medical bag and hastened to catch up with the soldiers headed towards Trenton.

The Americans weren't sure what to expect, whether there still was a chance to surprise the enemy. A foraging party of about thirty Americans had skirmished with a Hessian outpost Christmas night and Washington feared that might have put the enemy on alert. A Hessian regiment had marched out to investigate the sounds of gunfire but the Americans already had left, so the regiment turned around and returned to town. The other two regiments already had been given the holiday off and were languishing in their quarters.

There were other reasons for the Hessians to be alert, but since their commander chose to ignore them, so did the ordinary soldiers. Their commander was Colonel Johann Gottlieb Rall, a feisty professional who had distinguished himself at Fort Washington and White Plains. This day would prove him a better fighter than a commander.

British General James Grant at Brunswick had received word on Christmas Eve that the Americans were planning some sort of action against Trenton, although the information indicated it might only be a raiding party similar to the attack Haslet led against Roger's Rangers at Mamaroneck. Nevertheless, he sent a courier to alert Rall. The Hessian dismissed the warning, believing it unlikely that the Americans would make such an attempt against his trained force. He had three Hessian regiments and a company of British dragoons in his command and his previous encounters had left him with a disregard for the Americans' fighting ability.

Instead, Rall continued celebrating Christmas on into the twenty-sixth, as was the German fashion. He was at a supper party at the home of Abraham Hunt, a wealthy merchant, when a messenger appeared during the night with information that the Americans were, in fact, marching on the town. The staff attending the commander refused admittance. The messenger then wrote a note and asked that they give it to Rall, who just then came to the door, attracted by the loud conversation.

"I have a message for you, Colonel," the messenger said and handed him the note. Rall, annoyed at this interruption of his celebration, stuffed it in his pocket without a glance at its contents. He had forgotten about it when he finally went to bed, secure in his belief there was nothing to fear from the American army. The storm further convinced him there was no chance the attackers would be out and about to disturb the tranquility of the morning.

He was still sleeping when Washington's divisions approached Trenton just before eight o'clock.

There were three Hessian regiments and seventy British soldiers—1,400 in all—at Trenton under Rall's command, all expecting another uneventful day marred only by the dreary weather.

The first contact was made with the Hessian outposts.

The sentinels ran to the officer in charge, shouting in German that it was the enemy and calling on the Hessians to turn out ("Der Fiend! Heraus! Heraus!"). One of them ran into town and knocked on the door of the Stacey Potts house, which Rall was using as his headquarters. The sleeping commander was quickly roused and just as quickly dressed to confront this perplexing intrusion on his holiday.

It was already too late; the two American divisions had arrived almost simultaneously at opposite ends of town and had established dominant positions on both ends of King and Queen Streets, the main streets in Trenton.

Stirling's brigade, with the Delaware troops, deployed across the upper end of the two streets; Sullivan across the lower end. Other parts of Greene's division took positions east of town, guarding the Assunpink Creek bridge, the only route out of town. Mercer's brigade covered the west side of town.

Captain Thomas Forest placed four artillery pieces at the head of Queen Street and Captain Alexander Hamilton set up two guns facing down King Street.

The storm that had begun just before midnight continued to send snow, sometimes mixed with sleet, swirling around the scene. It could have been a picture perfect Christmas scene except for the violence that quickly disturbed the bliss of December 26.

The artillery began the attack. The cannons were loaded with grape shot and as Rall's soldiers tumbled out of their quarters, the lethal projectiles roared down the streets, shredding their ranks.

Movement of Americans and Their
Deployment for the Battle of Trenton
Map by John Mackenzie of britishbattles.com

The Hessian commander sent his own regiment to King Street and the regiment known as Lossberg to Queen Street. The third regiment, Knyphausen, was sent to face Sullivan.

Rall ordered two artillery pieces set up on King Street but the Virginia Continentals led by Captain William Washington and Lieutenant Monroe charged down the street and overran the position before the cannons could be fired. Monroe was wounded in the daring assault and treated by the same doctor who had confronted the marching columns earlier.

The Hessians had slightly better luck with their artillery on Queen Street, but those cannons, too, were soon silenced.

Gunsmoke filled the streets. Then, amidst the cacophony of gunfire and yelling soldiers, came the sound of music from the Hessian bands, the prominent kettle drums barely making themselves heard above the din of battle. The Hessian commanders had ordered the martial airs hoping to stiffen their men. Gunfire provided counterpoint to the music.

Rall, angered at the audacity of the Americans he had taken so lightly, ordered a bayonet charge. The artillery shot and rifle bullets tore through the ranks. His men hesitated, then fell back.

The Lossberg regiment tried a bayonet charge but some thirty of its soldiers fell from the deadly fire before they could even get close.

Meanwhile, Haslet had moved his soldiers down the street and deployed them in houses where the cover enabled them to keep their powder dry. They opened fire from the windows with deadly effect. Running men were almost obscured by the gunsmoke.

"We have them!" Haslet shouted, firing his pistols at the confused enemy soldiers who began seeking cover wherever they could find it. He was elated, a feeling shared by many Americans on this day. It was redemption after the long weeks of retreating.

Rall, too, now sensed that retreat was the only salvation. He spurred his horse towards the bridge over the Assunpink Creek only to find his way blocked. As the bewildered commander contemplated his next move he was shot twice in the side and fell from his horse.

With the only road over the Assunpink blocked, the frantic Hessians tried to ford the creek but found it too deep. Some fled into a field, into the face of Greene's soldiers and more lethal fire. They turned to a nearby orchard, but Americans were everywhere.

The firing trailed off as one after another of the Hessian soldiers pointed his rifle to the ground. Hessian officers raised their swords with their hats on the points, signaling surrender. A little more than an hour after the battle began, it was over.

A shout went up and down the American lines and the triumphant soldiers tossed their hats in the air in jubilation.

Haslet's own joy exceeded the feelings he had after subduing Roger's Rangers at Mamaroneck. This time there was none of the disappointment of an incomplete mission. The attack on Trenton had achieved everything the Americans had planned.

The mortally wounded Rall was picked up and carried into a nearby house. Washington and Greene visited him and granted him parole, a gracious gesture to a dying man. Also mortally wounded was Major Friedrich van Dechow, commander of the Knyphausen Regiment.

But there was disappointment as well as triumph for the Americans. The disappointments were due to the failure of two other parts of the plan, where commanders lacked the resolve and personal leadership of Washington.

One of the disappointments was the escape of about a third of the Hessian soldiers and a company of British dragoons who chose flight rather than fight and were able to get away before the Americans sealed off the escape routes.

Two other divisions were to participate in Washington's broad scheme. One, under Brigadier General James Ewing was to take 700 men across the river just below Trenton and guard any escape in that direction. Colonel John Cadwalader, temporarily promoted to brigadier general, would cross farther south, near Bristol, and attack Colonel Carl Von Donop's Hessian regiment at Mount Holly. Von Donop was in command of all the Hessian forces encamped in the Jersey towns along the Delaware.

Cadwalader, a member of a prominent Philadelphia family, commanded about 900 men, mostly from Pennsylvania but including Thomas Rodney's Dover Light Infantry Company which had arrived in camp only four days earlier, and a contingent from Rhode Island.

Ewing decided the weather was too severe to attempt the crossing and assumed Washington would decide to call off the attack. He kept his troops in quarters.

Cadwalader did make an attempt. When the crossing was nearly completed, however, Cadwalader decided it was impossible to unload his artillery because of ice blocking access to the river bank. Unwilling to do battle without his artillery, he ordered everybody back to Pennsylvania.

Rodney, thirty-two years old and anxious to see action, was a disappointed young man returning to camp. His troop had been the first to cross, assigned to secure the Jersey side. And they were the last to withdraw, covering for the division again. In all, his troop had spent six hours in Jersey and saw no action.

Without the support of Ewing's and Cadwalader's divisions, Washington faced his second disappointment. He had ordered the soldiers to take three days' rations, expecting to continue on to attack other British positions and maybe free all of Jersey from British control. Now he called his commanders together in Trenton to consider the next step.

"I deem it unwise to proceed on our original plan," he said. "We know that Ewing and Cadwalader's soldiers did not make the crossing and further contact with the enemy may expose us to superior numbers. We also have several hundred prisoners to encumber us."

Frustration showed on the faces of the officers. They were filled with the euphoria of victory and anxious to add to their laurels. But they had to concede the commander-in-chief's evaluation of their position.

And so they began loading the boats again for the return to Pennsylvania, still dealing with the weather conditions that had assaulted them for more than twelve hours. It took two days to complete the return, with nearly a thousand prisoners added to the transport.

Meanwhile, Cadwalader decided on the twenty-seventh to try again to cross over to Jersey. He had heard the sounds of battle the previous day, realized that Washington had carried out his part of the plan, and decided to fulfill his division's original role. This time he was successful, disembarking the last soldiers at three o'clock in the afternoon. He didn't learn until then that Washington's divisions were back in Pennsylvania.

"Well, I suppose we should return, too," he confided to Colonel Joseph Reed, Washington's adjutant, who had temporarily been assigned to Cadwalader as the second in command. "There may be too many Hessians around here for our small force."

"I would advise against returning," Reed said bluntly. "These soldiers have thrice endured the arduous journey across this river. Their spirits have been roused each time we've set foot in Jersey. To disappoint them once again would, I fear, diminish their fighting spirit. I suggest we proceed on to Burlington."

"General Cadwalader," another officer interjected. "I think such a move could be disastrous. We have no idea how many of the enemy might await us. And we are but a small part of the continental forces. I recommend we return to camp."

"No! No!" a few voices responded. "Push on! Push on!"

The officers fell to debating the point among themselves while Cadwalader consulted his own sense of the situation. He was conscious of the possibility his commander-in-chief might reproach him for his failure to participate in the assault on Trenton. Washington's disapproval, and even worse, contempt, was too much for a commander to contemplate.

"Gentleman," he interrupted the debate. "We'll go at least as far as Burlington. Our scouts say the town is undefended."

Burlington was, as reported, abandoned when they arrived at nine o'clock that evening.

Cadwalader now decided to push on to Bordentown. Since it was more likely an enemy force might be there, he dispatched a scouting party under Reed to check it out. Meantime, his soldiers would rest.

Reed reported back that Bordentown, too, had been deserted and at 4 A.M. on the twenty-eighth Cadwalader's main body set off for that town. They halted a half-mile out of town on word that Hessians also were on the march. Then came additional word that the enemy actually was marching away—fleeing—Bordentown. The Americans moved into town. It was with considerable pleasure they found the Hessians had abandoned supplies and equipment in their haste to leave.

Emboldened, Cadwalader pushed on after them until reality brought the pursuit to a stop. He considered that his men had been on forced marches for four days now and might not be fit for battle. He decided it was time to rest.

As Cadwalader's force rested and planned, Colonel Reed sent word to Washington that the enemy seemed to have disappeared. Perhaps, it was suggested, all of Jersey would now be open to the Americans.

The American command was obsessed now with the objective of clearing the enemy from Jersey, where abundant natural resources and settled towns and villages offered the promise of assistance to sustain an army.

For Haslet, however, came the realization that the days of glory for the Delaware battalion had ended.

He was resting his aching body in his headquarters on the twenty-seventh when a distressed Holland came in.

"Colonel," the adjutant informed him, "our soldiers are leaving."

"Leaving?" Haslet asked, bewildered.

"Yes. They're departing camp in great numbers. Everyone will be gone by sundown."

The information startled Haslet. Despite the rumors in his encampment, he had not given serious thought to the calendar.

"But their enlistments aren't up until the thirty-first," he said querulously.

The terms of enlistment had been a developing issue as the year neared its end. Haslet maintained the soldiers had enlisted for a year from the date they were enrolled, which would have taken most of them into January and even February and March. The prevailing opinion among the rank and file, however, was that they had agreed to serve until the end of the year 1776.

"Well, sir," Holland answered, "they feel nothing is going to happen before the end of the year, so they might as well start home now. And they are."

Haslet shook his head. He had hints that Washington was planning another foray into Jersey. Haslet had been thinking and planning a role his battalion might play.

Now he went outside his headquarters and stood silently as his soldiers passed by—not marching proudly in columns as he had seen them do so often in the past, but striding casually in small groups—waving and hollering their farewells.

"They're no longer soldiers," he thought to himself, "but friends and neighbors on the way home to their farms and shops." He waved back. He could not rouse himself to an effort to turn them back. There was a part of him that wished he were going with them. Never had the lure of Delaware and home been stronger in the months he had been away.

"Washington won't like this, but he must be told," Haslet said, finally, and Holland nodded.

Haslet mounted his horse and rode off for Washington's headquarters, now moved to the widow Hannah Stewart Harris' house in

Newtown, a bustling little town in Bucks County, about five miles from the river. Several officers also had found warm and pleasant quarters in the town.

Haslet found the general in conversation with Brigadier General Henry Knox, his artillery commander, and his aides. Washington smiled and greeted Haslet as he entered the room. The general was in a good mood.

After an exchange of greetings, Haslet came to the point of his visit.

"General, I'm embarrassed to report that my battalion has disappeared."

"Disappeared?" a perplexed Washington echoed.

"They've gone home," Haslet explained. "They felt there was no reason for them to wait the few days left in their terms. So, they've packed up and left. There are only a couple of officers and privates left."

"Damn!" Washington exploded, his cheerful mood vanished. "I'll send a guard after them and bring them back bound neck and heel."

He desperately needed soldiers of the quality of the Delaware battalion for the plans he was now making.

Haslet stood silently, waiting for Washington's temper to subside. They both knew it would be futile to chase after the vanished troops.

"I assure you, General," Haslet finally spoke up, "this is not the end of the Delaware battalion. They've merely gone home to recruit for a new regiment."

Washington reflected on Haslet's words.

"Well, I suppose I'll have to settle for that," he conceded. "John, your soldiers were fine fighting men. I'll only hope the new regiment emulates the fighting spirit of your 'Blue Hen's Chickens.'"

A smile lighted Washington's face as he used the pet name the army had applied to the Delaware battalion. Haslet also smiled at the familiarity. That was the first time he had heard Washington use the name.

"In fact, John, I think you should go back to Delaware yourself to take care of that recruitment. I've been told that you've agreed to command the new regiment. I certainly endorse that choice."

Washington turned around to a desk now and began writing on a piece of paper. When he finished he turned back to Haslet and handed it to him.

"Here," he said. "This is an order for you to return home to recruit."

"Well, I'm looking forward to seeing my family," Haslet replied. He hesitated a moment, then spoke a question that had been building for several weeks.

"Does this mean your excellency is unhappy with my leadership?" Washington was surprised by the question.

"Certainly not, John. Why would you think that?"

"Sometimes an officer is sent home to recruit when the command has lost confidence in that officer's leadership."

Washington looked aggrieved.

"That is definitely not the case with you, John. You're one of my finest field commanders. How could you entertain such a thought?"

"Well, there is the matter of the promotions to brigadier general. I felt my service warranted consideration but I was passed over. Colonel Smallwood was given preference over me. He certainly is a fine leader and deserving, but I felt diminished by the Congress' failure to choose me, particularly since I had been led to believe you also supported my promotion."

"John, the promotion had nothing to do with preferences, believe me. My regard for your leadership and the service you have performed for your country, your dedication to your country, places you second to none in my heart."

Although Haslet was four years older, the past months together had developed a bond between him and Washington, the kind of affection great leaders draw from their followers. He felt reassured at the general's words.

Unspoken was the fact that the larger Maryland colony had more influence in the Congress than Delaware.

"I need you, John. I need another fighting regiment like the one you led at Brooklyn Heights and Chatterton Hill and at Trenton. You can best do that, yourself, I think, and not leave it to others. Only you could rally the young men of Delaware to make the kind of sacrifice needed to secure the United States of America."

"As you wish, General," Haslet conceded.

"Now," Washington said, "I must plan our return to Jersey. There's an opportunity there to follow up Trenton by driving the enemy all the way back to New York. And if we're swift and decisive we may capture a fair amount of their supplies and equipment if we can precipitate a hasty departure on their part."

Haslet nodded.

"I would like to go with you," he said. "That would send me back to Delaware with a better story to tell."

Washington nodded and turned back to his planning.

The calendar was his biggest problem because it foretold the expiration of many enlistments. His was a vanishing army. He had urged his officers to push for an extension of time, but the word coming back to him was that many soldiers felt they had spent too long away from their farms, their shops, their trades, their families. They were anxious to leave. Home had more appeal than possible further victories.

Of the 2,400 men who had followed him to Trenton, Washington could count on only a third of that number now. He decided on a personal appeal.

The troops from Hugh Mercer's brigade were assembled and Washington rode out in front of them. Haslet, a commander without a command, could only watch, restless for action, anxious whether there would be enough soldiers available to fulfill Washington's hopes.

"My brave soldiers," Washington's voice boomed out. "You have just achieved a marvelous victory for your country at Trenton. From information I've received, it is possible all of Jersey is open to us, but I need soldiers to accomplish that. I plead with you to volunteer for one more month. That is the time we need and we'll offer you a bounty of $10 if you agree."

The drummers beat time for volunteers to step forward. There was no movement in the ranks.

Washington had turned and was riding back towards his staff officers, his move a gesture of confidence in a favorable response from the soldiers. The officers shook their heads as a signal there had been no volunteers.

He wheeled his horse around again and rode back and forth in front of the ranks.

Once again his voice boomed out:

"You have done all I asked you to do, my brave fellows, and more than could be reasonably expected; but your country is at stake—your wives and children, your homes, and all that you hold dear. You have worn yourselves out with fatigue and hardships, but we know not how to spare you. If you will consent to stay only one month longer, you will render that service to the cause of liberty and to your country which you probably never can do under any other circumstances."

There was a rustling in the ranks, then one soldier, a second, a third, then several more stepped forward until about 200 had indicated a favorable response to their commander's plea.

"Shall I enroll these men, your excellency?" an aide asked him.

"That won't be necessary," Washington responded. "Any man who will volunteer in such a case as this needs no enrollment to keep him to his duty."

Washington rode off to his headquarters.

He started his army across the Delaware again on the twenty-ninth. This time he did not have Glover's Marblehead regiment to handle the boats. The sailor side of these soldier/sailors finally had prevailed and the regiment decided it wanted to get into the more lucrative privateering business. Despite Washington's entreaties to stay a bit longer, they had voted to join the fleets of vessels sailing out of Delaware River ports in search of prizes on the high seas.

It took even longer, therefore, for the army to get across this time, two days—to the thirty-first. Their baggage wagons were left for last. As a consequence, the earlier arrivals had to camp in the open, huddling by campfires to keep warm.

On the final day of the year 1776 Washington received a copy of a resolution Congress adopted on December 27. Unique in American history, it gave the military commander almost dictatorial powers, free to conduct the war for American independence as he saw fit without awaiting Congressional approval.

In response, he wrote:

"The confidence which Congress have honored me with by these proceedings, has a claim to my warmest acknowledgements. At the same time I beg leave to assure them, that all my faculties shall be employed to direct properly the powers they have pleased to vest me with—and to advance those objects, and only those, which gave rise to this honorable mark of distinction."

The Hessian prisoners, meanwhile, had been sent on to Philadelphia, where on the thirtieth they were paraded through the streets before jubilant crowds. Never mind that the prisoners—clad in the handsome uniforms of dark blue, scarlet, or black that distinguished each of the three regiments—were more splendidly outfitted than their shabbily-dressed guards. The sight of the subdued foreigners was a tonic for the flagging patriot spirits.

There was hope after all!

Chapter Thirty-Six

Death at Princeton

John Haslet made himself comfortable at his quarters near Trenton on January 1, 1777, and penned a letter to Caesar Rodney.

His euphoria from the December 26 victory at Trenton was evident; the letter was effervescent. While he credited Virginians with most of the fighting, he noted proudly that Lord Stirling's brigade, which included the Delaware Continentals, "had the honor of fighting 100 Hessians to a surrender."

But the battalion had ceased to exist.

"Captain (Thomas) Holland, Ensign (John) Wilson, Dr. (Reuben) Gilder and myself are all who have followed the American cause (back) to Trenton, two privates excepted," he wrote.

Still, his optimism was irrepressible:

"We just now hear that the bridge on this side of Princeton is cut down and the enemy retiring. A sufficient number of troops are ready to drive them out of Jersey."

He reported suffering from piles and swollen legs from falling into the Delaware on the way back to Jersey "but no matter if we drive them to New York."

Then this strange comment: "If I return it will be to salute you, if not we shall meet in heaven."

A premonition?

Washington expected there would only be a token enemy presence in Jersey, scattered in posts along the route between Trenton and the North (Hudson) River.

The error of this assumption was quickly proven.

John Haslet: A Useful One

Even as Washington's forces completed recrossing the Delaware from Pennsylvania, a large British force, under the command of Lieutenant General Charles Cornwallis, was assembling to meet them.

Cornwallis was in a vengeful mood. He was all ready to sail to England and a reunion with his ailing wife when General William Howe summoned him to his headquarters in New York.

"Charles," the general announced, getting promptly to the point. "The rebels have had some small success against us in Trenton. They surprised the Hessians there and have taken nearly a thousand prisoners and all their supplies and equipment.

"Damn!" he said, his emotions overcoming his reserve. "It is unfathomable that these rebels and their bumbling officers could achieve such a triumph against professional soldiers. Perhaps we have placed too much faith in our Hessian allies."

"When did this happen?" an incredulous Cornwallis asked.

"On the twenty-sixth. A courier brought the news last night."

"Astounding!" Cornwallis commented. "Perhaps we've underestimated the Americans."

"Or overestimated the Hessians," Howe responded. "Whatever the reason, we must counter this impertinence immediately. We dare not give the rebels encouragement.

"You must cancel your trip and as quickly as possible put a force together and march to retake Trenton and put the rebels in their proper place."

Cornwallis nodded agreement.

So, as 1776 blended into 1777, he was en route to confront the unsuspecting Americans, intent on teaching them a lesson in the realities of British military superiority.

On January 1 he arrived in Princeton to assume command of the soldiers Major General James Grant had assembled there.

Washington, meanwhile, had taken over the Trenton home of loyalist John Barnes and was busying himself with plans for the Jersey campaign, unaware that the main enemy force was only a short day's march away. Unaware, that is, until he was warned of the large force assembling at Princeton.

Optimism dishearteningly changed to thoughts of survival.

Washington reacted accordingly. Cadwalader's 2,100 men, encamped just north of Trenton, were summoned at 2 A.M. on the second. Major General Thomas Mifflin already had come over with 1,600 Pennsylvania militia.

Cornwallis marched out of Princeton at dawn on January 2. It was an unseasonably warm day and progress was slow as soldiers slogged along the muddy roads. Their artillery carriages frequently became mired in the muck.

Washington now had about 5,000 soldiers, mostly militia. Cornwallis had about 5,500 regulars with him after posting 1,200 men at Princeton.

Washington's first move was to send Colonel Edward Hand and his Pennsylvania riflemen out to meet the enemy. The thirty-two-year-old Hand, a field commander of proven ability, had been in the Continental service since the siege of Boston.

His riflemen were waiting in the woods fronting a creek below Maidenhead when an unsuspecting party of Hessians rode up. There was a sudden volley from the woods and several Hessians fell from their horses.

Cornwallis, following with the main force, ordered his columns to spread out in a skirmish line across the creek from the riflemen. The two sides exchanged fire for more than half an hour with no casualties.

In the midst of all this, Washington rode up to Hand's position, Nathanael Greene and Henry Knox with him.

"Fine work, Colonel," Washington complimented the Pennsylvania commander. "It's important you continue to delay the enemy. I need time to position our forces at Trenton to meet them."

"We'll do our best, General," Hand assured him.

Washington and his entourage turned and rode swiftly back to Trenton.

Hand kept his promise, slowly withdrawing, stopping occasionally to exchange fire with the advancing British and Hessian soldiers. His tactics gave Washington an additional three hours to prepare.

He ordered the American forces deployed for three miles along the high bank of the Assunpink Creek on the opposite side from Trenton, feeling it was better to concede the town to the enemy than attempt to defend it against superior numbers. Besides, the creek's steep banks and numerous marshes made it a much more defensible position.

It was about five o'clock when the enemy finally reached Trenton, impressive columns of uniformed soldiers marching down King and Queen Streets only a week after the Americans had triumphantly swept them clean of Hessian soldiers.

The sun had set and the twilight was rapidly turning to night as Cornwallis attempted to cross the Assunpink Creek bridge.

The Americans put up a valiant defense. Thomas Rodney and his light infantry company from Dover were there, Rodney brandishing his sword at his men to get them to close ranks and face the onrushing enemy. Washington was there, too, sitting on his great white horse at the far end of the bridge, calmly observing the action. It was a sound-and-light show, the flashes from the muskets, cannons, and rifles illuminating the scene, the sounds deafening to all within hearing.

As British casualties mounted, the enemy probed upstream for places to ford but were driven away there, too. After suffering heavy casualties, Cornwallis decided to break off the attack, allow his men to enjoy the relative comfort of Trenton overnight while the Americans shivered through the night in the open fields across the Assunpink. And shiver they would. The relatively mild weather now was turning bitter again.

Settling before a roaring fire, enjoying a repast and drinks, Cornwallis contemplated finishing the American army on the morrow.

As he discussed the situation with his officers, Quartermaster General Sir William Erskine interjected a concern about the delay.

"If Washington is the general I think he is, there won't be any Americans left across the creek tomorrow," he said to Cornwallis.

"Unlikely," Cornwallis responded. "Where would they go? They can't escape across the Delaware. The river is almost frozen solid, almost unnavigable. And they've few boats available.

"They're trapped. They can move around the countryside tomorrow, as they wish, but they'll be like a worm wiggling to get away and we will squash them.

"Our soldiers have had a long day. A good night's rest will put them in good stead tomorrow, when I intend to bring this rebellion to an end and restore the Crown's rule over all of North America. Tomorrow I intend to bag the fox."

And so the royal forces bedded for the night. Cornwallis always seemed to have his soldiers' comfort in mind, an unusual concern among British generals, earning him the loyalty and affection of his troops.

There was sporadic cannon fire through the evening, then all fell silent well before midnight.

Haslet, meanwhile, had been made second in command in Mercer's brigade, which was stationed about two miles upstream, guarding the fords at what were known as Henry's Mill and Phillip's Mill.

Late in the evening, he went with Mercer to Washington's headquarters downstream for a council of war. "Well, gentlemen," Washington said to his officers. "We seem to have our backs to the water and our faces to the fire."

The officers merely nodded, waiting for their commander's thoughts to become clear.

"A familiar stance," Washington conceded. "I'm sure we all would have enjoyed a night's rest in Trenton. Our foes have deprived us of that pleasure, however. Well, we make the best of whatever conditions are left to us.

"Since they have possession of Trenton, I do not intend to contest them. After all, a good many of the houses have red tags on the doors. (Red tags were a profession of loyalty to the Crown.) It's obvious we can't remain here."

There was a lively discussion of their options. One was to retreat south, hoping to find a safe crossing back to Pennsylvania.

"That is fraught with danger," Washington observed. "An army on the run will find it extremely difficult to manage the crossing safely. Cornwallis is a much more energetic general than Howe. I would not expect him to tarry while we gather boats and make our way across the river."

The council fell silent again.

After a moment, Washington spoke again, firmly, finally revealing what had been in his mind all along.

"I propose we move out tonight and head for Princeton. We can take a back road. Cadwalader has mapped it for us."

Washington traced his finger across a paper with a crude map drawn on it.

"We should be able to subdue the garrison there. Then we shall go on to New Brunswick and seize the British supplies there. It would be a rich and fortuitous prize."

The boldness won quick approval of the council.

Haslet remembered the successful nighttime withdrawal from Brooklyn Heights last August, when they had the wide harbor to navigate and a much larger enemy force facing their lines. This, he thought, should be easier. And there would be no water to cross, thank God.

"We start immediately," Washington ordered. "Colonel Hitchcock, your detachment will begin digging entrenchments. Have your men work vigorously for they must appear to be doing the work of several thousand men, not just the few hundred in your detachment."

Daniel Hitchcock commanded about 400 seasoned soldiers from New England, primarily Rhode Island. He nodded. "We'll sound like a mighty army to the people across the creek," he promised.

Washington continued:

"I've ordered the supply wagons to Burlington, where I expect they will be safe until we can send for them. If necessary, they can be sent to safety across the river.

"Now, we need to muffle the carriages on our artillery because I don't intend to march without them. I don't need to tell you of the need for as much quiet movement as your men can manage."

He turned to Mercer.

"You'll lead the advance. Captain Rodney's troop will be in the front, along with the Red Feather Company from Philadelphia.

"Young Rodney is eager for action and has a well-trained company."

Washington dispatched the commanders to their tasks.

About 1 A.M. the American defenders began peeling away from the lines, reluctantly leaving their campfires to steal away in the cold night. Hancock's detachment did its job exceedingly well, making the enemy across the Assunpink believe thousands of American soldiers were digging in to meet a daylight assault.

The unseasonably warm weather at the beginning of the year had been replaced by more typical cold. Once again the weather blessed the patriots because the roads froze over, making it easier to move the artillery.

Haslet accompanied Mercer near the front of the line, the general riding while Haslet walked and after they seemed safely out of earshot of Trenton, they began to talk quietly.

"John, I understand the general ordered you back to Delaware to recruit. Why do you delay?"

"I hope to see the British and Hessians driven from Jersey before I return home. That would be, for me, a satisfactory conclusion to my service these past several months. And it makes a more appealing story to recruits. It's always much more attractive to be part of a victorious army."

"Agreed, John. But you could have been home with your family right now."

"I admit I miss them terribly, Hugh."

The moment admitted to familiarity between the general and his subordinate.

"But I will be going home soon enough. It will be good to see the children. And Jemima.

"I hope you have a chance to meet her and my family when the war is over and won, as I'm sure it will be. And see my plantation along the Mispillion. We'd just moved in to a new home when I was chosen to command the Delaware regiment, so I haven't spent much time there this past year, with all the business of the battalion and the Tories down in southern Delaware—they certainly kept us busy."

"I'll make it a point to visit," Mercer said.

They continued on silently for a while, each lost in his thoughts.

"What about you, Hugh? Any family?"

"No. No family."

"What happened after Duquesne?" Haslet asked. "When I left, you stayed behind in command of the fort."

"Yes. I stayed, in fact, for more than two years. It was a reasonably quiet time.

"My worst moment was an expedition up the Allegheny River to Fort Venango in March of '59. The waters were high and swift and we had a difficult time going upriver. I had to turn back."

(Venango was on the upper reaches of the Allegheny in northwestern Pennsylvania.)

"Then I heard that a part of my advance party had been ambushed. One of their boats came drifting down with five of my men in it, all scalped. One was still alive."

Mercer grimaced at the memory. His memory of those years was coming back in fragments.

"That summer we heard the French at Fort Venango were preparing to march on Duquesne—Fort Pitt as we renamed it. Our information was that over 1,000 soldiers and Indians were in the enemy expedition. That would have been more than twice the size of my garrison. But they turned back when they heard about the British victory at Niagara. They turned around and headed there instead.

"After that, except for an occasional encounter with the Indians—and they were minor—it was uneventful."

"We never supposed at the time that someday we would be fighting those British and hoping the French would be on our side," Haslet commented.

They lapsed into silence then as they continued along.

"John," Mercer finally broke the silence, "I heard you were concerned that Congress passed you over for brigadier general, that you thought you were out of favor with the general."

"Yes. I discussed it with him just before we left Pennsylvania."

"Don't be concerned," Mercer assured him. "The general holds you in high regard and has told me so."

"Thank you," Haslet said. It was reassuring, knowing that Mercer was a close friend of the commander-in-chief.

"You have to be aware that Washington is not a demonstrative man. Except when he's angry. Or when he's around the ladies," Mercer continued, smiling at some memory he did not share with Haslet.

They rode along again silently for a while until Mercer spoke again.

"Why did you come to this country, John?"

"Because I was led to believe from all I had heard that the only restrictions on a man's freedom here were his obligations to himself and his family and the only limits on his success were in his own willingness to work hard.

"I have not been disappointed."

He paused then added sharply:

"And I will not allow the British to deny me."

By now the first suggestion of daylight was appearing in the distant horizon.

"Looks like it will be a glorious day, " Mercer commented.

"For a change," Haslet added.

Scouts stopped to tell Mercer there had been no contact with the enemy so far.

"I wonder if the British all went to Trenton," Haslet said.

"Possibly," Mercer answered. "Although it's likely Cornwallis would have left some garrison to guard their supplies here. They may be off guard, thinking Cornwallis has us trapped at Trenton."

Mercer's assessment was partly right.

At that moment, just a mile or so away, British Lieutenant Colonel Charles Mawhood was leading the Seventeenth Regiment and portions of the Fifty-fifth Regiment down the main road, taking supplies and reinforcements to Cornwallis at Trenton. He had left the Fortieth Regiment and the rest of the Fifty-fifth behind to secure Princeton.

About a mile and a half south of Princeton the back road the American army had been following split, one part turning to the right and on to Princeton, the other following Stony Creek to intersect with the main road—called the Post Road—from Princeton to Trenton. Between the two roads was the 200-acre farm of Thomas Clarke.

Mercer headed along the Stony Creek towards the Post Road. It was to be his role to guard the Stony Creek bridge there and fight a delaying action against the expected pursuit by a chagrined Cornwallis.

The area was heavily wooded, with low hills, which hid from each other the various units now in motion: Mercer marching towards

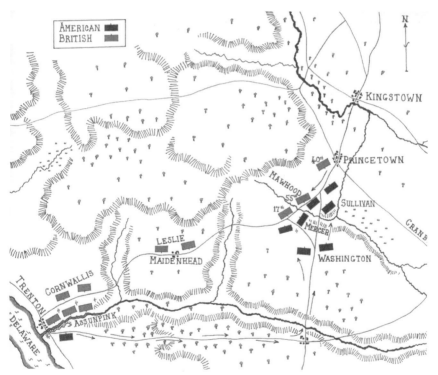

Retreat from Second Battle of Trenton
and Positions at Battle of Princeton
Map by John Mackenzie of britishbattles.com

the main road, Sullivan towards Princeton, and Mawhood towards Trenton.

The reflection of the rising sun off metal caught Mawhood's attention as the British troops moved just south of the Stony Creek bridge. He sent out scouts who quickly reported back that an undetermined number of rebel soldiers were on the march to Princeton.

Mawhood reined his horse around, summoned his two spaniels that had been scampering along beside their master, and ordered his troops to double time back across the bridge.

Probably these were rebels fleeing from the expected rout at Trenton, he reasoned, but prudence suggested he proceed warily.

He headed for an orchard on Clarke's property only to find that an advance detachment of Mercer's force, now aware of the British presence, had beaten him there and was deploying behind hedges. The British would have to face them from an open field.

Just as quickly as the soldiers on each side set in position, they opened fire, not more than forty yards apart. Each side had two pieces of artillery in support.

The firing lasted only fifteen minutes. Then Mawhood employed the ultimate British weapon: a bayonet charge.

Mercer's soldiers had held their positions well in the exchange of volleys but many were inexperienced militia. British soldiers kept their bayonets clean and shiny and the early morning sun sparkled off their bayonets, suggesting some occult power in them, as they quickly closed the gap between the two lines. It was a frightening sight. The militia broke and ran.

Mercer's horse was hit in the leg and pitched him to the ground as it fell. As he rose to his feet he simultaneously tried to rally his men and face the charging British.

Suddenly his position was overrun. He drew his sword to meet the enemy soldiers. A gun butt struck him hard on the head and he fell to the ground.

"Surrender, you damn rebel!" a British soldier demanded. Without waiting for an answer, he thrust his bayonet into Mercer's side. Six more thrusts followed and Mercer fell silent with wounds of the head and body.

Haslet, in another part of the field, pleaded with the fleeing men to stand and fight, but his plea went unheeded. He turned to meet the enemy and as he started to run towards Mercer, a bullet struck him in the forehead, killing him instantly.

One of the Delaware privates rushed to his side and lifted him to a sitting position, hoping to revive him. The soldier looked around, looking for someone who could help stay Haslet's death. Then he bowed his head in grief at the realization that this seemingly indestructible man who had inspired his men to take pride in being soldiers, who had showed compassion for their suffering, who had reassured them in defeat and complimented them in victory, lay dead in his arms. He gently lowered Haslet's body to the ground and sadly rose, his grief slowly adjusting to the situation around him.

Those of Mercer's troops not involved in the battle stood transfixed all this while, unable to figure what was happening, worrying why their comrades were rushing towards them from some danger they couldn't yet see, waiting for someone to tell them what to do. Cadwalader moved to stop the British advance but had to fall back. The British clearly were in command of the field.

Suddenly, a figure on a white horse emerged at full gallop from the other road, waving his hat in the air.

"Come on my brave soldiers," the figure entreated the Americans. "Follow me."

It was Washington, and the sight of this man sitting tall in his saddle, yelling out encouragement, had a mystical effect. Sullivan's soldiers fell in line, at first slowly, then with increasing urgency, finally breaking into a run and shouting taunts at the enemy confronting them.

Washington rode ahead of them at full speed, then stopped his mount between the two lines. There was another volley from the two sides.

Clouds of smoke rose over the scene, obscuring the commander-in-chief from view. One of his aides hid his eyes with his hat, expecting to see the general on the ground when the smoke rose.

Miraculously, he was still there, unharmed, sitting erect in his saddle, surveying the enemy position while continuing to encourage his soldiers to fight.

The Americans pressed on. Their numbers were growing as additional soldiers were brought on the battlefield. Now it was the British turn to panic. They started to retreat, then retreat became a disorderly scramble to get away from the Americans.

"Come on, soldiers," Washington shouted gleefully, "this is a fine fox hunt."

And off he dashed after the fleeing enemy.

From that point the battle belonged to the Americans.

Some British soldiers took refuge inside Nassau Hall but soon surrendered after Captain Alexander Hamilton pointed a cannon through the open front door.

In the meantime Washington realized that chasing enemy soldiers was not the appropriate sport for the commander-in-chief. He cut off his chase and rode back across the battlefield.

A body clothed in the blue coat of the First Delaware Continentals caught his eye. The blood soaking the snow caused him to catch his breath.

He stopped, dismounted and stared at the prone figure.

"John Haslet," he said, partly in recognition, partly in greeting, as if hoping the still figure would answer him. Washington paused to control his emotions, collect his thoughts. His eyes moistened.

"No one believed more passionately than you in independence for the American people and no one was readier to sacrifice for that belief," he said, his voice reverent.

"You were a great commander, John Haslet, and this general shall miss you very much. Miss not just your skills as a leader, but your companionship. I wish I could enjoy it longer but God has willed another service for you. God bless you."

Washington stood up, remounted, and rode off. There were other sad moments ahead. His good friend Hugh Mercer lay mortally wounded by a large oak tree.

(Mercer was carried off to the Thomas Clarke house and left in the care of Dr. Benjamin Rush. He died nine days later, he and Rush left undisturbed when the British reoccupied the town.)

The victors had been gathering up whatever equipment and supplies they could. Now it was time for the army to push on. Doubtlessly Cornwallis was headed rapidly back up the road when he found his quarry had escaped the trap at the Assunpink. Indeed, forward elements of Cornwallis' army were approaching even as the Americans marched out of town.

Washington relished the possibility of moving on to Brunswick and capturing that supply base. He had the bridges along the path of his march destroyed to delay Cornwallis' pursuit, hoping to gain enough distance between him and Cornwallis and enough time to conduct the assault. The recent successes had encouraged him to try for more but he realized his soldiers were too weary after more than two days on the march, so he abandoned the idea. Instead, he proceeded on to Morristown to spend the rest of the winter there.

The bodies of Mercer and Haslet were carried to Philadelphia and put on display in the State House yard as inspiration to the citizens, before being interred in the Presbyterian cemetery there.

Writing to Killen on January 27, Caesar Rodney commented:

"We know we lost a brave, open, honest, sensible man, one who loved his country's more than his private interest."

The victories at Trenton and Princeton energized the patriot cause throughout the colonies. Americans realized they could defeat the British and their mercenary allies. Furthermore, they had a commander-in-chief who could outwit the enemy, a commander whose steadfastness for the cause could carry the entire nation.

And there were repercussions far beyond the colonies. The boldness of Washington's maneuvers impressed rulers throughout Europe. The news brought the French closer to formalizing an alliance with the Americans.

A few days after Princeton, a rider stopped at the Three Runs Presbyterian Church at the Mispillion in lower Delaware. A group of boys were playing in the yard. The Reverend Alexander Houston, their pastor and schoolteacher, was observing them and walked over to the road to talk to the rider.

"Good morning," he said, "any news of the war?"

"Good news," the man responded. "Have you heard about Trenton?"

"I'm told we scored an important victory there," Houston said.

"Quite. Quite. And also at Princeton just a few days ago. Routed the British, took many prisoners, captured many supplies. The whole countryside is filled with joy at General Washington's victories. We hope this will mean a quick end to the war."

"That is a result to be prayed for," Houston conceded.

"Some sad news, however," the rider continued. "I'm en route to John Haslet's plantation with word for Mrs. Haslet that her husband was killed at Princeton."

The news was such a shock, Houston had to gasp for air.

Among the children, one child suddenly stopped playing, stood up and glanced at the rider with a questioning look on his face.

"John Haslet? Killed?" the boy asked.

"Yes, sadly it's true, boy," the rider answered.

The boy broke and ran across the fields, tears streaming down his face.

"Joseph. Wait!" Houston called out, but the boy paid no attention.

The minister shook his head sadly.

"That was John Haslet's son," he explained to the rider.

"Oh, I'm sorry, really sorry to have blurted out such news in his presence. But I had no idea a child of Haslet's was among your charges."

"I'm sure you didn't," Houston assured him. "Well, wait a moment and I'll go with you to Longfield. That's the Haslet plantation. Mrs. Haslet has not been well lately and she'll need comforting.

"Boys, you're dismissed for the day," he said to the remaining youngsters. "Be back here tomorrow."

Then Houston and the messenger rode off to Longfield.

Joseph's hysterical arrival home already had alarmed the household as Houston and the stranger approached. Jemima was trying to understand what her sobbing child was saying when she saw them. Her sense of foreboding nearly overwhelmed her as she stepped outside.

"Good morning, Reverend Houston," she said, "and good morning to you, sir."

The stranger removed his hat.

"Jemima, this man brings news, awful news."

"Is it about John?"

"Yes."

"What happened to him?"

"He was killed, ma'am," the messenger responded. "At Princeton. On January 3. He was rallying the soldiers against a British charge and a bullet caught him in the head."

The blunt words made Jemima's knees buckle.

Two female slaves who had come forth from the house on the arrival of the visitors caught her by the arms.

"Come inside, Miss Jemima," one said.

"She's not been well," she explained to Houston. "Best she lies down."

"I understand," Houston responded. "Is there anything I can do?"

"Polly is over at the other plantation," the woman said. "I'll have one of the men fetch her over here. I think Mr. Killen also should be notified. He'll know what else to do."

"I'll ride on up to Dover," Houston said. "I'll be back this evening to look in on you, Jemima."

Jemima did not respond and the two women helped her into the house and into her bed. Inside, Joseph's brother and sisters were trying to comprehend the words muffled by his sobs. The sight of their mother filled them with the terror of realizing something catastrophic had taken place that they didn't yet understand.

Jemima Haslet never arose again. Two weeks later she was dead. Joseph said she died of a broken heart.

The twenty-four-year-old Polly became mother to her much younger half brothers and half sisters. William Killen looked after the estate.

The Second Delaware Continentals went into service in 1777 under the command of David Hall who had been the senior captain under Haslet. It saw service at Brandywine, Germantown, Fort Mifflin, Monmouth, Stony Point, Paulus Hook, Camden, Cowpens, Guilford, Hobkirk's Hill, Ninety-Six, Eutaw Springs, and Yorktown and in innumerable minor skirmishes. After Hall was wounded at the Battle of Germantown in 1777, he gave intermittent service to the battalion until 1779 when Joseph Vaughn, another veteran of the First Continentals, took command. Robert Kirkwood, also a veteran of the First Continentals, succeeded him to the end of the war.

But John Haslet is the name most associated with the Blue Hen's Chickens.

Of his children, only Joseph and little Jemima produced children and only Jemima's children continued the Haslet line, if not the name.

On November 13, 1783, Polly married Robert McGarment, a member of Thomas Rodney's Light Infantry Company, in a ceremony in Philadelphia witnessed by two cousins from Ireland, one of them a child who would become the famous essayist William Hazlitt. ("Hazlitt" was one of the many variations in the spelling of the family name.) Polly had no children and died around the turn of the century.

Joseph became a farmer and politician, serving two nonconsecutive terms as governor of Delaware, one of them during the War of

1812. He died in 1823, during his second term. He was well regarded as a governor. Joseph had four children by two wives (the first wife died). Records of the Daughters of the American Revolution show their daughters Ann and Jemima had children, but that Ann wasn't married until 1848. The DAR shows Jemima marrying in 1835 and a grandson born in 1842.

John took up the practice of medicine like his father but never married. There is no record of the date of his death. Ann married John Patten, an officer in the Delaware Continentals, in December of 1788 but died two years later without children.

Daughter Jemima married George Monro, a prominent Wilmington physician, in 1793. They had three sons and five daughters, who in turn produced twenty-three children.

Jemima died in 1821, but it was probably some of her descendants who were in Dover in July 1841, when Haslet's remains were returned to Delaware for final honors.

Chapter Thirty-Seven

Finally at Rest

Daylight was a thin line on the horizon when the SS *Kent* nosed up to the wharf at Duck Creek Landing, a few miles north of Dover, Delaware, on Friday evening, July 2, 1841.

It had been several hours since the steamboat left Philadelphia with the remains of Delaware's Revolutionary War hero, John Haslet.

The trip downriver had been slowed by stops at New Castle and other landings along the way as hundreds of people lined the river banks to pay tribute to his memory, attracted by newspaper accounts and by the urging of community leaders.

This final journey for John Haslet had turned out to be a remarkable event, far more than anyone had expected back on January 18 when the planning started.

John Haslet, hero that he had been, certainly wasn't the best remembered Delawarean of the Revolutionary period.

Caesar Rodney had used his political skills to guide the three lower counties along the Delaware to support opposition to British rule. His midnight ride from Dover to Philadelphia to cast a key vote on the Declaration of Independence had become folk lore. John Dickinson's "Letters from a Pennsylvania Farmer" had provided intellectual stimulus to the pre-revolution ferment over colonial grievances with the British Parliament. And Thomas McKean mixed passion with his own political and intellectual contributions to the revolutionary fever of the 1770s. However, McKean and Dickinson had earned greater recognition serving the province of Pennsylvania. Allen McLane had been a war hero too, a romantic figure who served Washington as a spy. But his exploits were more individual whereas Haslet created a regiment that earned praise as one of the best—some said the best—regiment in the Continental army, one that fought throughout the war, down almost to the last man. They were the "Blue Hens," named for the bird said to have provided the fighting cocks that offered sport for the encampments in the early part of the war. The Delaware soldiers' smart blue uniforms and demonstrated fighting spirit made it seem natural to link them to that legendary bird.

After the Delaware Assembly voted to bring his remains from Philadelphia and have them placed "in some fitting and desirable spot within the limits of this state, " it was decided Dover, the capital, would be most appropriate rather than his home area of Three Runs (now Milford). Besides, his own church had ceased to exist more than twenty years before. He would be reinterred in the Presbyterian churchyard in Dover where there would be erected "a suitable monument with appropriate inscriptions and devices, prepared by a skillful artist and erected under their superintendence and direction, over his remains when so deposited."

The committee had planned to buy a plain coffin, transfer Haslet's remains, then leave Philadelphia without any ceremony, heading directly to Dover.

Irish pride overwhelmed these modest plans early on.

The Hibernian Society of Philadelphia saw an opportunity to glorify a native Irishman and seized the moment, transforming the Philadelphia phase of the event into a magnificent commemoration of the nation's sixty-fifth birthday anniversary, an opportunity seized to renew appreciation for the generation that had created the United States of America, all twenty-six of them.

And patriotic fervor can be epidemic.

All of that city's gentry responded to the society's request for a great turnout and thousands of spectators were attracted to the procession to the *Kent*'s wharf that morning.

Although there were far more people in Philadelphia than in the whole state of Delaware, his adopted homeland could not appear less grateful.

Now, some of its most prominent citizens gathered at the landing to welcome the remains and the considerable escort of civilian and military dignitaries from Maryland, Pennsylvania, and Delaware that had accompanied the hearse from Philadelphia.

There was Joseph Comegys, Dover's most successful lawyer, son of the recently-retired governor, and chairman of the reception committee. And also present was Dr. Henry Ridgely, chief marshal for the event.

One of the deputy marshals was Henry Hayes Lockwood, a graduate of West Point who now was making a career as a farmer. (Only twenty-seven, he would soon give up farming to join the navy, helped found the U. S. Naval Academy, and make a reputation as a teacher that served as a model for a character in Herman Melville's *White Jacket.*)

Most prominent, perhaps—certainly a center of attention—was twenty-five-year-old Anne Ridgely DuPont, daughter of Dr. Ridgely. As a member of two prominent Delaware families, she would automatically attract social attention, but she was blessed with a beauty, charm and self-confidence that drew the young and old to her company. The somber clothing she wore as appropriate to the occasion seemed only to accent her beauty. She had proved her competence by the way she took over after her mother's death in 1837 and helped her father raise her five younger siblings. Furthermore, she was a recent bride, married a few months earlier to Senator Charles I. DuPont, forty-four, son of a French diplomat, grandson of a prominent statesmen, and grand-nephew of the founder of the DuPont powder mill near Wilmington.

DuPont was a member of the legislative committee that saw to the arrangements for transferring Haslet's remains and had written the inscription that would adorn the memorial over his grave. He went to Philadelphia for the ceremonies there but had left the *Kent* at New Castle, picked up his three children from his first marriage, and raced downstate, barely reaching Duck Creek Landing ahead of the steamboat.

The crowd around his wife moved to a respectful distance to allow their enthusiastic reunion, then all turned to watch the *Kent* maneuver into the dock, lights from dockside torches illuminating the faces of the crowds on both the ship and the shore.

The landing procedure completed, the passengers filed down the gangway to greet and be greeted by those on shore.

General Thomas Fisher's son George took Major General Robert Patterson, commander of the Pennsylvania militia, to meet officers of the Delaware militia. Comegys joined them, then turned to greet the Hibernian Society delegation, expressing gratitude for the society's role in the Philadelphia tribute.

The other two members of the legislative committee on arrangements, Representatives William Huffington and Gardner Wright, briefed him on the Philadelphia ceremonies earlier in the day and Comegys nodded his head in appreciation and wonderment at the scenes they described.

By now the landing area was so crowded that people on the fringes disappeared into the shadows beyond the reach of the torchlights.

Finally, it was time for the final debarkation, the car carrying the remains of John Haslet.

The crowd moved back from the gangplank to make room for the militia honor guard flanking it. Grooms directed the horse-drawn car down the gangplank, a move requiring delicate execution that transfixed the spectators. Conversation had diminished to reverent murmurs. Within that car was the object of their efforts and, yet, known to them only through stories they had heard or read.

Those handful of people still alive who knew him were too old to be involved in this reception but would participate in Saturday's events.

With the hearse safely ashore, everyone moved to their carriages or horses for the trip to Dover, the militia on horseback shouldering torches to light the way.

And so they made their way down the road, the militia units marching to the moderate beat of the drummers. A full moon illuminating the fields and forests and the flickering shadows from the torches added an ethereal backdrop.

About a mile from town, dozens more people were waiting to greet the party. Bells could be heard tolling in Dover.

The procession marched around Dover Commons, the military band leading the way with the slow mournful beat of its drums. Torches flickered all around the square and lights from the buildings added a warm touch to the scene. And so they proceeded past Caesar Rodney's townhouse, past the hotel run in colonial times by Frenchie Battell—places where great events of those days had been discussed, action planned, results celebrated—past the tavern whose name had been abruptly changed from the King George to the George Washington when independence was proclaimed, and past the impressive Ridgely home, continuing on to the statehouse.

Comegys welcomed the visitors from Philadelphia, repeating publicly the state's appreciation of the acclaim that city offered for their distinguished son. The welcome was reciprocated and now the mahogany coffin bearing the remains was unloaded from the funeral car and carried slowly into the statehouse and placed on a catafalque in the courtroom. Under Anne Ridgely DuPont's supervision, the wives and daughters of the town's leaders had draped the room in black.

With the coffin in place, soldiers were stationed around the catafalque and remained there through the night.

Sunrise found the square filling with people arriving from all parts of the county, indeed from all parts of the state, for the event had been well promoted in the newspapers. People sensed this ceremony would make a lifetime memory and could scarcely pass up the opportunity to tell their posterity they were there on that glorious Independence commemoration (held on Saturday in 1841 because July 4 was a Sunday).

They formed a line outside the courthouse and shortly began to file in. In the normal practice of the times, the visitors were not there to stare at a closed coffin, but to see the mortal remains, the accepted way of paying respect to the dead. In fact, they saw only dust and ashes and remnants of a skeleton but imagination stimulated by stories handed down from the older generation and articles in the newspaper certified the life and gave meaning to the remains of John Haslet.

But Anne Ridgely DuPont could not bring herself to see. She stared at the coffin, her eyes moistening. She did not want to look inside at the skeletal remains lest it dissolve the image she had in her mind of a tall, handsome, officer in the blue jacket and beige trousers of a Delaware Continental, gallantly facing an onrushing tide of red uniforms. In her childhood she had read about him, heard stories about him from her grandfather, Charles Ridgely, and others who had been alive at the time. And she was slightly discomfited by a vague impression that her grandfather and Haslet had been rivals.

Now the stories were being revived and shared by the more knowledgeable among the spectators.

First among the viewers were the grandchildren, sons and daughters of Jemima Haslet Munro, youngest child of John Haslet. She was only a little over a year old when he died. In 1793 she was a teenage bride, marrying a prominent Wilmington physician, George Munro. Jemima had died in 1821, outliving her much older husband by just two years.

Following the grandchildren were the great-grandchildren, some of whom had traveled from new settlements out west of the Alleghenies for the occasion.

An old man in what appeared to be the faded blue uniform of the Delaware Continentals walked stiffly to the coffin and gazed inside. He stood erect, a middle-aged man and a teenaged boy on either side to steady him. The muscles of his face struggled to control the tears running down his cheeks, but he made no sounds. Then the old man saluted, turned, and shuffled out of the room, steadied by the hands of his companions.

There were a few more in the line of mourners who had known Haslet when he was alive and who had served in the war. They, too, found the experience very emotional, stirring a montage of memories.

So the line continued until all had a chance to gaze at the remains and reflect on the meaning of the man they represented.

Now, the Reverend Eliphalet Wheeler Gilbert, president of New Ark College, moved alongside the coffin and led the assemblage in prayer. When he had finished, John M. Clayton began his oration.

A former U. S. Senator, former chief justice of the state supreme court, Clayton came from Milford and was perhaps the most prominent public figure in the state at that time. His family had been in Delaware since the time of William Penn and an ancestor, William Clayton, served on Penn's first executive council in 1683. Claytons continued to be prominent in Delaware public life since and John's cousin Thomas also had served in the U. S. Senate.

(John M. Clayton earned an additional note in history as President Zachary Taylor's secretary of state, negotiating with British Diplomat Lytton Bulwer in 1850 the treaty that bears their names guaranteeing neutrality of any canal built across Central America, then being seriously discussed.)

A cum laude graduate of Yale Law School, forty-five, over six feet tall, he was an imposing figure as he talked of the life of John Haslet.

"Welcome home, John Haslet," he began, after acknowledging the distinguished guests in the courtroom. He paused, allowing time for his words to resonate through the crowd, for their meaning to make full impact. For local citizens, the words bound them to the man they honored and they were filled with the pride that this was not some stranger, but a friend, a neighbor.

"Allen McLane, Commodore McDonough, John Haslet all have brought honor to our state in serving their country," Clayton resumed. "And John Haslet was the first of that distinguished line.

"He was one of the choice spirits of the Revolution; one of the immortal band of heroes who, in the special providence of God, were made for that occasion, to release their country from oppression, to light a beacon fire of freedom for all the world, and set the example of a successful government enjoying a degree of liberty before then unknown among men.

"By his exertions and influence mainly, the Delaware Regiment was raised and mustered at Dover in 1776, one of the most distinguished regiments in the army of that immortal commander-in-chief, George Washington. He was at Washington's side at Brooklyn Heights, at White Plains, at Trenton, at Princeton. And when he fell at Princeton, it is said the great Washington himself shed tears over his corpse.

"If there be anything connected with the history of that celebrated and suffering corps to arouse the pride of Delawareans for heroic actions, or stimulate their gratitude for services rendered, the honor and the debt are chiefly due to the brave officers who organized and disciplined these troops and under whose head they fought. Haslet was not long among them, but he lived long enough to train this devoted band for action, to teach them how to fight and set them the example how, bravely, to die."

Clayton lowered his voice a bit now and continued:

"To those who believe in a special Providence—and what American can fail to recognize an almighty hand in the events of the revolution!—it would seem that the early martyrdom of Haslet was an appointed means for producing a great end and it is quite possible that Colonel Haslet in his death served the cause of his country more effectually than if he had not fallen.

"A poetic soul has written about John Haslet:

"Slowly and sadly they laid him down
From the field of his fame fresh and gory;
They carved not a line, they raised not a stone,
But they left him alone in his glory."

The poem was delivered with all the flourish a skilled orator commanded and now Clayton became less impassioned, more conversational.

"More than half a century has passed by since he was laid to rest in that lonely churchyard. The old church has even disappeared; and its site is now covered with warehouses and stores. The demands of trade and commerce clamored loudly for the room occupied by the silent dead, who unresistingly yield to the will of the living. The old grave yard is to be broken up. Those whose mortal remains there deposited, have the claims of kindred or friendship to watch over them, are being hurried off to other retired homes for the dead, lest they should be removed by the hands of the stranger and thrown into a promiscuous grave.

"But the State of Delaware could not leave it to filial piety or private friendship to save Haslet's bones from dishonor. Her legislature, in fulfillment of the desire of their citizens 'to cherish and preserve the memory of those of her brave and patriotic sons who died gallantly fighting under the banner of Washington, in defense of the liberties of their country,' directed a committee of their body to bring home the remains of Haslet and erect over them 'a suitable monument with appropriate inscriptions and devices.'

"And so he has returned home.

"There are among us today people who knew John Haslet personally, knew him as more than a soldier, but as a physician, legislator, and, yes, a family man. Among his children was one of our most prominent governors, Joseph Haslet, who guided the state through the War of 1812 and died in office not too many years ago, serving as Delaware's chief executive for a second time.

"None of John Haslet's children survive, unfortunately, but there are grandchildren and great grandchildren—some of whom have traveled great distances—with us today to honor him."

Clayton gestured towards the gathering of Haslet descendants facing the coffin and paused while the crowd acknowledged their presence.

"We owe men like John Haslet a singular debt. For it was they who undertook the seemingly hopeless fight against a tyrannical government that was sucking the lifeblood of freedom from the bones of colonial America.

"They proclaimed their birthrights as free men and when that government across the ocean turned deaf ears to their voices, they took up their rifles and confronted the forces of tyranny in battle across the great breadth of this nation, from New England to Georgia.

"Many fell along the way, among them our own hero, John Haslet. Others like David Hall and Joseph Vaughan and Robert Kirkwood picked up the baton and led the gallant soldiers of the Delaware Continentals—the fabled Blue Hens—in battle after battle until very few remained. But those few saw the birth of our nation, the confirmation of our birthright.

"This is a debt we owe that generation that can only be redeemed in similar service to this great nation. Those men inspired us. We must use that inspiration to build an even greater nation."

He paused again, to change the tempo and whispered the final words almost as a prayer.

"John Haslet left home, family friends—as dear to him as ours are to us—to face the peril of war and to lay down his life for his beliefs. We shall never forget what he and his compatriots did for us, to make this glorious celebration of America's independence possible."

The ceremony in the statehouse was finished, but the people stood silently, reverently in the chamber, reflecting on the meaning of John Haslet's life, and it was a little while before they began to file out to take their places for his final journey.

A band formed by the Philadelphia and Washington Greys took its place at the head of the procession followed by the remainder of their units as escorts to the funeral carriage.

Haslet's grandchildren and great-grandchildren assembled behind the carriage. Then came Gov. William Barkley Cooper, former Governor Joseph Comegys, judges, and other state officials.

The Hibernian delegation was next, ahead of the prominent Delawareans and Marylanders who lived in Philadelphia, had participated in the ceremony there, and had come to Dover to see the resolution of the solemn pageant.

The few Revolutionary soldiers in attendance followed them and then the Committee on Reception and Arrangements.

An assortment of prominent citizens from each county, from Pennsylvania and Maryland, and from Lewes completed the procession.

They moved slowly around the square to the funereal beat of the military drums, then proceeded to the First Presbyterian churchyard.

When all were assembled, the coffin was lifted from the carriage, carried to the grave site and there the military honor guard fired three volleys. Then the remains of Colonel John Haslet, commanding officer of the First Delaware Continentals, were lowered into the grave.

The crowd dispersed slowly, as if reluctant to leave Haslet alone once more.

DuPont stared thoughtfully, reverently at the gravesite and turned to Anne:

"He slept alone among strangers for so many years, but now he is among friends and fellow soldiers and won't be alone anymore."

When the people had dispersed, the stonecutters from the Philadelphia firm (John Struthers and Sons) moved in to complete the monument. On one side they placed the marble slab that had marked his grave in Philadelphia for so many years:

> In Memory of
> JOHN HAZLET, ESQUIRE,
> Colonel of the Delaware Regiment.
> Who Fell Gloriously at the battle of
> PRINCETON,
> In the Cause of
> AMERICAN INDEPENDENCE,
> January 3d, 1777.
> The General Assembly of the
> DELAWARE STATE,
> Remembering
> His virtues as a man—His merits as a citizen, and
> his service as a soldier, have caused this
> monumental stone, in testimony of their
> respect, to be placed over his grave.
> Anno MDCCLXXXIII

And on the other side, a new marble slab:

> ERECTED
> by the State of Delaware, as a Tribute of
> Respect to the Memory of
> Col. John Haslet,
> Whose remains, according to a resolution of the
> Legislature, passed on the 22d of February
> 1841, were removed from their resting place
> in the grave yard of the First Presby-
> terian Church of the City of Phil-
> adelphia, and here reinterred
> on Saturday, 3d July,
> 1841

The Presbyterian church and graveyard in Dover and the
Haslet Monument.
Photos by Fred B. Walters

Chapter Notes

Chapter One

This is based on accounts in the Philadelphia newspapers at the Pennsylvania State Library and the *Delaware Journal* on file at the University of Delaware.

The newspapers included verbatim accounts of Alderman Binns' speech. Rep. Huffington's remarks are created out of the newspaper accounts, which paraphrased them. The role of the Hibernian Society is based on meeting notes in John Hugh Campbell's *Friendly Sons of Saint Patrick,* published in 1892. Colonel Thomas Robinson's relationship to the notorious Tory is based on biographies in the *Biographical and Historical Encyclopedia of Delaware.* Newspaper accounts, however, made no mention of this connection. There was a prominent Robinson family in Wilmington during the colonial period but there doesn't seem to have been a descendant named Thomas.

I've depended upon Gary Laderman's *The Sacred Remains, American Attitudes Toward Death,* and James Farrell's *Inventing the American Way of Death,* for the passages in this chapter and throughout the book—particularly in Chapters Two and Thirty-Seven—on disposing of the dead.

Chapter Two

References to Haslet say he preached frequently in America. Although he studied religion at the University of Glasgow and was ordained a Presbyterian minister in 1752, notes of the Lewes Presbytery do not show him as a minister. He had cousins living along the Pennsylvania—Maryland border and the guess is he lived temporarily with them and sustained himself as an itinerant preacher, much in demand in the rural areas of the time.

The fact he recruited heavily from that area for his militia company and that he is listed in a 1761 newspaper ad as an agent for a New London church's lottery adds credibility to this theory.

Records of the Presbyterian Historical Society of Ireland, family accounts, and histories indicate Haslet emigrated from northern Ireland in 1757, five years after his first wife died. Most ship arrivals in Philadelphia from the province in that year were from Londonderry, although Newry remains a possibility. No ship arrivals in 1758 are listed until May and by then Haslet already had been commissioned in the Pennsylvania militia.

The account of the Forbes campaign is drawn from several sources, including the extensive collection of the papers of Henry Bouquet in the State Library of Pennsylvania. The dispute over the route to take is well documented in those letters, many of which were to or from Washington. Haslet's letter is often cited to describe the condition of the fort; it also is the earliest record of any of his correspondence in America. Haslet's remarks are based on comments in his letter. The scene that greeted the expedition, including the intertwined corpses of the Halketts and Francis Halkett's presence with the Forbes expedition, is mentioned in several sources. The tales of the twelve-year-old boy are mentioned in Haslet's letter and other sources. The dialogue between Forbes and his commanders is suggested by the historical evidence of the events discussed. As for the decision to choose Mercer to command the fort, Mercer himself mentioned his friendship to Washington years later and said he had moved to Virginia because of it.

The relationship between Haslet and McClughan is assumed from the fact he wrote a letter in 1759 supporting McClughan's bid for a captain's commission. The author likes to believe the friendship led to Haslet's decision to settle in Delaware.

Chapter Three

John Brinckle's deathbed scene is based on depositions on file in the Delaware State Archives by Haslet, Jemima, and Curtis Brinckle and his wife, plus copies of Brinckle's will on file in the same place. This chapter estab-

lishes Haslet in the Three Runs area of Kent/Sussex counties. A 1933 newspaper article, printed in connection with Christopher Ward's address to a meeting of the Sons of the Revolution, indicated Haslet served as a "lay lawyer, advising (clients and friends) in the administration of their affairs, making their wills, settling their estates, and acting as servener in drawing up legal documents and contracts."

Almost nothing is known of his activities from Fort Duquesne until this scene, however, although there is evidence in court records that he was in the area from 1760. He is listed in a newspaper ad in 1761 as a Kent County agent for a church lottery in nearby New London, Pennsylvania, and in 1762 he bid on property in Kent County. But his attendance at Brinckle's in September, 1764, is the first detailed account of his presence. However, beyond that nothing is known and the kitchen dialogue is the author's creation.

Reese Hammond's biography of Joseph Haslet, John's son, states that John Haslet emigrated with a brother and that presumably would be William, who settled in Maryland, at Greensboro, Caroline County. It would appear his brother Joseph emigrated much later, since he graduated from Glasgow in 1762. (There is a notice in the *Pennsylvania Gazette* in early 1764 of a letter waiting at the post office for "Joseph Haslet" and gives his residence as "Pennsylvania.") Like his oldest brother, he practiced medicine in Maryland, where he bought the property identified as "Fishingham," in Queen Anne County.

Chapter Four

It is not clear when Jemima Brinckle and John Haslet married, nor is there any information about any courtship. Marriage records in this period are practically nonexistent. The year 1765 is the first year Haslet shows on the Kent County tax rolls and that lends credibility to the supposition he had married Jemima that year and moved onto the Brinckle plantation. It is possible he lived in Sussex County until then but that county's tax records for that period are missing. It is known John and Jemima were married by May 20, 1766, when they filed an accounting, as husband and wife, of distributions from John Brinckle's estate to Reyneer Williams as administrator for the Cole children. There were four more accountings, through the year 1768. The identity of the slaves comes from Brinckle's will; otherwise, the chapter is conjecture.

Chapter Five

The stamp tax and the colonial reaction are based primarily on accounts from newspapers. They reported the colonial agents, including Benjamin Franklin, met with Grenville on February 2. Franklin's remarks are based on sentiments he expressed in his correspondence and the general sentiments of opponents to the tax at the time. Grenville's response is based on dispatches to the Philadelphia newspapers.

Although Delaware's reactions, including that in Sussex County, are matters of record, the account of the meeting at Three Runs church is the author's invention as a means to explain opposition to the tax and to introduce William Killen and Caesar Rodney, two principal figures in Haslet's life. For the discussion of medicine here and throughout the book I have depended upon Whitfield J. Bell Jr.'s *The Colonial Physician and other Essays*, Larry L. Burkhart's *The Good Fight: Medicine in Colonial Pennsylvania*, Lester Snow

King's *The Medical World of the Eighteenth Century*, Richard H. Shryock's report *Eighteenth Century Medicine in America*, in the proceedings of the American Antiquarian Society.

Chapter Six

The reaction to the stamp tax and its repeal are historical facts. The speeches in Parliament were reported in dispatches to American newspapers. The reaction in Philadelphia, including the scene at the London Coffee House, was published in the *Pennsylvania Gazette*. The author has taken dramatic license to place Haslet there at the time and the dialogue with Dr. Alison is the author's creation although the events discussed are historical. That he and Dr. Alison were acquainted is based on the letter he wrote in 1758 to the "Reverend Dr. Alison" with an account of the capture of Fort Duquesne. Haslet and Alison had quite similar backgrounds and I suspect Alison might have been among the first people Haslet saw when he arrived in America. It is not unlikely that Haslet visited Philadelphia occasionally. Delaware Archivist Leon deValinger, in his introduction to Volume 1 of *A Calendar of Ridgely Family Letters, 1742–1899*, writes of the colonial period that "Philadelphia continued to be . . . an important factor in the lives of the more prosperous Kent County residents . . . the mart of their commerce, the center from which came their books, newspapers, and contacts with inter-colonial and European affairs."

Haslet's bid on Kent County property owned by the Pennsylvania Land Company at its 1762 auction is based both on newspaper accounts and deeds in the Delaware Archives and filed with the Kent County Recorder of Deeds. The Pennsylvania Land Company was based in Philadelphia.

Chapter Seven

This chapter is mostly the author's imagination, fashioned from the scant information about Polly's immigration. It appears she was thirteen at the time. Since Haslet had married her mother in 1752 and, assuming Polly was born the following year, 1766 seems the likely year of her arrival. Samuel might have been a cousin, although reputable information identifies him as an uncle. Family genealogy lists a Samuel who had a son William who later died in Lancaster County. It is assumed that Polly would not have traveled alone so I decided to have William accompany her on the trip because it appears he arrived in America around this time. She might have sailed with Haslet's brother Joseph, but there is credible evidence that Joseph sailed in 1764, too early for Polly to have been with him. I am grateful to Michael Higgins of Belfast, a Haslet kin, whose research on the family and the Ireland of the 1770s helped in the writing of the reunion. The John Harris mentioned is the man for whom Harrisburg, Pennsylvania, is named. Information about the church comes from the Presbyterian Historical Society and from Julia Mullin's *The Presbytery of Limavady*.

The record of the Brady property acquisition and sale to Haslet is based on deeds on file in the Delaware State Archives. The descriptions of Kent County are based on several sources, including the histories of Delaware architecture and agriculture and historical writings and other material on file with the Milford Historical Society. Property advertisements in the Philadelphia newspapers also provided a picture of development in Kent County. The description of the Dickinson estate is based on an ad in the Philadelphia newspaper and from the Delaware archives. The estate today is largely as it existed in Haslet's time and is operated as a museum.

The account of the trip between Dover and Three Runs is the author's creation.

Throughout the book I've depended greatly upon Alice Morse Earle's, *Home Life in Colonial Days* (1898), and *Child Life in Colonial Days* (1899) for descriptions of colonial life.

Birth records for all the Haslet children are nonexistent, except for the last, Jemima, (November 7, 1775). Although some records say Joseph was born later, the biographies of Delaware governors give Joseph's birth year as 1766 and I have accepted that year. I have guessed that the Haslets didn't marry until late 1765, about a year after Jemima's first husband's death, and, therefore, speculate that her pregnancy began in early 1766. That is covered in Chapter Six. The medical information in this chapter is based on the books mentioned in the notes on Chapter Five.

Chapter Eight

The actions of the Massachusetts and New York legislatures and the reaction of Parliament are matters of historical record. So, too is Haslet's acquisition of the deed on the Mispillion property.

Although Haslet obviously went to Philadelphia to close his land deal, the meeting between him and Alison and McKean is the author's creation to establish what would become an important relationship with McKean. The subjects of their dinner table discussion are based on material drawn from G. S. Rowe's biography of McKean and Alan Heimert, introduction to *The Great Awakening*, edited with Perry Miller, (1967). The sentiments attributed to McKean about the schism in the church actually were contained in an anonymous analysis in the minutes of the Lewes Presbytery.

The University of Glasgow supplied information about the faculty at the time of Haslet's matriculation.

In writing about eighteenth century taverns, I've depended upon Peter Thompson's *Rum, Punch & Revolution, Taverngoing & public Life in 18th Century Philadelphia*, (1999).

The portion on the enactment of the Townshend duties is based on accounts in the contemporary Philadelphia newspapers.

Chapter Nine

The information about the Tennents is based primarily on the minutes of the Lewes Presbytery for the July meeting. Tennent's complaint against his wife and her response were published as advertisements in the Philadelphia newspapers. The minutes record Haslet's presence and outline Mrs. Tennent's complaints about her husband and the fact no action was taken in the absence of her husband and William McKay. The dialogue of the meeting is my creation.

Subsequent action on the Tennent matter is contained in the presbytery minutes on file at the Presbyterian Historical Society of America in Philadelphia.

The status of American-English relations is based on historical sources and newspaper accounts. The account of the Elizabethtown riot is based on a newspaper dispatch. The vignette about the eagle attack in Ireland was in the *Pennsylvania Gazette* for June 18, 1767.

Chapter Ten

Dickinson's letters are based on the actual newspaper articles in the *Pennsylvania Gazette*. The conversation at Haslet's dinner table is the author's creation. The meeting with Rodney also is the author's creation to move the story along, cover the important developments of 1768, and give a sense of the developing close relationship between the two men. The discussion is based on newspaper accounts and the history of

the period. The rivalry between Rodney and Charles Ridgley became evident in the years ahead.

Chapter Eleven

The seizure of Hancock's sloop and the crowd reaction is created from a newspaper account of the incident, the cause celebre of 1768. The Haslet scenes are the author's creation, but the events and opinions described are based on the historical record and the domestic moments are based on accounts of the lifestyles of the time. E. Dallas Hitchens made an extensive study of landholdings in the area and reported the presence of Cullen Town and a store run in the home of William Cullen. Mrs. McAllister's boarding school and its ad were real, but the vignette was created by the author to give the reader an idea of colonial education for young women.

Chapter Twelve

The information on the session of the Delaware Assembly is a matter of record. The message to the king is from the *Pennsylvania Gazette* of April 13, 1769. The dialogue at the assembly session is the author's creation, based on historical record of the events discussed. Rodney discussed his surgery in letters to his brother and friends. The division among the Delaware leadership as it developed in the period prior to and during the Revolution is recounted in several histories. The other events of 1768–69 are matters of historical record. The birth year of little John Haslet is variously given as 1768–1773. The author has chosen 1768 as the most logical year, one that is singled out in more than one record. There is almost no record of Haslet in these two years. The author guessed at his activities.

Chapter Thirteen

The account of McDougall's problems and the events leading up to and including the Boston Massacre are based on several newspaper accounts and Captain Preston's own account of the incident. These accounts do not mention the role of provocateur that historians have attributed to Samuel Adams. Some of the dialogue is from these accounts, other parts are the author's creation.

Haslet's meeting with Rodney is the author's creation. County records show that Haslet was elected to the legislature in the fall of 1770. It is assumed that opportunity came from Rodney, the county's political leader, and it is frequently mentioned that Haslet became a close political ally of Rodney.

Joseph Haslet's death was listed as 1770, but the month is not indicated. However, his will was probated in June. He was identified as a doctor. Information about Joseph's and William's settling in Maryland is contained in various church and legal documents in the archives in Dover and Annapolis It is the author's idea that William delivered the news to John Haslet.

Chapter Fourteen

Records of the fall 1770 session of the legislature are fairly complete and detail the challenge by John Clowes and the votes, although the dialogue of the debate is the author's concept. Clowes' background is provided by the newspapers and by the historical accounts of the period.

The appearance of Reverend George Whitefield in Philadelphia in May and his death in Boston on September 30 were recorded in the newspapers. His earlier illness while in England and the speculation he might never preach again also were reported in dispatches from London.

The Coleman anecdote was taken from a newspaper account.

The outcome of the Boston Massacre trials and the colonies' changing attitudes about the trade boycott are taken from newspaper accounts and the history of the period. Dialogue in this chapter is the author's impression of events that are part of the historical record, including the action in Delaware and other colonies concerning the committees of correspondence.

Chapter Fifteen

Events of 1771–73 are based on newspaper accounts and histories of the period. Haslet's activities are based on information in the archives and the record of the proceedings of the assembly for that period. The letter from James is created by the author using anonymous comments in a newspaper dispatch. It is not known exactly when daughter Ann was born, except it presumably was sometime in 1771. The resolution-writing meeting at McKean's is the author's creation, although the record shows McKean as the author of the resolution. The eulogy to Rebecca Killen was printed in the *Pennsylvania Gazette* (Philadelphia) of October 7, 1773, but the report does not identify the deliverer of the eulogy. The author has chosen to attribute it to Haslet since he and the Killens were close friends and Haslet had the pulpit in his background.

Chapter Sixteen

The action of the Delaware Assembly is based on the records. There was an extensive account in the newspaper on the *Polly* incident, including the identities of Gilbert Barclay and Captain Ayres, the ship's movement, the creation of the special merchants' committee, the confrontation with Barclay and Ayres.

The scenes and dialogues are created out of this account of the three days.

Chapter Seventeen

Haslet's winter of contentment is the author's creation based on accounts of life in the Milford area in that period and of colonial life in general for which I have drawn from Ms. Earle's works cited above.

Franklin's ordeal before the Privy Council is based on newspaper accounts, his own writings, and the history of the period. The debate in Parliament over the Boston Port Bill was constructed out of newspaper summaries.

Gage's instructions, his arrival in Boston and the first week of his rule as governor also are based on newspaper accounts. The author created the dialogue with Gage out of those accounts, which included quotes from Dartmouth and North.

Chapter Eighteen

The July 20 meeting at Dover is constructed from newspaper accounts, Caesar Rodney's letters, and a summary on file in the Delaware archives. There was a lengthy summary of Magaw's oration in the August 3 *Pennsylvania Gazette* and the author has used it to construct a speech. The dialogue of the meeting is the author's creation but the actions taken are matters of historical record. The resolution attributed to Haslet is in the newspaper account of the meeting, which does not identify the author. The information on the Sussex County meeting and the beginning of the idea to boycott English trade are based on the newspaper reports of the period.

Chapter Nineteen

The conversation between John Haslet, William Killen, and Thomas Rodney is constructed from letters between the Rodney brothers and newspaper accounts of the period. It is not known whether the three held such a meeting, but the letters make it clear that Thomas was acting as a stand-in for his brother Caesar. The scene on election day and the voting procedures are created from historical descriptions of elections. The outcome of the election is a matter of historical record. So are the proceedings of the Continental Congress and the militia rally issued by New Castle County at year's end. The Handerson deal was completed in early February so the author assumes negotiations were underway before the end of 1774.

Chapter Twenty

The letter by Robert Holliday and the subsequent action of the Committee of Correspondence is taken from the historical records and newspaper accounts of the time. Haslet's reaction and his passion for the patriot cause are assumed from accounts that indicated he became a focus of loyalist opposition in Kent and Sussex Counties. It also has been noted that Haslet was considered to be the man Rodney depended upon to get people straight on the matter of independence. As in most of this recreation of Haslet's life and times, the dialogue about the February 11 letter is the author's creation. The information in them, however, is a matter of record. The May 2 meeting and Holliday's apology are in the archives and newspaper accounts.

Haslet's purchase of the Handerson property is on record in both the Delaware Archives and the recorder of deeds for Kent County. It is a matter of record that Haslet's residence was located on that property and the home and auxiliary buildings are listed in a 1797 advertisement when son Joseph offered 430 acres north of Milford for sale. It is assumed that John Haslet and family had remained on the John Brinckle estate from the time he and Jemima married until probably early 1776, absent any contrary information. It does not seem logical he would have bought the home on the Handerson property if he already had a home on the adjacent tracts he purchased in the 1760s. This theory is supported by David Kenton of the Milford Historical Society.

The battles at Lexington and Concord and their immediate aftermath are matters of historical record. Haslet's reaction is imagined.

The status of militia in Delaware is unknown but the decision to begin organizing the militia and the call for the leaders to meet on May 20 are recorded in the archives and in newspaper accounts.

Chapter Twenty-one

The May militia meeting and Haslet's role in organizing the county militia are matters of historical record, as is the pledge signed at the meeting. The meeting between him and Caesar Rodney afterwards and the dialogue are the author's creation but the subjects discussed are based on newspaper accounts and the historical records. The creation of a continental army and George Washington's selection as commander-in-chief are historical facts. So are Delaware's movement to support it and Haslet's role in the Council of Safety meetings. It also is a matter or record that Haslet was offered the commission as colonel for the new Delaware battalion and accepted in a letter he wrote to Caesar Rodney, dated December 24.

The birth of baby Jemima Haslet on November 7, 1775, is recorded in the archives. (Hers is the only confirmed birth date in the family.) The family scene in which Jemima Haslet announces she is pregnant is the author's creation. The Killen daughter's death is recorded in the newspapers but there was confusion over her name. The newspaper identified her as Rebecca, but none of the three daughters listed in his biography were named Rebecca. The newspaper may have confused her with Killen's wife Rebecca who had died in 1773.

Chapter Twenty-two

Haslet's letter to Caesar Rodney is in the archives of the State of Delaware. It is a matter of record that opposition to the selection of officers to lead the Delaware battalion was led by Jacob Moore and supported by Simon Kollock and the other officers named. Kollock's later activities on behalf of the loyalist cause also are a matter of record. The record shows the Delaware Council of Safety convened January 9 and heard arguments on the appointments on the ninth and tenth. The record shows the absences on the first day as noted. (Caesar Rodney was not a member of the council but his brother Thomas was.) The dialogue at the meetings is the author's creation as is the final vote, which is not known.

The accounts of King George's speech and Parliament's reaction were printed in the newspapers of January 10, 1776. Paine's *Common Sense* and its instant impact are recorded in the newspaper accounts.

Christopher Ward, historian of the Delaware Continentals, gives Holland large credit for shaping the regiment. His background was provided in notes later by Enoch Anderson, an officer in the regiment, and Emerson Wilson, author of *Forgotten Heroes of Delaware*.

Haslet's move to the new plantation is assumed from the evidence of the property transactions and the inventory of his estate in 1777. The dialogue between him and Jemima is the author's creation. It is pure speculation that Polly took over management of the old plantation, but the inventory of Haslet's estate after his death suggests it was maintained as a home and the author is assuming it would be run by someone other than one of the slaves. The author chose Polly as that someone.

Chapter Twenty-three

The account of the engagement with the British tender involving Nehemiah Field's schooner is in contemporary newspapers. Haslet's own account is quoted in Thomas Scharf's *History of Delaware*. The dialogue has been added by the author.

The encounter with Thomas Robinson is the author's creation, assuming that because Haslet had gone to Lewes to investigate Tory activity he would have visited the county's most notorious loyalist. The incidents discussed are a matter of record, including Thomas Rodney's seizure of Robinson and Jacob Moore on their way to a legislative session.

The *Roebuck* engagement in May is reconstructed from newspaper accounts, which included eyewitness testimony later given by Americans being held prisoner on the *Roebuck*. The militia involvement at Fort Penn is detailed in a letter Haslet wrote on May 7 to Caesar Rodney.

The Congressional resolution is a matter of historical record and was the boldest step taken by that body so far.

Chapter Twenty-four

Rodney's letter to Haslet requesting he set up a meeting with Thomas Rodney, William Killen, and James Tilton to implement the May 15 Congressional resolution and expressing his sense of the need for such action is a matter of record. It's not known on what date they met, or where, but let-

ters at the end of May outline the agreed plan of action. The meeting at Haslet's plantation and the discussion have been created by the author, based on these letters and a later inventory of Haslet's estate.

The letters of Thomas Rodney and Haslet to Caesar Rodney are matters of public record, as are the votes of the Committee of Inspection and Observation. Haslet's accusation against John Clark also is a matter of record, although he may not have made it an issue before the committee. It is created here to provide background for the events following the meeting The dialogue at the committee meeting is the author's creation. The attack on Clark, Haslet's refusal to intercede, and Rodney's actions are based on historical accounts of the June 8 meeting and its aftermath.

Chapter Twenty-five

This chapter is based on known activities of the period: the threat from loyalists to attack Dover and Haslet's home, Thomas Rodney being roused at midnight on the message from Pope about the threat, Rodney's response, the stirring of Tory activity in the Lewes area, and the movement of militia units and the Delaware battalion. It is the author's idea that Killen went to Longfield and that Rodney sent Pope to protect the plantation. It is known that a militia unit was encamped later in the month at Three Runs.

Enoch Anderson's experiences in Sussex County are created out of accounts in the memoirs he wrote many years later. It is known from Haslet's correspondence that he was in Lewes during this period, that Rodney visited on the nineteenth of June for four days to make a report to the Delaware Assembly, that the Pennsylvania Regiment arrived on the twentieth, dispatched by the Congress.

The action by the Delaware Assembly on the fifteenth is a matter of record and the date was celebrated for some years as "Separation Day." The temporary peace arranged by Haslet at William Bradley's house is part of the historical record.

Chapter Twenty-six

There is some opinion that Rodney was still in Lewes when he was summoned to Philadelphia, but evidence suggests otherwise and later historians accept that he had been home a few days before the message from McKean arrived. The name of the courier, Jonathan Gray, is the author's invention. Weather conditions are a part of the record of the time, but there are only hints of Rodney's journey. It may be he traveled by carriage, but the author goes along with the preference as depicted by the statue in Wilmington showing a mounted Rodney. This account is created around the few pieces of information that exist. The action of the Continental Congress is, of course, a matter of history; the dialogue is added by the author.

The record and letters from Haslet and Thomas Rodney attest to the great celebration in Dover when the word arrived during a meeting of the Council of Safety to elect officers to the battalion. Available records, however, do not identify these officers. The description of the celebration is based on Thomas Rodney's letter to his brother and other historical accounts.

Chapter Twenty-seven

Haslet's presence in Lewes from July 6 is documented in his letters. His meeting with his officers and with Colonel David Hall and Henry Fisher is the author's conjecture but Hall's words are a paraphrase of the report, dated

July 6, he made to the Continental Congress. Haslet mentions the presence of eight ships in the Delaware Bay in a letter to Rodney and the author guesses he heard that from Fisher.

It is recorded that the Declaration of Independence was read to the battalion on July 10. History also records that Haslet gave an inspirational speech to his soldiers to prepare them for service with the Continental army, but the date is not known. Since the popular legend is that he gave the speech just before the battalion marched off to war, it is the author's conjecture that Haslet gave that speech following the reading of the Declaration. A famous painting hanging in the state archives building in Dover shows him leading the troops off to war from Dover Green, but that was done in 1915 and represents the artist's imagination. Records indicate they marched north from Lewes, and that Haslet followed them a week later, by boat. The movement of the battalion and of Haslet is based on the historical record.

The Battle of Charleston and the fruitless peace overtures from the Howe Brothers also are a matter of historical record. The scene between Washington and Howe's aide, Colonel Patterson, is recorded in the journals of the Continental Congress and published in newspapers of the period.

Chapter Twenty-eight

The records of the Kent County Recorder of Deeds and of the Register of Wills tell of Haslet's deal with the Rovells and of the contents of his will. Jemima Haslet was involved in the Rovell sale and the author decided to have the children accompany their parents to Dover to set up a final family farewell.

In placing Polly at the Brinckle Plantation in this and previous chapters, the author has been influenced by the inventory of the plantation in March

1777, following Haslet's death, that shows a still active farm, including three grown slaves. The oldest, Dollar, forty, is mentioned here. There was a separate inventory for Longfield.

The actions of the Delaware Assembly are recorded in the state's archives. The issue of taking arms out of the colony is mentioned in Haslet's letters but the author only assumes the resolution of the matter since the battalion did, in fact, march out of the colony before it was resolved. The Congressional record seems to support this view in that the Congress voted on August 5 to complete arms to the battalion and to send 193 arms to the colony "in lieu of so many had from them."

The battalion's arrival in Philadelphia on August 3 is mentioned in Caesar Rodney's letter to his brother Thomas. Rodney also mentioned compliments about the battalion from the delegates. Congress' decision to order the battalion to Amboy on August 8 is in the Congressional record.

Some historians dispute that the First Delaware Continentals became known as the "Blue Hen's Chickens," but rather were known as the "Delaware Blues," because of their uniforms. Nevertheless, the legend is repeated in several documents. It is known that the regiment liked cockfights and that Caldwell had brought some fighting cocks along with him. Whatever the truth, the story is part of the lore of the regiment.

The other events in the chapter and the conversations are the author's creation, although Rodney's opinions about the selection of delegates to the Constitutional Convention are based on his own writings.

Chapter Twenty-nine

The movement of the Delaware battalion during this period is reconstructed from various clues in the records of the state archives, the journals of the Continental Congress and historical accounts of the period.

A letter written by Gunning Bedford a few days after the battle of Long Island placed the arrival around the twenty-first. He said they stayed in camp for two or three days. Haslet, in a letter to Thomas Rodney, said that they went to Brooklyn Heights on the twenty-fifth. General Mercer's assignment as commander of the flying camp at Amboy is a matter of record. The story of his escape from the Indians during the French and Indian War may be anecdotal but it is included as an interesting part of his biography. The dialogue between Haslet and Mercer is the author's creation.

Chapter Thirty

The battalion's arrival and the dialogue between Washington and Haslet are the author's imagination, but the events mentioned are matters of historical record.

The court martial of Lieutenant Colonel Herman Zedwitz is based on the records of Peter Force for his *American Archives*, published in the early nineteenth century. Other material on Zedwitz is part of the record. He is not mentioned as part of the Life Guards conspiracy of June 1776, but he himself brought up his possible involvement in his letter to Governor Tryon and in his testimony at his trial. It's possible he made it up for purposes of his alleged attempt to deceive Tryon. It is not known how Haslet felt about his testimony or the reaction of other members of the board. Their comments are the author's conception; the dialogue in the trial itself is based on Force's material. The verdict is copied verbatim from that material.

Chapter Thirty-one

The events of the Battle of Long Island and the subsequent retreat is based on several accounts, particularly those of historians Henry Onderdonk Jr. in 1841, Christopher Ward, and Eric Manders.

Onderdonk included the tavern keeper story in his account, but the dialogue is the creation of this author. Washington's memorandum, the actions of the Delaware and Maryland regiments and of Atlee and Parsons, the desire of Clinton and Vaughan to keep fighting, the weather conditions and their impact on events are all matters of record. Much of the dialogue is the author's imagination but Washington's comments on the fighting at the stone house (which still exists in Brooklyn) and his distress at the premature withdrawal of Hand's command are all mentioned in histories of the battle.

Haslet's musings about the battle are based on a letter he wrote to Caesar Rodney on August 31. It is recorded that Washington waited until the last boat and Haslet casually mentioned in an October 4 letter to Thomas Rodney that "last of all crossed ourselves, thank God, in safety."

Chapter Thirty-two

Haslet's illness is mentioned in roster reports and letters. The visit by Tilton and Bedford is assumed by the author. The author has added punctuation to the letters for clarity; colonial writers paid little attention to this discipline of grammar.

The meeting between Admiral Howe and the congressional delegation is based on newspaper accounts.

The disposition of the troops after Long Island is based on the historical records. Washington's presence and action at Kip's Bay is a matter of record as are some of his comments, but the author added dialogue based on Washington's proven tendency to extreme displays of anger. The account of

the New York fire is based on the newspaper reports.

Haslet's attack on Rogers' Rangers is historical fact but the author created the scenes leading up to the attack. The barest of details is available on the unfortunate attack on the battalion on the way back from Mamaroneck by the Pennsylvania troops. The author has embellished these details.

Chapter Thirty-three

Details of the series of battles at White Plains are gathered from several historical accounts. Some are based on Haslet's recollection in a letter written shortly afterwards, but his role, including his forceful disposition of the artillery piece, and the actions of his regiment are supported by other records. These accounts state that Haslet virtually took command of the defense on Chatterton Hill.

The subsequent disposition of troops and the actions of General Lee are also matters of record.

Chapter Thirty-four

The movement of the armies during the November–December period are matters of historical record, which confirm that the Delaware battalion served as the rear guard as Stirling's brigade wended its way south. The capture of Fort Washington is based on the historical accounts as is Washington's presence at Fort Lee at the time.

The records of the Delaware Assembly state that Collins and West were sent to talk to Haslet and Patterson as part of the assembly's planning to raise a new battalion and it also is a matter of record that Haslet was the preferred commander for the new battalion. Haslet mentions meeting with them in his November 19 letter to Caesar Rodney. The dialogue is the author's creation and the reference to Asbury is inserted here by the author as an interesting footnote to the history of Delaware. There is no evidence he touched directly on Haslet's life but Asbury's role in the founding of the Methodist movement in America is a matter of record as is the importance of Kent County and Dover in that movement. The Reverend Philip Reading is inserted into the story here also to show how some Anglican clergy were affected by the Revolution.

Smallwood's promotion is recorded in the Congressional Journal and Haslet mentions in one of his letters that he thought Washington preferred him over Smallwood.

The behavior of Patterson's Delaware militia is in the record, as is Patterson's evaluation of their worthlessness. Anderson's impression of the lodgings at Princeton are based on the diary he wrote years later, but the conversation with Haslet is invented.

There are different versions of Washington's request to Thomas Paine, differing as to whether Paine already had started his pamphlet or began at Washington's insistence; the author chose to believe he already was writing it on the march from Fort Lee.

General Lee's behavior through all this is recorded in the historical accounts and revealed in his own letters. His capture is covered in several accounts at the time. It is a matter of record that Washington opened Lee's damning letter to Reed; the dialogue is based on that brief record.

The Honeyman incident is related in a nineteenth century history by William Stryker but the story has many skeptics. Details of his capture and escape were accepted by Stryker and this author has accepted it and created the scene and dialogue of the meeting inside Washington's headquarters. Rupert Hughes mentions Washington's proclivity for spies in his biography.

Finally, Haslet's meeting with his officers to push recruiting for the new battalion also is a matter of record, although, again, the dialogue is the author's contribution.

Chapter Thirty-five

Details of the Trenton expedition and the anecdotal material are contained in several excellent histories and in the accounts of several participants. The final roll call of the First Delaware Continental Battalion just before the battle is recorded in the military archives. The accounts also report that Washington ordered Paine's tract read to the troops before they embarked.

Monroe's account of the confrontation with the elderly doctor was given many years later when he was serving as President of the United States. The incident where Washington's horse slipped and was steadied by its rider is in one of the eyewitness accounts of the march.

The author has imagined Haslet's involvement in the battle, based on accounts of the disposition of the brigades. His letters provide only a broad view of his regiment's involvement in the battle. "Lord Stirling's brigade had the honor of fighting 1000 Hessians to a surrender," he wrote to Rodney (in what is believed to be his last letter before he was killed). "We should have gone on and panic struck they would have fled before us, but the inclemency of the weather rendered it impossible."

The movement of Cadwalader's division and other events to the end of the year, including Washington's plea to the troops to volunteer for additional service, are mentioned in the various accounts of the period.

The meeting between Washington and Haslet is the author's creation, based on a letter Haslet wrote to Caesar Rodney on January 1 from Trenton, in which he mentions his belief

408

that Washington preferred him over Smallwood and also that all but the handful of soldiers from his battalion had gone home. A copy of Washington's order for him to go home and recruit was found on his body at Princeton.

The Congressional resolution of December 27 and Washington's response are matters of record. The scene in Philadelphia when the Hessian prisoners were paraded through the town also is a matter of record. The prisoners were later dispersed to Lancaster County, Pennsylvania, and to Virginia.

Chapter Thirty-six

The events reported in this chapter are based on historical records. Howe's order to Cornwallis to cancel his trip is part of those records; the meeting between the two is the author's creation.

Sir William Erskine's advice against waiting overnight to attack Washington is from the various accounts of the Second Battle of Trenton as are the reservations of Cornwallis and his staff about continuing the attack that night. The rest of the conversation is created by the author. So is the meeting of Washington and his field commanders to plan another stealthy withdrawal from the trap poised by a British commander. The withdrawal, however, did occur as reported here.

Accounts say Haslet walked beside Mercer as they headed for Princeton and talked quietly. The author has imagined the substance of their conversation but the events discussed are matters of record.

The battle at Princeton is a compendium of several accounts. Historian Thomas Scharf, in his two-volume *History of Delaware* published in 1888, reported Private Peter Jacquett was at Haslet's side when he died but the only Jacquett on the roster of the Delaware Battalion was an officer, member of a prominent family that settled in Delaware when the Dutch ran the

colony. He is not among the five officers Haslet said in his January 1 letter to Caesar Rodney had accompanied him to New Jersey. He did, however, mention there were two privates with him. They were not identified in his letter.

In his *Recollections and Private Memoirs of Washington,* his adopted son George Washington Parke Custis reports Washington coming upon Haslet's body but does not elaborate. However, the popular legend of Haslet's death, repeated at the eulogy given at the July 2, 1841, ceremony in Philadelphia, is that the commander-in-chief wept over the corpse.

The incident at Three Runs Church where Joseph Haslet inadvertently overheard news of his father's death was in William Thompson Read's 1870 volume *Life and Correspondence of George Read, by His Grandson.*

Joseph Haslet said his mother died of a broken heart on news of his father's death. The archives record that William Killen took over management of the family affairs, but the author guesses that Polly, a grown woman many years older than her half-brothers and half-sisters, assumed the domestic role of her stepmother. The summary of their lives after 1777 is compiled from records in the Delaware State Archives, the Historical Society of Delaware, and the Morris Library at the University of Delaware.

Chapter Thirty-seven

This chapter is based primarily on the account in the *Delaware Journal* of July 9, 1841, the report of the Haslet Memorial Committee submitted to the Delaware House of Representatives on January 10, 1843, and from sources noted in Chapter One.

John Clayton's speech has not been preserved but the author borrowed generously from the *Journal's* account on the theory the reporter's words were inspired by that speech, if not actually a replication of it.

Profiles of the participants are based on Leon DeValinger's notes in *A Calendar of Ridgely Family Letters* and W. Emerson Wilson's *Forgotten Heroes of Delaware*. Records with the Historical Society of Delaware and in the Delaware archives list at least five veterans of the Revolutionary War era still alive at the time of the 1841 ceremonies. The *Journal* identified two in the procession but they are not among the five in the list and neither shows in the roster of the Delaware Continentals in the archives.

The Haslet genealogy comes from several sources, but there are disagreements over whether the line from Joseph continued, possibly confusing him with his Uncle Joseph. All seem to agree that Jemima's line continued. Birth and death records are incomplete but it would appear there were five grandchildren and eight great grandchildren alive in July, 1841. The accounts do not identify which of them attended the ceremony.

Bibliography

Auth, Stephen F. *The Ten Years' War: Indian-White Relations in Pennsylvania, 1755–1765.* New York : Garland Publications, 1989.

Anderson, Enoch. *Personal Recollections of Enoch Anderson.* Edited by Henry Hobart Bellas. Wilmington, Del.: Historical Society of Delaware, 1896.

Bell, Whitfield J. Jr. *The Colonial Physician and Other Essays.* New York: Science History Publications, 1975.

Bendler, Bruce. Colonial Delaware records, 1681–1713 / Bruce A. Bendler. Westminster, Md.: Family Line Publications, 1992.

Biographical and Genealogical History of the State of Delaware. Chambersburg, Pa.: J. M.Runk and Company, 1899.

Bouquet, Henry. *The Papers of Henry Bouquet.* Edited by Donald H. Kent and Autumn Leonard. Harrisburg: The Pennsylvania Historical and Museum Commission, 1978.

Brittingham, Hazel. *John Clowes Jr. 1730–1790: Broadkill Patriot: The Man, His Family, the Times.* Wilmington, Del.: Delaware Heritage Press, 1989.

Burkhart, Larry L. *The Good Fight: Medicine in Colonial Pennsylvania.* New York: Garland Pub., 1989.

Bushman, Claudia L., Harold B. Hancock, and Elizabeth Moyne Homsey. *Proceedings of the Assembly of the Lower Counties on Delaware, 1770–1776.* Newark, Del.: University of Delaware Press, 1986.

Campbell, John Hugh. *History of the Friendly Sons of St. Patrick and of the Hibernian Society for the Relief of Emigrants from Ireland.* Philadelphia: The Hibernian Society, 1892.

Chidsey, Donald Barr. *The French and Indian War: An Informal History.* New York, Crown 1969.

Clark, Raymond B. *Delaware Church Records.* St. Michaels, Md.: R.B. Clark, 1986.

Commager, Henry Steele, and Richard B. Morris, eds. *The Spirit of Seventy-Six: The Story of the American Revolution as Told by Participants.* New York: Da Capo Press, 1995.

Continental Congress. *Journals of the Continental Congress, 1774–1789.* Edited by Worthington C. Ford et al. 34 vols. Washington, D.C.: 1904–37.

Dalleo, Peter T. "'South of the Canal' in the 1840s as Described in the *Blue Hen's Chicken.*" In *Delaware History,* Fall-Winter 2000–2001, pages 121–137. Wilmington, Del.: Historical Society of Delaware.

DeValinger, Leon Jr., and Virginia E. Shaw, eds. *A Calendar of Ridgely Family Letters, 1742–1899.* 3 vols. Dover, Del.: Privately published for the Public Archives Commission, 1948.

Dickson, R.J. *Ulster Emigration to Colonial America, 1718–1775.* London: Routledge & Kegan Paul, 1966.

Dwyer, William M. *The Day is Ours!* New York : Viking Press, 1983.

Earle, Alice Morse. *Home Life in Colonial Days.* Stockbridge, Mass.: Berkshire Traveller Press/Berkshire House Publishers, 1898.

———. *Child Life in Colonial Days.* Stockbridge, Mass.: Berkshire Traveller Press/Berkshire House Publishers, c1992. 1899]

Farrell, James J. *Inventing the American Way of Death, 1830–1920.* Philadelphia: Temple University Press, 1980.

Force, Peter, ed. *American Archives:* consisting of a collection of authentick records, state papers, debates, and letters and other notices of publick affairs, the whole forming a documentary history of the origin and progress of the North American colonies; of the causes and accomplishment of the American revolution; and of the Constitution of government for the United States, to the final ratification thereof. In six series. Prepared and published under authority of an act of Congress. Washington, 1837–53.

Foster, R.F. *Modern Ireland, 1600–1972*. New York: Penguin Books, 1988.

Frank, William P. *Caesar Rodney, Patriot*. Wilmington, Del.: Delaware American Revolution Bicentennial Commission, 1975.

The George Washington Papers at the Library of Congress; *1776* *http://memory.loc.gov/ammem/gwhtml/1776.html*

Hall, Walter Phelps, and Robert Geenhalgh Albion. *A History of England and the British Empire*. Boston: The Atheneum Press, 1946.

Hancock, Harold B. *The Loyalists of Revolutionary Delaware*. Newark, Del.: The University of Delaware Press, 1977.

Haven, C.C. A new historic manual concerning the three battles at Trenton and Princeton, New Jersey, during the war for American independence, in 1776 and 1777. Trenton, NJ., W.T. Nicholson, printer, 1871.

Heimert, Alan. *The Great Awakening: Documents Illustrating the Crisis and Its Consequences*, edited by Alan Heimert and Perry Miller. Indianapolis: Bobbs-Merrill, 1967.

Herman, Bernard L. *Architecture and Rural Life in Central Delaware, 1700–1900*. Knoxville, Tenn.: University of Tennessee Press, 1987.

Herson, Jane McClellan. "The Development of Methodism in Delaware, 1739–1830." Master's thesis, University of Delaware, 1956.

Historical and Biographical Encyclopedia of Delaware, edited by J.M. McCarter and B.F. Jackson. Wilmington, Del.: Aldine Publishing and Engraving Co., 1882.

Hitchens, E. Dallas. *The Milford, Delaware, Area Before 1776*. Milford, Del.: Shawnee Printing, 1976.

Hoffecker, Carol E. *Delaware, a Bicentennial History*. New York: Norton, 1977.

Hughes, Rupert. *George Washington, the Human Being and the Hero*. 2 vols. New York: W. Morrow & Company, 1926.

Hynson, George B., ed. *Historical Etchings of Milford, Delaware, and Vicinity*. Milford, Del., Peninsular News & Advertiser Pub. Co., 1899.

Kent County Probate Records, 1680–1800. Leon deValinger Jr., compiler. Delaware Public Archives Commission, 1944.

Ketchum, Richard M. *The Winter Soldiers: The Battles for Trenton and Princeton*. Garden City, N.Y.: Doubleday, 1973.

Klett, Guy Soulliard. *Presbyterians in Colonial Pennsylvania*. Philadelphia: University of Pennsylvania Press, 1937.

King, Lester Snow. *The Medical World of the Eighteenth Century*. Chicago: University of Chicago Press, 1958.

Laderman, Gary. *The Sacred Remains, American Attitudes Toward Death, 1799–1883*. New Haven, Conn.: Yale University Press, 1996.

Letters of Members of the Continental Congress, edited by Edmund C. Burnett, 8 vols. Washington, D.C.: The Carnegie Institution of Washington, 1921–36.

Lossing, Benson J., ed. *Recollections and Private Memoirs of Washington by His Adopted Son, George Washington Parke Custis*. Philadelphia: Englewood Publishing Company, 1867.

Manders, Eric I. *The Battle of Long Island*. Monmouth Beach, N.J.: Philip Freneau Press, 1978.

Merril, Arthur A. *The Battle of White Plains*. Chappaqua, N.Y.: Analysis Press, 1976.

Messer, Peter C. "Treason Trials." *The Pennsylvania Magazine*, October 1999.

McMurtrie, Douglas C. *The Delaware Imprints of 1761*. Metuchen, N.J.: Priv. print., 1934.

Meltzer, Milton. *The American Revolutionaries: A History in Their Own Words*. New York: HarperCollins, 1987

Miers, Earl Schenck. *On Pale Rider*. Newark, Del.: Curtis Paper Company, 1964.

Morison, Samuel Eliot. *The Oxford History of the American People*. New York: Oxford University Press, 1965.

Mullin, Julia E. *The Presbytery of Limavady*. Limavady, Northern Ireland: North-West Books, 1989.

Munroe, John A. *Colonial Delaware: A History*. Millwood, N.Y.: KTO Press, 1978.

Newland, Samuel L., PhD. *The Pennsylvania Militia: The Early Years, 1669–1792*. Annville, Penna.: Pennsylvania Department of Military and Veterans Affairs, 1997.

Onderdonk, Henry Jr. *Revolutionary Incidents of Suffolk and Kings Counties; with an Account of the Battle of Long Island and the*

British Perisons and Prison-Ships at New York. Port Washington, N.Y.: Kennikat, 1970.

Passmore, Joanne O., Charles Maske, and Daniel E. Harris. *Three Centuries of Delaware Agriculture*. Dover, Del.: Delaware State Grange, 1978.

Peterson, Charles J. *The Military Heroes of the Revolution*. Philadelphia: J.B. Smith, 1858.

Read, William Thompson. *Life and Correspondence of George Read, by His Grandson*. Philadelphia: J.B. Lippincott & Co., 1870.

Rowe, G.S. *Thomas McKean, the Shaping of an American Republicanism*. Boulder, Col.: Associated University Press, 1978.

Ryden, George H. *Letters to and from Caesar Rodney*. Philadelphia: Pub. for the Historical Society of Delaware by the University of Pennsylvania Press, 1933.

Scharf, J. Thomas. *History of Delaware*. 2 vols. Philadelphia: L.J. Richards, 1888.

Scott, Joseph A. *A Geographical Description of the States of Maryland and Delaware*. Philadelphia: Printed by Kimber, Conrad, 1807.

Shryock, Richard. "Eighteenth Century Medicine in America." Proceedings of the American Antiquarian Society. Vol. 59, 1949.

Smith, Page. *John Adams*. 2 vols. Garden City, N. Y.: Doubleday, 1962.

————. *A New Age Now Begins*. 3 vols., New York: McGraw-Hill, 1976.

Thompson, Peter. *Rum, Punch and Revolution: Taverngoing and Public Life in Eighteenth Century Philadelphia*. Philadelphia: University of Pennsylvania Press, 1999.

Thompson, Ray. *Washington Along the Delaware: The Battles of Trenton and Princeton as Told by the Men Who Were There and Through Washington's Own Official Dispatches*. Fort Washington, Penna.: Bicentennial Press, 1970.

Tottle, Edward Loring. *War in the Woods, the Day the United States Began: July 9, 1755*. Windham, Me.: Educational Materials Company, 1991.

Tunis, Edwin. *Colonial Living*. Baltimore: The Johns Hopkins University Press, 1957.

Van Doren, Carl. *Benjamin Franklin*. New York: The Viking Press, 1938.

————. *Autobiographical Writings.* New York: The Viking Press, 1945.

VIRGINIA: "The Papers of George Washington," University of Virginia, Revolutionary War Series Documents; Washington's Revolutionary War Itinerary and the Location of His Headquarters, http://gwpapers.virginia.edu/documents/revolution/itinerary/1776.html site.

Waddell, Louis M., and Bruce D. Bomberger. *The French and Indian War in Pennsylvania 1753–1763.* Harrisburg, Penna.: The Pennsylvania Historical and Museum Commission, 1996.

Wallace, Martin. *A Short History of Ireland.* Belfast, Northern Ireland: The Appletree Press, 1973.

Ward, Christopher. *The Delaware Continentals 1776–1783* Wilmington, Del.: Historical Society of Delaware. 1941.

Ward, Christopher. *The War of the Revolution,* 2 vols. New York: Macmillan, 1952.

Ward, Matthew C. "Pennsylvania Captives Among the Ohio Indians, 1755–65." *Pennsylvania Magazine of History and Biography,* July 2001.

Waterston, Elizabeth. *Churches in Delaware During the Revolution.* Wilmington, Del.: Historical Society of Delaware, 1925.

Weis, Frederick Lewis. *The Colonial Clergy of Maryland, Delaware, and Georgia.* Lancaster, Mass.: Society of the Descendants of the Colonial Clergy, 1950.

Wheeler, Richard. *Voices of 1776.* New York: Crowell, 1972.

Whiteley, Hon. William G. *Papers of the Historical Society of Delaware* 2, no. 14 (1896).

Wilbur, C. Keith M.D. *The Revolutionary Soldier, 1775–1783.* Illustrated Living History Series. Old Saybrook, Conn.: The Globe Prequot Press, 1969.

————. *Revolutionary Medicine, 1700–1800.* Illustrated Living History Series. Old Saybrook, Conn.: The Globe Pequot Press, 1980.

Wilson, W. Emerson. *Forgotten Heroes of Delaware.* Cambridge, Mass.: Deltos Pub. Co., 1969.

Wise, Herbert Clifton. *Colonial Architecture.* Philadelphia, London: J.B. Lippincott Company, 1913.

Works Progress Administration (WPA). *Churches of Delaware.* Item 485, "Three Runs Presbyterian Church." Vol. 26, Delaware Archives.

About the Author

As a native Philadelphian, Fred Walters was exposed to colonial history early. A career in journalism nurtured his interest in how events shape our lives. When his interests in colonial history led to his discovery of the Revolutionary War hero John Haslet and he found that very little information had been published about him, Walters determined that someday he would learn all he could about John Haslet and write his story.

His career in journalism was jump-started when he began working for The Associated Press as a writer/reporter in his senior year at the University of Pennsylvania (after three and a half years in the U.S. Navy). Eleven years later he switched to broadcasting and has been a reporter, editor, and news executive for Metromedia in Philadelphia; for Westinghouse Broadcasting Company (since merged into CBS) in Harrisburg, Philadelphia, New York, and Los Angeles; and for ABC at its station in Detroit. As a news executive he developed and directed large, award-winning news staffs.

To commemorate the nation's Bicentennial he wrote and produced for the Westinghouse stations, in cooperation with the University of

Pennsylvania, a series of twelve, one-hour programs (*The Course of Human Events*) that won the National Headliners Award for 1976.

He has been a member of the Society of Professional Journalists since 1966, and was president of the Greater Philadelphia chapter in 1976 and 1977. He served as chairman of the society's 1975 national convention, held in Philadelphia.

He also was a member of the Pennsylvania Legislative Correspondents Association from 1957 to 1969, and its president from 1961 to 1963.